Essentials of Accounting for Governmental and Not-for-Profit Organizations

Tenth Edition

Paul A. Copley,
Ph. D., CPA

KPMG Professor
Director, School of Accounting
James Madison University

McGraw-Hill
Irwin

The McGraw·Hill Companies

McGraw-Hill
Irwin

ESSENTIALS OF ACCOUNTING FOR GOVERNMENTAL AND NOT-FOR-PROFIT
ORGANIZATIONS, TENTH EDITION

ISBN 978-0-07-352705-5
MHID 0-07-352705-X

Vice President and Editor-in-Chief: *Martin Lange*
VP SEM, EDP, Central Publishing Services: *Kimberly Meriwether David*
Editorial Director: *Stewart Mattson*
Publisher: *Tim Vertovec*
Sponsoring Editor: *Donna Dillon*
Marketing Manager: *Dean Karampelas*
Development Editor: *Emily Hatteberg*
Project Manager: *Melissa M. Leick*
Design Coordinator: *Brenda Rolwes*
Cover Designer: *Studio Montage, St. Louis, Missouri*
USE Cover Image Credit: *Eyewire (Photodisc)/PunchStock*
Senior Production Supervisor: *Laura Fuller*
Media Project Manager: *Suresh Babu/Balaji Sundararaman, Hurix Systems Pvt. Ltd.*
Compositor: *MPS Limited, A Macmillan Company*
Typeface: *10.5/12pt Times Roman*
Printer: *R. R. Donnelley*

Library of Congress Cataloging-in-Publication Data

Copley, Paul A.
    Essentials of accounting for governmental and not-for-profit organizations / Paul A. Copley. — 10th ed.
        p. cm.
    Includes index.
    ISBN 978-0-07-352705-5
    1.   Administrative agencies—United States—Accounting. 2.   Nonprofit organizations—United States—
Accounting. I.   Title.
    HJ9801.H39 2011
    657'.83500973—dc22

                                                                                    2009054187

www.mhhe.com

Preface

Thank you for considering the tenth edition of *Essentials of Accounting for Governmental and Not-for-Profit Organizations*. The tenth edition is updated for recent changes including:

- GASB *Statement 54: Fund Balance Reporting and Governmental Fund Type Definitions.*

- FASB *Statement 164, Not-for Profit Entities: Mergers and Acquisitions.*

- IRS Form 990 *Return of Organization Exempt From Income Tax.*

In addition, the text includes a new chapter on Federal Government reporting.

I have used the text with stand-alone, three semester-hour classes, with half-semester GNP courses, and as a module in advanced accounting classes. It is appropriate for accounting majors or as part of a public administration program. The coverage is effective in preparing candidates for the CPA examination.

The focus of the text is on the preparation of external financial statements. Among the more challenging aspects of state and local government reporting is the preparation of government-wide financial statements. Our approach is similar to that used in practice. Specifically, day-to-day events are recorded at the fund level using the basis of accounting for fund financial statements. Governmental activities are recorded using the modified accrual basis. The fund-basis statements are then used as input in the preparation of government-wide statements. The preparation of government-wide statements is presented in an Excel worksheet. This approach has two advantages: (1) it is the approach most commonly applied in practice, and (2) it is an approach familiar to students who have studied the process of consolidation in their advanced accounting classes. State and local government reporting is illustrated using an ongoing example integrated throughout Chapters 2 through 8 and 13.

Additional features of the text are available on the instructor or student Web sites and include:

- A continuous homework problem throughout Chapters 2 through 8 and 13.

- Instructor's guide.

- Suggested quiz and examination questions and problems.

- PowerPoint slides.

- Excel-based assignments.

- An additional practice set.

I thank Sandra Bitenc, University of Texas—Arlington; Angele Brill, Castleton State College; Richard C. Brooks, West Virginia University; Bradley Childs, Belmont University; Dori Danko, Grand Valley State University; Gertrude Eguae-Obazee, Albright College; Gladys Gomez, University of Mary Washington; Marina Grau, Houston Community

College; David J. Harr, George Mason University; Maggie Houston, Wright State University; Tom Hrubec, Franklin University; Mary Jepperson, Saint John's University; Beth Kern, Indiana University South Bend; John Lasik, Central Washington University; Rodney A. Oglesby, Drury University; Jim Shelton, Harding University; Chuck Smith, Iowa Western Community College; D. Terry Balkaran, Queens College; and Bradley Trimble, Columbus State Community College for reviewing the ninth edition and providing suggestions. I wish to thank my colleague Loretta Manktelow; co-author of the *Instructor's Guide* and author of the *Test Bank* as well as Maggie Houston of Wright State University for her work on the online quizzes. Finally, I am indebted to the many users of the text for their comments. Additional comments and suggestions are welcome and can be addressed to me at copleypa@jmu.edu.

Paul A. Copley

In memory of those lost:
— Northern Illinois University, February 14, 2008
— Virginia Tech, April 16, 2007

Contents

Introduction to Accounting and Financial Reporting for Governmental and Not-For-Profit Organizations

The truth is that all men having power ought to be mistrusted.

If men were angels, no government would be necessary. If angels were to govern men, neither external nor internal controls on government would be necessary. James Madison, fourth president of the United States and principal author of the U.S. Constitution

Learning Objectives

- Obtain an overview of financial reporting for nonbusiness entities.
- Distinguish between private and public sector organizations.
- Identify the sources of authoritative accounting standards for various public and private sector organizations.
- Define the 11 fund types used by state and local governments.

In its relatively short existence, the United States has grown to be the largest and most successful economy in history. Why then would a country founded on the principles of free markets and private investment rely on governments to provide many goods and services? The answer lies in understanding the incentives of a free enterprise economy. There are many services that simply cannot be priced in a way that naturally encourages commercial entrepreneurs to enter the marketplace. Commonly this is because the service is subject to free-riding. For example, public safety and a clean environment benefit every citizen, whether or not they contribute to its cost. Because there is no practical means for businesses to sell this service, governments are called upon through the political process to provide those services that citizens demand. In other instances, free market incentives do not align with public interest. For example, society finds it desirable to provide a K–12 education to all its citizens, not just those with the ability to pay.[1]

Although the majority of products and services are provided by either businesses or governments, in some circumstances private organizations are formed to provide goods or services without the intent of earning a profit from these activities. Examples include public charities, trade associations, and civic groups. Again, the goods or services they provide often cannot be priced in a way that encourages commercial entrepreneurship. For example, a public radio broadcast cannot be effectively restricted to only those individuals choosing to support the public radio station. While this explains why the services are not provided by businesses, why aren't governments called upon to provide them?

In some instances, obstacles exist that prevent government involvement. For example, the U.S. Constitution provides for separation of church and state. Therefore, any group that wishes to promote religious activities must do so through private organizations rather than through government. More commonly the reason is lack of political influence. Support for the arts may be important to a group of individuals but unless that group is sufficiently large to influence the political process, it is unlikely that elected officials will use government funds for that purpose. However, support for the arts could still be provided by forming a charitable foundation with no relationship to the government and having the foundation solicit donations from that segment of the public who finds the arts important.

The organizations introduced in the preceding paragraphs are the focus of this book: governmental and not-for-profit organizations. They are distinguished from commercial businesses by the absence of an identifiable individual or group of individuals who hold a legally enforceable residual claim to the net assets. Throughout the text a distinction will be made between **public** and **private** organizations. Public organizations are owned or controlled by governments. Private organizations are not owned or controlled by governments and include businesses as well as private not-for-profit organizations. **Not-for-profit organizations** lack a residual ownership claim and the organization's purpose is something other than to provide goods and services at a profit.

Because significant resources are provided to governments and not-for-profit organizations, financial reporting by these organizations is important. To paraphrase the James Madison quotation provided at the beginning of the chapter, because humans (not angels) operate governments, controls are necessary. Financial reports that reflect the policies and actions of governmental managers are an effective means to control the actions of those entrusted with public resources. To be effective, external financial reports must be guided by a set of generally accepted accounting

---

[1] The branch of economics that studies the demand for government services is termed *public choice*.

principles. The generally accepted accounting principles for governmental and private not-for-profit organizations are the subject of this book. The first nine chapters of the text deal with public sector (state and local government) organizations and Chapters 10, 11, and 12 deal primarily with private not-for-profit organizations. Chapter 13 discusses auditing and tax-related issues unique to governments and private not-for-profits and also evaluates performance of these entities. Chapter 14 describes financial reporting by the federal government.

GENERALLY ACCEPTED ACCOUNTING PRINCIPLES

Organisms evolve in response to characteristics of their environment. Similarly, accounting principles evolve over time as people find certain practices useful for decision making. Further, we expect organisms in different environments to evolve differently. Similarly, if the environments in which governments and not-for-profits operate differ in important ways from that of commercial enterprises, we would expect the accounting practices to evolve differently.

The Governmental Accounting Standards Board published a document titled *Why Governmental Accounting and Financial Reporting Is—and Should Be— Different* (http://www.gasb.org/white_paper_full.pdf). This white paper identifies five environmental differences between governments and for-profit business enterprises and describes how those differences manifest in differences in the objectives and practice of financial reporting.

1. **Organizational Purposes.** While the purpose of a commercial business is to generate a profit for the benefit of its owners, governments exist for the well-being of citizens by providing public services—whether or not the services are profitable undertakings. Since taxes and many other government revenues are not equivalent to sales, the excess of revenues over expenses cannot be interpreted as an effectiveness measure in the manner of business net income.

Whereas the purpose of government operations differs greatly from commercial businesses, the purpose of governmental accounting is the same—to provide information that is useful to stakeholders in making decisions. However, governments have vastly different sets of users of accounting information. Like businesses, governments have creditors who are interested in assessing the creditworthiness of the government. Citizens and businesses, both within the government's jurisdiction and those considering relocation to the jurisdiction, are also stakeholders who rely on governmental reporting to make economic decisions. In addition, governments receive resources from other governments and grantors who may require financial reports and audits as a condition of the grant. Since this diverse set of resource providers have varying interests, the information needs of one group may not meet the needs of another. The result is that governments report far more disaggregated information than commercial enterprises.

2. **Sources of Revenues.** Net income is a universally accepted measure of business performance. The calculation of net income begins with sales. A sale

occurs when an independent party perceives that the service offered both provides value and is fairly priced. Net income then simply determines whether this measure of demand (sales) exceeds the cost of providing the service and is an accepted measure of performance for business organizations. On the other hand, governments derive many of their resources from taxes. Individuals and businesses pay taxes to avoid penalty, not voluntarily because they perceive government services to be of value and fairly priced. Since taxes do not involve an earnings process, the timing of the recognition of tax revenue is not always clear.

3. **Potential for Longevity.** Because the U.S. and state constitutions grant state and local governments the ability to tax, governments very rarely go out of business. This long-term view of operations changes the focus of accounting from one of near-term recovery of amounts invested in assets to a longer-term focus on the sustainability of services and the ability to meet future demand. As a result, short-term fluctuations in the value of assets or liabilities are less likely to be recognized in government financial statements. For example, changes in the fair value of assets in employee pension plans are not recognized in the short term.

4. **Relationship with Stakeholders.** Taxes are generated through the legislative process by officials elected by the citizens. Because citizens and businesses are then required to pay these taxes, governments have an obligation to demonstrate accountability for these public funds. Whereas a business can use its resources as it deems appropriate, governments frequently receive resources that are restricted to a particular purpose. For example, a city may collect a telephone excise tax legally restricted to operating a 911 emergency service. In an effort to provide assurance that resources are used according to legal or donor restrictions, governments use **fund accounting.** A fund represents part of the activities of an organization that is separated from other activities in the accounting records to more easily demonstrate compliance with legal restrictions or limitations.

5. **Role of the Budget.** Many businesses prepare budgets, but these are for planning and control purposes and are rarely made available to creditors or investors. In contrast, government budgets are expressions of public policy and often carry the authority of law, preventing public officials from spending outside their budgetary authority. The increased importance of budgets is reflected in government financial reports by a required report comparing budgeted and actual amounts.

For these and other reasons, the accounting practices of governmental organizations evolved differently from those of businesses. As you will see in later chapters, the accounting practices of not-for-profit organizations more closely resemble those of commercial businesses. However, the not-for-profit environment shares some important characteristics with governments. Similar to governments, not-for-profits do not have residual owners. "Investors" in not-for-profits are diverse and include donors, volunteers, and members. In addition, as with governments, the excess of revenues over expenses is not an effective measure of organizational performance. Finally, like governments, not-for-profits receive resources with donor-imposed restrictions.

√ **ILLUSTRATION 1–1**   Summary of Standards-Setting Organizations

Reporting Organization	Standards Setting Board
Federal government	Federal Accounting Standards Advisory Board (FASAB)
State and local governments	Governmental Accounting Standards Board (GASB)
Public not-for-profits	Governmental Accounting Standards Board (GASB)
Private not-for-profits	Financial Accounting Standards Board (FASB)
Investor-owned businesses	Financial Accounting Standards Board (FASB)

Further complicating this issue is the fact that we have three levels of government (federal, state, and local) and not-for-profits may be either publicly or privately owned. This is important because different standards-setting bodies have authority for establishing reporting standards for these groups. Illustration 1–1 summarizes the various organizational types and the bodies with primary standard-setting authority.

Accounting and financial reporting standards for the federal government are recommended by the Federal Accounting Standards Advisory Board (FASAB). Recommendations of the FASAB are reviewed and become effective unless objected to by one of the **principals, the U.S. Government Accountability Office (GAO), the U.S. Department of the Treasury,** or the **U.S. Office of Management and Budget (OMB).** These standards apply to financial reports issued by federal agencies and to the Consolidated Financial Report of the United States Government. Accounting and financial reporting standards for the federal government are illustrated in Chapter 14.

Accounting and financial reporting standards for state and local governments in the United States are set by the **Governmental Accounting Standards Board (GASB).** The GASB also sets accounting and financial reporting standards for governmentally related not-for-profit organizations, such as colleges and universities, health care entities, museums, libraries, and performing arts organizations that are owned or controlled by governments. Accounting and financial reporting standards for profit-seeking businesses and for nongovernmental not-for-profit organizations are set by the **Financial Accounting Standards Board (FASB).**

The GASB and the FASB are parallel bodies under the oversight of the **Financial Accounting Foundation (FAF).** The FAF appoints the members of the two boards and provides financial support to the boards by obtaining contributions from business corporations; professional organizations of accountants and financial analysts; CPA firms; debt-rating agencies; and state and local governments. Because of the breadth of support and the lack of ties to any single organization or government, the GASB and the FASB are referred to as "independent standards-setting bodies in the private sector." Standards set by the FASAB, GASB, and FASB are the primary sources of **generally accepted accounting principles (GAAP)** as the term is used in accounting and auditing literature.

FASAB, GASB, and FASB standards are set forth primarily in documents called **Statements.** From time to time, the boards find it necessary to expand on standards in documents called **Interpretations.** Boards also issue **Technical Bulletins** to explain the application of standards in certain situations or industries. Because FASB, GASB, and FASAB Statements, Interpretations, and Technical Bulletins do not cover all possible transactions, government and not-for-profit entities may need to refer to other publications for guidance. However, these other publications do not take precedence over standards issued by the standard-setting boards. The result is that financial statement preparers follow a hierarchy of generally accepted accounting standards. Until recently this hierarchy was established by the **American Institute of Certified Public Accountants (AICPA).** However each of the standard-setting organizations has now published its own hierarchy of GAAP. This hierarchy is summarized in Illustration 1–2. The final category includes practices that have evolved within an industry without specific authoritative action by any standard-setting body.

Some organizations possess certain characteristics of both governmental and nongovernmental not-for-profit organizations, and it is necessary to determine whether those organizations are governmental or nongovernmental for purposes of applying GAAP, in accord with the hierarchy shown in Illustration 1–2. For this reason, the FASB and GASB agreed upon a definition of a government. As reproduced in the AICPA *Audit and Accounting Guide: Not-for-Profit Organizations,* the definition is as follows:

Public corporations and bodies corporate and politic are governmental organizations. Other organizations are governmental organizations if they have one or more of the following characteristics:

    a. Popular election of officers or appointment (or approval) of a controlling majority of the members of the organization's governing body by officials of one or more state or local governments;

    b. The potential for unilateral dissolution by a government with the net assets reverting to a government; or

    c. The power to enact and enforce a tax levy.

Furthermore, organizations are presumed to be governmental if they have the ability to issue directly (rather than through a state or municipal authority) debt that pays interest exempt from federal taxation.

OBJECTIVES OF ACCOUNTING AND FINANCIAL REPORTING

All three standards-setting organizations—the Federal Accounting Standards Advisory Board, the Financial Accounting Standards Board, and the Governmental Accounting Standards Board—take the position that the establishment of accounting and financial reporting standards should be guided by conceptual considerations so that the body of standards is internally consistent and the standards address broad issues expected to be of importance for a significant period of time. The cornerstone of a conceptual framework is said to be a statement of the objectives of financial reporting.

ILLUSTRATION 1–2   GAAP Hierarchy

Category	FASB Statement 162 Nongovernmental Entities (commercial and private not-for-profits)	GASB Statement 55 State and Local Governments	FASAB (Exposure Draft) Federal Government and Agencies
A.	• FASB *Statements and Interpretations*, • FASB *Staff Positions*, and • AICPA *Accounting Research Bulletins* and *Accounting Principles Board Opinions* that are not superseded by actions of the FASB.	• GASB *Statements and Interpretations*.	• FASAB *Statements and Interpretations*, • AICPA and FASB pronouncements specifically made applicable to federal governmental entities by FASAB Statements or Interpretations.
B.	• FASB *Technical Bulletins* and, • if cleared by the FASB, *AICPA Industry Audit and Accounting Guides and Statements of Position*.	• GASB *Technical Bulletins* and, • if cleared by the GASB, *AICPA Industry Audit and Accounting Guides and Statements of Position*.	• FASAB *Technical Bulletins* and, • if specifically made applicable to federal governmental entities by the AICPA and cleared by the FASAB, *AICPA Industry Audit and Accounting Guides and Statements of Position*.
C.	• AICPA *Practice Bulletins* that have been cleared by the FASB, and • consensus positions of the FASB *Emerging Issues Task Force*.	• AICPA *Practice Bulletins* that have been cleared by the GASB.	• AICPA AcSEC *Practice Bulletins* if cleared by the FASAB. • *Technical releases* of the FASAB Accounting and Auditing Policy Committee.
D.	• Implementation guides (Q&As) published by the FASB staff, • AICPA *Accounting Interpretations, Industry Audit and Accounting Guides and Statements of Position* not cleared by the FASB, and • practices that are widely recognized and prevalent either generally or in the industry.	• Implementation guides (Q&As) published by the GASB staff, and • practices that are widely recognized and prevalent in state and local governments.	• Implementation guides published by the FASAB staff, and • practices that are widely recognized and prevalent in the federal government.

7

Objectives of Accounting and Financial Reporting for the Federal Government

The Federal Accounting Standards Advisory Board (FASAB) was established to recommend accounting and financial reporting standards to the principals—the U.S. Office of Management and Budget, the U.S. Department of the Treasury, and the U.S. Government Accountability Office. The FASAB has issued six **Statements of Federal Financial Accounting Concepts (SFFACs).** These concepts apply to financial reporting for the federal government as a whole and for individual reporting agencies.

SFFAC 1, *Objectives of Federal Financial Reporting,* outlines four objectives that should be followed in federal financial reporting. The first, budgetary integrity, indicates that financial reporting should demonstrate accountability with regard to the raising and expending of moneys in accord with the budgetary process and laws and regulations. The second, operating performance, suggests that financial reporting should enable evaluation of the service efforts, costs, and accomplishments of the reporting entity. The third, stewardship, reflects the concept that financial reporting should enable an assessment of the impact on the nation of the government's operations and investments. Finally, the fourth, systems and controls, indicates that financial reporting should reveal whether financial systems and controls are adequate.

Other federal government accounting concept statements include:

- SFFAC 2—*Entity and Display,*
- SFFAC 3—*Management's Discussion and Analysis,*
- SFFAC 4—*Intended Audience and Qualitative Characteristics for the Consolidated Financial Report of the United States Government,*
- SFFAC 5—*Definitions of Elements and Basic Recognition Criteria for Accrual-Basis Financial Statements,* and
- SFFAC 6—*Distinguishing Basic Information, Required Supplementary Information, and Other Accompanying Information.*

Objectives of Financial Reporting by Not-for-Profit Entities

FASB has issued seven concepts statements, including one dedicated to nonbusiness entities. In its *Statement of Financial Accounting Concepts No. 4,* the FASB identifies the information needs of the users of nonbusiness financial statements. These include providing information that is useful to present and potential resource providers in the following:

- Making decisions about the allocation of resources to those organizations,
- Assessing the services that a nonbusiness organization provides and its ability to continue to provide those services,
- Assessing management's stewardship and performance, and
- Evaluating an organization's economic resources, obligations, and effects of changes in those net resources.

Objectives of Accounting and Financial Reporting for State and Local Governmental Units

The Governmental Accounting Standards Board was established in 1984 as the successor to the National Council on Governmental Accounting (NCGA). In 1987 the GASB issued its *Concepts Statement No. 1, Objectives of Financial Reporting,* for state and local governments. In that statement the Board noted the following:

> Accountability requires governments to answer to the citizenry—to justify the raising of public resources and the purposes for which they are used. Governmental accountability is based on the belief that the citizenry has a right to know, a right to receive openly declared facts that may lead to public debate by the citizens and their elected representatives. Financial reporting plays a major role in fulfilling government's duty to be publicly accountable in a democratic society.[2]

Financial reports of state and local governments, according to the Governmental Accounting Standards Board, are used primarily to: (1) compare actual financial results with the legally adopted budget; (2) assess financial condition and results of operations; (3) assist in determining compliance with finance-related laws, rules, and regulations; and (4) assist in evaluating efficiency and effectiveness.

Concepts Statement No. 3, Communication Methods in General Purpose External Financial Reports that Contain Basic Financial Statements, was issued in 2005. The Statement defines methods of presenting information in financial reports and presents the following disclosure hierarchy:

1. Recognition in the **basic financial statements:** Assets, liabilities, revenues, expenses or expenditures, and other elements of a financial statement that can be measured with sufficient reliability should be recorded in the financial statements.

2. Disclosure in **notes to the financial statements:** Notes enhance the user's understanding of items in the financial statements and may include management's objective explanations. Disclosure in the notes is not an adequate substitute for recognition in the financial statements when an event can be measured reliably.

3. Presentation as **required supplementary information (RSI):** RSI is information the GASB has determined is *essential* for placing financial statement and note information in an appropriate context. The information must be objective and does not include predictions or subjective assessments.

4. Presentation as (other) supplementary information: This is information that is *useful* (but not essential) for placing financial statement and note information in an appropriate context. The GASB does not require supplementary information, unless identified as RSI.

Concepts Statement No. 4, Elements of Financial Statements provides key definitions, including:

- *Assets* are resources with present service capacity that the government presently controls,

[2] Governmental Accounting Standards Board, *Concepts Statement No. 1, Objectives of Financial Reporting* (Norwalk, CT., 2001).

- *Liabilities* are present obligations to sacrifice resources that the government has little or no discretion to avoid,
- *Net position* is the residual of all other elements presented in a statement of financial position,
- *Inflows of resources* are acquisitions of net assets by the government that are applicable to the reporting period, and
- *Outflows of resources* are consumption of net assets by the government that are applicable to the reporting period.

Concepts statements 2 and 5 relate to the reporting of service efforts and accomplishments reporting. These statements recognize the limitations of traditional financial statements which are not well designed for evaluating the government's effectiveness in delivering public services. Service efforts and accomplishments reporting will be more fully described in Chapter 13.

STATE AND LOCAL GOVERNMENT FINANCIAL REPORTING

GASB *Concepts Statements* stress that accounting and reporting standards for state and local governments should meet the financial information needs of many diverse groups: citizen groups, legislative and oversight officials, and investors, and creditors. The *Concepts Statements* also make clear that reporting standards for governments recognize that decisions made by these groups involve political and social decisions as well as economic ones. Accordingly, governmental financial reporting standards are much more inclusive than FASB standards, which consider the needs of only investors and creditors concerned with economic decisions.

Comprehensive Annual Financial Report

The discussion of financial reporting in the GASB *Codification* Sec. 2200 sets standards for the content of the comprehensive annual financial report of a state or local government reporting entity. A **comprehensive annual financial report (CAFR)** is the government's official annual report prepared and published as a matter of public record. In addition to the basic financial statements and other financial statements, the CAFR contains introductory material, an auditor's report, certain RSI, schedules necessary to demonstrate legal compliance, and statistical tables. Chapter 2 presents an extensive discussion and illustration of the basic financial statements and the other major components of the CAFR.

Illustration 1–3 presents an overview of the financial reporting process for state and local governments. While a business will typically have a single general ledger, the activities of governments are broken down into subunits called *funds*. A typical town or county government could have a dozen funds while cities and states

ILLUSTRATION 1–3   **Financial Reporting Process for State and Local Governments**

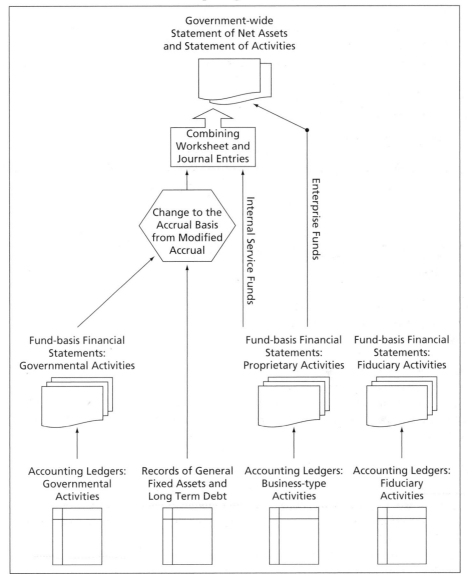

generally have many more. Each fund requires its own general ledger and general journal. These are represented at the bottom of Illustration 1–3. In addition, records are kept of general fixed assets and long-term debt.

Governments have two levels of financial statement reporting. The first is the fund-basis financial statements. Fund-basis statements are presented for three categories of activities: governmental, proprietary, and fiduciary. These categories and the funds comprising each are described in detail later in this chapter. While the fund-basis statements present an in-depth record of individual activities of the government, it is difficult for the financial statement user to pull this disaggregated information together and form an overall view of the government's finances. For that reason, governments are required to present government-wide financial statements. The government-wide statements combine the governmental and business-type activities of the government for the purpose of presenting an overall picture of the financial position and results of operations of the government. An important feature of the government-wide financial statements is that they are prepared using a common measurement focus and basis of accounting.

Measurement Focus and Basis of Accounting

State and local governments prepare their financial reports using two general accounting methods. One method assumes an economic resources measurement focus and the accrual basis of accounting, and the other method assumes a flow of current financial resources measurement focus and modified accrual accounting. Each of these two methods is discussed below.

Economic Resources Measurement Focus and the Accrual Basis of Accounting
The government-wide statements and the fund statements for proprietary funds and fiduciary funds use the economic resources measurement focus and the accrual basis of accounting. **Measurement focus** refers to *what* items are being reported in the financial statements. An economic resource measurement focus measures both current and long-term assets and liabilities and is the measurement focus used by commercial businesses. A balance sheet prepared on the economic resource focus reports the balances in fixed assets and long-term liabilities. **Basis of accounting** determines *when* transactions and events are recognized in the accounting records. The accrual basis of accounting recognizes revenues when they are earned (and are expected to be realized) and recognizes expenses when the related goods or services are used up. Again, this is the basis of accounting used by commercial businesses.

Current Financial Resources Measurement Focus and the Modified Accrual Basis of Accounting   The fund statements for governmental funds are presented using the current financial resources measurement focus and modified accrual basis of accounting. Many of the transactions in governmental funds are nonexchange in nature; that is, they are activities undertaken in response to the needs of the public. Activities reported in governmental funds are heavily financed by taxes and involuntary contributions from persons (and organizations) who do not receive services in direct proportion to the contribution they make. GASB standards provide that accounting systems of governmental funds are designed to measure (a) the extent to which financial resources obtained during a period are sufficient to cover claims incurred during that period against financial resources and (b) the net financial resources available for future periods. Thus, governmental funds are said to have a **flow of current financial resources measurement**

focus, as distinguished from the government-wide, proprietary fund, and fiduciary fund statements, which have a flow of economic resources measurement focus. Activities of governmental funds are said to be **expendable;** that is, the focus is on the receipt and expenditure of resources. These resources are further defined as expendable resources, generally but not totally restricted to current assets and liabilities.

    Modified accrual accounting, as the term implies, is a modification of accrual accounting. As will be discussed much more fully in Chapters 3, 4, and 5, revenues are generally recognized when *measurable* and *available* to finance the expenditures of the current period. Expenditures (not expenses) are recognized in the period in which the fund liability is incurred. Long-term assets, with minor exceptions, are not recognized; the same is true of most long-term debt. Capital (fixed) assets and long-term debt are not reported in governmental funds. It should be noted that governmental *funds* are reported using the modified accrual basis of accounting; however, governmental-type *activities* are reported in the government-wide statements using the accrual basis of accounting, including fixed assets and long-term debt. As shown in Illustration 1–3, the governmental activities fund-basis financial statements and the records of general fixed assets and long-term debt serve as inputs to the government-wide financial statements. The governmental activities balances are changed through combining worksheets and journal entries to reflect an economic resource measurement focus and the accrual basis of accounting before being presented in the government-wide financial statements.

Fund Structure for State and Local Government Accounting and Reporting

Traditionally, state and local government financial reporting has been based on **fund accounting.** Fund accounting and reporting permit governmental managers to demonstrate compliance with legal and contractual requirements. Fund accounting and the term **fund,** are defined by the GASB as follows:

> Governmental accounting systems should be organized and operated on a fund basis. A fund is defined as a **fiscal and accounting entity** with a self-balancing set of accounts recording cash and other financial resources, together with all related liabilities and residual equities or balances, and changes therein, which are segregated for the purpose of carrying on specific activities or attaining certain objectives in accordance with special regulations, restrictions, or limitations.[3]

    Note that the definition of the word *fund* requires that two conditions must be met for a fund, in a technical sense, to exist: (1) there must be a **fiscal entity**—assets set aside for specific purposes, and (2) there must be a double-entry **accounting entity** created to account for the fiscal entity.

---

[3] National Council on Governmental Accounting, Statement No. 1, par 2. (Norwalk, CT).

outlay : tiền fỉ' tổn

State and local governments use 11 fund types. These fund types are organized into three categories: governmental funds, proprietary funds, and fiduciary
funds.

*Finance
& modified*

Governmental Funds   Five fund types are classified as **governmental funds:**

1. The **General Fund** accounts for most of the basic services provided by the government. Technically, it accounts for and reports all financial resources not accounted for and reported in another fund.
2. **Capital projects funds** account for and report financial resources that are restricted, committed, or assigned to expenditure for capital outlays. As such, it
   accounts for the purchase or construction of major capital improvements (except)
   those purchased or constructed by a proprietary (and less commonly, fiduciary)
   fund.
3. **Debt service funds** account for and report financial resources that are restricted,
   committed, or assigned to expenditure for principal and interest, other than interest or principal on proprietary or fiduciary activities.
4. **Special revenue funds** account for and report the proceeds of specific revenue sources that are restricted or committed to expenditure for a specified
   purpose other than debt service or capital projects. These include activities
   funded by federal or state grants or by taxes specifically restricted to certain
   activities. *Ex motor fuel tax limited by law to Hwy & constructing repair*
5. **Permanent funds** account for and report resources that are restricted to the
   extent that only earnings, and not principal, may be used for purposes that support the reporting government's programs.

Every government will have a single General Fund but may have multiple funds in
each of the other categories. Accounting for the General Fund and special revenue
funds is discussed in Chapters 3 and 4, while capital project, debt service, and permanent fund accounting is illustrated in Chapter 5.

Proprietary Funds   Two types of funds used by state and local governments are
classified as **proprietary funds.** The term indicates that the funds are used to
account for a government's ongoing organizations and activities that are similar
to those often found in the commercial sector. Proprietary funds are discussed in
Chapter 6. There are two types of proprietary funds:

1. **Enterprise funds** are used when resources are provided primarily through the
   use of sales and service charges to parties external to the government. Examples
   of enterprise funds include water and other utilities, airports, swimming pools,
   and transit systems.
2. **Internal service funds** account for services provided by one department of a
   government to another, generally on a cost-reimbursement basis. In some cases,
   these services are also provided to other governments. Examples of internal service funds include print shops, motor pools, and self-insurance funds.

Fiduciary Funds   **Fiduciary funds,** sometimes known as **trust** ⌄
funds, account for resources for which the government is acting as a c⌄
disbursing agent or as a trustee. Fiduciary funds are covered in Chapter 7.
types of fiduciary funds exist:

1. **Agency funds** are used to account for situations in which the government is acting as a collecting/disbursing agent. An example would be a county tax agency
fund, where the county collects and disburses property taxes for other taxing
units within the county, such as independent school districts.
2. **Pension (and other employee benefit) trust funds** are used to account
for pension and employee benefit funds for which the governmental unit is the
trustee.
3. **Investment trust funds** account for the external portion of investment pools
reported by the sponsoring government.
4. **Private-purpose trust funds** report all other trust arrangements under which
principal and income benefit individuals, private organizations, or other
governments.

Illustration 1–4 summarizes the fund types, basis of accounting, and required fund-
basis financial statements for each fund category. The table is presented in reverse
order to assist in identifying the appropriate fund to record a given transaction.
Starting at the top, determine whether a given transaction is a fiduciary activity. If it
is, identify which of the four fiduciary fund types is appropriate and do not consider

ILLUSTRATION 1–4   Summary of Funds Used by State and Local Governments

Fund Category	Fund	Basis of Accounting	Fund-basis Financial Statements
Fiduciary	Private-Purpose Trust Investment Trust Pension Trust Agency	Accrual	• Statement of Fiduciary Net Assets • Statement of Changes in Fiduciary Net Assets
Proprietary	Internal Service Enterprise	Accrual	• Statement of Net Assets • Statement of Revenues, Expenses, and Changes in Net Assets • Statement of Cash Flows
Governmental	Permanent Debt Service Capital Project Special Revenue General	Modified accrual	• Balance Sheet • Statement of Revenues, Expenditures, and Changes in Fund Balances

the proprietary or governmental-type funds. If it is not fiduciary, determine whether it is a proprietary activity, and if it is, determine whether it is internal service or enterprise. Any transaction that is not fiduciary or proprietary must be a governmental activity. Again, start at the top of the governmental activity funds and determine first whether the transaction meets the definition of a permanent fund. If it does not, move down through the list. Any transaction that has not been identified as a permanent, debt service, capital projects, or special revenue fund transaction must be accounted for in the General Fund.

Number of Funds Required

In the GASB Summary Statement of Principles, the principle that follows the definition of fund types is often overlooked. This principle states that *governmental units should establish and maintain those funds required by law and sound financial administration.* If state law and/or agreements with creditors do not require the receipt of revenues that are raised solely for a defined purpose and if administrators do not feel that use of a separate fund is needed to be able to demonstrate that revenues were raised solely for that particular purpose, the General Fund should be used.

Budgetary Accounting

GASB standards recognize that state laws generally require administrators of state agencies and of local governmental units to obtain the appropriate legislative body's formal approval of all plans to raise revenues and make expenditures. Additionally, it is common for state agencies to be given the responsibility for monitoring the financial plans and financial operations of local governmental units within the state. Therefore, GASB standards contain the following three-part budgetary principle:

1. An annual budget(s) should be adopted by every governmental unit.
2. The accounting system should provide the basis for appropriate budgetary control.
3. Budgetary comparisons should be included in the appropriate financial statements and schedules for governmental funds for which an annual budget has been adopted.

Part 1 of the principle is not an accounting or financial reporting principle, but it is a necessary precondition to parts 2 and 3. A budget, when adopted according to procedures specified in state laws, is binding upon the administrators of a government. Accordingly, a distinctive characteristic of governmental accounting is the formal reporting of the legally approved budget compared with actual results for the General Fund and all major special revenue funds that have a legally adopted annual budget. This report is included as a part of required supplementary information (RSI) in the CAFR. The nature and operation of accounting and budgetary reporting are explained in appropriate detail in Chapter 3.

ADDITIONAL RESOURCES

Individuals interested in studying the original sources of GAAP may consult the GASB **Codification**.[4] The *Codification* lists GASB pronouncements by topic; alternatively, you may consult the GASB *Original Pronouncements* that provide the information in statement order.[5] All of these sources are described on the GASB Web site (www.gasb.org) which also provides information regarding current activities, including exposure drafts of new standards.

The **American Institute of Certified Public Accountants (AICPA)** provides guidance regarding state and local governmental accounting and auditing, especially in its *Audit and Accounting Guide: State and Local Governmental Units*.[6] The AICPA Web site is www.aicpa.org.

The **Government Finance Officers Association** of the United States and Canada (GFOA) is the professional organization of the preparers of governmental financial statements. Detailed guidance is available in their publication, *Governmental Accounting, Auditing, and Financial Reporting*.[7] The GFOA Web site is www.gfoa.org.

Now that you have finished reading Chapter 1, complete the multiple choice questions provided on the text's Web site (www.mhhe.com/copley10e) to test your comprehension of the chapter.

[4] Governmental Accounting Standards Board, *Codification of Governmental Accounting and Financial Reporting Standards* (Norwalk, CT: GASB).

[5] Governmental Accounting Standards Board, *Original Pronouncements: Governmental Accounting and Financial Reporting Standards* (Norwalk, CT: GASB).

[6] American Institute of Certified Public Accountants, *Audit and Accounting Guide: State and Local Governmental Units* (New York, AICPA, 2007).

[7] Stephen J. Gautier, *Governmental Accounting, Auditing, and Financial Reporting Using the GASB 34 Model* (Chicago: Government Finance Officers Association, 2001).

Questions and Exercises

1–1 Obtain a copy of a recent Comprehensive Annual Financial Report (CAFR). These may be obtained by writing the director of finance in a city or county of your choice. Your instructor may have one available for you, or you may obtain one from the GASB Web site: www.gasb.org. It would be best, but not absolutely necessary, to use a CAFR that has a Certificate of Excellence in Financial Reporting from the Government Finance Officers Association. You will be answering questions related to the CAFR in Chapters 1 through 9. Answer the following questions related to your CAFR.

    a. What are the inclusive dates of the fiscal year?

    b. Write the name and address of the independent auditor. Is the auditor's opinion unqualified? If not, describe the qualification. Is the opinion limited to the basic financial statements, or does the opinion include combining and individual fund statements?

c. Is the report separated into the three distinct sections: introductory, financial, and statistical? Does the report have a "single audit" section at the end? (A few CAFRs include their single audit report in the CAFR—see Chapter 13 for more detail of the single audit requirements.)

d. Does the report contain an organization chart? A table of contents? A list of principal officials? A letter of transmittal? Is the letter of transmittal dated and signed by the chief financial officer? List the major items of discussion in the letter of transmittal.

e. Does the report include a Management's Discussion and Analysis? List the major items of discussion.

f. Does the report include the government-wide statements (Statement of Net Assets and Statement of Activities)?

g. Does the report reflect fund financial statements for governmental, proprietary, and fiduciary funds? List those statements. List the major governmental and proprietary funds (the funds which have separate columns in the governmental and proprietary fund statements).

1–2   Identify and describe the five environmental differences between governments and for-profit business enterprises as identified in the Governmental Accounting Standards Board's *Why Governmental Accounting and Financial Reporting Is—and Should Be—Different.*

1–3   Identify and briefly describe the three organizations that set standards for state and local governments, the federal government, and nongovernmental not-for-profit organizations.

1–4   What is the definition of a government as agreed upon by the FASB and GASB?

1–5   Describe the "hierarchy of GAAP" for state and local governments, the federal government, and nongovernmental not-for-profit organizations.

1–6   Accounting and financial reporting for state and local governments use, in different places, either the economic resources measurement focus and the accrual basis of accounting or the current financial resources measurement focus and the modified accrual basis of accounting. Discuss the differences in measurement focus and basis of accounting related to (*a*) the conceptual differences, (*b*) differences in revenue recognition, (*c*) differences in expense/expenditure recognition, (*d*) differences in recognition of fixed assets, and (*e*) differences in the recording of long-term debt.

1–7   Distinguish between private and public sector organization.

1–8   GASB considers budgetary accounting and reporting to be important. List the principles outlined by GASB related to budgetary accounting and reporting.

1–9   Go to the GASB Web site (www.gasb.org). What is the mission of GASB?

1–10 For each of the items below, identify which fund would be used to account for the item and provide a justification for your answer.

   a. A city government issued general obligation bonds to finance the construction of a new jail.

   b. A state government collected a tax of $1.00 per pack of cigarettes which is (by law) required to be used to fund health and fitness programs in public schools.

   c. A county government expended $1 million to expand the water treatment plant.

   d. A donor provided investments totaling $4 million to create an endowment, the earnings of which will be used to provide scholarships.

   e. A donor provided $50,000 to be used to purchase newspaper and magazine subscriptions for the public library. There is no requirement that the original principal may not be spent.

   f. A city government sold surplus street maintenance trucks for $10,000.

Continuous Problem

1–C. Chapters 2 through 9 deal with specific knowledge needed to understand accounting and financial reporting by state and local governments. A continuous problem is available on the text's Web site (www.mhhe.com/copley10e) to keep the entire accounting area in perspective. The problem assumes the government is using fund accounting for its internal record-keeping and then at year-end makes necessary adjustments to prepare the government-wide statements. The problem covers all of the funds of the City of Everlasting Sunshine. At appropriate stages, preparation of the fund and government-wide statements are required. The following funds are included in this series of problems.

> General
> Special revenue—Street and Highway Fund
> Capital projects—City Hall Annex Construction Fund
> Debt service—City Hall Annex Debt Service Fund
> Debt service—City Hall Debt Service Fund
> Internal service—Stores and Services Fund
> Enterprise—Water and Sewer Fund
> Agency—Tax Collection Fund
> Investment trust—Area Investment Pool Fund
> Private-purpose—Student Scholarship Fund
> Pension trust—Fire and Police Retirement Fund

Overview of Financial Reporting for State and Local Governments

Particulars on government expenditures and taxation should be plain and available to all if the oversight by the people is to be effective. Thomas Jefferson, third president of the United States and author of the Declaration of Independence

Learning Objectives

- Obtain an overview of the contents of a governmental financial report.
- Define the governmental reporting entity.
- Illustrate the basic financial statements for a state or local government.

C hapters 3 through 9 of this text describe and illustrate detailed accounting and financial reporting requirements for state and local governments. The purpose of this chapter is to provide background information so students may better understand the material that follows. This chapter presents a detailed look at financial statements and certain required schedules.

State and local governments are encouraged to prepare a **Comprehensive Annual Financial Report (CAFR).** According to the GASB *Codification* Sec. 2200:

> A comprehensive annual financial report should be prepared and published, covering all funds and activities of the primary government (including its blended component units) and providing an overview of all discretely presented component units of the reporting entity—including introductory section, management's discussion and analysis (MD&A), basic financial statements, required supplementary information other than MD&A, combining and individual fund statements, schedules, narrative explanations, and statistical section.

While governments are encouraged to prepare a complete CAFR, the GASB has identified a set of statements and disclosures that are required to be in compliance with generally accepted accounting principles (GAAP). The minimum required contents of a governmental financial report appear in Illustration 2–1.

ILLUSTRATION 2–1   Required Contents of Governmental Financial Report.

1. Management's Discussion and Analysis

2. Basic Financial Statements

   a. Government-wide Financial Statements

                    Government-wide Statement of Net Assets—Illustration 2–5
                    Government-wide Statement of Activities—Illustration 2–6

   b. Fund Basis Financial Statements   *work most:*
                   Governmental Type Funds ＊ *General fund : payroll --*
                   Balance Sheet—Illustration 2–7b
                   Statement of Revenues, Expenditures and Changes in
                      Fund Balances—Illustration 2–8b
                   Reconciliation of governmental statements to
                      government-wide statements— Illustration
                      2–7a and Illustration 2–8a

                   Proprietary Funds
                   Statement of Net Assets—Illustration 2–9
                   Statement of Revenues, Expenses and Changes in
                      Fund Net Assets—Illustration 2–10
                   Statement of Cash Flows—Illustration 2–11

                   Fiduciary Funds
                   Statement of Fiduciary Net Assets—Illustration 2–12
                   Statement of Changes in Fiduciary Net Assets—Illustration 2–13

   c. Notes to the Financial Statements—Illustration 2–14

3. Required Supplementary Information (Other than MD&A)

                   Information about infrastructure assets using the modified
                      approach—Illustration 2–15
                   Budgetary comparison schedule (General and major Special
                      Revenue Funds)—Illustration 2–16
                   Schedule of funding progress of pension plans
                   Schedule of employer contributions of pension plans
                   Schedules required for external financing pools

The remainder of this chapter presents (1) a discussion of the financial reporting entity, (2) an overview of the CAFR contents, and (3) a detailed presentation of the Comprehensive Annual Financial Report, including illustrative statements.

THE GOVERNMENTAL REPORTING ENTITY

One of the most fundamental accounting issues is identifying the accounting entity. This is made more difficult by the fact that general-purpose governments such as states, counties, and large cities typically are complex organizations that include semiautonomous boards, commissions, and agencies created to accomplish projects or activities that, for one reason or another (generally restrictive clauses in state constitutions or statutes), may not be carried out by a government as originally constituted. For many years, separate annual reports were issued for each legal entity.

GASB *Statement 14, The Financial Reporting Entity,* establishes that the **financial reporting entity** is the primary government together with its component units. The **primary government** can be a state government, a general-purpose local government such as a city or county, or a special purpose government such as a school district. **Component units** are legally separate organizations for which the elected officials of the primary government are *financially accountable*. In addition, a component unit can be an organization for which the nature and significance of its relationship with a primary government are such that exclusion would cause the reporting entity's financial statements to be misleading or incomplete.

Statement 14 provides guidance in determining when a primary government has financial accountability for another organization. First, the primary government either appoints a voting majority of the governing body of the other organization or members of the primary government's governing body hold a majority of the seats of the other organization's board. Second, the relationship meets one of the following two criteria: (component units)

1. The other organization provides either a financial burden or benefit to the primary government; or
2. The primary government can impose its will on the other organization.

A financial burden exists, for example, if the primary government is responsible for liabilities or accumulated deficits of the other organization. A financial benefit exists, for example, if the primary government is entitled to the other organization's assets. Examples of the ability to impose its will include the right to replace the other organization's management or to approve its budget.

Once it is determined that an organization is a component unit of a primary government, the issue becomes how to include its financial information in the primary government's financial reports. GASB standards provide two methods for including component unit financial information with that of the primary government. The first is known as **blending,** because the financial information becomes part of the financial statements of the primary government. Blended organizations are reported as though they were funds of the primary government. Blending is appropriate only when the component unit is so intertwined with the primary government that they are in substance the same entity. This may be the case if the two entities' governing boards are identical or if the component unit provides services solely to the primary government.

More commonly, component units are reported using **discrete presentation.** In discrete presentation, the financial information of the component is presented in a column, apart from the primary government and not included in the totals reported for the primary government. Discretely presented component units appear as separate columns in the government-wide statements. If there is more than one component unit, combining statements are provided showing financial information for each component unit.

REPORTING BY MAJOR FUNDS

In addition to the government-wide statement, governments are required to prepare fund financial statements within the three categories of funds: governmental, proprietary, and fiduciary. Because governments may have many governmental and proprietary funds, governments are only required to present separate columns for each **major fund.** The General Fund is always considered a major fund. Other governmental funds are considered major when both of the following conditions exist:

1. total assets, liabilities, revenues, *or* expenditures of that individual governmental fund constitute 10 percent of the total for the governmental funds category, *and*
2. total assets, liabilities, revenues, *or* expenditures of that individual governmental fund are 5 percent of the total of the governmental and enterprise categories, combined.

Similar tests are applied to determine major enterprise funds. Additionally, a government may designate any fund major if reporting that fund separately would be useful. Any funds not reported separately are aggregated and reported in a single column under the label *nonmajor funds*. If the reporting government is preparing a complete CAFR, a schedule showing the detail of nonmajor funds is provided in the other supplementary information section.

OVERVIEW OF THE COMPREHENSIVE ANNUAL FINANCIAL REPORT (CAFR)

The Comprehensive Annual Financial Report has three major sections: introductory, financial, and statistical. The CAFR is to include blended component units and discretely presented component units. An outline of the CAFR was presented in Illustration 2–1. Information appearing in the CAFR is described and illustrated in the following sections, beginning with the Introductory Section, Illustration 2–2.

**Example Comprehensive Annual Financial Report
Introductory Section**

Introductory Section

The Introductory Section of a CAFR includes the table of contents, a letter of transmittal from the preparer (typically the government's Finance Director), a list of government officials, and an organizational chart. If a government received a Certificate of Achievement for Excellence in Financial Reporting from the Government Finance Officers Association in the prior year,[1] the introductory section will include a reproduction of that certificate. The introductory section is <u>not audited</u>.

ILLUSTRATION 2–2   Introductory Section of CAFR

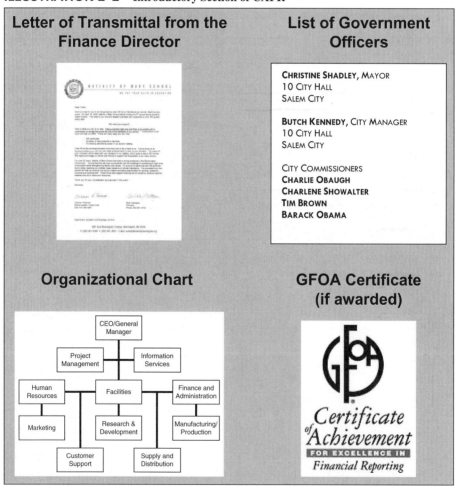

[1] The Government Finance Officers Association of the United States and Canada sponsors a Certificate program to encourage and promote excellent financial reporting. To receive that certificate, a government must have an unqualified audit opinion and have its report reviewed, using an extensive checklist, by independent reviewers who are experienced in financial reporting. See www.gfoa.org

Financial Section: Auditor's Report

The auditor's report (Illustration 2–3), placed at the beginning of the financial section, normally expresses an opinion on the basic financial statements. Like other audits, CPAs are required to conduct government audits according to auditing standards issued by the American Institute of Certified Public Accountants. In addition, specialized governmental auditing standards must be followed. These standards are issued by the Government Accountability Office (GAO). GAO is an agency of the federal government and is the investigative arm of Congress. Governmental auditing standards are discussed in more detail in Chapter 13.

ILLUSTRATION 2–3   Independent Auditor's Report

Kelly & Koch, LLC
Certified Public Accountants

We have audited the accompanying financial statements of the governmental activities, the business-type activities, the aggregate discretely presented component units, each major fund, and the aggregate remaining fund information of the City of Salem as of and for the year ended December 31, 2012, which collectively comprise the City's basic financial statements as listed in the table of contents. These financial statements are the responsibility of the City of Salem's management. Our responsibility is to express opinions on these financial statements based on our audit.

We conducted our audit in accordance with auditing standards generally accepted in the United States of America. Those standards require that we plan and perform the audit to obtain reasonable assurance about whether the financial statements are free of material misstatement. An audit includes examining, on a test basis, evidence supporting the amounts and disclosures in the financial statements. An audit also includes assessing the accounting principles used and significant estimates made by management, as well as evaluating the overall financial statement presentation. We believe that our audit provides a reasonable basis for our opinions.

In our opinion, the financial statements referred to above present fairly, in all material respects, the respective financial position of the governmental activities, the business-type activities, the aggregate discretely presented component units, each major fund, and the aggregate remaining fund information of the City of Salem as of December 31, 2012, and the respective changes in financial position and cash flows, where applicable, thereof for the year then ended in conformity with accounting principles generally accepted in the United States of America.

Additional paragraphs address required supplementary information, other supplementary information, and the statistical tables.
Illustration 13–2 provides an example of a complete (unqualified) opinion.

[Signature] [Date]

Management's Discussion and Analysis (MD&A)

The MD&A (Illustration 2–4) provides an opportunity for the government to provide, in plain terms, an overview of the government's financial activities. This section is considered **Required Supplementary Information,** which means that it is required and entails some auditor responsibility, but not as much as the basic financial statements. Auditors review the material to establish that it is not misleading in relation to the basic statements but do not include the MD&A in the scope of the audit. A number of specific items must be included:

1. A brief discussion of the financial statements.
2. Condensed financial information derived from the government-wide financial statements, comparing the current year with the prior year. GASB *Statement 34* identifies 14 specific items for discussion.
3. An analysis of the government's overall financial position and results of operations to assist users in assessing whether financial position has improved or deteriorated as a result of the year's operations.
4. An analysis of balances and transactions of individual funds.
5. An analysis of significant variations between original and final budget amounts and between final budget amounts and actual results for the General Fund.
6. A description of significant capital asset and long-term debt activity during the year.
7. A discussion by governments that use the modified approach to report infrastructure assets (discussed in Chapter 8), that includes: discussion of changes in the condition of infrastructure assets, comparison of assessed condition with the condition level established by the government, and disclosure of the difference between the amount needed to maintain infrastructure assets and the amount actually expended.
8. A description of any known facts, decisions, or conditions that would have a significant effect on the government's financial position or results of operations.

GASB *Statement 37* makes it clear that MD&A is limited to the preceding eight items. However, governments may expand the discussion of these items if deemed appropriate.

ILLUSTRATION 2–4 Management's Discussion and Analysis

Financial Highlights
Highlights for the City of Salem's government-wide Financial Statements

- The City's total net assets of governmental activities were $38.4 million at December 31, 2012. Net assets for the business-type activities were $47.9 million.
- Total revenues of governmental activities exceeded total expenses by $3.3 million.
- The City's total debt at December 31, 2012, was $62.2 million, a net increase of $6.5 million. The City issued $9.7 million in general obligation bonds during 2012 to renovate the courthouse.

Overview of the Financial Statements

The financial section of this annual report consists of four parts: (1) management's discussion and analysis, (2) the basic financial statements, (3) required supplementary information, and (4) other supplementary information.

The basic financial statements include two kinds of statements that present different views of the City:

- The government-wide financial statements provide readers with a broad overview of the City's finances, including long-term and short-term information about the City's overall financial status.
- The fund financial statements focus on the individual parts of the City government, reporting the City's operations in more detail than the government-wide statements.

Government-wide Financial Statements

The government-wide financial statements report information about the City of Salem as a whole using accounting methods similar to those used by private-sector companies. The statement of net assets and the statement of activities are the government-wide statements. These statements include all of the government's assets and liabilities using the accrual basis of accounting. All revenues and expenses are reported, regardless of when cash is received or paid.

The City's total net assets exceeded liabilities by $86 million at December 31, 2012. The largest portion of the City's net assets (70%) reflects its investments in capital assets, less accumulated depreciation and any related outstanding debt used to acquire those assets. The City uses these assets to provide services to its citizens and customers, therefore these assets are not available for future spending. Presented below is a table comparing the three categories of net assets for the City's governmental, business-type, and component unit activities for fiscal years 2011 and 2012.

Management's discussion and analysis continues typically for 10 or more pages.

Statement of Net Assets

The Statement of Net Assets (Illustration 2–5) presents the asset, liability, and net asset balances (measured on the accrual basis and economic resources measurement focus) for the entity's governmental and business-type activities. Together, the governmental and business activities comprise the primary government. Similar information is presented in a separate column for the government's discretely presented component units. Fiduciary activities, however, are not included in the government-wide statements. Prior year balances may be presented, but are not required.

Assets are generally reported in order of liquidity. A classified approach (presenting separate totals for current and noncurrent items) may be used, but is not required. Note in particular that capital assets (property and equipment) are presented in the governmental activities column. This will not be the case when we examine the governmental fund basis financial statements. The capital assets include infrastructure and are reported net of accumulated depreciation. Similarly, long-term debt is presented in the governmental activities column of the government-wide Statement of Activities, but is not presented for governmental funds in the fund basis balance sheet.

The difference between assets and liabilities is called net assets and is reported in three categories. **Invested in capital assets, net of related debt** is computed by taking the capital assets, less accumulated depreciation, and deducting outstanding debt that is related to the financing of capital assets. Liabilities incurred to finance operations (including long-term liabilities for compensated absences or employee benefits) would not be deducted. **Restricted net assets** include resources that are restricted by (*a*) external parties, including creditors, grantors, contributors, or by laws or regulations of other governments; or (*b*) laws or constitutional provisions of the reporting government. The remaining amount, **unrestricted net assets,** is a "plug" figure that is determined by deducting the balances of the other two categories from the overall excess of assets over liabilities.

$$\text{Net } A = A - L$$

Invested in capital,
net of debt
$$= (\text{Capital } A - \text{Acc. Dep.}) - \text{debt related to financing capital } A \quad (\text{Except finace operating})$$

Restricted N/A =

Unrestricted N/A = Overall excess of A over L − Bal. of other 2 categories

Example Comprehensive Annual Financial Report
Financial Section: Basic Financial Statements
Government-wide Financial Statements: Statement of Net Assets

ILLUSTRATION 2–5 Statement of Net Assets

CITY OF SALEM
Statement of Net Assets
As of December 31, 2012

	Governmental Activities	Business-type Activities	Primary Government	Component Units
Assets	Primary Government			*separate Co.*
Cash and cash equivalents	$ 8,242,998	$ 4,814,724	$13,057,722	$ 84,733
Investments	3,312,992	10,350,334	13,663,326	———
Inventory	1,072,963	30,779	1,103,742	———
Receivables (net):				
Taxes receivable	2,872,611	———	2,872,611	———
Accounts receivable	722,215	2,657,326	3,379,541	———
Due from other governments	1,328,448	———	1,328,448	———
Restricted assets	3,933,126	2,295,043	6,228,169	———
Capital assets (net of accumulated depreciation)	65,690,373	48,894,402	114,584,775	11,197,985
Total assets	87,175,726	69,042,608	156,218,334	11,282,718
Liabilities				
Accounts payable	2,425,447	493,849	2,919,296	710
Accrued liabilities	4,340,108	473,168	4,813,276	———
Noncurrent liabilities due within one year	2,164,521	1,342,717	3,507,238	———
Noncurrent liabilities due in more than one year	39,834,882	18,858,187	58,693,069	———
Total liabilities	48,764,958	21,167,921	69,932,879	710
Net assets				
Invested in capital assets net of related debt	23,690,970	28,693,498	52,384,468	11,197,985
Restricted	3,933,126	———	3,933,126	———
Unrestricted	10,786,672	19,181,189	29,967,861	84,023
TOTAL NET ASSETS	$38,410,768	$47,874,687	$86,285,455	$11,282,008

Government-wide Statement of Activities

Note the general format of the Statement of Activities (Illustration 2–6). Expenses are measured on the accrual basis and reported first. Expenses for governmental activities are reported initially, followed by the business-type activities and the component units (reading from top to bottom). Direct expenses, including depreciation, are required to be reported by function (General Government, Judicial Administration, etc.). Although rarely done, governments may allocate indirect expenses to functions. However, the government is required to show a separate column for these allocated amounts. Depreciation that relates to assets serving multiple functions may be allocated as an indirect expense, charged in total to general government, or displayed in a separate line.

Interest on long-term debt would be included in direct expenses if the interest related to a single function. Most interest, however, cannot be identified with a single function and should be shown separately. Interest incurred during construction of capital projects is capitalized and included in the capital asset on the Statement of Net Assets.

Revenues that can be directly associated with functions are deducted, and a net expense or revenue is presented. General revenues are presented in the lower right-hand section of the statement, and the change in net assets is computed. General revenues include tax revenues and those revenues that are not associated directly with a particular function or program. All taxes levied by the government, including those restricted to a particular purpose, are reported as general revenues. Program revenues include charges for services, operating grants, taxes levied by a state and shared with the local government, and capital grants and contributions. Charges for services include charges by enterprise funds as well as fines and forfeits. Grants and contributions are typically resources provided by other governments.

Contributions to endowments and extraordinary items (items that are both unusual *and* infrequent) are reported separately after general revenues. However, **special items** (items within the control of management but which are unusual in nature *or* infrequent in occurrence) are shown in a separate line within general revenues.

The Statement of Activities is a consolidated statement within columns (governmental activities, business-type activities, and component units), which means that interfund services provided and used and transfers between two governmental funds are eliminated. Transfers between governmental and business-type activities are displayed in the general revenues section and offset.

ILLUSTRATION 2–6   Statement of Activities

CITY OF SALEM
Statement of Activities
For the Year Ended December 31, 2012

Functions/Programs	Expenses	Program Revenues Charges for Services	Program Revenues Operating Grants and Contributions	Program Revenues Capital Grants and Contributions	Net (Expense) Revenue and Change in Net Assets Governmental Activities	Net (Expense) Revenue and Change in Net Assets Business-type Activities	Net (Expense) Revenue and Change in Net Assets Total	Net (Expense) Revenue and Change in Net Assets Component Units
Governmental activities								
General government	$ 3,734,068	$ 1,144,018	$ 263,178	$ —	$ (2,326,872)		$ (2,326,872)	$
Judicial administration	1,433,650	56,497	1,002,525	—	(374,628)		(374,628)	
Public safety	9,265,997	275,492	750,109	277,700	(7,962,696)		(7,962,696)	
Public works	6,167,650	—	2,903,982	1,853,091	(1,410,577)		(1,410,577)	
Health and welfare	4,436,534	—	2,861,389	4,203	(1,570,942)		(1,570,942)	
Education	9,292,427	—	73,300	—	(9,219,127)		(9,219,127)	
Parks and recreation	3,217,236	604,359	302,672	500	(2,309,705)		(2,309,705)	
Community development	1,720,121	51,611	298,495	156,361	(1,213,654)		(1,213,654)	
Interest on long-term debt	1,422,428				(1,422,428)		(1,422,428)	
Total governmental activities	40,690,111	2,131,977	8,455,650	2,291,855	(27,810,629)		(27,810,629)	
Business-type activities								
Water	6,041,987	6,385,233		3,109,692		3,452,938	3,452,938	
Solid waste	2,556,633	2,351,433	6,594	2,085,064		1,886,458	1,886,458	
Parking	481,869	261,107				(220,762)	(220,762)	
Total business-type activities	9,080,489	8,997,773	6,594	5,194,756		5,118,634	5,118,634	
Total primary government	49,770,600	11,129,750	8,462,244	7,486,611	(27,810,629)	5,118,634	(22,691,995)	
Component units								
Industrial development authority	4,322,849	9,979	20,000	4,193,964				(98,906)
				General revenues				
				Property taxes	15,382,482		15,382,482	
				Sales taxes	5,729,224		5,729,224	
				Hotel and meals taxes	4,998,045		4,998,045	
				Grants	2,724,725		2,724,725	1,172
				Miscellaneous	1,611,886	729,488	2,341,374	
				Transfers	615,062	(615,062)		
				Total general revenues	31,061,424	114,426	31,175,850	1,172
				Change in net assets	3,250,795	5,233,060	8,483,855	(97,734)
				Net assets, beginning	35,159,973	42,641,627	77,801,600	11,379,742
				Net assets, ending	$38,410,768	$47,874,687	$86,285,455	$11,282,008

Governmental Funds: Balance Sheet

Illustration 2–7b presents a Balance Sheet for the governmental funds, including the General, special revenue, capital projects, and debt service funds. The City of Salem does not have a permanent fund or it would be presented here as well. Each of the city's governmental funds is considered a major fund and presented separately. If the city had multiple smaller funds, they would be aggregated and reported in a single column labeled *nonmajor funds*.

The governmental fund statements are prepared using the current financial resources focus and the modified accrual basis of accounting. For this reason, capital assets and long-term debt do not appear on the balance sheet. The excess of assets over liabilities is labeled *fund balance*, an account title used only in the governmental funds. All other funds and the government-wide statements label the difference between assets and liabilities as *net assets*.

Several features of the Balance Sheet should be noted. First, a total column is required. Secondly, fund balance is displayed within the categories of nonspendable, restricted, committed, assigned and unassigned. These will be more fully described in later chapters, but represent varying degrees of constraint placed on the use of the (net) resources of governmental funds.

Finally, total fund balances reported in the total column ($12,922,626) must be reconciled to total net assets ($38,410,768) presented in the governmental activities column of the government-wide Statement of Net Assets. The reconciliation is presented separately in Illustration 2–7a (*below*). These amounts differ because the two statements have different bases of accounting and because most internal service funds are included in the governmental activities column on the government-wide statements

ILLUSTRATION 2–7a   Reconciliation to (Government-wide) Statement of Net Assets

Fund Balance reported in the Governmental Funds Balance Sheet	$12,992,626
Amounts reported for governmental activities in the Statement of Net Assets are different because:	
Capital Assets used in government operations are not financial resources and therefore are not reported in the funds	65,621,772
Some liabilities are not due and payable in the current period and are not reported in fund liabilities	(41,999,403)
The assets and liabilities of internal service funds in included in governmental activities for the Statement of Net Assets	436,475
Receivables on the statement of net assets that do not provide current financial resources are reported as deferred revenue in the funds.	1,359,298
Net Assets of Governmental Activities in the Statement of Net Assets	$38,410,768

ILLUSTRATION 2–7b   Governmental Funds Balance Sheet

CITY OF SALEM
Balance Sheet
Governmental Funds
As of December 31, 2012

Assets	General Fund	Special Revenue Fund	Courthouse Renovation Fund	Debt Service Fund	Total Governmental Funds
Cash and cash equivalents	$6,408,214	$627,837	$895,300	$230,000	$8,161,351
Investments	3,312,992	——	——	——	3,312,992
Receivables (net)					
Taxes receivable	2,872,611	——	——	——	2,872,611
Accounts Receivable	679,215	14,177	——	——	693,392
Due from Other Governments	1,085,184	——	243,264	——	1,328,448
Supplies inventory	23,747	——	——	——	23,747
Restricted Assets	3,933,126	——	——	——	3,933,126
TOTAL ASSETS	$18,315,089	642,014	1,138,564	230,000	$20,325,667
Liabilities					
Accounts payable	2,085,358	70,000	207,134	——	2,362,492
Accrued liabilities	543,064	——	19,398	——	562,462
Deferred Revenues	4,408,087	——	——	——	4,408,087
Total Liabilities	7,036,509	70,000	226,532	——	7,333,041
Fund Balance =A —L					
Nonspendable					
- Supplies inventory	23,747	——	——	——	23,747
Restricted					
- Intergovernmental grants	——	312,000	500,000	——	812,000
- Bond sinking fund	——	——	——	230,000	230,000
Committed					
- Rainy day fund	4,500,000	——	——	——	4,500,000
- Courthouse renovation	——	——	380,000	——	380,000
Assigned					
- School lunch program	——	260,014	——	——	260,014
- Other capital projects	680,500	——	32,032	——	712,532
- Other purposes	236,800	——	——	——	236,800
Unassigned	5,837,533	——	——	——	5,837,533
TOTAL FUND BALANCE	11,278,580	572,014	912,032	230,000	12,992,626
TOTAL LIABILITIES AND FUND BALANCE	$18,315,089	$642,014	$1,138,564	$230,000	$20,325,667

Governmental Funds: Statement of Revenues, Expenditures, and Changes in Fund Balance

Illustration 2–8b presents the operating statement for the same governmental funds appearing in the balance sheet. Again, the statement is prepared using the current financial resources measurement focus and the modified accrual basis of accounting. Revenues are reported by source and expenditures (not expenses) are reported by character: current, debt service, and capital outlay. Within the current category, expenditures are presented by function: general government, judicial administration, public safety, and so on. Within the debt service category, expenditures are displayed as interest or principal.

Following revenues and expenses, other financing sources and uses are displayed. These reflect interfund transfers and the proceeds of issuing debt. Most of the items appearing in this section are eliminated when preparing the government-wide financial statements. Like all operating statements, reconciliations to the balance sheet are required. In this case, the operating statement is reconciled to total fund balances by adding the beginning of year fund balance.

The excess of revenues and other sources over expenditure and other uses ($1,485,357) is reconciled to the change in net assets ($3,250,795) for the governmental activities column in the government-wide statement of activities. This reconciliation would normally appear at the bottom of the statement of revenues, expenditures, and changes in fund balance, but is presented in Illustration 2–8a due to space considerations.

ILLUSTRATION 2–8a   Reconciliation to Statement of Activities

Amounts reported for governmental activities in the Statement of Activities are different because of the following:	
Excess of revenues and other sources over (under) expenditures and other uses.	$(1,485,357)
Governmental funds report the cost of capital assets as expenditures, while they are capital assets in the government-wide statements.	10,924,818
Debt proceeds provide current financial resources to the governmental funds but are liabilities in the government-wide statements.	(9,675,400)
Depreciation is not recorded in the governmental funds, but is expensed in the Statement of Activities.	(1,691,116)
Income earned by Internal Service funds is included in governmental activities on government-wide statements.	23,964
Payments of principal on long-term debt are expenditures in the governmental funds but reduce the liability in the government-wide statements.	1,155,326
Property taxes expected to be collected more than 60 days after year end are deferred in the governmental funds.	3,998,560
Change in net assets of governmental activities	$3,250,795

ILLUSTRATION 2–8b Governmental Funds Statement of Revenues, Expenditures, and Changes in Fund Balance

CITY OF SALEM
Statement of Revenues, Expenditures, and Changes
in Fund Balances—Governmental Funds
For the Year Ended December 31, 2012

	General	Special Revenue	Courthouse Renovation	Debt Service	Total Governmental
Revenues					
Property taxes	$15,361,830	$ ——	$ ——	$ ——	$15,361,830
Other local taxes	11,761,522	——	——	——	11,761,522
Charges for services	1,601,435	291,243	——	——	1,892,678
Intergovernmental	7,098,698	3,456,194	441,548	——	10,996,440
Miscellaneous	1,262,549	——	——	——	1,262,549
Total revenues	37,086,034	3,747,437	441,548	——	41,275,019
Expenditures					
Current:					
General government	3,353,502	——	——	——	3,353,502
Judicial administration	1,456,734	1,981,144	——	——	3,437,878
Public safety	8,216,347	——	——	——	8,216,347
Public works	4,602,273	——	——	——	4,602,273
Health and welfare	4,418,294	——	——	——	4,418,294
Education	8,887,834	——	——	——	8,887,834
Parks and recreation	3,055,325	——	——	——	3,055,325
Community development	899,209	1,093,804	——	——	1,993,013
Capital outlay	——	——	10,924,818	——	10,924,818
Debt service:					
Principal	——	——	——	1,155,326	1,155,326
Interest	——	——	——	924,818	924,818
Total expenditures	$34,889,518	3,074,948	10,924,818	2,080,144	50,969,428
Revenues over (under) expenditures	2,196,516	672,489	(10,483,270)	(2,080,144)	(9,694,409)
Other financing sources (uses)					
Issuance of debt	——	——	9,675,400	——	9,675,400
Transfers from other funds				2,080,144	2,080,144
Transfers (to) other funds	(3,256,899)	(289,593)	——	——	(3,546,492)
Total other financing sources (uses)	(3,256,899)	(289,593)	9,675,400	2,080,144	8,209,052
Excess of revenues and other sources over (under) expenditures and other uses	(1,060,383)	382,896	(807,870)	——	(1,485,357)
Fund balance— Beginning of Year	12,338,963	189,118	1,719,902	230,000	14,487,983
Fund balance—End of Year	$11,278,580	$572,014	$912,032	$230,000	$12,992,626

(handwritten notes: "Reconcile", "= To B/S")

Proprietary Funds: Statement of Net Assets

Illustration 2–9 presents a Statement of Net Assets for the proprietary funds. Again, major funds must be presented in separate columns. An enterprise fund is considered major if: (*a*) assets, liabilities, revenues, *or* expenses are 10 percent or more of the total for all enterprise funds, *and* (*b*) its assets, liabilities, revenues, *or* expenses are 5 percent or more of the total of the governmental and enterprise categories, combined. In this case, the parking enterprise fund does not meet the requirements, but the government chooses to display it separately rather than label it a nonmajor fund.

Internal service funds are also presented in a separate column in the proprietary fund statement of net assets. However, internal service funds do not follow the procedures described for major funds. Governments with more than one internal service fund combine the funds into one column for the Statement of Net Assets. Detailed financial statements for each internal service fund are included in the other supplementary information.

The proprietary funds report using the economic resources measurement focus and the accrual basis of accounting. Since this is the same as the government-wide statements, reconciliations between the two sets of statements are typically not needed. In this example, you should be able to trace amounts reported in the total column for the enterprise funds to the business activities column of the statement of net assets.

GASB requires a classified balance sheet where separate totals are reported for current and noncurrent assets and liabilities. Both noncurrent assets and liabilities are presented. The excess of assets over liabilities is reported as net assets, in the same manner as the government-wide statement of net assets. In particular, net assets are reported as: (1) invested in capital assets net of related debt, (2) restricted, or (3) unrestricted. Illustration 2–9 uses a "net asset" format (assets minus liabilities equal net assets), but a balance sheet format is also acceptable (assets equal liabilities plus net assets).

Example Comprehensive Annual Financial Report
Financial Section: Basic Financial Statements
Proprietary Funds Statements: Statement of Net Assets

ILLUSTRATION 2–9 Proprietary Funds: Statement of Net Assets

CITY OF SALEM
Statement of Net Assets—Proprietary Funds
As of December 31, 2012

	Business-type Activities—Enterprise Funds				Governmental Activities—Internal Service
Assets	Water	Solid Waste	Parking	Total	Fund
Current assets:					
Cash and cash equivalents	$3,801,978	$ 847,889	$164,857	$4,814,724	$81,647
Investments	4,433,039	5,917,295	———	10,350,334	———
Inventory	30,779	———	———	30,779	330,759
Receivables (net)	———	———	———	———	———
Accounts receivable	2,307,643	342,394	7,289	2,657,326	———
Due from other funds	———	———	———	———	28,824
Restricted assets	1,394,787	900,256	———	2,295,043	———
Total current assets	11,968,226	8,007,834	172,146	20,148,206	441,230
Noncurrent assets:					
Capital Assets (net of accumulated depreciation)	37,975,852	4,611,754	6,306,796	48,894,402	68,603
Total assets	$49,944,078	$12,619,588	$6,478,942	$69,042,608	$509,833
Liabilities					
Current liabilities:					
Accounts payable	317,131	174,087	2,631	493,849	62,958
Accrued liabilities	437,363	25,854	9,951	473,168	3,309
Total current liabilities	754,494	199,941	12,582	967,017	66,267
Liability for landfilll closure and postclosure care costs	———	2,063,637	———	2,063,637	———
Capital leases payable					7,091
Bonds payable	16,114,097	———	2,023,170	18,137,267	———
Total noncurrent liabilities	16,114,097	2,063,637	2,023,170	20,200,904	7,091
Total liabilities	16,868,591	2,263,578	2,035,752	21,167,921	73,358
Net assets $= A - L$					
Invested in capital assets net of related debt	21,861,755	4,611,754	4,283,626	30,757,135	61,512
Restricted	1,394,787	900,256	———	2,295,043	———
Unrestricted	9,818,945	4,844,000	159,564	14,822,509	374,963
TOTAL NET ASSETS	$33,075,487	$10,356,010	$4,443,190	$47,874,687	$436,475

$= P.31$

Proprietary Funds: Statement of Revenues, Expenses, and Changes in Fund Net Assets

Illustration 2–10 presents a Statement of Revenues, Expenses, and Changes in Fund Net Assets for the propriety funds. GASB requires that operating revenues and expenses be reported first, followed by operating income or loss. Note that depreciation expense is separately displayed as an operating expense. Nonoperating revenues and expenses are reported after operating income. Interest revenue and expense are nonoperating.

Capital contributions, additions to endowments, special and extraordinary items, and transfers appear after the nonoperating revenues and expenses. Capital contributions frequently represent contributions of capital assets by neighborhood and commercial property developers. The change in net assets is reconciled to the statement of net assets by adding the beginning balance of net assets for the period.

Note that the $436,475 total net assets appearing at the bottom of the Internal Service Fund columns in this statement and the Statement of Net Assets (Illustration 2–9) appears in the reconciliation at the bottom of the Governmental Funds balance sheet (Illustration 2–7a). That is because the internal service fund's assets and liabilities (net assets) are reported as governmental activities in the government-wide statement of net assets.

Example Comprehensive Annual Financial Report
Financial Section: Basic Financial Statements
Proprietary Funds Statements: Statement of Revenues, Expenses,
and Changes in Fund Net Assests

ILLUSTRATION 2–10   Proprietary Funds: Statement of Revenues, Expenses, and Changes in Fund Net Assets

CITY OF SALEM
Statement of Revenues, Expenses, and Changes in Fund Net Assets—Proprietary Funds
For the Year Ended December 31, 2012

	Business-type Activities—Enterprise Funds				Governmental Activities—Internal Service Fund
	Water	Solid Waste	Parking	Total	
Operating revenues					
Charges for services	$6,335,022	$2,292,322	$261,088	$8,888,432	$663,162
Miscellaneous	45,499	58,827	———	104,326	———
Total revenues	6,380,521	2,351,149	261,088	8,992,758	663,162
Operating expenses					
Personnel services	1,576,088	1,164,629	126,466	2,867,183	591,010
Repairs and maintenance	389,271	50,296	———	439,567	2,698
Contractual services	1,107,169	439,355	———	1,546,524	34,622
Depreciation	1,374,214	353,411	153,097	1,880,722	6,654
Utilities	186,195	1,173	40,619	227,987	100
Other	699,009	332,110	63,766	1,094,885	4,256
Landfill closure costs	———	215,659	———	215,659	———
Total operating expenses	5,331,946	2,556,633	383,948	8,272,527	639,340
Operating income (loss)	1,048,575	(205,484)	(122,860)	720,231	23,822
Nonoperating revenues (expenses)					
Interest Income	452,718	279,924	1,558	734,200	700
State aid	23,746	6,878	———	30,624	———
Interest expense	(710,042)	———	(97,901)	(807,943)	(558)
Total nonoperating revenue	(233,578)	286,802	(96,343)	(43,119)	142
Income before contributions and transfers	814,997	81,318	(219,203)	677,112	23,964
Capital contributions	3,085,946	2,085,064	———	5,171,010	———
Transfers in	———	———	179,440	179,440	———
Transfers out	(92,300)	(702,202)	———	(794,502)	———
Change in net assets	3,808,643	1,464,180	(39,763)	5,233,060	23,964
Net assets—beginning of year	29,452,090	8,842,556	4,346,981	42,641,627	412,511
Net assets—end of year	$33,260,733	$10,306,736	$4,307,218	$47,874,687	$436,475

Proprietary Funds: Statement of Cash Flows

Proprietary funds are the only funds that report a Statement of Cash Flows, presented here in Illustration 2–11. Several differences exist between the GASB format cash flow statement and the FASB format required of commercial businesses:

1. GASB requires governments to prepare cash flows from operating activities on the direct method.
2. The reconciliation of income to cash flows from operating activities of the proprietary fund, which appears in the bottom section of the statement, begins with operating income, not net income (or total change in net assets).
3. The statement has four sections, rather than the three observed in FASB format statements. These include:

   • Operating activities are those associated with operating income. As a result, cash flows from interest expense, interest revenue, and investment income do not appear in the operating activities section.
   • Noncapital-related financing activities involve the borrowing and payment (including interest) of loans for purposes other than financing capital additions, chiefly, borrowing for operations.
   • Capital and related financing include grants and debt transactions (including interest) used to finance capital additions.
   • Investing activities involve the acquisition and sale of investments as well as cash received from investment income.

One purpose of a cash flow statement is to help in explaining changes between the beginning and ending balances of assets and liabilities. Differences resulting in cash inflows and outflows are reflected in the body of the statement. However, some investing, capital, and financing activities may not affect cash. Capital leases, for example, result in a capital asset and a long-term liability, but do not involve cash at the inception. Noncash investing, capital, and financing activities, such as this, are disclosed below the cash flow statement. Illustration 2–11 presents another example of a noncash capital-related transaction, the contribution to the city of $5,171,000 of capital assets by developers or other governments. The amounts of such contributions are disclosed at the bottom of the cash flows statement.

ILLUSTRATION 2–11   Proprietary Funds: Statement of Cash Flows

CITY OF SALEM
Statement of Cash Flows
Proprietary Funds
For the Year Ended December 31, 2012

	Business-type Activities—Enterprise Funds				Governmental Activities— Internal Service
	Water	Solid Waste	Parking	Total	Funds
Cash flows from operating activities					
Cash received from customers	$6,388,018	$2,343,431	$259,946	$8,991,395	$649,426
Cash paid to suppliers	(2,490,241)	(822,363)	(80,137)	(3,392,741)	(630,437)
Cash paid to employees	(948,035)	(764,032)	(99,517)	(1,811,584)	———
Other	(588,974)	(322,472)	(50,430)	(961,876)	———
Net cash provided by operating activities	2,360,768	434,564	29,862	2,825,194	18,989
Cash flows from noncapital financing activities					
Operating grants received	———	6,594	———	6,594	———
Transfers from other funds	———	———	179,440	179,440	———
Transfers to other funds	(92,300)	(702,202)	———	(794,502)	———
Net cash provided by noncapital financing activities	(92,300)	(695,608)	179,440	(608,468)	———
Cash flows from capital and related financing activities					
Acquisition of capital assets	(543,169)	(456,179)	———	(999,348)	———
Principal paid on long-term debt	(1,014,887)	———	(128,420)	(1,143,307)	(3,719)
Interest paid	(535,567)	———	(95,961)	(631,528)	———
Net cash provided from capital and related financing activities	(2,093,623)	(456,179)	(224,381)	(2,774,183)	(3,719)
Cash flows from investing activities					
Interest received	287,725	279,924	1,558	569,207	700
Net cash provided from investing activities	287,725	279,924	1,558	569,207	700
Increase in cash	462,570	(437,299)	(13,521)	11,750	15,970
Cash and cash equivalents beginning of year	9,167,234	8,102,739	178,378	17,448,351	65,677
Cash and cash equivalents end of year	9,629,804	7,665,440	164,857	17,460,101	81,647
Reconciliation of operating income to net cash provided by operating activities:					
Operating income	1,048,575	(205,484)	(122,860)	720,231	23,822
Depreciation	1,374,214	353,411	153,097	1,880,722	6,654
(Increase) decrease in receivables	21,097	122,828	(375)	143,550	(13,736)
(Increase) decrease in inventory	———	———	———	———	(46,535)
Increase (decrease) in accounts payable	(83,118)	———	———	(83,118)	48,784
Increase in landfill closure liability	———	163,809	———	163,809	———
Net cash provided by operating activities	$2,360,768	$434,564	$29,862	$2,825,194	$18,989
Noncash investing, capital, and financing activities:					
Contributions of capital assets from developers	$3,085,946	$2,085,064	$———	$5,171,000	$———

Example Comprehensive Annual Financial Report
Financial Section: Basic Financial Statements
Fiduciary Funds Statements: Statement of Fiduciary Net Assets;
Statement of Changes in Fiduciary Net Assests

Fiduciary: Statement of Fiduciary Net Assets

Illustration 2–12 presents a Statement of Fiduciary Net Assets. Fiduciary funds are reported by fund type, not major funds. GASB requires that fiduciary fund statements be included for all trust and agency fund types and for component units that are similar in nature. GASB also requires, if separate GAAP basis financial statements are not issued for individual pension and other employee benefit plans, that those reports be included in the notes to the basis financial statements.

The fiduciary funds use the economic resources measurement focus and may include capital and other noncurrent assets and long-term liabilities. Note in Illustration 2–12 that the excess of assets over liabilities is labeled *net assets* and the statement indicates that the net assets are held in trust for some purpose.

Fiduciary: Statement of Changes in Fiduciary Net Assets

Illustration 2–13 presents a Statement of Changes in Fiduciary Net Assets. Note that the agency fund does not appear in this statement. That is because assets equal liabilities in agency funds (zero net assets). Although fiduciary funds use accrual accounting, the activity accounts are not labeled Revenues and Expenses. Rather the terms *additions* and *deductions* are used to reflect the fact that the government has only custody of the resources. Recall also that fiduciary funds are not included in the government-wide financial statements.

Trust funds frequently have substantial investments activities. GASB requires that investments be reported at fair market value. Changes in the value of investments are reflected in the Statement of Changes in Fiduciary Net Assets as *increase (decrease) in the fair value of investments*. In the case of the City of Salem, this totals $163,050.

ILLUSTRATION 2–12 Statement of Fiduciary Net Assets

CITY OF SALEM
Statement of Fiduciary Net Assets
As of December 31, 2012

Assets	Employee Pension Trust	Private-purpose Trust	Agency Fund
Cash and cash equivalents	$ 172,000	$12,500	$2,369,000
Interest and dividends receivable	13,690	——	——
Investments at fair value			
Corporate bonds	2,725,600	——	——
Corporate stocks	6,852,300	——	——
U.S. government securities	1,325,000	900,256	——
TOTAL ASSETS	$11,088,590	912,756	2,369,000
Liabilities			
Accounts payable	$ 105,000	7,600	——
Due to other governments			2,369,000
Total liabilities	105,000	7,600	2,369,000
Net assets			
Held in trust for pension benefits	10,983,590	——	——
Held in trust for other purposes	——	905,156	——
TOTAL NET ASSETS	$10,983,590	$905,156	$ ——

ILLUSTRATION 2–13 Statement of Changes in Fiduciary Net Assets

CITY OF SALEM
Statement of Changes in Fiduciary Net Assets
For the Year Ended December 31, 2012

Additions	Employee Pension Trust	Private-purpose Trust
Contributions:		
Plan members	$ 912,000	$ ——
Employer	1,600,000	——
Individuals	——	100,000
Total contributions	2,512,000	100,000
Investment income:		
Interest	18,560	8,500
Dividends	63,000	——
Increase in fair value of investments	163,050	——
Total investment income	244,610	8,500
Total additions	2,756,610	108,500
Deductions		
Administrative expenses	12,900	——
Benefits	883,600	7,600
Refunds of contributions	35,000	——
Total deductions	931,500	7,600
Change in net assets	1,825,110	100,900
Net assets—beginning of year	9,158,480	804,256
Net assets—end-of-year	$10,977,590	$905,156

Notes to the Financial Statements

The notes to the financial statements are an integral part of the basic financial statements. As presented in Illustration 2–14, the first note is a summary of the significant accounting policies and the first of these is generally a description of the reporting entity. Any event significant to understanding and interpreting the financial statements should be described in the notes, whether or not it is specifically required by GASB standards. Following is a description of typical contents to the notes:

1. Summary of significant accounting policies, including:

   - A brief description of the component units and their relationship to the reporting entity.
   - A description of the activities reported in each of the following columns presented in the basic financial statements: major funds, internal service funds, and fiduciary fund types.
   - A description of the government-wide statements and the measurement focus and basis of accounting used in the government-wide statements.
   - The revenue recognition policies used in the fund financial statements, including the length of time used to define *available* for purposes of revenue recognition in the governmental fund financial statements.
   - The policy for eliminating internal activity in the government-wide statement of activities.
   - The policy for capitalizing assets and for estimating the useful lives of those assets.
   - A description of the types of transactions included in program revenues and the policy for allocating indirect expenses to functions (if applicable) in the statement of activities.
   - The policy for defining operating and nonoperating revenues of proprietary funds.
   - The policy for applying FASB pronouncements issued after November 30, 1989, to business-type activities and to enterprise funds of the primary government.
   - The definition of cash and cash equivalents used in the statement of cash flows for the proprietary funds.
   - The government's policy with regard to restricted and unrestricted resources when an expense is incurred for purposes for which both restricted and unrestricted resources are available.

2. Description of cash deposits with financial institutions.
3. Investments.
4. Contingent liabilities.
5. Encumbrances outstanding.

Example Comprehensive Annual Financial Report
Financial Section: Basic Financial Statements
Notes to the Financial Statements

ILLUSTRATION 2–14   Notes to the Financial Statements

1. Summary of Significant Accounting Policies

The City of Salem was established as a town in 1861 and incorporated as a city by an act of the State Legislature in 1930. The City has an area of 19.9 square miles and a population of 23,875, according to the 2010 Census. The City provides a full range of services, including general government, judicial administration, public safety, public works, health and welfare, education, parks and recreation, community development, water utility, refuse disposal, and parking facilities.

The financial statements of the City have been prepared in accordance with accounting principles generally accepted (GAAP) in the United States applicable to governmental units as specified by the Governmental Accounting Standards Board. The following is a summary of the more significant accounting policies of the City:

A. The Financial Reporting Entity

As required by GAAP, these financial statements present the City (primary government) and its component unit. The Salem Industrial Development Authority is reported as a separate and discretely presented component unit of the City. The City has no blended component units.

The Salem Industrial Development Authority has the responsibility to promote industry and develop trade by inducing manufacturing, industrial and other commercial enterprises to locate or remain in the City. The City appoints all seven members of the Authority's Board of Directors. In addition the City issued $10 million in general obligation bonds in 2004 to provide a capital grant to the Authority. As a result, the Authority imposes a financial burden on the City. Complete financial statements of the Authority may be obtained from the Salem Industrial Development Authority's offices, located at 10 West Main Street.

The notes typically continue for 20 or more pages.

6. Effects of events subsequent to the date of the financial statements.
7. Annual pension cost and net pension obligation.
8. Violations of finance-related legal and contractual provisions and actions taken to address violations.
9. Debt service requirements.
10. Commitments under noncapitalized (operating) leases.
11. Construction and other significant commitments.
12. Required disclosures about capital leases.
13. Required disclosures about long-term liabilities.
14. Deficit fund balances or net assets of individual nonmajor funds.
15. Interfund receivables and payables.
16. Disclosures about donor-restricted endowments.
17. For component units, the nature and amount of significant transactions with other units of the reporting entity.

Of course, the disclosures just listed are not required when they do not apply. For example, lease disclosures are not applicable if the government has no noncancelable leases.

Required Supplementary Information Other than MD&A

Recall that required supplementary information appears in two parts of the financial section: the MD&A precedes the basic financial statements and certain required supplementary information (RSI) schedules follow the notes. Among the required schedules are the following: information required when using the modified approach to infrastructure, budgetary comparison schedule, pension schedules (illustrated in Chapter 7), and schedules of risk management activities.

Modified Approach for Reporting Infrastructure As an alternative to depreciating infrastructure assets, governments may choose to use a modified approach (described in Chapter 8). Governments that choose to use the modified approach must present a schedule of the assessed condition of infrastructure assets and a schedule comparing the estimated cost to maintain infrastructure assets with the amounts actually expended. These schedules are part of the RSI and are presented in Illustration 2–15.

ILLUSTRATION 2–15 **Required Schedules When Using the Modified Approach for Infrastructure**

CITY OF SALEM
Condition Rating of City's Street System

	Fiscal Years 2006–2009 % of Streets	Fiscal Years 2010–2012 % of Streets
Excellent to Good	35	85
Fair	26	13
Poor to Substandard	39	2

Comparison of Needed-to-Actual Maintenance Expenditures for City's Street System

	2009	2010	2011	2012
Needed to maintain	$ 1,113,851	$1,251,518	$1,406,200	$1,580,000
Actual amount expended	$ 1,111,346	1,248,703	1,403,037	1,576,446

The City has an ongoing street rehabilitation program, funded in the General Fund, that is intended to improve the condition rating of the City's streets. The rehabilitation program is formulated based on deficiencies identified as part of its Asset Management System.

Budgetary Comparison Schedule Illustration 2–16 presents a budgetary comparison schedule, which is required of the General Fund and each major special revenue fund that has a legally adopted budget. This schedule includes the original budget, the final appropriated budget, and the actual results computed on the same basis as the budget. When the basis of accounting used in the budget differs from that in the statement of revenues, expenditures, and changes in fund balance, the two must be reconciled in the schedule or in notes to the RSI. In the case of the City of Salem, the city uses the GAAP basic for budgeting and no reconciliation is required. Governments have the option of reporting a budget comparison statement as part of the basic financial statements rather than this schedule in the RSI.

Example Comprehensive Annual Financial Report
Financial Section: Required Supplementary Information
Other than Management's Discussion and Analysis

ILLUSTRATION 2–16 Schedule of Revenues, Expenditures, and Changes in Fund Balance—Budget and Actual: General Fund

CITY OF SALEM
Schedule of Revenues, Expenditures, and Changes in Fund Balance—
Budget and Actual: General Fund
For the Year Ended December 31, 2012

	Budgeted Amounts		Actual Amounts Budgetary Basis	Variance with Final Budget
Revenues	Original	Final		
Property taxes	$14,666,000	$14,666,000	$15,361,830	$695,830
Other local taxes	11,562,500	11,562,500	11,761,522	199,022
Charges for services	1,613,011	1,613,011	1,601,435	(11,576)
Intergovernmental	7,892,080	8,047,907	7,098,698	(949,209)
Miscellaneous	1,504,977	1,388,385	1,262,549	(125,836)
Total revenues	37,238,568	37,277,803	37,086,034	(191,769)
Expenditures				
Current				
General Government	3,567,838	3,489,870	3,353,502	136,368
Judicial Administration	1,321,048	1,497,845	1,456,734	41,111
Public Safety	7,753,002	8,325,564	8,216,347	109,217
Public Works	4,541,651	4,984,353	4,602,273	382,080
Health and Welfare	4,823,267	4,440,167	4,418,294	21,873
Education	8,963,248	8,929,725	8,887,834	41,891
Parks and Recreation	2,983,861	3,097,528	3,055,325	42,203
Community Development	872,594	904,168	899,209	4,959
Total expenditures	34,826,509	35,669,220	34,889,518	779,702
Revenues over (under) expenditures	2,412,059	1,608,583	2,196,516	587,933
Other financing sources (uses):				
Transfers (to) other funds	(3,560,000)	(3,257,000)	(3,256,899)	101
	(3,560,000)	(3,257,000)	(3,256,899)	101
Excess of revenues and other sources over (under) expenditures and other uses	(1,147,941)	(1,648,417)	(1,060,383)	588,034
Fund balance— beginning of year	12,338,963	12,338,963	12,338,963	——
Fund balance— end of Year	$11,191,022	$10,690,546	$11,278,580	$588,034

Example Comprehensive Annual Financial Report
Financial Section: <u>Other</u> Supplementry Information

Combining Statements

A complete CAFR presents combining statements to reflect its nonmajor funds whenever a nonmajor column is used in one of the fund statements. Any fund that was not large enough to be reported as a major fund will be presented in the combining statement. The total column in the combining statements will be the same as the *nonmajor funds* column in the basic financial statements.

Example Comprehensive Annual Financial Report
Statistical Section

Statistical Information

Governments wishing to present the more complete comprehensive annual financial report (CAFR) will include a statistical section. This section is not part of the CAFR's financial section and, like the introductory section, is not audited. Governments typically present 10 years of information in each table or schedule. The purpose of the statistical section is to provide historical (trend) information and additional detail to help the financial statement user better understand and assess a government's economic condition. Failure to include the statistical section will not result in a qualified or adverse audit opinion.

GASB *Statement 44, Economic Condition Reporting: The Statistical Section* (May 2004), provides guidance on the content of the statistical section. Statistical information, when presented, should be presented in five categories.

1. *Financial trends information* assists users in understanding how a government's financial position has changed over time.
2. *Revenue capacity information* is used to assess the government's ability to generate revenue from its own sources (i.e., taxes, service charges, and investments).
3. *Debt capacity information* is used to assess a government's debt burden and ability to take on more debt.
4. *Demographic and economic information* describes a government's socioeconomic environment and is used to interpret comparisons across time and between governments.
5. *Operating information* provides contextual information about a government's operations such as number of government employees, volume and usage of capital assets, and indicators of the demand for government services.

The sources of information and important assumptions must be described. Governments may provide other information as long as it is consistent with the objectives of improving the understanding and assessment of a government's economic condition.

SPECIAL-PURPOSE GOVERNMENTS

The reporting outlined in previous sections is for general-purpose governments, such as states, municipalities, and counties. However, many governments are special purpose, including school districts, sanitary districts, public employee retirement systems, tollway systems, and fire protection districts. How financial information is reported by special-purpose governments depends on whether those governments are governmental or business-type in nature, or both. GASB *Statement 34* provides the following definitions:

> Governmental activities generally are financed through taxes, intergovernmental revenues, and other nonexchange revenues. These activities are usually reported in governmental funds and internal service funds. Business-type activities are financed in whole or in part by fees charged to external parties for goods or services. These activities are usually reported in enterprise funds.

Special-purpose governments that have more than one governmental activity, or that have both governmental and business-type activities, are required to present both government-wide and fund reporting, as described previously. This reporting includes MD&A, the basic financial statements and notes, and RSI. Special-purpose governments that have only one governmental program may combine the fund and government-wide statements, using separate columns and a reconciliation, or use other simplified approaches. See Illustrations 9–2 and 9–3 for examples. Special-purpose governments that have only business-type activities should report only the financial statements required for enterprise funds. These would include:

- MD&A
- Statement of Net Assets, or Balance Sheet
- Statement of Revenues, Expenses, and Changes in Fund Net Assets
- Statement of Cash Flows
- Notes to the Financial Statements
- RSI, other than MD&A, as appropriate.

Special-purpose governments that are fiduciary only in nature, such as public employee retirement systems (PERS), are to prepare only those statements required for fiduciary funds, including MD&A, a Statement of Fiduciary Net Assets, a Statement of Changes in Fiduciary Net Assets, and notes to the financial statements.

PUBLIC COLLEGES AND UNIVERSITIES

GASB *Statement 35, Basic Financial Statements—and Management's Discussion and Analysis—for Public Colleges and Universities. Statement 35* requires that public colleges and universities report in a manner consistent with *Statement 34.* These institutions choose between reporting as business-type activities (only), governmental activities (only), or as governmental and business-type activities. The latter would most likely be chosen only by community colleges with the power to tax. Most other institutions report as business-type activities. Illustrative financial statements are provided in *Statement 35*. Accounting for public colleges and universities is discussed, along with accounting for other governmental not-for-profit organizations, in Chapter 9.

OTHER GOVERNMENTAL NOT-FOR-PROFIT ORGANIZATIONS

Certain not-for-profit organizations may be determined to be governmental in nature for accounting purposes, under the definition outlined in Chapter 1. This might include foundations of public colleges and universities, public schools, and other governmental units. Museums, performing arts organizations, and public health organizations might also be considered governmental. The general rule is the same as it is for public colleges and universities and for special-purpose governments. Required reports would depend on whether the entity is considered governmental, business-type, or governmental and business-type in nature. An exception is made for certain not-for-profit governmental units that had been following the provisions of GASB *Statement 29*. Not-for-profit governmental entities using prior accounting and reporting principles under AICPA Statement of Position 78–10 or under the AICPA Audits of Voluntary Health and Welfare Guide (see Chapter 10) may choose to report as business-type activities, even if the criteria are not met. This is to avoid requiring those governmental not-for-profits to create modified accrual accounting statements.

Now that you have finished reading Chapter 2, complete the multiple choice questions provided on the text's Web site (www.mhhe.com/copley10e) to test your comprehension of the chapter.

Questions and Exercises

2–1. Using the Comprehensive Annual Financial Report obtained for Exercise 1–1, answer the following questions.

   a. Compare the items discussed in the MD&A in your CAFR with the list of items in this chapter. Which topics listed in this chapter are not in your CAFR? Which topics are in your CAFR that are not listed in this chapter? Do you think your CAFR has a reasonably complete discussion?

   b. From the MD&A in your report, write a short summary of (1) the financial condition of your government, (2) a comparison of revenues compared with the prior year, (3) a comparison of expenses compared with the prior year, and (4) a comparison of budgeted and actual activity.

   c. From the Statement of Net Assets, write down the following: (1) unrestricted net assets—governmental activities; (2) unrestricted net assets—business-type activities; (3) restricted net assets by restriction—governmental activities; (4) restricted net assets by restriction—business-type activities; and (5) unrestricted and restricted net assets—component units.

d. From the Statement of Activities, write down the following: (1) net program expense (or revenue)—governmental activities; (2) net program expense (or revenue)—business-type activities; (3) net program expense (or revenue)—component units; (4) change in net assets—governmental activities; (5) change in net assets—business-type activities; and (6) change in net assets—component units. Do the ending net asset figures in this statement agree with the net asset figures in the Statement of Net Assets?

e. From the Statement of Revenues, Expenditures, and Changes in Fund Balances for Governmental Funds, identify the names of the major governmental funds.Write down the net change in fund balance for each major fund.

f. From the governmental fund statements, take one major fund (other than the General Fund) and prove, using the 10 percent and 5 percent criteria described in this chapter, that the fund is required to be reported as a major fund.

g. From the Statement of Revenues, Expenses, and Changes in Fund Net Assets list the major enterprise funds. For each, write down: (1) the operating income, (2) the net income (loss) before contributions and (3) the change in net assets.

2–2. With regard to GASB rules for the financial reporting entity, answer the following:

a. Define the financial reporting entity.

b. Define and give an example of a primary government.

c. Define and give an example of a component unit.

d. Define and describe the two methods of reporting the primary government and component units in the financial reporting entity.

2–3. With regard to the Comprehensive Annual Financial Report (CAFR):

a. What are the three major sections?

b. List the government-wide statements. Indicate the measurement focus and basis of accounting used for the government-wide statements.

c. List the governmental fund statements. Indicate the measurement focus and basis of accounting used for the governmental fund statements.

d. List the proprietary fund statements. Indicate the measurement focus and basis of accounting used for the proprietary fund statements.

e. List the fiduciary fund statements. Describe the measurement focus and basis of accounting used for the fiduciary fund statements.

f. Outline the reports and schedules to be reported as required supplementary information.

2–4. Describe the test for determining whether a governmental fund is a major fund. Describe the test for determining whether an enterprise fund is a major fund.

2–5. Describe how the cash flow statement of an enterprise fund differs in format from the cash flow statements of private-sector organizations such as commercial businesses.

2–6. Describe the net asset classification appearing on the government-wide statement of net assets.

2–7. The following information is available for the preparation of the government-wide financial statements for the city of Southern Springs as of April 30, 2012:

Cash and cash equivalents, governmental activities	$ 1,880,000
Cash and cash equivalents, business-type activities	850,000
Receivables, governmental activities	559,000
Receivables, business-type activities	1,330,000
Inventories, business-type activities	520,000
Capital assets, net, governmental activities	12,500,000
Capital assets, net, business-type activities	10,340,000
Accounts payable, governmental activities	650,000
Accounts payable, business-type activities	659,000
Noncurrent liabilities, governmental activities	5,350,000
Noncurrent liabilities, business-type activities	3,210,000
Net assets, invested in capital assets, net, governmental activities	8,123,000
Net assets, invested in capital assets, net, business-type activities	7,159,000
Net assets, restricted for debt service, governmental activities	754,000
Net assets, restricted for debt service, business-type activities	223,000

From the preceding information, prepare, in good form, a Statement of Net Assets for the city of Southern Springs as of April 30, 2012. Include the unrestricted net assets, which are to be computed from this information. Include a total column.

2–8. The following information is available for the preparation of the government-wide financial statements for the city of Northern Pines for the year ended June 30, 2012:

Expenses:	
General government	$10,300,000
Public safety	22,900,000
Public works	11,290,000
Health and sanitation	6,210,000
Culture and recreation	4,198,000
Interest on long-term debt, governmental type	621,000
Water and sewer system	11,550,000
Parking system	419,000
Revenues:	
Charges for services, general government	1,110,000
Charges for services, public safety	210,000
Operating grant, public safety	698,000
Charges for services, health and sanitation	2,555,000
Operating grant, health and sanitation	1,210,000
Charges for services, culture and recreation	2,198,000
Charges for services, water and sewer	12,578,000
Charges for services, parking system	398,000
Property taxes	27,112,000
Sales taxes	20,698,000
Investment earnings, business-type	319,000

Special item—gain on sale of unused land, governmental type	1,250,000
Transfer from governmental activities to business-type activities	688,000
Net assets, July 1, 2011, governmental activities	11,222,000
Net assets, July 1, 2011, business-type activities	22,333,000

From the previous information, prepare, in good form, a Statement of Activities for the city of Northern Pines for the year ended June 30, 2012. Northern Pines has no component units.

2–9. The following General Fund information is available for the preparation of the financial statements for the city of Eastern Shores for the year ended September 30, 2012:

Revenues:	
Property taxes	$27,000,000
Sales taxes	13,216,000
Fees and fines	1,124,000
Licenses and permits	1,921,000
Intergovernmental	868,000
Investment earnings	654,000
Expenditures:	
Current:	
General government	8,192,000
Public safety	24,444,000
Public works	6,211,000
Health and sanitation	1,693,000
Culture and recreation	2,154,000
Debt service—principal	652,000
Debt service—interest	821,000
Proceeds of long-term, capital-related debt	2,210,000
Transfer to special revenue fund	1,119,000
Special item—proceeds from sale of land	821,000
Fund balance, October 1, 2011	13,211,000

From the information given above, prepare, in good form, a General Fund Statement of Revenues, Expenditures, and Changes in Fund Balances for the city of Eastern Shores General Fund for the Year Ended September 30, 2012.

2–10. The following water and sewer fund information is available for the preparation of the financial statements for the City of Western Sands for the year ended December 31, 2012:

Operating revenues—charges for services	$18,387,000
Operating expenses:	
Personal services	6,977,000
Contractual services	2,195,000
Utilities	888,000
Repairs and maintenance	1,992,000
Depreciation	5,922,000
Interest revenue	129,000

Interest expense	834,000
Capital contributions	1,632,000
Transfer to general fund	965,000
Net assets, January 1, 2012	10,219,000

From the information given above, prepare, in good form, a Water and Sewer Fund column for the proprietary fund Statement of Revenues, Expenses, and Changes in Fund Net Assets for the year ended December 31, 2012.

2–11. Use the CAFR information for the City of Salem (Illustrations 2–2 through 2–16) to find the following items. In your answer, both indicate which financial statement contained the information and the item and the dollar amount.

	Information Item	Statement	$ Amount
Ex	Amounts due from other governments to support governmental activities	Balance Sheet— Governmental Funds	$1,328,448
A.	Total capital outlay for the courthouse renovation		
B.	Total cash paid for capital additions for the Solid waste fund		
C.	Interest paid (not expense) on general long-term debt		
D.	Interest paid (not expense) on water department debt		
E.	Capital asset (net) for the government's component units		
F.	Contributions received for use by the private purpose trust		
G.	Noncurrent liabilities associated with governmental activities that are due in more than one year.		
H.	Noncash contributions of capital assets for the Water department.		

2–12. Use the CAFR information for the City of Salem (Illustrations 2–2 through 2–16) to find the following items. Each item will appear in two separate financial statements. In your answer indicate *both* financial statements that contained the information item and the dollar amount.

	Information Item	Statements		$ Amount
Ex	Investments held by the Enterprise funds	Statement of Net Assets—Proprietary Funds	Government-wide Statement of Net Assets	$10,350,334
A.	Total fund balance of the Special Revenue Fund			
B.	Net assets available for employee pensions			
C.	Operating income for the Internal Service Funds			
D.	Total net assets of the primary government			

Modified Accrual Accounting: Including the Role of Fund Balances and Budgetary Authority

When the people become involved in their government, government becomes more accountable, our society is stronger, more compassionate, and better prepared for the challenges of the future. Arnold Schwarznegger, 38th Governor of California

Sure there are dishonest men in local government. But, there are dishonest men in national government too. Richard M. Nixon, 37th President of the United States and the only president to resign the office.

Learning Objectives

- Describe the basic accounts used by governmental funds.
- Identify the recognition criteria for revenues and expenditures under the modified accrual basis.
- Apply fund balance classifications for governmental funds.
- Prepare journal entries for the expenditures cycle using both budgetary and activity accounts.

The most distinguishing feature of governmental accounting is the use of the modified accrual basis (and current financial resources measurement focus) of accounting.[1] Although the use of modified accrual accounting is limited to one type

---

[1] The term *modified accrual* is used throughout this chapter to represent both the current financial resources measurement focus and the modified accrual basis of accounting.

of fund (i.e., governmental funds) and then only to the fund-basis statements, this does not mean it is inconsequential. Recall that every general purpose government will have (at least) a General Fund, and the General Fund is commonly the largest fund when measured in terms of government expenditures. Further, since most tax revenue is received by the General and other governmental funds, these funds are of particular interest to taxpayers.

Before describing exactly what the modified accrual basis is, it may be useful to describe what it is not. The modified accrual basis is not equivalent to the cash basis. Governmental funds record receivables (e.g., taxes receivable) and recognize revenues before collection, which is not true of a cash-basis system. Similarly, governmental funds record many liabilities (e.g., salaries payable) and accrue expenditures when payable, rather than waiting until payment occurs. The modified accrual basis is also not merely a "light" version of the accrual basis, differing only in its failure to recognize long-term assets and liabilities.

The modified accrual basis is a distinct system of accounting that contains financial statement elements that appear nowhere else. Among these are *expenditures* and *fund balances*. At the same time, the modified accrual basis contains other elements that are shared with the accrual basis, such as assets and liabilities. Although revenues appear in the financial statements of accrual and modified accrual funds, revenues follow different recognition criteria between the two bases. Finally, there are no *expenses* in modified accrual funds. The following sections describe the account structure and recognition criteria for governmental funds. The modified accrual basis evolved from the demand for accountability over public resources and is therefore closely tied to the budget function. Budgetary accounting is illustrated in the appendix to this chapter.

MODIFIED ACCRUAL ACCOUNTS

Balance Sheet Accounts

Illustration 3–1 provides the typical account structure for a governmental fund using modified accrual accounting. Panel 1 displays the Balance Sheet accounts. Because governmental funds report under the current financial resources measurement focus, long-term assets are not presented. Generally speaking, the assets represent cash and assets that may be expected to be converted into cash in the normal course of operations. Similarly, these funds report only those liabilities that will be settled with current financial resources. Therefore, long-term liabilities are not reported in governmental funds.

The account category, **Fund Balance,** is unique to governmental funds. Neither property owners nor voters have a legal claim on any excess of fund assets over liabilities; therefore, Fund Balance is not analogous to the capital of an investor-owned entity. However, Fund Balance serves a purpose similar to retained earnings, in that activity accounts are closed to this account at the end of each accounting period. While mathematically comparable to retained earnings, fund balances are very different in interpretation. Because only current financial resources and claims against

ILLUSTRATION 3–1   Account Structure of Governmental Funds

Panel 1. Accounts that are not closed at year-end (Balance Sheet)

Assets	Liabilities
Cash and cash equivalents	Accounts payable
Investments	Accrued liabilities
Receivables:	Deferred revenues
Taxes receivable	
Accounts receivable	**Fund Balances**
Due from other governments	Nonspendable
Supplies inventories	Restricted
Restricted assets (typically cash)	Committed
	Assigned
	Unassigned

Panel 2. Accounts that are closed at year-end   *temp.*

Budgetary Accounts	Financial Statement Activity Accounts
Estimated Revenues	**Revenues**
	Tax revenues
	Charges for services
Appropriations	**Expenditures**
	Current
	Capital outlay
	Debt service
Estimated other financing sources	**Other financing sources**
	Transfers in
	Debt proceeds
Estimated other financing uses	**Other financing uses**
	Transfers out
Encumbrances	

---

those resources are recognized in these funds, the difference between assets and liabilities (fund balance) represents the net resources of the fund that are currently available for future spending. However, even current financial resources vary in the extent to which government managers have discretion over their future use, and this is reflected by assigning fund balance to five categories (nonspendable, restricted, committed, assigned, and unassigned).

A recent GASB pronouncement (GASB *Statement 54 Fund Balance Reporting and Governmental Fund Type Definitions*) establishes reporting requirements for fund balances.[2] GASB *Statement 54* establishes five new categories of fund balance

---

[2] GASB *Statement 54* is required for fiscal years ending in June 2011 and later.

while eliminating the previous categories of reserved and unreserved. The standard affects only the equity section of the balance sheet of governmental funds. It does not change the reporting of net assets of proprietary and fiduciary funds or the government-wide Statement of Net Assets.

The new standard is GASB's response to credit market participants who sought greater information about the availability of reported fund balances. In particular, bond investors and rating agencies wish to understand the extent to which the net financial resources of governmental funds are constrained and how binding those constraints are. For example, fund resources can be restricted by creditors, donors, or granting agencies. Resources may also be formally committed by elected officials to specific activities. Alternatively, constraints may merely be nonbinding indications of management's intent to use resources for a particular purpose. *Statement 54* establishes new fund balance classifications to reflect these varying levels of constraint.

Nonspendable Fund Balances Illustration 3–2 summarizes the reporting requirements for fund balances under *Statement 54*. The first step in applying *Statement 54* is to identify those fund resources that are **nonspendable.** (This is identified as step 1 in the illustration.) Inventories and prepaid items typically appear in governmental funds because they are current assets. However, these resources are nonspendable because they are used in operations rather than converted into cash. The principal (corpus) of a permanent fund that may not be spent but is required to be maintained would also be classified as nonspendable. Other examples include assets held for sale and long-term receivables, which are sometimes reported in governmental funds.

The remaining resources (net of liabilities) of the fund include cash and items expected to be converted into cash in the next period. These "spendable" resources are further classified according to the nature of any constraints imposed on their use, using a hierarchy of constraints. The hierarchy ranges from "restricted" for the most constrained to "unassigned" for the least.

Restricted Fund Balances **Restricted fund balance** (item 2a in the illustration) represents the net resources of a governmental fund that are subject to constraints imposed by external parties or law. Restrictions arising from external parties include debt covenants (such as a requirement for a sinking fund) or constraints imposed by legislation or federal and state agencies on the use of intergovernmental revenues. Restrictions can also result from legally enforceable requirements that resources be used only for specific purposes. For example, some states permit cities and counties to propose taxes on the sale of prepared food and beverages. If approved by the voters, the referendum commonly restricts the use of the tax proceeds (typically to capital projects). The unexpended resources derived from this tax would be displayed as restricted fund balance.

The net position (i.e., equity) section of the government-wide Statement of Net Assets (GASB 34) classifies net assets within three categories, including *restricted net assets*. With one exception, those resources classified as restricted net assets

ILLUSTRATION 3–2 Diagram of GASB *Statement 54*

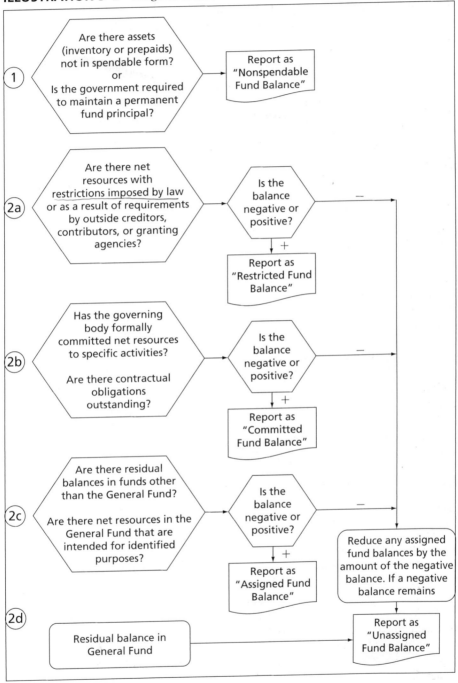

in the government-wide statements would also be classified as restricted fund balance in the fund basis statements. The exception is permanent fund principle. These resources are classified as restricted net assets under GASB 34 and nonspendable fund balance under GASB 54.

Committed Fund Balances **Committed fund balance** (item 2b in the illustration) represents the net resources of a governmental fund that the governing body has specified for particular use. To be classified as committed, the resources should have been designated through ordinance or resolution by the government's highest level of authority (e.g., state legislature, city council, or county board of supervisors). Committed resources differ from restricted in that the constraint is imposed by a government upon itself. GASB 54 also provides that amounts representing contractual obligations of a government should also be classified as committed fund balance, provided that existing resources in the fund have been specifically committed for use in satisfying the contractual obligation. The statement offers no examples of such contractual obligations, but it seems reasonable that they would be of sufficient significance to involve the formal action of the governing board. For example, board approval of large construction contracts would typically represent commitment of the funds.

Assigned Fund Balances **Assigned fund balance** (item 2c in the illustration) represents the net resources of governmental funds that the government intends for a specific purpose. Assigned resources differ from committed in that the committed resources require a formal action by the governing body of the government. Constraints imposed on assigned resources are more easily modified or removed. For governmental funds other than the General Fund, this is the category for all (positive) residual fund balances. The rationale is that the act of recording resources in special revenue, capital projects, debt service, or permanent funds is evidence of the government's intent to use the resources for a specific purpose. Resources in the General Fund may also be assigned to a specific purpose if that is the intent of the government. Intent may be expressed through the governing body by means other than ordinance or resolution or by committees or individuals with the authority to assign resources to specific activities. Assignment within the General Fund implies an intended use that is more limited than merely support of the general purposes of the government.

Unassigned Fund Balances **Unassigned fund balance** (item 2d in the illustration) is the residual category for the General Fund. Within the General Fund, governments should not report assigned fund balance amounts if the assignment for specific purpose results in a negative unassigned fund balance. Negative fund balances could occur if expenditures for a specific purpose exceed the resources available in the fund. However, *Statement 54* does not permit the reporting of negative restricted, committed, or assigned fund balances. If this occurs, the government should reduce any assigned fund balances (in that fund) by the amount of the negative balance. If a deficit remains once all assigned fund balances are zero, the remaining negative amount should be reported as unassigned fund balance.

Statement 54 also provides guidance on the classification of *budget stabilization* or *rainy day* funds. Rainy day funds are amounts set aside for future periods of economic downturn. Such stabilization amounts that meet certain criteria are classified as committed or (less commonly) restricted, if imposed externally or by law. Rainy day funds are classified as committed only if they are created by a resolution or ordinance that identifies the specific circumstances under which the resources may be expended. Rainy day amounts that are available "in emergencies" or in periods of "revenue shortfalls" would not be classified as committed unless the emergency or shortfall condition is specified and of a magnitude to distinguish it from events that occur routinely. Rainy day funds not meeting these conditions are reported as unassigned fund balance in the General Fund.

Illustration 3–3 provides an annotated example of fund balance reporting for the City of Salem example used in Chapter 2. Note that the governmental funds balance sheet is the only financial statement affected by *Statement 54*.

Financial Statement Activity Accounts

Panel 2 of Illustration 3–1 presents activity and budgetary accounts for governmental funds. The activity accounts reflect sources and uses of funds; examples are given in detail in Chapters 4 and 5. Revenues and Other Financing Sources are sources (or inflows) of financial resources while Expenditures and Other Financing Uses represent uses (or outflows) of financial resources. **Other Financing Sources** include transfers in from other funds and the proceeds of long-term borrowing. **Revenues** are defined as all other inflows and include taxes, charges for services, and amounts provided by other entities such as the state or federal government. Because taxes and many other revenues do not involve exchange transactions, governments cannot determine the point at which these revenues are earned. Therefore, revenue recognition occurs when the resulting resources are deemed to be both measureable and *available* to finance expenditures of the current period. Revenue recognition for specific types of nonexchange transactions is described later in this chapter.

Expenditure is a term that replaces both the terms *costs* and *expenses* used in accounting for commercial businesses. **Expenditures** are recognized when a liability is incurred that will be settled with current financial resources in the fund. Expenditures may be for salaries (current), land, buildings, or equipment (capital) or for payment of interest and principal on debt (debt service). Transfers out of a fund to other funds are classified as **Other Financing Uses.** An example of the use of transfer accounts occurs when a portion of the taxes recognized as revenue by the General Fund is transferred to a debt service fund that will record payments of interest and principal on general obligation debt. The General Fund would record the taxes as *Tax Revenue* and the amounts transferred to the debt service fund as *Other Financing Uses—Transfers Out*. The debt service fund would record the receipt of the transfer as *Other Financing Sources—Transfer In* and the subsequent payments of interest and principal as *Debt Service Expenditures*. Thus, use of the transfer accounts achieves the desired objective that revenues are recognized in the fund that levied the taxes (i.e., General Fund) and expenditures are recognized in the fund that expends the cash (i.e., debt service fund).

ILLUSTRATION 3–3   Example of Fund Balance Reporting

CITY OF SALEM
Balance Sheet—Fund Balance Section
Governmental Funds
As of December 31, 2012

	General Fund	Special Revenue Fund	Courthouse Renovation Fund	Debt Service Fund	Total Governmental Funds
FUND BALANCE					
Nonspendable					
Supplies inventory	23,747				23,747
Restricted					
Intergovernmental grants		312,000	500,000		812,000
Bond sinking fund				230,000	230,000
Committed					
Rainy day fund	4,500,000				4,500,000
Courthouse renovation			380,000		380,000
Assigned					
School lunch program		260,014			260,014
Other capital projects	680,500		32,032		712,532
Other purposes	236,800				236,800
Unassigned	5,837,533				5,837,533
TOTAL FUND BALANCE	11,278,580	572,014	912,032	230,000	12,992,626

This amount equals the balance of supplies inventories in the asset section of the balance sheet.

These represent resources that are restricted by outside parties through grant agreements and bond covenants.

These represent resources that are restricted by City Council as a reserve for revenue shortfalls (General Fund) and by contractual obligation (capital projects fund).

These include the residual balance of the special revenue, and capital projects funds. It also includes amounts assigned within the General Fund by expressed intent (e.g., by purchase orders).

This is the residual balance of the General Fund.

Budgetary Accounts

GASB standards require governments to present a comparison of budgeted and actual results for the General Fund and special revenue funds with legally adopted budgets. Although GASB standards guide the format of this comparison, the GASB does not prescribe budgetary accounting practices and does not require governments to maintain budgetary accounts. Budgetary accounts do not appear in the general purpose financial statements.[3] Nevertheless, governments typically record budgets, and governmental accounting systems are designed to assure compliance with budgets.

The accounts appearing in the left-hand side of Illustration 3–1, Panel 2 serve this budgetary (rather than external reporting) function of the government. A government may raise revenues only from sources allowed by law. Laws commonly establish the maximum amount of a tax or set a maximum tax rate. Revenues to be raised pursuant to law during a budget period are set forth in an **Estimated Revenues** budget. Resources raised by the government may only be expended for purposes and in amounts approved by the governing body or legislature. This is known as the appropriations process. An **Appropriations** budget, when enacted into law, is the legal authorization for the government to incur liabilities for purposes specified in the appropriations statute or ordinance. The amount expended may not exceed the amount appropriated for each purpose. In this manner, a government budget has the effect of law by limiting spending to approved levels. **Estimated Other Financing Sources** and **Estimated Other Financing Uses** are budgetary accounts reflecting anticipated inflows and outflows of resources from sources other than revenues and spending. When a purchase order or contract is issued as authorized by an appropriation, the government recognizes this commitment as an **encumbrance.** An encumbrance is not a liability because the goods or services have merely been ordered, not received. The process by which a government moves from budgetary authority to expending fund resources is described in the following section.

EXPENDITURE CYCLE

Illustration 3–4 depicts the expenditure cycle and corresponding journal entries for the General Fund or a special revenue fund with a legally adopted budget. To save space, we demonstrate journal entries using control accounts for activity (revenues and expenditures) and budgetary accounts (estimated revenues, appropriations, and encumbrances). Entries to control accounts would be supported with detailed entries in subsidiary accounts. These summarized postings are adequate to demonstrate the accounting concepts addressed. With the development of drop-down menus and other technological improvements, many accounting

---

[3] GASB *Statement 54* eliminated the reporting of *Budgetary Fund Balance—Reserve for Encumbrances* within the fund balance section of governmental fund balance sheets, removing the only instance of budgetary accounts appearing in the general purpose financial statements.

ILLUSTRATION 3–4   Expenditure Cycle

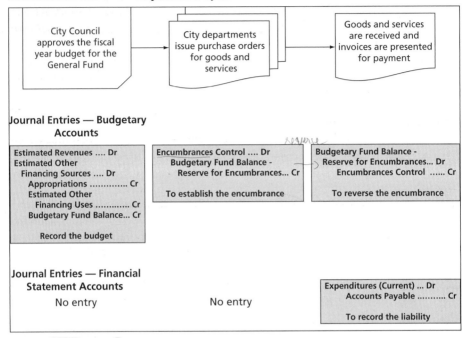

information systems have discontinued the use of control accounts. You may wish to use detailed accounts (for example revenues by source) when preparing end-of-chapter exercises.

The process begins with the governing board or legislature approving a budget. At first glance the budgetary accounts may appear to have balances opposite what would be expected—*Estimated Revenues* have debit balances and *Appropriations* have credit. However, the entry is designed to reflect the anticipated effect on the fund's net resources (**Budgetary Fund Balance**) if everything went according to expectations. Because budgeted revenues and other financing sources exceed budgeted expenditures and other uses, fund balance is expected to increase (credit). However, if budgeted expenditures and other uses are expected to exceed budgeted revenues and other financing sources, Budgetary Fund Balance would be debited in the entry. The appendix to this chapter presents more detailed budgetary entries, including budget amendments.

A department (such as police or health) cannot commit the government to expend resources until it is granted budgetary authority through its appropriations. Once that authority exists, departments can begin to commit resources by placing purchase orders or signing contracts. These commits are reflected in the budgetary accounts through the recording of *Encumbrances* and the corresponding *Budgetary Fund Balance—Reserve for Encumbrances*. GASB *Statement 54* requires that significant encumbrances be disclosed in the notes along with required disclosures about other commitments. However, there is no separate reporting of encumbrances within the fund balance section of the governmental funds balance sheet. Rather, encumbered resources should be reported within the restricted, committed, or assigned categories in a manner consistent with the criteria for those classifications.

GASB *Statement 54* provides no examples as guidance on how to classify encumbered amounts. At the very least, the existence of an encumbrance suggests that the government has an expressed intent to use resources for a particular purpose and therefore these resources should *not* be classified as *unassigned*. Encumbrance accounting may also be used in the case of contractual obligations, such as construction contracts. GASB *Statement 54* requires that resources obligated to contractual obligations be classified as *committed*. We will examine the relation of encumbrances to the classification of fund balances in more detail in Chapters 4 and 5.

Once goods or services are received, the government has a liability. At this point, two journal entries are necessary. The first reverses the encumbrance at its original amount. Since the government has incurred an actual liability, it is no longer necessary to reflect a commitment for the outstanding purchase orders or contracts. The second entry records the liability (Accounts Payable) and an Expenditure in the amount of the invoice. Recall that expenditures may be for current operations, capital assets, or debt service, including payment of principal on long-term debt.

Governments can choose not to record encumbrances for all expenditures, particularly those that are relatively predictable in amount. For example, salaries may be initially recorded only as expenditures when due without having been formally encumbered. At the end of the budget period unencumbered, unexpended appropriations lapse, that is, administrators no longer have the authority to incur liabilities under the expired appropriations. In nearly all cases, administrators continue to have the authority to disburse cash in payment of liabilities legally incurred (and recorded as expenditures) in a prior period. However, appropriations that are encumbered may or may not carry forward to the next accounting period, depending on the government's policy. If they do not carry forward and must be appropriated again in the following year, the encumbrances are said to **lapse.** The entry to record a lapsed encumbrance is the same as the reversal entry when a good or service is received (debit *Budgetary Fund Balance—Reserve for Encumbrances* and credit *Encumbrances—Control*).

REVENUE RECOGNITION FOR NONEXCHANGE TRANSACTIONS

Under modified accrual accounting, revenues are recognized when they are both **measurable** and **available** to finance expenditures of the current period. Many governmental revenues result from nonexchange transactions. **Nonexchange transactions** are transactions in which a government receives resources without directly giving equal value in exchange. These are in contrast to exchange transactions, such as the purchase of goods or services. The most common forms of nonexchange transactions are tax revenues and intergovernmental grants. Most of the activities of governmental funds are supported by revenues generated through nonexchange transactions. Before a government may recognize revenue resulting from nonexchange transactions, it must meet a number of **eligibility requirements.** The eligibility requirements are as follows:

1. **Required Characteristics of Recipients.** The recipient must have the characteristics specified by the provider. For example, a state can provide funding on a per student basis to public schools. In order to recognize this revenue, the entity must be a public school as defined by state laws.

2. **Time Requirement.** If time requirements (for expenditure) are specified by the resource provider or legislation, those time requirements must be met. For example, a state can provide funding to support park districts for the next fiscal year. In that case, the revenue would not be recognized by the park districts until that fiscal year. If the resource provider does not specify time requirements, then no condition exists and the revenue would be recognized as soon as other eligibility requirements are met.

3. **Reimbursement.** For those grants and gifts that are payable only upon the incurrence of qualifying outlays, revenues would be recognized only when the expenditures have been incurred.

4. **Contingencies.** Resources pledged that have a contingency attached are not recognized as revenue until the contingency has been met. For example, if a donor indicates that $100,000 will be donated to build an addition to the city library when funds in an equal amount have been pledged by others, that revenue would be recognized only after the "matching" $100,000 has been raised from other donors.

Illustration 3–5 identifies the four types of nonexchange transactions and describes when revenues resulting from these transactions are recognized under the modified accrual basis of accounting. The last column of Illustration 3–5 provides representative journal entries, illustrating the application of the *measurable and available* recognition criteria. In some cases, revenues resulting from nonexchange transactions are recognized in different periods in the fund basis and government-wide financial statements. For this reason, we will revisit this illustration in Chapter 8, which deals with the preparation of government-wide statements.

Imposed nonexchange transactions are taxes and other assessments imposed by governments that are not derived from underlying transactions. Examples include property taxes, special assessments, and fines and forfeits. A special rule applies to property taxes. Property taxes collected within 60 days after the end of the fiscal year may be deemed to be *available* and recorded as revenue in the year assessed, rather than the year collected. Amounts expected to be collected more than 60 days after year-end are not recognized as revenue when assessed, but as deferred revenue (a liability).

ILLUSTRATION 3–5 Classes and Timing of Recognition of Revenue from Nonexchange Transactions

Type	Description and Examples	Modified Accrual Basis (Governmental Fund Basis)	Representative Transactions	Example Journal Entry (Governmental Fund Basis Reporting)
Imposed Nonexchange Revenues	Taxes and other assessments that do not result from an underlying transaction. Examples include property taxes and special assessments imposed on property owners. Also includes fines and forfeits.	Record the receivable (and an allowance for uncollectibles) when an enforceable claim exits. Revenues should be recognized in the period for which the taxes are levied (i.e., budgeted), but are also subject to the availability rule. Property tax revenues expected to be collected > 60 days after year-end are deferred.	1. Property taxes levied 2. Deferral of portion expected to be collected > 60 days after year-end	1. Taxes Receivable ....Dr Estimated Uncollectible Taxes ......Cr Revenues Control ....Cr 2. Revenues Control ....Dr Deferred Revenues—Property Taxes..Cr
Derived Tax Revenues	These are taxes assessed on exchange transactions conducted by businesses or citizens. Examples include sales, income, and excise taxes.	Record the receivable when the taxpayer's underlying transaction takes place. Revenues should be recognized when available and measurable. Revenues not expected to be collected in time to settle current liabilities are deferred (i.e., available and measurable criteria).	1. Income tax withholdings are received. 2. Additional income taxes expected to be received after year end. Part of this will not be received in time to be available to settle current liabilities.	1. Cash ....Dr Revenues Control ....Cr 2. Taxes Receivable ....Dr Revenues Control ....Cr Deferred Revenues—Income Taxes ..Cr
Government-mandated Nonexchange Transactions	Grants from higher levels of government (federal or state) given to support a program. Since the program is required, the lower-level government has no choice but to participate.	The recognition rules are the same for mandated and voluntary nonexchange grants. Record the revenue when all eligibility requirements have been met. In the case of reimbursement grants, revenue is recognized only when qualified expenditures have been incurred. In the case of advanced funded grants, recognize revenues as qualified expenditures are incurred.	**Reimbursement-type grant:** 1. Incur qualified expenditures. 2. Recognize revenue. **Advance funded grant:** 3. Receipt of advance funding. 4. Incur expenditures and recognize revenue in an equal amount.	1. Expenditures Control ....Dr Accounts Payable/Cash ......Cr 2. Due from grantor ....Dr Revenues Control ....Cr 3. Cash .... Dr Deferred Revenues—Grants ....Cr 4a. Expenditures Control ...Dr Accounts Payable/Cash ......Cr 4b. Deferred Revenues— Grants ....Dr Revenues Control ....Cr
Voluntary Nonexchange Transactions	Donations and grants given to support a program. Since the program is not required, the receiving government voluntarily agrees to participate.			

Derived tax revenues result from taxes assessed on exchange transactions. Examples include taxes on retail sales, income, and gasoline. The amounts due are recorded in the time period the underlying transaction took place. For example, revenues due from taxes on the sale of gasoline should be recorded along with a receivable (from the retailers) in the month that the gasoline was sold. The revenue is recognized at the time of the exchange transaction provided the cash is expected to be collected shortly after the current fiscal year. If collection is expected to take place after the period considered *available* to pay current period liabilities (e.g., 60 days), it should be credited to deferred revenue of the current period.

Government mandated and **voluntary nonexchange transactions** are recorded as revenue when the eligibility requirements have been met. Generally this is when the receiving government has made qualifying expenditures under the grant agreement. Once qualifying expenditures have been made, the government records the grant revenue. The two types of grants differ in whether or not the government has the ability to refuse to participate. For example, government-mandated grants are typically from higher levels of government (federal or state) given to support a required program. Because the program is required, the lower-level government has no choice but to accept. For example, a state may require school systems to mainstream certain students in the schools and provide funds to carry out this mandate.

SUMMARY

The current financial resource measurement focus and modified accrual basis of accounting are unique to the governmental funds of state and local governments. The focus is on the flow of financial resources rather than income measurement. Key elements include:

- **Revenues.** Inflows of net financial resources from sources other than interfund transfers and debt proceeds. Revenues are recognized when they are both measurable and available to finance current expenditures.
- **Expenditures.** Outflows of net financial resources from sources other than interfund transfers that are recognized when a governmental fund incurs a liability pursuant to budgetary authority provided by appropriation.
- **Fund balance.** The net position (assets less liabilities) of a governmental fund and can be classified as nonspendable, restricted, committed, assigned, or unassigned.

The General Fund and many special revenue funds record budgets and their accounting systems are designed to assure compliance with budgets. Budgetary accounting is illustrated in the appendix to this chapter.

Now that you have completed reading Chapter 3, complete the multiple choice questions provided on the text's Web site (www.mhhe.com/copley10e) to test your comprehension of the chapter.

APPENDIX: BUDGETARY ACCOUNTING ILLUSTRATED

Budgets And Budgetary Accounts

The fact that budgets are legally binding upon administrators has led to the incorporation of budgetary accounts in the General Fund and in special revenue funds for which annual budgets are adopted.

As indicated earlier, governments are required to report budget-actual comparisons as schedules in Required Supplementary Information. Governments may elect instead to provide those comparisons as one of the basic statements rather than as a schedule. The schedule (or statement) must provide the original budget; the final budget; and the actual amounts of revenues, expenditures, and other financing sources and uses. A variance column between the final budget and actual amounts is encouraged but not required. The format of the schedule (or statement) may be that of the budget document, or in the form used for the Statement of Revenues, Expenditures, and Changes in Fund Balances (see Illustration 2–16).

Whichever approach is used, *the amounts in the Actual column are to be reported on the basis required by law for budget preparation, even if that basis differs from the basis provided in GASB standards.* For example, in some states revenues must be budgeted on the cash basis. If the Budget and Actual columns of the budget-actual comparison schedule differ from GASB standards, the heading of the statement should so indicate. Standards further require that, either on the face of the budgetary comparison schedule or in a separate schedule, the amounts in the Actual column of the budgetary comparison schedule must be reconciled with the amounts shown in the Combined Statement of Revenues, Expenditures, and Changes in Fund Balances prepared in conformity with GAAP.

To facilitate preparation of the budgetary comparison schedule, accounting systems of governmental funds incorporate **budgetary accounts.** The general ledger accounts needed to provide appropriate budgetary control are **Estimated Revenues, Appropriations, Estimated Other Financing Sources** and **Estimated Other Financing Uses** control accounts, supported by subsidiary accounts as needed.

At the beginning of the budget period, the Estimated Revenues control account is debited for the total amount of revenues expected to be recognized, as provided in the Revenues budget. The amount of revenue expected from each source specified in the Revenues budget is recorded in a subsidiary ledger account so that the total of subsidiary ledger detail agrees with the debit to the control account, and both agree with the adopted budget. If a separate entry is to be made to record the Revenues budget, the general ledger debit to the Estimated Revenues control account is offset by a credit to Budgetary Fund Balance. The account title, *Budgetary* Fund Balance, is used through the text to identify journal entries to establish or amend the budget. In practice, many governments make budget entries directly to Fund Balance. Since the budgetary accounts are closed at year-end, the choice of account title has no financial statement effect.

The credit balance of the Budgetary Fund Balance account is the total amount expected to be available to finance appropriations. Consequently, the accounting entry to record the legally approved appropriations budget is a debit to Budgetary Fund Balance and a credit to Appropriations for the total amount appropriated for the activities accounted for by the fund. The Appropriations control account is supported by a subsidiary ledger kept in the same detail as provided in the appropriations ordinance, so that the total of the subsidiary ledger detail agrees with the credit to the Appropriations control account, and both agree with the adopted budget.

Recording the Budget

Assume the amounts appearing below have been legally approved as the budget for the General Fund of a city government for the fiscal year ending December 31, 2012. As of January 1, 2012, the first day of the fiscal year, the total Estimated Revenues should be recorded in the General Fund general ledger accounts, and the amounts that are expected to be recognized during the year from each revenue source specified in the budget should be recorded in the subsidiary ledger accounts. If the budget provided for other financing sources, such as transfers in, Entry 1 would indicate a debit to Estimated Other Financing Sources. An appropriate entry would be as follows:

	General Ledger		Subsidiary Ledger	
	Debits	Credits	Debits	Credits
1. Estimated Revenues Control	1,350,000			
Estimated Other Financing Source Control ..	0			
Budgetary Fund Balance		1,350,000		
Revenues Ledger:				
Taxes			$882,500	
Licenses and permits			125,500	
Intergovernmental revenues			200,000	
Charges for services			90,000	
Fines and forfeits			32,500	
Miscellaneous revenues			19,500	

Subsidiary ledgers provide for the capture of detailed data specific to a business process. With the development of drop-down menus and other technological improvements, many accounting information systems have discontinued subsidiary ledgers. To save space throughout future chapters, we will demonstrate journal entries using control accounts to summarize revenue, expenditure, encumbrance, and budgetary accounts as if subsidiary ledgers are in use. These summarized postings are adequate to demonstrate the accounting concepts addressed.

The total Appropriations legally approved for 2012 for the General Fund of the same governmental unit should also be recorded in the General Fund general ledger accounts, and the amounts that are appropriated for each function itemized in the budget should be recorded in subsidiary ledger accounts. An appropriate entry would be as follows:

	General Ledger		Subsidiary Ledger	
	Debits	Credits	Debits	Credits
2. Budgetary Fund Balance	1,300,000			
Appropriations Control		1,225,500		
Estimated Other Financing				
Uses Control		74,500		
Appropriations Ledger:				
General government				$129,000
Public safety				277,300
Highways and streets				84,500
Sanitation				50,000
Health				47,750
Welfare				51,000
Culture and recreation				44,500
Education				541,450
Other Financing Uses Ledger:				
Transfers out				74,500

It is acceptable to combine the two entries illustrated and make one General Fund entry to record Estimated Revenues, Appropriations, and Estimated Other Financing Uses; in this case there would be a credit to Budgetary Fund Balance for $50,000 (the amount by which Estimated Revenues exceeds Appropriations and Estimated Other Financing Uses).

Accounting for Revenues

During a fiscal year, actual revenues should be recognized in the general ledger accounts of governmental funds by credits to the Revenues Control account (offset by debits to receivable accounts for revenues susceptible to accrual or by debits to Cash for revenues that are recognized when the cash is collected). The general ledger Revenues Control account supported by Revenues subsidiary ledger accounts is kept in exactly the same detail as kept for the Estimated Revenues subsidiary ledger accounts. For example, assume that the General Fund of the government for which budgetary entries are illustrated in the preceding section collected revenues in cash from the following sources in these amounts:

	General Ledger		Subsidiary Ledger	
	Debits	Credits	Debits	Credits
3. Cash..............................	1,314,500			
Revenues Control.....................		1,314,500		
Revenues Ledger:				
Taxes				$881,300
Licenses and permits				103,000
Intergovernmental revenues...........				186,500
Charges for services................				91,000
Fines and forfeits				33,200
Miscellaneous revenues				19,500

Periodically throughout the year, elected officials and government managers will compare Estimated Revenue subsidiary accounts with actual Revenues subsidiary accounts. If revenues fail to reach the levels anticipated when the budget was enacted, budget revisions may be warranted to prevent the government from deficit spending. Illustration 3–6 shows the Licenses and Permits Revenue subsidiary ledger in a typical spreadsheet format. Because Estimated Revenues are recorded with debits and actual Revenues with credits, summing the two amounts provides a measure of the variance from expectations. In this case, Licenses and Permits Revenue did not meet expectations and a budget revision was deemed necessary. Since the budget is recorded at the beginning of the year and actual revenues are recognized throughout the year, *Estimated Revenues Not Yet Realized* will commonly have a net debit balance.

ILLUSTRATION 3–6   Revenues Ledger

	NAME OF GOVERNMENT			
	Revenues Ledger			
	General Fund: Licenses and Permits Revenue			
	2012 Fiscal Year			
Transaction	Reference	Estimated Revenues	Actual Revenues	Estimated Revenues Not Yet Realized [= Sum]
(1)	Initial budget	$125,500		$125,500
(3)	Collections		($103,000)	$ 22,500
(7)	Budget revision	($ 22,500)		$ 0
		$103,000	($103,000)	$ 0

$ Amounts in ( ) denote credits.

Budgetary Fund Bal. ↓ 22.5
Estimated Rev.   22.5

Accounting for Encumbrances and Expenditures

An appropriation is considered to be **expended** when authorized liabilities are incurred. Purchase orders and contracts are commitments that will result in liabilities when the goods or services are received or the contracts executed. Such expected liabilities are called **encumbrances.** In order to keep track of purchase orders and contracts outstanding, it is recommended that the Encumbrance Control account (and the subsidiary account for the specific appropriation encumbered) be debited and the Budgetary Fund Balance—Reserve for Encumbrances account credited for the amount of each purchase order or contract issued.

When goods or services are received, two entries are necessary: (1) Budgetary Fund Balance—Reserve for Encumbrances is debited, and Encumbrances Control (and the proper subsidiary account) is credited for the amount entered in these accounts when the encumbrance documents were issued; and (2) Expenditures Control (and the proper subsidiary account) is debited and a liability account is credited for the amount to be paid. In order to accomplish the necessary matching of Appropriations, Encumbrances, and Expenditures, it is necessary that subsidiary ledger classifications of all three correspond exactly.

The following entries illustrate accounting for Encumbrances and Expenditures for the General Fund. Entry 4 reflects purchase orders issued pursuant to the authority contained in the General Fund appropriations; assumed amounts chargeable to each function for which purchase orders are issued on this date are shown in the debits to the Encumbrances subsidiary accounts.

	General Ledger		Subsidiary Ledger	
	Debits	Credits	Debits	Credits
4. Encumbrances Control...............	500,100			
Budgetary Fund Balance—Reserve				
for Encumbrances...............		500,100		
Encumbrances Ledger:...............				
General government...............			$ 73,200	
Public safety......................			115,100	
Highways and streets..............			34,600	
Sanitation........................			29,300	
Health...........................			16,500	
Welfare..........................			18,700	
Culture and recreation............			14,800	
Education........................			197,900	

Estimate

Entries 5a and 5b illustrate entries required to record the receipt of some of the items for which purchase orders were recorded in Entry 4. Note that Entry 4 is made for the amounts estimated at the time purchase orders or other commitment documents are issued. When the purchase orders are filled, the actual amount approved by the government for payment to the supplier often differs from the estimated amount recorded in the Encumbrances account (and subsidiary ledger accounts) because some items may have been unavailable, prices of items have changed, and so on. Since the Encumbrances Control account was debited in Entry 4 for the estimated amount, the Encumbrances Control account must be credited for the same estimate, to the extent that purchase orders are filled (or canceled). The balance remaining in the Encumbrances Control account, therefore, is the estimated dollar amount of purchase orders outstanding.

Entry 5a shows the entry necessary on the assumption that most purchase orders recorded in Entry 4 have now been filled but purchase orders for general government and education remain outstanding. Expenditures, however, should be recorded at the actual amount the government agrees to pay the vendors who have filled the purchase orders. Entry 5b shows the entry necessary to record the liability for invoices approved for payment. The fact that estimated and actual amounts differ causes no accounting difficulties as long as goods or services are received in the same fiscal period as ordered.[4] The accounting treatment required when encumbrances outstanding at year-end are filled or canceled in a following year is illustrated in Chapter 4.

	General Ledger		Subsidiary Ledger	
	Debits	Credits	Debits	Credits
5a. Budgetary Fund Balance—				
Reserve for Encumbrances.	492,300			
Encumbrances Control		492,300		
Encumbrances Ledger:.				
General government				$ 68,300
Public safety				115,100
Highways and streets				34,600
Sanitation				29,300
Health				16,500
Welfare				18,700
Culture and recreation				14,800
Education				195,000
5b. Expenditures Control	491,800			
Accounts Payable		491,800		
Expenditures Ledger:				
General government			$ 69,100	
Public safety			115,100	
Highways and streets			34,400	
Sanitation			29,300	
Health			16,600	
Welfare			18,700	
Culture and recreation			14,800	
Education			193,800	

The encumbrance procedure is not always needed to make sure that appropriations are not overexpended. For example, although salaries and wages of government

[4] Many governments would require an additional approval (frequently in the form of a revised encumbrance) for amounts in excess of the original purchase order.

employees must be chargeable against valid and sufficient appropriations in order to give rise to legal expenditures, many governments do not find it necessary to encumber the departmental personal services appropriations for estimated payrolls of recurring, relatively predictable amounts. Entry 6 shows the recording of expenditures of appropriations for salaries and wages not previously encumbered.

	General Ledger		Subsidiary Ledger	
	Debits	Credits	Debits	Credits
6. Expenditures Control.	663,600			
Accounts Payable		663,600		
Expenditures Ledger:				
General government			$ 47,805	
Public safety			143,295	
Highways and streets			51,000	
Sanitation			26,950	
Health			27,900	
Welfare			28,100	
Culture and recreation			26,100	
Education			312,450	

Illustration 3–7 shows a subsidiary ledger for the Education Department that supports all three general ledger control accounts: Appropriations, Encumbrances, and Expenditures. Again the ledger is presented in spreadsheet format.

ILLUSTRATION 3–7   Subsidiary Ledger for the Education Department

NAME OF GOVERNMENT
Appropriations, Expenditures, and Encumbrances Ledger
General Fund: Education Department
2012 Fiscal Year

Transaction	Reference	Appropriations	Encumbrances	Expenditures	Unexpended Appropriation Balance [= SUM]
(2)	Budget	($541,450)			($541,450)
(4)	Purchase orders issued		$197,900		($343,550)
(5)	Invoices received and approved for payment		($195,000)	$193,800	($344,750)
(6)	Payrolls			$312,450	($ 32,300)
		($541,450)	$ 2,900	$506,250	($ 32,300)

$ Amounts in ( ) denote credits.

Outstanding at yr-end

Because Appropriations are recorded as credits and Encumbrances and Expenditures as debits, summing the amounts results in "Unexpended Appropriations Balance." This may be interpreted as how much the Education Department may continue to expend and remain within its budget. The purpose of encumbrance accounting is to prevent governments from overspending. This becomes apparent in Illustration 3–7. At the time a purchase order is issued (transaction 4), the encumbrance is recorded in this subsidiary ledger as a debit, thereby reducing the balance appearing in the unexpended appropriation column. The $2,900 appearing at the bottom of the encumbrances column represent purchase orders outstanding at year-end.

Budget Revisions

In most cases, governments will prepare and adopt budget revisions. Assume the government in this example decided to revise the Estimated Revenues budget downward by $36,000 and the Appropriations Budget upward by $8,000:

	General Ledger		Subsidiary Ledger	
	Debits	Credits	Debits	Credits
7. Budgetary Fund Balance	44,000			
Estimated Revenues Control		36,000		
Appropriations Control.		8,000		
Revenues Ledger:.				
Licenses and permits				$22,500
Intergovernmental revenues				13,500
Appropriations Ledger:.				
Highways and streets				1,000
Sanitation				7,000

Budget revisions would require adjustments to the budgetary accounts and balances in the subsidiary ledgers (Illustrations 3–6 and 3–7).

Budgetary Comparison Schedule

Illustration 3–8 presents a budgetary comparison schedule as it might be prepared by the government in the example. Assume a transfer out in the amount of $74,500 as provided in the budget. This schedule would be included as a part of Required Supplementary Information or could be prepared as a basic financial statement.

Expenditure Actual = (Encum. Issued ÷ Encu. filled) + Expenditures.

ILLUSTRATION 3-8   Budgetary Comparison Schedule

				Variance with Final
			Actual	Budget
	Budgeted Amounts		Amounts	Positive
			(Budgetary	(Negative)
	Original	Final	Basis)	

NAME OF GOVERNMENTAL UNIT
Budgetary Comparison Schedule
General Fund
For the Year Ended December 31, 2012

	Original	Final	Actual Amounts (Budgetary Basis)	Variance with Final Budget Positive (Negative)
Revenues:				
Taxes	$ 882,500	$ 882,500	$ 881,300	$ (1,200)
Licenses and permits	125,500	103,000	103,000	———
Intergovernmental revenues	200,000	186,500	186,500	———
Charges for services	90,000	90,000	91,000	1,000
Fines and forfeits	32,500	32,500	33,200	700
Miscellaneous revenues	19,500	19,500	19,500	———
Total revenues	1,350,000	1,314,000	1,314,500	500
Expenditures and encumbrances:				
General government	129,000	129,000	121,805	7,195
Public safety	277,300	277,300	258,395	18,905
Highways and streets	84,500	85,500	85,400	100
Sanitation	50,000	57,000	56,250	750
Health	47,750	47,750	44,500	3,250
Welfare	51,000	51,000	46,800	4,200
Culture and recreation	44,500	44,500	40,900	3,600
Education	541,450	541,450	509,150	32,300
Total expenditures and encumbrances	1,225,500	1,233,500	1,163,200	70,300
Excess (deficiency) of revenues over expenditures and encumbrances	124,500	80,500	151,300	70,800
Other financing sources (uses): transfers out	(74,500)	(74,500)	(74,500)	———
Net change in fund balance	50,000	6,000	76,800	70,800
Fund balance—beginning	332,000	350,000	350,000	———
Fund balance—ending	$ 382,000	$ 356,000	$ 426,800	$70,800

(13200 - 6830) + 69100 + 47805

Classification of Estimated Revenues and Revenues

A revenue budget is necessary for administrators to determine whether proposed expenditures can be financed by resources available to the budgeting jurisdiction. The budget should include all sources, including interfund transfers and bond issue proceeds as well as taxes, licenses and permits, fees, forfeits, and other revenue sources. It should be emphasized that a government may raise revenues only from sources that are available to it by law.

The primary classification of governmental revenue is by **fund.** Within each fund the major classification is by source. Within each major source class it is desirable to have as many secondary classes as are needed to facilitate revenue budgeting and accounting. Commonly used major revenue source classes are:

Taxes	Charges for services
Licenses and permits	Fines and forfeits
Intergovernmental revenues	Miscellaneous revenues

Examples of secondary classes of tax revenues include property taxes, sales taxes, and excise taxes.

Classification of Appropriations and Expenditures

Recall that an appropriation, when enacted into law, is an authorization to incur liabilities on behalf of the government for goods, services, and facilities to be used for purposes specified in the appropriation ordinance, or statute, in amounts not in excess of those specified for each purpose. When liabilities authorized by an appropriation have been incurred, the appropriation is said to be expended. Classification by fund is, of course, essential. Within each fund one or more of the following classification schemes is used to meet the needs of financial statement users: (1) function or program, (2) organization unit, (3) activity, (4) character, and (5) object. Common terminology and classifications should be used consistently throughout the budget, the accounts, and the financial reports of each fund.

Examples of classifications by **function** are general government, public safety, and highways and streets. While most governments report by function, others report by program, such as protection of persons and property and environmental protection. Programs are often performed by more than one department; consequently, program expenditures often cross departmental lines. Reporting expenditures by departments (e.g., police or health) is the most common form of classification by **organizational unit. Activities** are specific and distinguishable lines of work performed by organizational units. Examples of activities are solid waste collection and solid waste disposal, both in the Public Works Department. Classification by **character** deals with the time period involved and includes current expenditures, capital outlays, and debt service. Classification by **object** reports the inputs, or the item or service received, such as personal services, supplies, other services and charges, capital outlays, and debt service. Generally, more detailed object classes are used for each of the major categories.

Questions and Exercises

3–1. Using the annual report obtained for Exercise 1–1, answer the following questions.

    a. Look at the Statement of Revenues, Expenditures, and Changes in Fund Balances for the governmental funds. List the revenue source classes. Do they agree with those sources discussed in this chapter? Are expenditures reported by character? List the functional classifications under the current character classification. Do those classifications agree with those listed in the example shown in this chapter? Are Other Financing Sources and Uses presented separately? Does your report show transfers in? Transfers out? Capital leases? Proceeds of bonds?

    b. Look at the Budgetary Comparison Schedule in the RSI section of your annual Report (or Budgetary Comparison Statement, if that is used by your government) for the General Fund. Is the budgetary format used, or is the schedule in the format used for the Statement of Revenues, Expenditures, and Changes in Fund Balances? Does the report reflect the original budget, revised budget, and actual figures? Are variance columns presented comparing the actual with the revised budget and comparing the original with the revised budget? Is a reconciliation between the budgetary basis of accounting and GAAP presented on the budgetary comparison schedule or in a separate schedule? What are the major differences, if any? Are budgetary comparison schedules (or statements) presented for special revenue funds? Are all special revenue funds included?

    c. Look at the note that describes the basis of budgeting (usually in the Summary of Significant Accounting Policies). Is the budget prepared on the GAAP basis or some other basis? Are the differences, if any, between the budgetary basis and GAAP clearly explained? Does the note indicate that encumbrance accounting is used? Do unexpended encumbrances lapse at year-end? If unexpended encumbrances lapse, are they normally reappropriated in the following year? Do the notes describe the budget calendar (a separate note may have this information)? Do the notes describe the legal level of budgetary control and the levels at which certain budget revisions might be made? Were budget revisions necessary during the year?

3–2. The City of Oxbow General Fund has the following net resources at year-end:

- $100,000 unexpended proceeds of a state grant required by law to be used for health education.
- $15,000 of prepaid insurance.
- $500,000 rainy day fund approved by city council for use under specified circumstances.

- $25,000 of contractual obligations for capital projects.
- $50,000 unexpended proceeds of a tax required by law to be used for emergency 911 services.
- $550,000 to be used to fund government operations in the future.

Required: Prepare the fund balance section of the Balance Sheet.

3–3. How should rainy day funds be reported under GASB *Statement 54?*

3–4. Prepare budgetary entries, using general ledger accounts only, for each of the following unrelated situations:

a. Anticipated revenues are $10 million; anticipated expenditures and encumbrances are $9.8 million.

b. Anticipated revenues are $9.8 million; anticipated expenditures and encumbrances are $10 million.

c. Anticipated revenues are $10 million; anticipated transfers from other funds are $1.3 million; anticipated expenditures and encumbrances are $9.8 million; anticipated transfers to other funds are $1.2 million.

d. Anticipated revenues are $9.8 million; anticipated transfers from other funds are $1.2 million; anticipated expenditures and encumbrances are $10 million; anticipated transfers to other funds are $1.3 million.

3–5. For each of the summarized transactions for the Village of Sycamore General Fund, prepare the general ledger journal entries. The year is January 1–December 31, 2012.

a. The budget was formally adopted, providing for estimated revenues of $1,000,000 and appropriations of $980,000.

b. Revenues were received, all in cash, in the amount of $1,010,000.

c. Purchase orders were issued in the amount of $500,000.

d. Of the $500,000 in (c), purchase orders were filled in the amount of $490,000; the invoice amount was $480,000 (not yet paid).

e. Expenditures, not encumbered, amounted to $460,000 (not yet paid).

f. Amounts from (d) and (e) are paid in cash.

3–6. a. Distinguish between (1) exchange and (2) nonexchange transactions.

b. Identify and describe the four eligibility requirements for a government to recognize revenue in a nonexchange transaction.

c. GASB *Statement 33* classifies nonexchange transactions into four categories. List the four categories, give an example of each, and outline asset and revenue recognition criteria for each.

3–7. a. Outline revenue recognition criteria under modified accrual accounting. Include specific requirements for property tax revenue.

b. Outline expenditure recognition criteria under modified accrual accounting.

3–8. Distinguish between the (1) GAAP basis and (2) budgetary basis of reporting for the General Fund.

3–9. The City of South Dundee budget for the fiscal year ended June 30, 2012, included an appropriation for the police department in the amount of $16,000,000. During the month of July 2011, the following transactions occurred (in summary):

Purchase orders were issued in the amount of $600,000.

Of the $600,000 in purchase orders, $580,000 were filled, with invoices amounting to $575,000. *reverse to replace w. actual 575*

Salaries, not encumbered, amounted to $798,000.

A budget appropriations reduction in the amount of $20,000 was approved by the city council.

Prepare an appropriations, expenditures and encumbrances ledger for the police department for the month of July, in a format similar to Illustration 3–7.

3–10. The Budgetary Comparison Schedule for the City of Vienna appears below. Several items of information are missing (denoted**).

CITY OF VIENNA
Budgetary Comparison Schedule
General Fund
For the Year Ended December 31, 2012

	Budgeted Amounts		Actual Amounts (Budgetary Basis)	Variance with Final Budget Positive (Negative)
	Original	Final		
Revenues:				
Taxes	$3,200,000	**	$3,400,000	$100,000
Licenses	900,000	900,000	**	(2,000)
Intergovernmental	500,000	500,000	500,000	0
Miscellaneous	100,000	104,000	105,000	1,000
Total revenues	4,700,000	**	**	99,000
Expenditures and encumbrances				
General government	**	**	925,000	15,000
Parks	2,500,000	2,500,000	2,400,000	100,000
Health and welfare	1,200,000	1,204,000	**	54,000
Total expenditures and encumbrances	**	**	**	169,000
Net change in fund balance	50,000	160,000	428,000	268,000
Fund balance—beginning	332,000	350,000	350,000	0
Fund balance—ending	$ 382,000	$510,000	$778,000	$268,000

Required:

a. Determine the missing amounts.

b. During the year, the City made a single budget revision. Prepare the journal entry to record that revision.

3–11. Appearing below is the subsidiary ledger for the public safety department of the City of Boone. After the first month of the year, five entries have been made to the ledger.

Transaction	Appropriations	Encumbrances	Expenditures	Unexpended Appropriation Balance [= SUM]
1	($254,000)*			($254,000)
2		$18,000		($236,000)
3		($15,000)	$14,500	($236,500)
4			11,000	($225,500)
5	$17,000			($208,500)
	($237,000)	$3,000	$25,500	($208,500)

* $ amounts in ( ) denote credits.

Describe the most likely event that led to each of the postings (items 1–5).

3–12. Following are transactions and events of the General Fund of the City of Springfield for the fiscal year ended December 31, 2012.

1. Estimated revenues (legally budgeted)

Property taxes	$5,000,000
Sales taxes	4,000,000
Licenses and permits	1,500,000
Miscellaneous	500,000

2. Appropriations Spending

General government	$5,000,000
Culture and recreation	4,500,000
Health and welfare	1,000,000

3. Revenues received (cash)

Property taxes	$4,783,541
Sales taxes	4,501,009
Licenses and permits	1,700,000
Miscellaneous	800,000

4. Encumbrances issued (includes salaries and other recurring items)

	Estimated
General government	$5,100,000
Culture and recreation	4,650,000
Health and welfare	905,000

5. Goods and services received (paid in cash)

	Estimated	Actual
General government	$5,100,000	$5,035,450
Culture and recreation	4,650,000	4,610,000
Health and welfare	905,000	891,550

6. Budget revisions

Increase appropriations:

General government	$100,000
Culture and recreation	150,000

7. Fund balance—Unrestricted on January 1, 2012, was $735,000. There were no outstanding encumbrances at that date.

a. Record the transactions using appropriate journal entries.

b. Prepare a budgetary comparison schedule for the General Fund.

3–13. The town council of Riverside met in December 2011. The council estimated revenues for 2012 to be $750,000 from property taxes and $150,000 from business licenses. The appropriations budget from the council was as follows:

General government	$500,000
Parks and recreation	110,000
Sanitation	90,000
Streets and sidewalks	160,000

In 2012, heavy spring rains caused some flooding near the river. As a result, a picnic area at River's Edge Park was ruined and several damaged shops had to shut down. The council adopted an upward revision of $22,000 for the parks and recreation budget and reduced the estimated revenues from business licenses by 10 percent.

The General Fund began the year with a balance of $22,888. During 2012, tax collections totaled $748,800 and revenues from business licenses were $137,202. Expenditures were $499,200 for general government, $131,345 for parks and recreation, $91,600 for sanitation, and $157,333 for streets and sidewalks. There are no outstanding encumbrances at year-end.

1. Prepare a budgetary comparison schedule for the General Fund for 2012.

3–14. Presented here are several transactions and events of the General Fund of Johnson County. All transactions and events relate to calendar year 2012.

1. Estimated revenues from the following sources were legally budgeted.

Sales taxes	$6,000,000
Fines and forfeits	2,000,000
Licenses and permits	1,750,000
Intergovernmental revenues	350,000
Total	$10,100,000

2. Appropriations for the following functions were legally budgeted.

General government	$2,100,000
Public safety	3,890,000
Culture and recreation	700,000
Health and welfare	3,000,000
Total	$9,690,000

the year, revenues were received in cash from the following

~~s~~ taxes	$ 5,930,000
~~s~~ and forfeits	1,990,000
~~n~~ses and permits	1,740,000
~~r~~governmental revenues	385,000
~~T~~otal	$10,045,000

4. During the year, contracts and purchase orders were issued as follows:

General government	$ 450,000
Public safety	800,000
Culture and recreation	280,000
Health and welfare	500,000
Total	$2,030,000

5. Goods and services (these are a portion of the total ordered in transaction 4) were received, as follows:

	Estimated	Actual
General government	$ 450,000	$ 452,000
Public safety	500,000	510,000
Culture and recreation	275,000	276,000
Health and welfare	500,000	500,000
Total	$1,725,000	$1,738,000

6. A budget revision was approved by the County Commission. Estimated revenues for intergovernmental revenues were increased by $35,000. Appropriations for general government were increased by $100,000.

7. Vouchers were issued for items not previously encumbered, primarily personal services, in the following amounts:

General government	$1,747,000
Public safety	3,080,000
Culture and recreation	418,000
Health and welfare	2,500,000
Total	$7,745,000

a. Record the transactions in general journal form. Include subsidiary accounts as illustrated in this chapter.

b. Open budgetary, revenue, expenditure, and encumbrance general ledger control accounts and post the transactions. You may use T-accounts.

c. Open Revenue and Appropriations, Expenditures, and Encumbrances subsidiary ledgers. Post the transactions. Prove that the control account balances agree with the related subsidiary ledger accounts.

d. Assume a beginning Fund Balance—Unreserved of $150,000. Prepare a budgetary comparison schedule for the General Fund. Include encumbrances with expenditures. Use Illustration 3–8 as an example.

e. Assuming that encumbered appropriations do *not* lapse at the end of the budget year, how much of the appropriations, by function, did lapse at the end of 2012? Show computations in good form.

Excel-Based Problems

. Microsoft Excel templates are available on the text Web site for use with problems 3–15 and 3–16 (www.mhhe.com/copley10e).

3–15. The Budgetary Comparison Schedule for the City of Salem appears in Illustration 2–16. Assume the general and subsidiary ledgers for the General Fund were lost after a water pipe burst. You are charged with reproducing the journal entries that took place during the year ended December 31, 2012.

Use the excel file provided to prepare summary journal entries, including subsidiary ledger entries, for the following events.

a. Record the original budget.

b. Record the revisions to the budget.

c. Record the actual revenues.

d. Record the encumbrances, assuming all expenditures originated as encumbrances and the encumbrance and expenditure are equal in amount.

e. Record the actual expenditures and reversal of the associated encumbrance.

You should follow the format of the entries provided in entries 1 to 7 of the appendix to Chapter 3.

3–16. The City of Grafton's records reflected the following budget and actual data for the General Fund for the fiscal year ended June 30, 2012.

1. Estimated revenues:

Taxes (Property)	$3,000,000
Licenses and permits	800,000
Intergovernmental revenues	300,000
Miscellaneous revenues	200,000

2. Revenues:

Taxes (Property)	$3,000,000
Licenses and permits	801,320
Intergovernmental revenues	293,000
Miscellaneous revenues	198,000

3. Appropriations:

General government	$ 900,000
Public safety	2,000,000
Health and welfare	1,400,000

4. Expenditures of 2012 appropriations:

General government	$ 880,000
Public safety	1,949,000
Health and welfare	1,398,000

5. Encumbrances of 2012 appropriations, outstanding as of June 30, 2012.

General government	$18,000
Public safety	50,000

6. Transfer to debt service fund:

Budget	$600,000
Actual	600,000

7. Budget revisions approved by the city council:

Estimated revenues:

Decrease intergovernmental revenues	$10,000
Decrease miscellaneous revenues	3,000

Appropriations:

Decrease general government	2,000

8. Total fund balance at July 1, 2011, was $1,038,000.

Required: Use the Excel file provided to prepare a budgetary comparision schedule for the City of Grafton for the fiscal year ended June 30, 2012. Include outstanding encumbrances with expenditures. Use the formula feature (e.g., sum, =, etc.) of Excel to calculate the amounts in cells shaded blue.

Continuous Problem

Available on the text's Web site (www.mhhe.com/copley10e).

Accounting for the General and Special Revenue Funds

It is evident from the state of the country, from the habits of the people, from the experience we have had on the point itself, that it is impracticable to raise any considerable sums by direct taxation. (Alexander Hamilton, first Secretary of the Treasury, commenting on how to finance government operations)

It's not pretty, but it's our system of government. And it works. It's like sausage: no one wants to see it made, and it will eventually destroy your heart. (Stephen Colbert, political satirist and television host)

Learning Objectives

- Apply the modified accrual basis of accounting in the recording of typical transaction of a General or special revenue fund.
- Prepare closing entries and classify fund balances within the framework of GASB *Statement 54.*
- Prepare the fund-basis financial statements for a General or special revenue fund.

Modified accrual accounting is illustrated in Chapter 3 along with the use of budgetary accounts. This chapter applies that knowledge by recording common transactions and events in the operation of the General Fund and a special revenue fund of a hypothetical local government, the Village of Elizabeth. We will continue with the Village of Elizabeth in Chapters 5 through 8, demonstrating governmental, proprietary, and fiduciary fund accounting. Chapters 4 through 7 present the required fund-basis financial statements and Chapter 8 illustrates the preparation of government-wide financial statements. In the interest of clarity of presentation, subsidiary ledgers are not illustrated throughout this chapter for the budgetary and operating statement accounts, but keep in mind that subsidiary accounts or more detailed general ledger accounts for revenues, expenditures, and budgetary accounts would be required in actual situations.

Recall from Chapter 1 the following fund definitions, as prescribed by GASB *Statement 54:*

- **General Fund** Accounts for and reports all financial resources not accounted for and reported in another fund.
- **Special Revenue Funds** Account for and report the proceeds of specific revenue sources that are *restricted or committed* to expenditure for specified purpose other than debt service or capital projects.
- **Debt Service Funds** Account for and report financial resources that are *restricted, committed, or assigned* to expenditure for principal and interest.
- **Capital Projects Funds** Account for and report financial resources that are *restricted, committed, or assigned* to expenditure for capital outlays.

The purpose of fund accounting is to segregate those financial resources that have constraints or limitations on their use so that the government may demonstrate compliance with those limitations. However, many resources have no limitations on their use and do not require segregation. The General Fund accounts for any resources not reported in one of the other (limited-use) funds. Every general-purpose government will have one, and only one, General Fund. Special revenue funds are an example of a fund established because of constraints placed on the use of government resources. Note, however, that special revenue funds are not used if the resources are required to be used to acquire capital assets or for the payment of interest and principal on long-term debt.

GASB *Statement 54* provides particular guidance for the use of special revenue funds. Specifically, the standard requires that special revenue funds be used only if a substantial portion of the resources are provided by one or more *restricted* or *committed* (not *assigned*) revenue sources. Although other resources may supplement a special revenue fund, assignment of resources is not sufficient for the establishment of a special revenue fund. In this respect, special revenue funds are notably different from debt service and capital project funds. Further, if the government expects that a substantial portion of the resources supporting a special revenue fund's activities will no longer be derived from restricted and committed revenue sources, the government should discontinue the use of a special revenue fund and report the fund's remaining resources in the General Fund.

OVERVIEW OF MODIFIED ACCRUAL ACCOUNTING

Governmental fund financial statements are prepared on the **modified accrual basis of accounting.** Under modified accrual accounting, revenues are recognized when they are both **measurable** and **available** to finance expenditures of the current period. The term *measurable* means that the government is able to determine or reasonably estimate the amount. For example, property taxes are measurable before collection because the government determines the amount assessed and estimates any portion that will ultimately prove to be uncollectible. The term *available* means the amount is expected to be collected within the current period or soon enough thereafter to be used to pay liabilities of the current period.

The term *expenditure* rather than *expense* is used in modified accrual accounting. **Expenditures** are decreases in net financial resources and are generally recognized when the related liability is incurred. Expenditures may be for current purposes (such as salaries or supplies) for capital outlay, or for debt service (principal or interest). GASB *Interpretation 6, Recognition and Measurement of Certain Liabilities and Expenditures in Governmental Fund Financial Statements,* clarifies when expenditures should be recognized when using modified accrual accounting.

Generally, expenditures are recorded and fund liabilities are recognized when goods and services are received, regardless of whether resources are available in the fund. The most important exception is that debt service expenditures for principal and interest are recorded when *due.* This means that debt service expenditures are not accrued, but are recognized and fund liabilities are recorded on the maturity date.

According to *Interpretation 6,* expenditures for claims and judgments, compensated absences, special termination benefits, and landfill closure and postclosure care costs of governmental funds should be recognized to the extent that the liabilities are going to be paid with available resources; additional amounts are reported as (long-term) liabilities in the government-wide statements.

INTERFUND TRANSACTIONS

Interfund transactions are transactions between individual funds. Interfund transactions are of particular interest to financial statement preparers and users because failure to report these transactions properly results in two funds being misstated. Additionally, because most of these transactions are eliminated in the government-wide statements, it is particularly important they be identified in the accounts of the affected funds. Like related party transactions, transactions between funds of the same government may not be assumed to be arm's length in nature. An arm's length transaction is one in which both parties act in their own self-interest and are not subject to pressure or influence. GASB standards require that interfund transactions be classified into two categories, each with two subcategories. Journal entries to record interfund transactions are based on these classifications. **Reciprocal interfund activity** is the internal counterpart to exchange and exchange-like transactions and includes **interfund loans** and **interfund services provided and used.** **Nonreciprocal interfund activity** includes **interfund transfers** and **interfund reimbursements.** The accounting for interfund transactions is described below and summarized in Illustration 4–1.

Interfund Loans

Interfund loans are resources provided from one fund to another with the requirement for repayment. The fund providing the resources records an interfund receivable (*Due from Other Funds*) and the fund receiving the resources records an interfund payable (*Due to Other Funds*). Long-term loans use the terms *Advance to Other Funds* and *Advance from Other Funds.* Interfund loan receivables and payables are separately reported on the balance sheets of the affected funds.

ILLUSTRATION 4–1 Summary of Interfund Transactions

Interfund Transaction	Description	Example Journal Entry: Fund Making the Payment	Example Journal Entry: Fund Receiving the Payment
Interfund Loans	In an interfund loan, resources are provided from one fund to another with the expectation they will be repaid.	Due from Other Fund ...Dr Cash ....Cr If the loan is long-term, *Advance to Other Funds* is used in place of *Due from Other Funds*.	Cash ....Dr Due to Other Fund ....Cr If the loan is long-term, *Advance from Other Funds* is used in place of *Due to Other Funds*.
Interfund Services	The most common examples are where a governmental fund purchases services from an internal service (or enterprise) fund.	Expenditures ....Dr Cash ....Cr If the fund receiving the service is a proprietary fund, *Expense* is used in place of *Expenditure*.	Cash ....Dr Operating Revenue— Charges for Services ....Cr
Interfund Transfers	In an interfund transfer, resources are provided from one fund to another **without** the expectation they will be repaid.	Other Financing Uses— Transfers Out ....Dr Cash ....Cr	Cash ....Dr Other Financing Sources— Transfers In...............Cr
Interfund Reimbursement	In an interfund reimbursement, one fund initially records a purchase that belongs in another fund.		Expenditures ....Dr Cash ....Cr
	The fund where the purchase correctly belongs reimburses the fund that made the payment and the paying fund reverses its initial entry.	Expenditures ....Dr Cash ....Cr If the fund is a proprietary fund, *Expense* is used in place of *Expenditure*.	Cash ....Dr Expenditures ....Cr If the fund is a proprietary fund, *Expense* is used in place of *Expenditure*.

Interfund Services Provided and Used

Interfund services provided and used represent transactions involving sales and purchases of goods and services between funds. An example is the sale of water from a water utility (enterprise) fund to the General Fund. In these transactions, one fund records a revenue (enterprise, in this example) and the other fund records an expenditure or expense (the General Fund). Sometimes called **quasi-external transactions,** these transactions are reported as if they were transactions with parties outside the government.

Interfund Transfers

Interfund transfers represent flows of cash or other assets without a requirement for repayment. An example would be an annual transfer of resources from the General Fund to a debt service fund. Interfund transfers act (in terms of debits and credits) as if they are revenues or expenditures (expenses) but are classified as other financing sources (the debt service fund) and other financing uses (the General Fund).

Interfund Reimbursements

Interfund reimbursements represent repayments to the funds that initially recorded expenditures or expenses by the funds responsible. For example, assume the General Fund had previously debited expenditures to acquire some supplies, but the supplies should have been charged to a special revenue fund. The reimbursement entry would have one fund (the special revenue fund) debit an expenditure (or expense) and the other fund (the General Fund) credit an expenditure or expense.

ILLUSTRATIVE CASE—GENERAL FUND

Illustration 3–1 (in Chapter 3) presents a Governmental Fund Account Structure that can be used as a guide when studying the following illustrative case and other journal entries in Chapters 4 and 5. Assume that at the beginning of fiscal year 2012, the Village of Elizabeth's General Fund had the following balances in its accounts:

	Debits	Credits
Cash	$100,000	
Taxes Receivable—Delinquent	400,000	
Estimated Uncollectible Delinquent Taxes		$ 40,000
Interest and Penalties Receivable on Taxes	25,000	
Estimated Uncollectible Interest and Penalties		10,000
Accounts Payable		135,000
Deferred Revenues—Property Taxes		20,000
Due to Federal Government		30,000
Budgetary Fund Balance—Reserve for Encumbrances *outstanding fr last yr*		45,000
Fund Balance		245,000
Totals	$525,000	$525,000

The Deferred Revenues—Property Taxes account reflects the portion of the $400,000 in taxes receivable that have not yet been recognized as a revenue. The Budgetary Fund Balance—Reserve for Encumbrances account represents the amount of purchase orders and contracts, related to the prior year, that remain open at the beginning of 2012.

Recording the Budget

At the beginning of fiscal year 2012, it is necessary to record the budget (assuming that all legal requirements have been met). If the total estimated revenue budget is $6,200,000, the total appropriations are $5,200,000, the total planned transfer to debt service funds is $204,000, and a planned transfer to establish an internal service fund is $596,000, the necessary entry to record the budget would be as follows (keeping in mind that appropriate subsidiary ledger detail would be required in actual situations):

	Debits	Credits
1. Estimated Revenues Control	6,200,000	
Appropriations Control		5,200,000
Estimated Other Financing Uses Control _204 +596_		800,000
Budgetary Fund Balance _1 (6,200 - 5,200 - 800)_		200,000

Re-establishment of Encumbrances

Assuming the $45,000 in purchase orders at the beginning of the year will be honored, it is necessary to re-establish the encumbrances. As we will see later in this chapter (entry 30), outstanding encumbrances are closed to Fund Balance. Re-establishing the encumbrance in the following year can be accomplished by reversing the effect of that entry.

2. Encumbrances Control (*prior year*)	45,000	
Fund Balance		45,000

Recording Prior-Year Property Taxes as Revenues

GASB standards for property tax revenue recognition under the modified accrual basis of accounting provide that revenue should not be recognized for property taxes expected to be collected more than 60 days beyond the end of the fiscal year. In fact, some governments defer all of their property taxes receivable at year-end. At the end of 2011, the Village of Elizabeth deferred $20,000 in property taxes, and that amount is reflected in the beginning trial balance as a liability. Since these taxes will be available for 2012 expenditures, entry 3 recognizes that amount as a revenue for 2012 (see entry 27 for the current year deferral):

	Debits	Credits
3. Deferred Revenues—Property Taxes	20,000	
Revenues Control		20,000

Recognize Rev. for prior yr

Tax Anticipation Notes Payable

In the trial balance of the General Fund of the Village of Elizabeth, liabilities (Accounts Payable and Due to Federal Government) total $165,000. Cash of the General Fund on the date of the trial balance amounts to $100,000. Although some collections of delinquent taxes receivable are expected early in the year, payrolls and other liabilities are incurred and must be paid before substantial amounts of cash will be collected. Accordingly, it may be desirable to arrange a short-term loan. The taxing power of the Village is ample security for a short-term debt. Local banks customarily meet the working capital needs of governmental units by accepting a "tax anticipation note" (a short-term note) from the government officials. If the amount of $200,000 is borrowed at this time the necessary entry is as follows:

4. Cash.	200,000	
Tax Anticipation Notes Payable		200,000

Because the loan is short term, it is reflected as a liability of the fund.

Payment of Liabilities as Recorded

Checks were drawn to pay the accounts payable and the amount due to the federal government as of the end of the previous year:

5. Accounts Payable	135,000	
Due to Federal Government	30,000	
Cash.		165,000

Encumbrance Entry

In addition to the $45,000 encumbrance outstanding at the beginning of the year, purchase orders for materials and supplies are issued in the amount of $826,000. The general ledger entry to record the encumbrances for the purchase orders is as follows (subsidiary ledger detail is omitted from this example but should be recorded by an actual governmental unit):

6. Encumbrances Control	826,000	
Budgetary Fund Balance—Reserve for Encumbrances		826,000

Recording Property Tax Levy

Assume the gross amount of the current property tax levy is $3,265,306. After considering local economic conditions and the Village's tax collection policies, it is estimated that 2 percent of these taxes will be uncollectible. Therefore, the following entry is made at the time of the tax levy:

	Debits	Credits
7. Taxes Receivable—Current	3,265,306	
Estimated Uncollectible Current Taxes		65,306
Revenues Control		3,200,000

Keep in mind that the account Revenues Control is a control account in the General Fund general ledger. It is supported by a subsidiary ledger in the manner illustrated in Chapter 3. Taxes Receivable—Current is also a control account and is supported by a subsidiary ledger organized by parcels of property according to their legal descriptions.

Collection of Delinquent Taxes

Delinquent taxes are subject to interest and penalties that must be paid at the time the tax bill is paid. It is also permitted for a government to accrue the amount of the penalties at the time that the taxes become delinquent. Interest is also computed and recorded at year-end. Interest must also be accrued for the period from the date of last recording to the date when a taxpayer pays the delinquent taxes. In the current year, the Village of Elizabeth collected delinquent taxes in the amount of $330,000, on which interest and penalties of $20,000 had been accrued at the end of 2011; further $3,000 additional interest was collected for the period from the first day of 2012 to the dates on which the delinquent taxes were collected. Entry 8a records the additional interest as revenue of 2012; entry 8b records the collection of the delinquent taxes and the total interest and penalties owed on them.

8a. Interest and Penalties Receivable on Taxes	3,000	
Revenues Control		3,000
8b. Cash...	353,000	
Taxes Receivable—Delinquent.........................		330,000
Interest and Penalties Receivable on Taxes		23,000

Collection of Current Taxes

Collections during 2012 of property taxes levied are $2,700,000. Since the revenue was recognized at the time the receivable was recorded, the following entry would be made:

9. Cash..	2,700,000	
Taxes Receivable—Current		2,700,000

Other Revenues

At the time of sale, sales taxes are paid to retailers who then submit them to the state government. Although the entire amount collected is paid to the state, it is common that a portion of the tax is revenue to the state government and the remaining portion is revenue to the local government. Assume that retailers must submit sales taxes by the 10th of the following month to the state government and the state pays the local governments their share within 30 days. During the year, $1,350,000 of sales taxes resulting from 2012 sales are received from the state government. An additional $60,000 for sales during the final week of 2012 are expected to be received in January 2013.

	Debits	Credits
10. Cash..	1,350,000	
Due from State Government............................	60,000	
Revenues Control		1,410,000

Revenues from licenses and permits, fines and forfeits, intergovernmental revenue, charges for services, and other sources not susceptible to accrual are recognized on the cash basis. Collections for the year are $1,450,000.

11. Cash...	1,450,000	
Revenues Control		1,450,000

Repayment of Tax Anticipation Notes

As tax collections begin to exceed current disbursements, it becomes possible for the Village of Elizabeth to repay the local bank for the money borrowed in tax anticipation notes (entry 4). Just as borrowing money did not involve the recognition of revenue, the repayment of the principal is merely the extinguishment of short-term debt of the General Fund and not an expenditure. Payment of interest, however, must be recognized as an expenditure. Assuming the interest is $5,000, the entry is as follows:

12. Tax Anticipation Notes Payable........................	200,000	
Expenditures Control	5,000	
Cash...		205,000

Recognition of Expenditures for Encumbered Items

Some of the materials and supplies ordered last year and this year (see entries 2 and 6) were received. Invoices for the items received totaled $820,300; related purchase orders totaled $821,000. After inspection of the goods and supplies, the invoices were approved for payment. Since the purchase orders had been recorded as encumbrances against the appropriations, it is necessary to reverse the encumbered amount and to record the expenditure in the amount of the actual liability:

	Debits	Credits
13a. Budgetary Fund Balance—Reserve for Encumbrances	821,000	
Encumbrances Control (*prior year*)		45,000
Encumbrances Control		776,000
13b. Expenditures Control (*prior year*)	45,000	
Expenditures Control	775,300	
Accounts Payable		820,300

The designation of expenditures as relating to a prior year is desirable, since expenditures arising from 2011 encumbrances would typically not be reflected in the Budgetary Comparison Schedule for fiscal year 2012. Instead, they would have been reflected in the previous year's Budgetary Comparison Schedule.

Payrolls and Payroll Taxes

The gross pay of employees of General Fund departments amounted to $3,345,000. The Village of Elizabeth does not use the encumbrance procedure for payrolls. The gross pay is charged against the appropriations of the individual departments through a subsidiary ledger (not presented). Deductions from gross pay for the period amounted to $78,000 for employees' state income tax withholdings and $686,000 due to the federal government ($430,000 for federal income tax withholdings and $256,000 for the employees' share of FICA and Medicare taxes). Assuming the liability for net pay is processed through the accounts payable system, the entries to record the payroll and subsequent payment are as follows:

14a. Expenditures Control.	3,345,000	
Due to Federal Government		686,000
Due to State Government		78,000
Accounts Payable		2,581,000
14b. Accounts Payable	2,581,000	
Cash.		2,581,000

The Village is liable for the employer's share of FICA tax and Medicare tax ($256,000) and for contributions to additional retirement funds established by state law (assumed to amount to $167,000 for the year). The Village's liabilities for its contributions are recorded:

	Debits	Credits
15. Expenditures Control	423,000	
Due to Federal Government		256,000
Due to State Government		167,000

Payment on Account and Other Items

Payment is made on $770,000 of the outstanding accounts payable, and the amounts due the state and federal governments are paid in full:

	Debits	Credits
16. Accounts Payable	770,000	
Due to Federal Government	942,000	
Due to State Government	245,000	
Cash.		1,957,000

Correction of Errors

No problems arise in the collection of current taxes if they are collected as billed; the collections are debited to Cash and credited to Taxes Receivable—Current. Sometimes, even in a well-designed and well-operated system, errors occur and must be corrected. If, for example, duplicate tax bills totaling $1,200 were sent out for the same piece of property, the following entry would be required. (The error also caused a slight overstatement of the credit to Estimated Uncollectible Current Taxes in entry 7, but the error in that account is not considered material enough to correct.)

	Debits	Credits
17. Revenues Control	1,200	
Taxes Receivable—Current		1,200

    Audit procedures may disclose errors in the recording of expenditures during the current year or during a prior year. If the error occurred during the current year, the Expenditures Control account and the proper subsidiary ledger account can be debited or credited as needed to correct the error. If the error occurred in a prior year, however, the Expenditures account in error has been closed to Fund Balance, so theoretically the correcting entry should be made to that account. As a practical matter, immaterial changes resulting from corrections of prior period errors may be recorded in the current period Revenues or Expenditures accounts.

Amendment of the Budget

Comparisons of budgeted and actual revenues by sources and comparisons of departmental or program appropriations with expenditures and encumbrances, as well as an interpretation of information that was not available at the time the budgets were originally adopted, may indicate the desirability or necessity of amending the budget during the fiscal year. For example, assume that the revenues budget was increased by $50,000 in the Charges for Services source category and that the appropriation for the Public Works Department was increased by $100,000. The amendments to the budget would be recorded when they were legally approved, as follows:

	Debits	Credits
18. Estimated Revenues Control......................................	50,000	
Budgetary Fund Balance.......................................	50,000	
Appropriations Control.....................................		100,000

Corresponding changes would be made in the subsidiary ledger accounts as illustrated in the appendix to Chapter 3.

Interfund Transactions

Interfund Services Provided and Used   Interfund services provided and used are recognized as revenues or expenditures (or expenses in the case of proprietary funds) of the funds involved in the same manner as they would be recognized if the transactions involved outside organizations.

Water utilities ordinarily provide a city with fire hydrants and water service for fire protection at a flat annual charge. A government-owned water utility expected to support the cost of its operations by user charges should be accounted for as an enterprise fund. Fire protection is logically budgeted as an activity of the fire department, a General Fund department. Assuming that the amount charged by the water utility to the General Fund for hydrants and water service was $80,000, the General Fund entry would be as follows:

19. Expenditures Control	80,000	
Due to Water Utility Fund		80,000

The account *Due to Water Utility Fund* is a current liability. The enterprise fund would also record this transaction (see enterprise fund entry 1 in Chapter 6).

Another common transaction for the General Fund is the receipt of supplies or services from an internal service fund established to provide purchasing and distribution services to other government departments. Assume that the General Fund received $377,000 in supplies from the Supplies Fund and later made a partial payment of $322,000 in cash. The entries would be as follows:

20a. Expenditures Control......................................	377,000	
Due to Supplies Fund		377,000
20b. Due to Supplies Fund	322,000	
Cash...		322,000

The internal service fund would also record this (see internal service fund entries 5b and 7 in Chapter 6).

Interfund Transfers   Some transactions are labeled as "other financing sources (uses)—transfers" in order to avoid reporting revenues and expenditures more than once in the governmental unit. Assuming that the General Fund made the budgeted transfer to a Debt Service Fund for the payment of debt service, the General Fund entry would be as follows:'

	Debits	Credits
21a. Other Financing Uses—Transfers Out Control.	204,000	
Due to Debt Service Fund.		204,000

When the cash is transferred, the entry would be as follows:

21b. Due to Debt Service Fund.	204,000	
Cash.		204,000

The debt service fund will make a corresponding entry to record the transfer. See debt service entry 19 in Chapter 5.

Other transfers are nonroutine transactions, often made to establish or liquidate a fund. Assume that the General Fund made a permanent transfer of $596,000 to establish an internal service fund. The General Fund entry would be as follows:

22. Other Financing Uses—Transfers Out Control.	596,000	
Cash.		596,000

See internal service fund entry 1 in Chapter 6.

Interfund Reimbursements   Assume that $20,000 of the expenditures in entry 13b related to supplies used for road maintenance that should have been charged to the Motor Fuel Tax Fund, a special revenue fund. It was decided that $20,000 cash would be moved from the Motor Fuel Tax Fund and that the transaction would be treated as an interfund reimbursement. Accordingly, $20,000 is charged to the Motor Fuel Tax Fund (see entry 3 in the Special Revenue Fund section of this chapter) and General Fund expenditures are reduced by $20,000.

23. Cash.	20,000	
Expenditures Control		20,000

Write-off of Uncollectible Delinquent Taxes

Government officials should review aged schedules of receivables periodically in order to determine the adequacy of allowance accounts and to authorize the write-offs of items judged to be uncollectible. Although the levy of property taxes creates a lien against the underlying property in the amount of the tax, accumulated taxes may exceed the market value of the property, or in the case of personal property (e.g., cars), the property may be removed from the jurisdiction of the government. When delinquent taxes are deemed to be uncollectible, the related interest and penalties must also be written off. If the treasurer of the Village of Elizabeth received approval to write off delinquent taxes totaling $30,000 and related interest and penalties of $3,000, the entry would be as follows:

	Debits	Credits
24. Estimated Uncollectible		
Delinquent Taxes	30,000	
Taxes Receivable—Delinquent		30,000
Estimated Uncollectible.		
Interest and Penalties	3,000	
Interest and Penalties Receivable on Taxes		3,000

When delinquent taxes are written off, the tax bills are retained in the files, although they are no longer subject to general ledger control, because changes in conditions may make it possible to collect the amounts in the future. If collections of write-off taxes are made, the amounts should be returned to general ledger control by making an entry that is the reverse of the write-off entry, so that the procedures described in entries 8a and 8b may be followed.

Reclassification of Current Taxes

Assuming that all property taxes levied by the Village of Elizabeth for 2012 were to have been paid by property owners before the end of the year, any balance of taxes receivable at year-end is properly classified as delinquent, rather than current. The related allowance for estimated uncollectible taxes also should be reclassified to the delinquent classification. A review should be made at this time to ensure that the estimated uncollectible amount is reasonable in relation to the delinquent taxes. Assuming the estimate is reasonable, the entry would be as follows:

25. Taxes Receivable—Delinquent.	564,106	
Taxes Receivable—Current		564,106
Estimated Uncollectible Current Taxes.	65,306	
Estimated Uncollectible Delinquent Taxes.		65,306

Accrual of Interest and Penalties

Delinquent taxes are subject to interest and penalties. The amount of interest and penalties earned in 2012 by the General Fund of the Village of Elizabeth and not yet recognized is $56,410, but it is expected that only $39,490 of that can be collected. The entry would be as follows:

	Debits	Credits
26. Interest and Penalties Receivable on Taxes	56,410	
Estimated Uncollectible Interest and Penalties		16,920
Revenues Control.		39,490

Deferral of Property Tax Revenue

A review of the taxes receivable subsidiary ledger indicated that approximately $40,000 would probably be received more than 60 days beyond the end of the fiscal year. The sixty-day rule requires that the $40,000 be deferred:

27. Revenues Control	40,000	
Deferred Revenues—Property Taxes		40,000

Special Item

GASB standards require that extraordinary items and special items be reported separately after other financing sources and uses. Extraordinary items are significant transactions or other events that are both unusual and infrequent. **Special items** are significant transactions or other events that are *either* unusual or infrequent but *within* the control of management. Assume the Village sold land for $300,000.

28. Cash.	300,000	
Special Item—Proceeds from Sale of Land		300,000

The reduction in the land account would be reported in the government-wide financial statements. Because governmental funds report only current financial resources, land does not need to be removed from the General Fund's assets.

Preclosing Trial Balance

Illustration 4–2 presents the general ledger control accounts after all journal entries have been posted. Note that only Balance Sheet accounts have beginning balances (denoted *bb*). It is often useful to prepare a trial balance before proceeding with the

ILLUSTRATION 4–2 General Ledger Control Accounts

CASH

bb	100,000		
(4)	200,000	(5)	165,000
(8)	353,000	(12)	205,000
(9)	2,700,000	(14)	2,581,000
(10)	1,350,000	(16)	1,957,000
(11)	1,450,000	(20)	322,000
(23)	20,000	(21)	204,000
(28)	300,000	(22)	596,000
	443,000		

TAXES RECEIVABLE

bb	400,000		
(7)	3,265,306	(8)	330,000
		(9)	2,700,000
		(17)	1,200
		(24)	30,000
	604,106		

TAXES RECEIVABLE ESTM' UNCOLLECT'

		bb	40,000
(24)	30,000	(7)	65,306
			75,306

INTR & PENALTY REC.

bb	25,000		
(8)	3,000	(8)	23,000
(26)	56,410	(24)	3,000
	58,410		

ESTM' UNCOLLECT' INTR & PEN REC.

		bb	10,000
(24)	3,000	(26)	16,920
			23,920

DUE FROM STATE GOV

bb	60,000		
		(10)	60,000

ACCOUNTS PAYABLE

		bb	135,000
(5)	135,000	(13)	820,300
(14)	2,581,000	(14)	2,581,000
			50,300

NOTES PAYABLE

		bb	200,000
(12)	200,000		
			-

DUE TO STATE GOV

		bb	78,000 (14)
(16)	245,000		167,000 (15)
			-

DUE TO FEDR GOV

		bb	30,000
(5)	30,000	(14)	686,000
(16)	942,000	(15)	256,000

DUE TO OTHER FUNDS

		bb	-
(20)	322,000	(19)	80,000
(21)	204,000	(20)	377,000
		(21)	204,000
			135,000

DEFERRED REVENUE

		bb	20,000
(3)	20,000	(27)	40,000
			40,000

ESTIMATED REV' CONTROL

(1)	6,200,000		
(18)	50,000		
	6,250,000		

APPROPRIATIONS CONTROL

		(1)	5,200,000
		(18)	100,000
			5,300,000

ESTIMATED OTHER FINAN USES CONTROL

		(1)	800,000
			800,000

REVENUES CONTROL

		(3)	20,000
		(7)	3,200,000
		(8)	3,000
		(10)	1,410,000
		(11)	1,450,000
		(26)	39,490
(17)	1,200		
(27)	40,000		
			6,081,290

2011 EXPENDITURES CONTROL

			-
(13)	45,000	(23)	45,000

2012 EXPENDITURES CONTROL

(12)	5,000		
(13)	775,300		
(14)	3,345,000		
(15)	423,000	(23)	20,000
(19)	80,000		
(20)	377,000		
	4,985,300		

2011 ENCUMBRANCES CONTROL

			-
(2)	45,000	(13)	45,000

2012 ENCUMBRANCES CONTROL

			-
(6)	826,000	(13)	776,000
			50,000

OFU TRANSFERS OUT CONTROL

(21)	204,000		
(22)	596,000		
	800,000		

BUDGETARY FUND BALANCE

		bb	
(18)	50,000	(1)	200,000
			150,000

BUDGETARY FUND BALANCE— RESERVE FOR ENCUMBRANCES

		bb	45,000
(13)	826,000	(6)	826,000
			45,000

UNRESERVED FUND BALANCE

		bb	245,000
		(2)	45,000
			290,000

OFS SPECIAL ITEM PROCEEDS SALE LAND

			-
		(28)	300,000
			300,000

* bb denotes beginning balance at January 1, 2012.

ILLUSTRATION 4–3   Preclosing Trial Balance

VILLAGE OF ELIZABETH
General Fund
Trial Balance
As of December 31, 2012

	Debits	Credits
Cash	$443,000	
Taxes Receivable—Delinquent	604,106	
Estimated Uncollectible Delinquent Taxes		$75,306
Interest and Penalties Receivable on Taxes	58,410	
Estimated Uncollectible Interest and Penalties		23,920
Due from State Government	60,000	
Accounts Payable		50,300
Due to Water Utility Fund		80,000
Due to Supplies Fund		55,000
Deferred Revenues—Property Taxes		40,000
Budgetary Fund Balance—Reserve for Encumbrances		50,000
Fund Balance		290,000
Estimated Revenues Control	6,250,000	
Revenues Control		6,081,290
Appropriations Control		5,300,000
Estimated Other Financing Uses Control		800,000
Budgetary Fund Balance		150,000
Expenditures Control (*prior year*)	4,985,300	
Expenditures Control (*prior year*)	45,000	
Encumbrances Control (*prior year*)	50,000	
Other Financing Uses—Transfers Out Control	800,000	
Special Item—Proceeds from Sale of Land		300,000
	$13,295,816	$13,295,816

year-end closing entries and financial statements. Illustration 4–3 presents the pre-closing trial balance for the General Fund at December 31, 2012.

Closing Entries

The essence of the closing process for the General Fund or special revenue funds of a state or local government is the transfer of the balances of the operating statement accounts and the balances of the budgetary accounts for the year to the Fund Balance account. Note that the first closing entry has the effect of reversing the entry to record the budget (entry 1) and the entry to amend the budget (entry 18). After the closing entries are posted, the Fund Balance account represents the net amount of resources available for appropriation.

	Debits	Credits
29. Appropriations Control.	5,300,000	
Estimated Other Financing Uses Control	800,000	
Budgetary Fund Balance.	150,000	
Estimated Revenues Control.		6,250,000

	Debits	Credits
30. Revenues Control	6,081,290	
Special Items—Proceeds from Sale of Land.	300,000	
Expenditures Control (*prior year*)		45,000
Expenditures Control (*prior year*)		4,985,300
Other Financing Uses—Transfers Out Control		800,000
Encumbrances Control		50,000
Fund Balance		500,990 ←—plus in

After the closing entries are posted to the general ledger, the excess of fund assets over liabilities is represented in two fund balance accounts:

- *Fund Balance* $790,990 ($290,000 beginning balance plus $500,990 from the closing entry #30) and
- *Budgetary Fund Balance—Reserve for Encumbrances* $50,000.

These amounts must be reported within the five categories of fund balance. The General Fund has no unused supplies or prepaid expenses, so there are no *Nonspendable* resources in this example. Assume that the Village received a grant of $350,000 from the state that is restricted to qualifying expenditures associated with public works. At year-end, $75,000 of this grant remained unexpended and is reported as *Restricted Fund Balance*. Assume also that the Village Council has formally *committed* $100,000 of the remaining fund balance to capital projects improving the communication equipment of the police, fire, and EMT programs. The balance of Budgetary Fund Balance—Reserve for Encumbrances represents purchase orders outstanding at year end that will be paid next year from the General Fund. For purposes of fund balance reporting, these purchase commitments reflect an expressed intent by the government to use $50,000 of the General Fund's net resources for specific purposes and should be reported as *Assigned Fund Balance*. The residual amount of the fund's net resources ($615,990) is reported as *Unassigned Fund Balance*. These amounts are summarized as follows:

	Total $	Non-spendable	Restricted	Committed	Assigned	Unassigned
Fund Balance	$790,990	——	$75,000	$100,000	——	$615,990
Budgetary Fund Balance— Reserve for Encumbrances	$50,000	——	——	——	50,000	——
Total Fund Balances	$840,990	0	$75,000	$100,000	$50,000	$615,990

Some governments may choose to allocate these amounts to individual fund balance accounts through journal entry. Our approach will be to determine the components of fund balance in the manner illustrated above and present the totals directly in the balance sheet. In this way we reduce the number of accounts necessary to record changes in overall fund balance.

Year-End Financial Statements

The Balance Sheet for the General Fund of the Village of Elizabeth as of the end of 2012 is shown in Illustration 4–4. If the General Fund has both a due from and a due to another fund, it is permissible to offset these amounts, provided they are with the same fund. (It should be emphasized, however, that it is not acceptable to offset a receivable from one fund against a payable to a different fund.)

The General Fund is also required to report a Statement of Revenues, Expenditures, and Changes in Fund Balance. Illustration 4–5 presents the actual revenues and actual expenditures that resulted from transactions illustrated in this chapter, including the expenditure of $45,000 relating to a 2011 encumbrance (entry 13). Note that the expenditures do not include the current encumbrances outstanding

ILLUSTRATION 4–4   Balance Sheet for the General Fund

VILLAGE OF ELIZABETH General Fund Balance Sheet As of December 31, 2012		
Assets		
Cash		$443,000
Taxes Receivable—Delinquent	$604,106	
Less: Estimated Uncollectible	75,306	528,800
Interest and Penalties Receivable on Taxes	58,410	
Less: Estimated Uncollectible	23,920	34,490
Due from State Government		$60,000
Total Assets		1,066,290
Liabilities and Fund Equity		
Liabilities:		
Accounts Payable	$50,300	
Due to Water Utility Fund	80,000	
Due to Supplies Fund	55,000	
Deferred Revenues—Property Taxes	40,000	
Total Liabilities		$225,300
Fund Balance:		
Restricted for Public Works	75,000	
Committed to Capital Projects	100,000	
Assigned for Other Purposes	50,000	
Unassigned	615,990	
Total Fund Balances		840,990
Total Liabilities and Fund Balances		$1,066,290

ILLUSTRATION 4–5   Statement of Revenues, Expenditures, and Changes in Fund Balance

VILLAGE OF ELIZABETH General Fund Statement of Revenues, Expenditures, and Changes in Fund Balance For the Year Ended December 31, 2012		
Revenues (amounts assumed):		
Property taxes	$3,178,800	
Interest and penalties on delinquent taxes	42,490	
Sales taxes	1,410,000	
Licenses and permits	540,000	
Fines and forfeits	430,000	
Intergovernmental revenue	350,000	
Charges for services	100,000	
Miscellaneous revenues	30,000	
Total revenues		$6,081,290
Expenditures (amounts assumed):		
General government	810,000	
Public safety	2,139,500	
Public works	630,000	
Health and welfare	480,100	
Parks and recreation	527,400	
Contribution to retirement funds	423,000	
Miscellaneous expenditures	20,300	
Total expenditures		(5,030,300)
Excess of revenues over expenditures		1,050,990
Other financing uses:		
Transfers out		(800,000)
Special item:		
Proceeds from sale of land		300,000
Net change in fund balance		550,990
Fund balance, January 1, 2012		290,000
Fund balance, December 31, 2012		$ 840,990

of $50,000, because GASB standards specify that encumbrances are not to be reported as expenditures (except in statements on schedules prepared in conformity with budgetary practices instead of generally accepted accounting principles [GAAP]).

Information shown in Illustration 4–5 would be presented in columnar form with other government type funds in the Statement of Revenues, Expenditures, and Changes in Fund Balances for governmental funds (see Chapter 5).

Illustration 4–6 presents the budgetary comparison schedule for the General Fund that would appear in the required supplementary information. Note the required reconciliation between the budgetary basis and GAAP basis reporting of expenditures appearing at the bottom of the schedule. Additional differences may exist and would require similar explanation.

ILLUSTRATION 4–6 Budgetary Comparison Schedule

VILLAGE OF ELIZABETH				
Budgetary Comparison Schedule				
General Fund				
For the Year Ended December 31, 2012				

	Budgeted Amounts		Actual Amounts (BUDGETARY BASIS)*	Variance with Final Budget Positive (Negative)
	Original	FINAL		
Revenues:				
Property taxes	$3,000,000	$3,000,000	$3,178,800	$178,800
Interest and penalties	30,000	30,000	42,490	12,490
Sales taxes	1,763,000	1,763,000	1,410,000	(353,000)
Licenses and permits	550,000	550,000	540,000	(10,000)
Fines and forfeits	420,000	420,000	430,000	10,000
Intergovernmental	350,000	350,000	350,000	———
Charges for services	50,000	100,000	100,000	———
Miscellaneous	37,000	37,000	30,000	(7,000)
Total revenues	6,200,000	6,250,000	6,081,290	(168,710)
Expenditures and Encumbrances:				
General government	821,000	821,000	765,000	56,000
Public safety	2,240,000	2,240,000	2,139,500	100,500
Public works	540,000	640,000	630,000	10,000
Health and welfare	528,000	528,000	480,100	47,900
Parks and recreation	628,000	628,000	577,400	50,600
Contribution to retirement funds	423,000	423,000	423,000	———
Miscellaneous	20,000	20,000	20,300	(300)
Total expenditures and encumbrances	5,200,000	5,300,000	5,035,300	264,700
Excess (deficiency) of revenues Over expenditures & encumbrances	1,000,000	950,000	1,045,990	95,990
Other financing sources (uses)				
Special item: sale of land	———	———	300,000	300,000
Transfers to other funds	(800,000)	(800,000)	(800,000)	———
Net change in fund balance	200,000	150,000	545,990	395,990
Fund balance, beginning	290,000	290,000	290,000	———
Fund balance, ending	$490,000	$440,000	$ 835,990	$395,990

Budget to GAAP Differences*	General Government Expenditures	Parks and Recreation Expenditures	Total Fund Balance Dec. 31, 2012
Budgetary Basis	$765,000	$577,400	$835,990
Encumbrances outstanding 12-31-2011	45,000		(45,000)
Encumbrances outstanding 12-31-2012	———	(50,000)	50,000
GAAP Basis	810,000	527,400	840,990

Explanation: Encumbrances for goods and services ordered but not received are reported in the year the orders are placed for budgetary purposes, but are reported in the year received for GAAP purposes.

ILLUSTRATIVE CASE—SPECIAL REVENUE FUND

Special revenue funds are used when it is desirable to provide separate reporting of resources that are *restricted or committed* to expenditure for a specified purpose other than debt service or capital projects. Resources appropriately reported within proprietary or fiduciary funds are also excluded from special revenue funds. Governments should attempt to keep the number of special revenue and other funds to a reasonable number. Often a functional classification in the General Fund is adequate to meet the information needs of users interested in assuring compliance with resource limitations.

Commonly, special revenue funds are used for intergovernmental grants in which the federal or state government provides resources to local governments. The legislation providing these resources typically imposes restrictions on the use of intergovernmental revenues. Special revenue funds may also be necessary in the case of taxes that require the government to use the tax proceeds to support specific activities. An example is the emergency 911 surcharge commonly paid by consumers to phone service providers. These taxes are collected by the phone company and remitted to city or county governments. The taxes are required by law to be used for the support of the 911 emergency phone network.

Assume the Village of Elizabeth maintains a motor fuel tax fund, as required by state law. Revenues include state motor fuel tax receipts and state reimbursement grants. Expenditures are incurred for road repairs and maintenance. A legally adopted annual budget is not required or used. Assume, at the beginning of 2012, the motor fuel tax fund has cash of $212,500 offset by fund balance in the same amount.

Motor Fuel Tax Revenues

During 2012, the State notified the Village that $650,000 in motor fuel taxes will be awarded. Records show $575,000 was received in cash; the remainder is due from the state and should be received within 60 days of the end of the fiscal year. Motor fuel taxes are a derived tax revenue; under modified accrual accounting, the amount that can be recognized is the amount that is measurable and available.

	Debits	Credits
1. Cash	575,000	
Due from State Government	75,000	
Revenues Control		650,000

Expenditures for Road Repairs

Also during 2012, expenditures for road repairs amounted to $605,000, of which $540,000 was paid in cash. Note that encumbrance accounting might be used but is omitted for the sake of brevity.

	Debits	Credits
2. Expenditures Control	605,000	
Cash		540,000
Accounts Payable		65,000

Reimbursement to General Fund

Entry 23 in the General Fund example related to supplies, originally charged to expenditures by the General Fund, that were for road repairs and should be charged to the motor fuel tax fund. The corresponding interfund reimbursement entry to charge the motor fuel tax fund and to reimburse cash to the General Fund is

3. Expenditures Control	20,000	
Cash		20,000

Reimbursement Grant Accounting

Assume the State awarded the Village a grant of $450,000 for major repairs to three Village intersections. The funds will be released by the State only as work is completed, as a reimbursement. This represents an eligibility requirement under GASB *Statement 33*. Accordingly, grant revenues and receivables would be recognized as expenditures are incurred. During 2012, expenditures in the amount of $350,000 were incurred, of which $280,000 was paid. The State had remitted $300,000 cash as of the end of 2012.

4. Expenditures Control	350,000	
Cash		280,000
Accounts Payable		70,000
5. Due from State Government	350,000	
Revenues Control		350,000
6. Cash	300,000	
Due from State Government		300,000

Closing Entry

At year-end, the Motor Fuel Tax Fund would prepare the following closing entry:

7. Revenues Control	1,000,000	
Expenditures Control		975,000
Fund Balance		25,000

After the closing entries are posted to the general ledger, the excess of fund assets over liabilities is $237,500 ($212,500 beginning balance plus $25,000 from the closing entry 7). As with the General Fund, these amounts must be reported within the five categories of fund balance. The motor fuel tax fund has no unused supplies or prepaid expenses, so there are no *Nonspendable* resources in this example. All of the resources in this fund are required by state law to be used for road repairs and maintenance under the public works department. This represents a restriction imposed by an outside entity and the net resources are reported as *Restricted Fund Balance*. Had the Village supplemented the motor fuel tax fund with resources that were not restricted or committed, the residual balance would be reported as *Assigned Fund Balance*. Only the General Fund may report a positive *Unassigned Fund Balance*.

Year-End Financial Statements

Illustration 4–7 & 4–8 reflect the Balance Sheet and the Statement of Revenues, Expenditures, and Changes in Fund Balances for the motor fuel tax fund.

ILLUSTRATION 4–7   Balance Sheet for Motor Fuel Tax Fund

VILLAGE OF ELIZABETH Motor Fuel Tax Fund Balance Sheet As of December 31, 2012	
Assets	
Cash	$247,500
Due from State Government	125,000
Total Assets	$372,500
Liabilities and Fund Equity	
Liabilities:	
Accounts Payable	$135,000
Fund Balance:	
Restricted for Road Repair	237,500
Total Liabilities and Fund Equity	$372,500

ILLUSTRATION 4–8   Statement of Revenues, Expenses, and Changes in Fund Balances

VILLAGE OF ELIZABETH Motor Fuel Tax Fund Statement of Revenues, Expenditures, and Changes in Fund Balances For the Year Ended December 31, 2012	
Revenues:	
Motor Fuel Taxes	$ 650,000
State Reimbursement Grant	350,000
Total Revenues	1,000,000
Expenditures:	
Public Works	975,000
Net Change in Fund Balance	25,000
Fund Balance, January 1, 2012	212,500
Fund Balance, December 31, 2012	$ 237,500

RECOGNITION OF INVENTORIES IN GOVERNMENTAL FUNDS

In most cases, supplies inventories are insignificant relative to governmental fund balances. Generally accepted accounting principles permit two methods of accounting for inventories. Under the **purchases method,** Expenditures are debited when supplies are received. No adjustment is made to Expenditures to reflect the use of supplies. At the end of the period, the Supplies Inventory account is debited and *Nonspendable Fund Balance* is credited to reflect the balance of unused supplies on hand. Under this method, Expenditures equals the amount of supplies purchased (not used) during the period.

An alternative is the method used by commercial businesses, the **consumption method.** Under this method, Supplies Inventory is debited when inventories are acquired. When supplies are consumed, the Expenditures account is debited and Supplies Inventory credited, with the result that expenditures equal the amount of supplies used during a period. A portion of the post-closing fund balance (equal to the unused Supplies Inventory) is classified as *Nonspendable Fund Balance* in the fund balances section of the Balance Sheet. The consumption method is preferable because it requires no adjustment to supplies expense when preparing the government-wide statements.

Now that you have finished reading Chapter 4, complete the multiple choice questions provided on the text's Web site (www.mhhe.com/copley10e) to test your comprehension of the chapter.

Questions and Exercises

4–1. Using the annual financial report obtained for Exercise 1–1, answer the following questions:

  a. Look at the General Fund column of the Balance Sheet for governmental funds. What are the major assets? Liabilities? What reserves have been established for fund balance? Are any designations shown? Are taxes receivable offset by Deferred Revenues? Are the amounts the same? (If so, this would indicate cash accounting for property taxes.)

  b. Look at the General Fund column of the governmental funds Statement of Revenues, Expenditures, and Changes in Fund Balances. Prepare a schedule showing percentages of revenues by source. Prepare a schedule showing percentages of expenditures by function. Does your government have significant transfers in or out? Can you identify the fund that provides or receives these resources? Does your government have any other financing sources or uses? Special and/or extraordinary items?

  c. Does your government report any special revenue funds as major funds in the governmental fund statements? What are they? What are the major revenue sources? Expenditure functions?

  d. Review the notes to the financial statements to determine the measurement focus and basis of accounting used to prepare the governmental fund financial statements. Do the notes describe modified accrual accounting in a manner consistent with this book? Which revenue sources are subject to accrual? Are expenditures generally recognized when goods and services are received? Which specific modifications to accrual accounting are mentioned in the notes?

e. Look at the General Fund column of the governmental fund statements from the point of view of a financial analyst. Is the Fund Balance as of the balance sheet date larger or smaller than at the beginning of the year? Are reasons for the change apparent from the statements? Compute a ratio of fund balance/general fund revenues and compare it with your class members'.

4–2. The Village of Seaside Pines prepared the following General Fund Trial Balance as of December 31, 2012, the last day of its fiscal year.

	Debits	Credits
Accounts Payable		$45,000
Allowance Uncollectible Taxes		12,000
Appropriations		485,000
Budgetary Fund Balance		30,000
Cash	$190,000	
Deferred Revenue		19,000
Due from Capital Projects Fund	5,000	
Due to Debt Service Fund		17,000
Encumbrances	60,000	
Estimated Revenue	550,000	
Estimated Other Financing Uses		35,000
General Government Expenditures	175,000	
Other Revenues		38,000
Property Tax Revenue		503,000
Public Safety Expenditures	247,000	
Budgetary Fund Balance— Reserve for Encumbrances		60,000
Supplies Inventory	7,000	
Tax Anticipation Note Payable		100,000
Taxes Receivable	202,000	
Transfer Out (to Internal Service Fund)	33,000	
Fund Balance		125,000
Totals	$1,469,000	$1,469,000

a. Prepare the closing entries for December 31. (It is not necessary to use control accounts and subsidiary ledgers.)

b. Prepare the Statement of Revenues, Expenditures, and Changes in Fund Balance for the General Fund for the year ended December 31.

c. Prepare the Fund Balance Section of the December 31 Balance Sheet assuming there are no restricted or committed net resources and the outstanding encumbrances are for capital additions.

4–3. On January 1, 2012, the first day of its fiscal year, the City of Carter received notification that a federal grant in the amount of $650,000 was approved. The grant was restricted for the payment of wages to teenagers for summer employment. The terms of the grant permitted reimbursement only after qualified expenditures have been made; the grant could be used over a two-year period in equal amounts of $325,000 each. The following data pertain to operations of the Summer Employment Grant Fund, a special revenue fund of the City of Carter, during the year ended December 31, 2012.

Show entries in general journal form to record the following events and transactions in the accounts of the Summer Employment Grant Fund:

1. The budget was recorded. It provided for Estimated Revenues for the year in the amount of $325,000, and for Appropriations in the amount of $325,000.
2. A temporary loan of $325,000 was received from the General Fund.
3. During the year, teenagers earned and were paid $312,000 under terms of the Summer Employment program. An additional $5,000 is accrued as payable on December 31. Recognize the receivable and revenue (include the $5,000 of wages payable).
4. Each month a properly documented request for reimbursement was sent to the federal government; checks for $298,000 were received.
5. Necessary closing entries were made.

4–4. The Town of Quincy's fiscal year ends on June 30. The following data relate to the property tax levy for the fiscal year ended June 30, 2012. Prepare journal entries for each of the dates as indicated.

   a. The balance in deferred property tax revenue was $182,000 at the end of the previous year. This was recognized as revenue in the current year in a reversing journal entry.
   b. On July 1, 2011, property taxes in the amount of $10,000,000 were levied. It was estimated that 3 percent would be uncollectible. The property taxes were intended to finance the expenditures for the year ended June 30, 2012.
   c. October 31, $4,600,000 in property taxes were collected.
   d. December 31, $4,800,000 in additional property taxes were collected.
   e. Receivables totaling $12,000 were deemed to be uncollectible and written off.
   f. On June 30, $175,000, was transferred from Revenues Control to Deferred Revenues, because it was not expected to be collected within 60 days.

4–5. Prepare journal entries in the General Fund of the Brownville School District.

   a. The District had outstanding encumbrances of $13,000 for band instruments from the previous year. It is the District's policy to re-establish those encumbrances in the subsequent year.

Purchase has been given but not been received at the end of yr.

    b. The District ordered textbooks at an estimated cost of $87,000.

    c. The band instruments arrived at an invoice price of $12,500 plus $225 shipping.

    d. Textbooks originally estimated to cost $77,000 were received with an invoice price of $76,900. The remaining portion of the order is backordered.

    e. A contract was signed with a CPA to provide the annual audit in the amount of $11,000.

4–6. The following information was abstracted from the accounts of the General Fund of the City of Rome after the books had been closed for the fiscal year ended June 30, 2012.

	Postclosing Trial Balance June 30, 2011	Transactions July 1, 2011 to June 30, 2012		Postclosing Trial Balance June 30, 2012
		Debits	Credits	
Cash	$700,000	$1,820,000	$1,867,000	$653,000
Taxes Receivable	40,000	1,880,000	1,828,000	92,000
	$740,000			$745,000
Allowance for				
Uncollectible Taxes	$ 8,000	$ 8,000	$ 10,000	$ 10,000
Accounts Payable	132,000	1,852,000	1,740,000	20,000
Fund Balance:				
Budgetary Fund Balance—				
Reserve for Encumbrances	——		70,000	70,000
Unreserved	600,000		45,000	645,000
	$740,000			$745,000

During the year, purchase orders were placed in the amount of $1,070,000. These purchase orders were filled in the amount of $1,000,000 leaving $70,000 open at year-end. There were no transfers into the General Fund, but one transfer out. Prepare journal entries to record the budgeted and actual transactions for the fiscal year ended June 30, 2012. Include closing entries.

(AICPA, adapted)

4–7. The following transactions relate to the General Fund of the City of Buffalo Falls for the year ended December 31, 2012:

    1. Beginning balances were: Cash, $150,000; Taxes Receivable, $200,000; Accounts Payable, $50,000; and Fund Balance, $300,000.

    2. The budget was passed. Estimated revenues amounted to $2,000,000 and appropriations totaled $1,980,000. All expenditures are classified as General Government.

    3. Property taxes were levied in the amount of $1,200,000. All of the taxes are expected to be collected before February 2013.

4. Cash receipts totaled $1,200,000 for property taxes and $740,000 from other revenue.

5. Contracts were issued for contracted services in the amount of $900,000.

6. Contracted services were performed relating to $765,000 of the contracts with invoices amounting to $759,000.

7. Other expenditures amounted to $950,000.

8. Accounts payable were paid in the amount of $1,700,000.

9. The books were closed.

Required:

a. Prepare journal entries for the above transactions.

b. Prepare a Statement of Revenues, Expenditures, and Changes in Fund Balance for the General Fund.

c. Prepare a Balance Sheet for the General Fund assuming there are no restricted or assigned net resources and outstanding encumbrances are committed by contractual obligation.

4–8. The General Fund trial balance of the City of Cordes as of January 1, 2012, was as follows:

	Debits	Credits
Cash	$20,000	
Taxes Receivable—Delinquent	77,200	
Estimated Uncollectible Taxes—Delinquent		$ 9,200
Accounts Payable		16,000
Budgetary Fund Balance—Reserve for Encumbrances		8,500
Fund Balance		63,500
	$97,200	$97,200

The following data pertain to General Fund operations for the City of Cordes for the fiscal year ended December 31, 2012:

1. Budget adopted:

Revenues:	
Property Taxes	$420,800
Fines, Forfeits, and Penalties	160,000
Miscellaneous Revenues	20,000
	$600,800
Expenditures and Other Financing Uses:	
Public Safety	$390,000
General Government	120,000
Culture and Recreation	54,000
Transfers Out	30,000
	$594,000

2. Encumbrances outstanding at the end of 2011 were re-established.

3. Property taxes of $430,000 were levied. Two percent of the tax levy is expected to be uncollectible.

4. Purchase orders issued in 2012:

Public Safety	$152,000
General Government	80,000
Culture and Recreation	54,000
	$286,000

5. Cash collections and transfers:

Delinquent Taxes	$ 39,200
Current Taxes	368,000
Fines, Forfeits, and Penalties	154,000
Miscellaneous Revenues	20,000
Transfers In	18,000
	$599,200

6. Purchase orders issued in 2012 were filled in the following amounts:

	Estimated	Actual
Public Safety	$149,000	$148,400
General Government	80,000	80,000
Culture and Recreation	54,000	54,000
	$283,000	$282,400

7. Purchase orders issued in 2011 in the following amounts were filled in 2012:

	Estimated	Actual
Public Safety	$8,500	$8,400

8. Additional accounts payable for salaries and wages (not encumbered):

Public Safety	$230,000
General Government	37,000
	$267,000

9. Accounts paid amounted to $570,000; the transfer out, $30,000, was made in cash.

10. Reclassify Taxes Receivable—Current and Estimated Uncollectible Taxes—Current as delinquent.

Required:

a. Prepare journal entries to record the effects of the foregoing data. Omit explanations and subsidiary accounts.

b. Prepare closing entries.

c. Prepare for the General Fund of the City of Cordes

(1) A Statement of Revenues, Expenditures, and Changes in Fund Balance for the year ended December 31, 2012.

(2) A Balance Sheet as of December 31, 2012, assuming there are no restricted or committed net resources and the only assigned net resources are the outstanding encumbrances.

4–9. The following transactions relate to Newport City's special revenue fund.

1. In 2012, Newport City created a special revenue fund to help fund the 911 emergency call center. The center is to be funded through a legally restricted tax on cellular phones. No budget is recorded.

2. During the first year of operations, revenues from the newly imposed tax totaled $450,000. Of this amount, $380,000 has been received in cash and the remainder will be received within 60 days of the end of the fiscal year.

3. Expenditures (salaries) incurred through the operation of the 911 emergency call center totaled $370,000. Of this amount, $320,000 was paid before year-end.

4. During the year the state government awarded Newport City a grant to reimburse the City's costs (not to exceed $150,000) for the purpose of training new 911 operators. During the year, the City paid $147,500 (not reflected in the expenditures above) to train new operators for the 911 emergency call center and billed the state government.

5. $134,000 of the amount billed to the state had been received by year-end.

   a. Prepare the journal entries for the above transactions. It is not necessary to use control accounts and subsidiary ledgers. Prepare Closing entries for year-end.

   b. Prepare a Statement of Revenues, Expenditures, and Changes in Fund Balance for the Special Revenue Fund.

   c. Prepare a Balance Sheet, assuming there are no committed or assigned net resources.

4–10. Assume at the beginning of 2012, the Ashlawn Village Street and Highway Fund (a special revenue fund) has cash of $300,000 offset by assigned fund balance in the same amount.

1. During the year, the State notified the Village that $450,000 for the street and highway fund will be awarded for work performed on several bridges over the next two years. The grant is a cost reimbursement arrangement (no budget entry is necessary).

2. During the year, the Village signed contracts for bridge repairs that amounted to $340,000.

3. The bridge repairs were completed and an invoice was received for $333,000, of which $320,000 was paid in cash.

4. The special revenue fund reimbursed the General Fund for a payment the General Fund made on behalf of the Street and Highway Fund in the amount of $7,000. This amount is not related to the bridge repairs under the state grant.

5. The state government paid the Village $300,000 on work completed under the grant before year-end.

   a. Prepare the journal entries for the above transactions. Prepare Closing entries for year-end.

   b. Prepare a Statement of Revenues, Expenditures, and Changes in Fund Balance for the Special Revenue Fund.

   c. Prepare a Balance Sheet.

Excel-Based Problems

4–11. Jefferson County General Fund began the year 2012 with the following account balances:

	Debits	Credits
Cash	$132,348	
Taxes Receivable	47,220	
Allowance for Uncollectible Taxes		$ 500
Supplies	660	
Budgetary Fund Balance		
Reserve for Encumbrances		4,800
Deferred Property Taxes		22,000
Wages Payable		970
Fund Balance		151,958
Totals	$180,228	$180,228

During 2012, Jefferson experienced the following transactions:

1. The budget was passed by the County Commission, providing estimated revenues of $250,000 and appropriations of $180,000 and estimated other financing uses of $40,000. Classify expenditures in the General Fund as either General Government or Capital Outlay. Make entries directly to these and the individual revenue accounts; do not use subsidiary ledgers.

2. The encumbrances outstanding at December 31, 2011, were re-established.

3. The deferred revenue at December 31, 2011, is recognized as revenue in the current period.

4. Property taxes in the amount of $260,000 were levied by the County. It is estimated 0.5% (1/2 of 1 percent) will be uncollectible.

5. Property tax collections totaled $247,000. Accounts totaling $950 were written off as uncollectible.

6. Encumbrances were issued for supplies in the amount of $36,000.

7. Supplies in the amount of $39,800 were received. Jefferson County records supplies as an asset when acquired. The related encumbrances for these items totaled $40,000 and included the $4,800 encumbered last year. The County paid $35,650 on accounts payable during the year.

8. The County contracted to have alarm systems (capital assets) installed in the administration building at a cost of $46,600. The systems were installed and the amount was paid.

9. Paid wages totaling $131,970, including the amount payable at the end of 2011. (These were for general government operations.)

10. Paid other general government operating items of $7,600.

11. The General Fund transferred $38,500 to the debt service fund in anticipation of bond interest and principle payments.

Additional Information

12. Wages earned but unpaid at the end of the year amounted to $2,200.

13. Supplies of $250 were on hand at the end of the year. (Supplies are used for general government operations.)

14. A review of property taxes receivable indicates that $17,500 of the outstanding balances would likely be collected more than 60 days after year-end and should be deferred.

Required

Use the Excel template provided on the textbook Web site to complete the following requirements. A separate tab is provided in Excel for each of these steps.

a. Prepare journal entries to record the information described in items 1 to 14.

b. Post these entries to T-accounts.

c. Prepare closing journal entries; post to the T-account provided. Classify fund balances assuming there are no restricted or committed net resources and the only assigned net resources are the outstanding encumbrances.

d. Prepare a Statement of Revenues, Expenditures, and Changes in Fund Balance for the General Fund for the year ending 2012. Use Excel formulas to calculate the cells shaded in blue.

e. Prepare a Balance Sheet for the General Fund as of December 31, 2012. Use Excel formulas to calculate the cells shaded in blue.

4–12. The State Government administers a special revenue fund, the *Fish and Game Fund*. By legislation, revenue in this fund can be used only for the purpose of protection, propagation, and restoration of sport fish and game resources and the expenses of administering sport fish and wildlife programs. Revenues are received from the sale of State sport fishing and hunting licenses and special permits as well as money received in settlement of a claim or loss caused by damage to fish and game purposes. The fund began in 2012 with the following balances:

	Debits	Credits
Accounts Payable		$55,000
Cash	$200,000	
License Fees Receivable	125,000	
Budgetary Fund Balance—		
Reserve for Encumbrances		36,000
Supplies	9,000	
Fund Balance		216,000
Wages Payable		27,000
Total	$334,000	$334,000

1. The State adopted a budget for the Fish and Game Fund providing estimated revenues of $1,400,000, appropriations of $1,680,000, and anticipated transfers from the State's General Fund of $300,000. All expenditures, other than capital expenditures, are to be charged to *Current Expenditures—Wildlife Management.*

2. The beginning Budgetary Fund Balance—Reserve for Encumbrances represents outstanding purchase orders for hatchery supplies that will be received in the current year. It is the State's policy to honor outstanding purchase orders from the previous year.

3. Hunting and fishing licenses are sold by outfitters and outdoor equipment retailers and are remitted to the State by the 15th of the following month. During 2012, the State received $1,150,000 in cash for licenses, which includes the amount accrued at the end of the previous year. In addition, it is estimated $137,000 will be received in January 2013 for December 2012 sales.

4. During the year, the State received an additional $255,000 for fines levied against individuals violating state hunting and fishing laws.

5. The State operates fish hatcheries for its stocking program. During the year, the State placed orders totaling $260,000 for hatchlings, feed, and other supplies. These are in addition to the outstanding purchase orders from 2011.

6. The State received supplies at an invoice cost totaling $286,000 for hatchery supplies. The related encumbrances for these items totaled $289,000 (this includes the $36,000 issued in 2011).

7. Payments of accounts payable totaled $303,000 in 2012.

8. The General Fund provided $300,000 to the *Fish and Game Fund* for the acquisition of a new fish hatchery. This amount was received in 2012.

9. A purchase order was awarded to Aquatics Construction Company for the new hatchery in the amount of $305,000. The contract was completed and capital expenditures for the new hatchery were paid in the amount of $305,000.

10. Wages were paid during the year in the amount of $990,000. This includes the unpaid amounts accrued at the end of the previous year.

11. Unpaid wages related to the last pay period of 2012 totaled $42,000 and will be paid in January 2013.

12. At December 31, the unused hatchery supplies on hand totaled $6,700.

Required

Use the Excel template provided. A separate tab is provided in Excel for each of these steps.

a. Prepare journal entries to record the information described in items 1 to 12.

b. Post these entries to T-accounts.

c. Prepare closing journal entries; post to the T-account provided. Classify fund balances assuming all spendable net resources are classified as Restricted

d. Prepare a Statement of Revenues, Expenditures and Changes in Fund Balance for the Special Revenue Fund for the year ending 2012.

e. Prepare a Balance Sheet for the Special Revenue Fund as of December 31, 2012.

Continuous Problem

Available on the text's Web site (www.mhhe.com/copley10e).

Accounting for Other Governmental Fund Types: Capital Projects, Debt Service, and Permanent

It rivals anything in the history of the world built by men. (Matthew Amorello, chairman of the Massachusetts Turnpike Authority on the completion of Boston's "Big Dig," a $14.6 billion underground highway. Since opening, the project has gained notoriety for a criminal investigation into faulty materials and problems with hundreds of leaks. In July 2006, 12 tons of ceiling tiles fell to the roadway, killing one person.)

I place . . . public debt as the greatest of the dangers to be feared. Thomas Jefferson, 3rd president of the United States, whose administration negotiated the Louisiana Purchase, financing 80 percent of the purchase with government debt.

Learning Objectives

- Apply the modified accrual basis of accounting in the recording of typical transactions of capital projects, debt service, and permanent funds.
- Prepare the fund-basis financial statements for governmental funds.
- Record capital lease transactions related to governmental operations.
- Classify and identify appropriate fund reporting for trust agreements.

Chapter 4 describes accounting and financial reporting for the General Fund and special revenue funds. This chapter describes and illustrates the accounting for the remaining governmental funds: capital projects, debt service, and permanent.

ILLUSTRATION 5–1 Summary of Governmental Type Funds

Fund Name	Modified Accrual Basis	Financial Resource Focus	Record Budgets	Encumbrances	Fund Description	Fund Term
General Fund	✓	✓	✓	✓	Accounts for all financial resources not required to be reported in another fund.	Indefinite life.
Special Revenue	✓	✓	✓	✓	Accounts for legally restricted revenue sources, other than those restricted for capital projects or debt service.	For each period that a substantial portion of the resources are provided by one or more *restricted* or *committed* revenue sources.
Capital Projects	✓	✓		✓	Accounts for financial resources to be used for acquisition or construction of major capital facilities (other than those financed by proprietary or fiduciary funds).	From the period resources are first provided until the capital facility is complete.
Debt Service	✓	✓			Accounts for financial resources to be used for payment of interest and principal on general long-term debt (not needed for debt paid from proprietary or fiduciary funds).	From the period funds are first accumulated until the final interest and principal payment is made.
Permanent	✓	✓			Accounts for resources that are legally restricted to the extent earnings (but not principal) may be used to support government programs.	Indefinite life, beginning with the initial contribution.

*Debt service funds are required to report only *matured* interest and principal payments as current liabilities. Unmatured principal installments and accrued interest, although due shortly after year-end are not required to be reported as liabilities in the debt service fund until due.

Representative transactions and fund-basis financial statements are presented for the Village of Elizabeth.

Illustration 5–1 provides a summary of governmental funds. Many of the practices described in Chapter 4 apply to capital projects, debt service, and permanent funds. All of the governmental funds use the modified accrual basis of accounting and the current financial resources measurement focus. Budgets are typically not recorded for capital projects, debt service, and permanent funds. Similarly, encumbrance accounting is typically not used for debt service and permanent funds.

Governmental fund types account for revenues, other financing sources, expenditures, and other financing uses that are for capital outlay and debt service purposes, as well as for current purposes. General fixed assets that are acquired with governmental fund resources are recorded as expenditures in the governmental funds but are displayed as capital assets in the government-wide financial statements. Similarly, the proceeds of general long-term debt incurred for governmental activities are recorded as other financing sources in governmental funds but the liability is displayed as long-term debt in the government-wide statements.

Since long-term liabilities are not recorded in the governmental funds, payments of principal are recorded as expenditures, rather than reductions of outstandings liabilities. Capital projects funds and debt service funds, in particular, are used to acquire major fixed assets and to issue and service long-term debt, although the General Fund may also be used for these purposes. Adjustments needed to record the general fixed assets and long-term debt transactions prior to preparing the government-wide statements are identified in this chapter but are illustrated more fully in Chapter 8 of this text. The general fixed assets and long-term debt for the Village of Elizabeth are included in the government-wide statements illustrated in Chapter 8.

Permanent funds reflect resources that are restricted so that principal may not be expended and earnings are used to benefit the government or its citizenry. If both earnings and principal may be expended, the activities should be reported in a special revenue fund. In this chapter, a cemetery perpetual care fund is used to illustrate permanent funds.

CAPITAL PROJECTS FUNDS

A major source of funding for capital projects funds is the issuance of long-term debt. In addition to debt proceeds, capital projects funds may receive: grants from other governmental units, proceeds of dedicated taxes, transfers from other funds, gifts from individuals or organizations, or a combination of several of these sources.

Capital projects funds differ from General Funds in that a capital projects fund exists only for the duration of the project for which it is created. In some jurisdictions, governments are allowed to account for all capital projects within a single capital projects fund. In other jurisdictions, laws require each project to be accounted for by a separate capital projects fund. Even in jurisdictions that permit the use of a single fund, managers may prefer to use separate funds to enhance control over individual projects. In such cases, a fund is created when a capital project or a series of related projects is legally authorized; it is closed when the project or series is completed.

GASB standards require capital project fund-basis statements to be reported using the modified accrual basis of accounting. Proceeds of debt issues should be recognized by a capital projects fund at the time the debt is actually incurred, rather than at the time it is authorized, because authorization of an issue does not guarantee its sale. Proceeds of debt issues are recorded as **Proceeds of Bonds** or **Proceeds of Long-Term Notes** rather than as Revenues and are reported in the Other Financing Sources section of the Statement of Revenues, Expenditures, and Changes in Fund Balances. Similarly, revenues raised by the General Fund or a special revenue fund and transferred to a capital projects fund are recorded as Transfers In and reported in the Other Financing Sources section of the operating statement. Taxes or other revenues raised specifically for a capital project are recorded as revenues of the capital projects fund. Grants, entitlements, or shared revenues received by a capital projects fund from another governmental unit are considered revenues of the capital projects fund, as is interest earned on temporary investments of the capital projects fund.

Expenditures of capital projects funds generally are reported in the capital outlay character classification in the Governmental Funds Statement of Revenues, Expenditures, and Changes in Fund Balances. Capital outlay expenditures result in additions to the general fixed assets reported in the government-wide Statement of Net Assets. Even though budgetary reporting is not required for capital projects funds, encumbrance accounting is used.

Illustrative Case

The following case illustrates representative transactions of a capital projects fund. Assume that early in 2012 the Village Council of the Village of Elizabeth authorized an issue of $1,200,000 of 8 percent 10-year regular serial tax-supported bonds to finance construction of a fire station addition. The total cost of the fire station addition was expected to be $2,000,000, with $600,000 to be financed by grants from other governmental units and $200,000 to be transferred from an enterprise fund of the Village of Elizabeth. The project would utilize land already owned by the Village and was to be done partly by a private contractor and partly by the Village's own working force. Completion of the project was expected within the year. Transactions and entries are illustrated next. For economy of time and space, vouchering of liabilities and entries in subsidiary ledger accounts are not illustrated.

The $1,200,000 bond issue, which had received referendum approval by taxpayers, was officially approved by the Village Council. No formal entry is required. A memorandum entry may be made to identify the approved project and the means of financing it.

The sum of $100,000 was borrowed from the National Bank for defraying engineering and other preliminary costs incurred before bonds could be sold. The notes will be repaid in the current period and are recorded as a liability in the capital project fund.

	Debits	Credits
1. Cash..	100,000	
Bond Anticipation Notes Payable.......................		100,000

The receivables from the enterprise fund and the other governmental units were recorded; receipt was expected during the current year.

	Debits	Credits
2. Due from Other Funds.................................	200,000	
Due from Other Governmental Units.....................	600,000	
Other Financing Sources—Transfers In		200,000
Revenues Control		600,000

Total purchase orders for supplies, materials, items of minor equipment, and contracted services required for the project amounted to $247,698.

	Debits	Credits
3. Encumbrances Control	247,698	
Budgetary Fund Balance—Reserve for Encumbrances		247,698

A contract was issued for the major part of the work to be done by a private contractor in the amount of $1,500,000.

	Debits	Credits
4. Encumbrances Control	1,500,000	
Budgetary Fund Balance—Reserve for Encumbrances		1,500,000

Special engineering and miscellaneous preliminary costs that had not been encumbered were paid in the amount of $97,500.

	Debits	Credits
5. Construction Expenditures	97,500	
Cash..		97,500

When the project was approximately half-finished, the contractor submitted billing for a payment of $750,000. The following entry records conversion of a commitment (Encumbrances) to a liability, eligible for payment upon proper authentication. Contracts Payable records the status of a claim under a contract between the time of presentation and verification for payment.

	Debits	Credits
6. Budgetary Fund Balance—Reserve for Encumbrances	750,000	
Construction Expenditures	750,000	
Encumbrances Control		750,000
Contracts Payable		750,000

The transfer ($200,000) was received from the enterprise fund, and $300,000 was received from the other governmental units.

	Debits	Credits
7. Cash.	500,000	
Due from Other Funds.		200,000
Due from Other Governmental Units		300,000

The bond issue, dated January 2, was sold at a premium of $12,000 on that date. In this example, as is generally the case, the premium must be used for debt service and is not available for use by the capital projects fund; therefore, the premium is transferred to the debt service fund. Entry 8a records the receipt by the capital projects fund of the proceeds of the bonds, and 8b records the transfer of the premium amount to the debt service fund.

8a. Cash *Receipt by capital project fund*	1,212,000	
Other Financing Sources—Proceeds of Bonds		1,200,000
Other Financing Sources—Premium on Bonds		12,000
8b. Other Financing Uses—Transfers Out	12,000	
Cash.		102,500
transfer premium to debt service fund		

If bonds were sold at a discount, either the difference would be made up by a transfer from another fund, or the capital projects fund would have fewer resources available for the project. Generally, bond issue costs would be involved and would be recorded as expenditures.

If bonds were sold between interest dates, the government would collect from the purchaser the amount of interest accrued to the date of sale, because a full six months' interest would be paid on the next interest payment date. Interest payments are made from debt service funds; therefore, cash in the amount of accrued interest sold at the time of bond issuance should be recorded in the Debt Service Fund.

The Village of Elizabeth's Capital Projects Fund pays the bond anticipation notes and interest (assumed to amount to $2,500), and records the following journal entry:

9. Bond Anticipation Notes Payable.	100,000	
Interest Expenditures.	2,500	
Cash.		102,500

Entry 1

The contractor's initial claim (see entry 6) was paid, less a 5 percent retention. Retention of a contractually stipulated percentage from payments to a contractor is common until the construction is completed and has been inspected for conformity with specifications and plans.

	Debits	Credits
10. Contracts Payable	750,000	
Cash..		712,500
Contracts Payable—Retained Percentage.....................		37,500

Upon final acceptance of the project, the retained percentage is paid. In the event that the government finds it necessary to spend money correcting deficiencies in the contractor's performance, the payment is charged to Contracts Payable—Retained Percentage.

Disbursements for items ordered at an estimated cost of $217,000 (included in the amount recorded by entry 3) amounted to $216,500.

	Debits	Credits
11. Budgetary Fund Balance—Reserve for Encumbrances	217,000	
Construction Expenditures	216,500	
Encumbrances Control		217,000
Cash..		216,500

Assume the contractor completes construction of the fire station and bills the Village of Elizabeth for the balance on the contract:

	Debits	Credits
12. Budgetary Fund Balance—Reserve for Encumbrances	750,000	
Construction Expenditures	750,000	
Encumbrances Control		750,000
Contracts Payable		750,000

Assume the amount remaining from other governmental units was received:

	Debits	Credits
13. Cash..	300,000	
Due from Other Governmental Units........................		300,000

Invoices for goods and services previously encumbered in the amount of $30,698 were received and approved for payment in the amount of $30,500. Additional construction expenditures, not encumbered, amounted to $116,500. The entire amount was paid in cash.

	Debits	Credits
14. Budgetary Fund Balance—Reserve for Encumbrances	30,698	
Construction Expenditures	147,000	
Encumbrances Control		30,698
Cash...		147,000

Assuming that inspection revealed only minor imperfections in the contractor's performance, and upon correction of these, the contractor's bill and the amount previously retained were paid, entry 15 should be made:

	Debits	Credits
15. Contracts Payable—Retained Percentage	37,500	
Contracts Payable	750,000	
Cash...		787,500

After entry 15 is recorded, $36,500 in cash remained in the capital projects fund. That amount was transferred to a debt service fund for the payment of bonds:

	Debits	Credits
16. Other Financing Uses—Transfers Out	36,500	
Cash...		36,500

Upon completion of the project and disposition of any remaining cash, the following closing entry was made:

	Debits	Credits
17. Revenues Control	600,000	
Other Financing Sources—Transfers In	200,000	
Other Financing Sources—Proceeds of Bonds	1,200,000	
Other Financing Sources—Premium on Bonds	12,000	
Construction Expenditures		1,961,000
Interest Expenditures		2,500
Other Financing Uses—Transfers Out...................		48,500

Financial statements for the Fire Station Addition Capital Projects Fund are presented as part of the Governmental Funds Balance Sheet (Illustration 5–3) and the Governmental Funds Statement of Revenues, Expenditures, and Changes in Fund Balances (Illustration 5–4) provided near the end of this chapter. Because the Village's fire station project was completed and the remaining resources transferred to the debt service fund, there are no balances remaining in the fund and it does not appear in the governmental funds Balance Sheet (Illustration 5–3). However, the assets, liabilities, and fund balances of major capital projects continuing into the next period would appear in governmental fund Balance Sheets. Fund balances of capital projects funds are classified among the categories identified in GASB *Statement 54:* Nonspendable, Restricted, Committed, or Assigned. In the case of capital projects funds, it is common for net resources to be classified as *Restricted.* For example, the bond issue may be the result of a referendum in which the voters both approved the debt issue and established its intended use. Intergovernmental grants and taxes dedicated to capital improvements are also likely to be classified as *Restricted.* Resources not meeting the definition of restricted are likely to be reported as Committed Fund Balance. GASB *Statement 54* requires that resources intended to fulfill contractual obligations (such as long-term construction contracts) be reported as Committed. Any remaining net resources would be reported as Assigned, the residual classification for funds other than the General Fund.

The addition to the fire station, excluding interest, will be capitalized and shown as an addition to the capital assets in the government-wide financial statements. In addition, the $1,200,000 in bonds will be recorded as a liability in the government-wide statements. See Chapter 8 for the adjustments necessary as a result of this project.

OTHER ISSUES INVOLVING ACQUISITION OF CAPITAL ASSETS

Acquisition of General Fixed Assets by Lease Agreements

FASB *SFAS No. 13* defines and establishes accounting and financial reporting standards for a number of forms of leases including **operating leases** and **capital leases.** GASB *Statement No. 13* accepts the FASB's *SFAS No. 13* definitions of these two forms of leases and prescribes accounting and financial reporting for lease agreements of state and local governments. If a noncancelable lease meets any one of the following criteria, it is a **capital** lease:

1. The lease transfers ownership of the property to the lessee by the end of the lease term.
2. The lease contains an option to purchase the leased property at a bargain price.
3. The lease term is equal to or greater than 75 percent of the estimated economic life of the leased property.
4. The present value of rental or other minimum lease payments equals or exceeds 90 percent of the fair value of the leased property.

If none of the criteria are met, the lease is classified as an **operating** lease by the lessee. Rental payments under an operating lease for assets used by the governmental funds are recorded by the governmental funds as current expenditures of the period. The GASB has issued specific guidelines for state and government entities with operating leases with scheduled rent increases (*Statement No. 13*). Discussion of this special case is beyond the scope of this text.

If a government acquires general fixed assets under a capital lease agreement, the asset should be recorded in the government-wide financial statements at the inception of the agreement at the lesser of (1) the present value of the rental and other minimum lease payments or (2) the fair value of the leased property. For example, assume a government signs a capital lease agreement to pay $10,000 on January 1, 2012, the scheduled date of delivery of certain equipment to be used by an activity accounted for by a special revenue fund. The lease calls for annual payments of $10,000 at the beginning of each year thereafter; that is, January 1, 2013, January 1, 2014, and so on.

There are 10 payments of $10,000 each, for a total of $100,000, but capital outlays under capital leases are recorded at the **present value** of the stream of annual payments, using the rate "the lessee would have incurred to borrow over a similar term the funds necessary to purchase the leased asset." Assuming the rate to be 10 percent, the present value of the 10 payments is $67,590. If the fair value of the leased property is more than $67,590, the asset should be reported in the government-wide statement at $67,590, and the liability for $57,590 ($67,590 less the payment of $10,000 at inception) should also be reported in the government-wide statements. GASB standards also require a governmental fund be used to record the following entry at the inception of the capital lease:

	Debits	Credits
Expenditures—Capital Outlay..........................	67,590	
Other Financing Sources—Capital Lease Agreements		57,590
Cash		10,000

Rental payments during the life of the capital lease are recorded in a governmental fund (such as a debt service fund) as illustrated later in this chapter.

Construction of General Fixed Assets Financed by Special Assessment Debt

A special assessment is a tax levy that is assessed only against certain taxpayers—those taxpayers who are deemed to benefit from the service or project paid for by the proceeds of the special assessment levy. Special assessments may be either service types or construction types. Service-type special assessments, such as an assessment to downtown businesses for special garbage removal or police protection, would be accounted for in the appropriate fund, often the General or a special revenue fund.

Construction-type special assessment projects account for longer-term projects that often require debt financing. For example, assume that a government issued $500,000 in debt to install street lighting and build sidewalks in a newly annexed subdivision. Five-year special assessment bonds were issued to finance the project, which is administered by the city. Since city law requires that the provision of lighting and sidewalks is the responsibility of property owners, a special assessment (property tax) is levied against the property owners in that subdivision for a five-year period. The proceeds of the assessment are used to pay the principal and interest on the debt.

Special assessment projects may be accounted for in one of two ways. If the government is either primarily or secondarily liable for the payment of debt principal and interest, the project is accounted for as if it were a governmental project. A capital projects fund should account for the proceeds of the debt and the construction expenditures. The capitalized cost of the project will be recorded in the government-wide statements. The debt should be recorded in the government-wide statements, and the special assessment tax levy and debt service expenditures should be recorded in a debt service fund, as illustrated for general government debt in this chapter.

Alternatively, if the government is not liable for the special assessment debt directly or through guarantee, the special assessment is accounted for in an agency fund. Accounting for agency and other fiduciary funds is discussed and illustrated in Chapter 7.

DEBT SERVICE FUNDS

As we just observed, major capital additions are commonly financed through bond or other debt issues. Another fund type, the **debt service fund,** is used to account for financial resources that are intended to provide payments of interest and principal as they come due. Debt service funds are not created for debt issues where the activities of proprietary funds are intended to generate sufficient cash to make interest and principal payments.

If taxes and/or special assessments are levied specifically for payment of interest and principal on long-term debt, those taxes are recognized as revenues of the debt service fund. More commonly, undesignated taxes are levied by the General Fund and transferred to a debt service fund to repay debt. In that case, the taxes are recorded as revenues by the General Fund and as transfers to the debt service fund. Because the amounts of bond issues and the associated capital projects are often approved by the voters, bond premiums and unexpended capital project resources are generally required by state law to be transferred to debt service funds.

The Modified Accrual Basis—As Applied to Debt Service Funds

GASB standards require debt service accounting to be on the same modified accrual basis of accounting as General, special revenue, and capital project funds. One peculiarity of the modified accrual basis as applied to debt service accounting is that interest on long-term debt is not accrued; it is recognized as an expenditure in the year in which the interest is legally due. For example, if the fiscal year of a government ends on December 31, and the interest on its bonds is payable on April 1 and October 1 of each year, interest payable would *not* be reported as a liability in the Balance Sheet of the Debt Service Fund prepared as of December 31. The rationale is that, since interest is not legally due until April 1 of the following year, resources need not be expended in the current year. The same reasoning applies to principal amounts that mature in the next fiscal year; expenditures and liabilities are recognized in the debt service fund in the year for which the principal is legally due. The only exception permitted by GASB is that if a government has resources available for payment in a debt service fund and the period of time until interest or principal payment is due is no more than one month, then the interest or principal payment may be accrued.

Additional Uses of Debt Service Funds

Debt service funds may be required to service, in addition to term and serial bonds, debt arising from the use of notes, capital leases, or warrants having a maturity more than one year after the date of issue. Although each issue of long-term debt is a separate obligation, all debts to be serviced from tax revenues may be accounted for by a single debt service fund, if permitted by state laws and covenants with creditors. If more than one debt service fund is required by law, as few funds of this type should be created as possible.

In some jurisdictions, there are no statutes that require the debt service function to be accounted for by a debt service fund. Whether or not required by statute or local ordinance, bond indentures or other agreements with creditors are often construed as requiring the use of a debt service fund. Unless the debt service function is very simple, it may be argued that good financial management would dictate the establishment of a debt service fund even when it is not legally required. If neither law nor sound financial administration requires the use of debt service funds, the function may be performed within the accounting and budgeting framework of the General Fund. In such cases, the accounting and financial reporting standards discussed in this chapter should be followed for the debt service activities of the General Fund.

Debt Service Accounting for Serial Bonds

The principal on serial bonds is paid over the term of the bonds, rather than in a lump sum at the end. Usually the government designates a bank as fiscal agent to handle interest and principal payments for each debt issue. The assets of a debt service fund may, therefore, include Cash with Fiscal Agent, and the expenditures, and liabilities may include amounts for the service charges of fiscal agents.

There are four types of serial bonds: regular, deferred, annuity, and irregular. If the total principal of an issue is repayable in a specified number of equal installments over the life of the issue, it is a **regular** serial bond issue. If the first installment is delayed for a period of more than one year after the date of the issue, but thereafter installments fall due on a regular basis, the bonds are known as **deferred serial bonds.** If the amount of annual principal repayments is scheduled to increase each year by approximately the same amount that interest payments decrease (interest decreases, of course, because the amount of outstanding bonds decreases) so that the annual debt service payments remain relatively uniform over the term of the issue, the bonds are called **annuity** serial bonds. **Irregular** serial bonds may have any pattern of repayment that does not fit the other three categories.

trative Case—Regular Serial Bonds

Acc unting for regular serial bonds is illustrated by a debt service fund created to pay principal and interest for the fire station project for the Village of Elizabeth discussed earlier in this chapter. Recall that, early in 2012, the Village Council of the Village of Elizabeth authorized an issue of $1,200,000 of 8 percent tax-supported bonds. At the time of authorization, no formal entry is required in the capital projects fund; at that time, a memorandum entry may be made in the capital projects fund and provision made to account for debt service of the new debt issue in a debt service fund.

Assume that the bonds in this example are dated January 2, 2012, that interest payment dates are June 30 and December 31, and that the first of the 10 equal annual principal payments will be on December 31, 2012.

The bonds were sold on January 2, 2012, at a premium of $12,000, which was recorded in the capital projects fund (see entry 8a of this chapter). The premium was transferred to the debt service fund (see entry 8b):

	Debits	Credits
18. Cash	12,000	
Other Financing Sources—Transfers In.		12,000

While GASB standards do not require the reporting of budget-actual schedules for debt service funds, prudence would dictate internal budgetary planning. Assuming the $12,000 amount was known at the time of budgetary planning, the following would reflect debt service needs related to this project:

Semiannual Interest, June 30 ($1,200,000 × 08 × $6/12$)	$ 48,000
Semiannual Interest, December 31 ($1,200,000 × .08 × $6/12$)	48,000
Principal, December 31 ($1,200,000/10)	120,000
Total Cash Needed	216,000
Less: Premium	12,000
Cash Needs (Net) for 2012	$204,000

Assume cash was transferred from the General Fund in the amount of $204,000 (see entries 21a and 21b of Chapter 4):

19. Cash	204,000	
Other Financing Sources—Transfers In.		204,000

On June 30, $48,000 was paid to a local bank to make the first interest payment. An expenditure and a liability were also recorded:

	Debits	Credits
20a. Cash with Fiscal Agent.	48,000	
Cash		48,000
20b. Expenditures—Bond Interest.	48,000	
Matured Interest Payable		48,000

When the fiscal agent reports that checks have been issued to all bondholders, entry 21 is made:

21. Matured Interest Payable	48,000	
Cash with Fiscal Agent.		48,000

On December 31, the next interest payment of $48,000 is due; also on that date, a principal payment of $120,000 is due. The debt service fund pays $168,000 to the local bank for payment and records the expenditures and liabilities for principal and interest:

22a. Cash with Fiscal Agent	168,000	
Cash		168,000
22b. Expenditures—Bond Principal	120,000	
Expenditures—Bond Interest	48,000	
Matured Bonds Payable		120,000
Matured Interest Payable		48,000

The bank reported that all payments had been made as of December 31, 2012:

23. Matured Bonds Payable	120,000	
Matured Interest Payable	48,000	
Cash with Fiscal Agent.		168,000

It should be noted that, if principal and/or interest payment dates were other than at the end of the fiscal year, for example, May 1 and November 1, accruals would *not* be made for the fund financial statements, following modified accrual accounting. However, accruals for interest would be made when preparing the government-wide financial statements.

Entry 16 of the capital projects fund illustration in this chapter reflected a transfer of $36,500 to the debt service fund, representing the unused construction funds. The corresponding entry is made in the debt service fund:

	Debits	Credits
24. Cash.	36,500	
Other Financing Sources—Transfers In.		36,500

At year-end, the debt service fund would reflect the following closing entry:

	Debits	Credits
25. Other Financing Sources—Transfers In.	252,500	
Expenditures—Bond Principal.		120,000
Expenditures—Bond Interest.		96,000
Fund Balance.		36,500

Financial statements for the Fire Station Addition Debt Service Fund are presented as part of the Governmental Funds Balance Sheet (Illustration 5–3) and the Governmental Funds Statement of Revenues, Expenditures, and Changes in Fund Balances (Illustration 5–4) provided near the end of this chapter. Fund balances of debt service funds are classified among the categories identified in GASB *Statement 54:* Restricted, Committed, or Assigned. Unexpended resources transferred to the debt service fund from the General Fund would typically be classified as *Assigned Fund Balance.* In the case of term bonds, debt agreements may require a government to set aside cash in a sinking fund. If a sinking fund is required by creditors or law, the unexpended resources would be classified as *Restricted.*

OTHER ISSUES INVOLVING PAYMENT OF LONG-TERM DEBT

Debt Service Accounting for Deferred Serial Bonds

If a government issues bonds other than regular serial bonds, debt service fund accounting is somewhat more complex than just illustrated. A government that issues deferred serial bonds will normally have several years without principal repayment during which, if it is fiscally prudent, amounts will be accumulated in the debt service fund for payment when the bonds mature. If this is the case, debt service fund cash should be invested in order to earn interest revenues. Material amounts of interest receivable on investments should be accrued at year-end.

Debt Service Accounting for Term Bonds

Term bond issues mature in their entirety on a given date, in contrast to serial bonds, which mature in installments. Term bond debt service requirements may be determined on an actuarial basis or on less sophisticated bases designed to produce approximately level payments during the life of the issue. The annuity tables used for an actuarial basis assume that the investments of a debt service fund earn interest at a given percentage. Accounting for a term bond debt service fund would be similar to the method of accounting for a deferred serial bond issue.

Debt Service Accounting for Capital Lease Payments

Earlier in this chapter, the section headed "Acquisition of General Fixed Assets by Lease Agreements" gave an example of the necessary entry in a governmental fund at the inception of a capital lease.

Commonly, governments use the General or a debt service fund to record capital lease payments. Like an annuity serial bond, part of each lease payment is interest at a constant rate on the unpaid balance of the lease obligation, and part is a payment on the principal. Each annual payment on the capital lease in this example amounts to $10,000; for the payment on January 1, 2013, assuming $5,759 is payment of interest ($57,590 × .10) and $4,241 is payment on principal, the entry in the Debt Service Fund would be as follows:

	Debits	Credits
Expenditures—Interest	5,759	
Expenditures—Principal	4,241	
Cash		10,000

As indicated previously in this chapter, a worksheet entry would be made for the government-wide statements, recording the fixed asset and capital lease obligation at the present value of lease payments. As a result of the above transaction, the capital lease obligation would be reduced by $4,241.

For the payment on January 1, 2014, the interest would be ($57,590 − $4,241 = $53,349) × .10, or $5,335 (rounded), and the principal expenditure would be $4,665 ($10,000 − $5,335).

Bond Refundings

Governments occasionally refund bonds, that is, issue new debt to replace old debt. This may be to obtain better interest rates, to get away from onerous debt covenants, or to change the maturity of the debt. A **current refunding** exists when new debt is issued and the proceeds are used to call the existing debt. Assume a government wishes to refund debt with a new bond issue of $10,000,000. The entries to record the replacement of the old debt with new would be:

Cash	10,000,000	
Other Financing Sources—Refunding of Existing Debt		10,000,000
Other Financing Uses—Refunding of Existing Debt	10,000,000	
Cash		10,000,000

Alternatively, an **advance refunding** exists when the proceeds are placed in an escrow account pending the call date or the maturity date of the existing debt. In this case, the debt is said to be **defeased** for accounting purposes. That means the old debt is not reported in the financial statements and is replaced by the new debt. Extensive note disclosures are required for both current and advance refundings.

PERMANENT FUNDS

Governments sometimes receive donations or other resources from individuals, estates, and private or public organizations. Commonly these donations take the form of trusts. Trusts are accounted for in a number of different funds, depending on the nature and terms of the agreement. Illustration 5–2 summarizes accounting for trusts. Initially, it is important to determine whether the trust benefits the government or its citizenry. Second, it is important to determine whether the trust principal is to be maintained or may be expended. Trusts that generate income for the benefit of the government or its citizens and require the principal to be maintained are reported in permanent funds. (Similar funds whose earnings benefit individuals, private organizations, or other governments are *private-purpose trust funds,* discussed in Chapter 7.) An example of a permanent fund is a cemetery perpetual care fund, which provides resources for the ongoing maintenance of a public cemetery.

ILLUSTRATION 5–2   Summary of Government Trust Accounting

Purpose of Trust	Trust Description	Appropriate Fund
Trust is to be used to benefit the government or its citizenry. *Examples:* Cemetery perpetual care or funds established to support libraries, museums, or zoos.	*Expendable:* Trust does not distinguish between earnings and principal. Both may be expended for the purpose provided.	Special revenue fund
	Nonexpendable: Trust stipulates that earnings only (not principal) may be expended for the purpose provided.	Permanent fund
Trust is to benefit individuals, private organizations, or other governments. *Examples:* Scholarship funds or funds intended to benefit families of police or fire fighters killed on duty.	Although these are most commonly nonexpendable, there is no requirement that they be so.	Private-purpose trust fund

Assume that, early in 2012, Richard Lee, a citizen of the Village of Elizabeth, drove by the Village Cemetery and was distressed by the poor level of maintenance. He entered into an agreement with Village officials on April 1, to provide $300,000 to the Village, with the stipulation that the $300,000 be invested, the principal never be expended, and the earnings be used to maintain the Village Cemetery. Accordingly, the Lee Cemetery Perpetual Care Fund was established, and the following entry was made:

	Debits	Credits
26. Cash..	300,000	
Revenues—Additions to Permanent Endowments...........		300,000

The funds were immediately invested in ABC Company bonds, which were selling at par. The bonds carried an annual interest rate of 8 percent and paid interest on April 1 and October 1:

	Debits	Credits
27. Investments—Bonds.....................................	300,000	
Cash...		300,000

On October 1, $12,000 interest was received:

28. Cash..	12,000	
Revenues—Investment Income—Interest................		12,000

During 2012, $11,000 was expended for cemetery maintenance:

29. Expenditures—Cemetery	11,000	
Cash...		11,000

Modified accrual accounting permits interest revenues to be accrued at year-end. The amount is $6,000 ($300,000 \times .08 \times \frac{3}{12}$):

30. Accrued Interest Receivable............................	6,000	
Revenues—Investment Income—Interest................		6,000

GASB *Statement 31* requires that investments with determinable fair values be recorded at fair value. On December 31, 2012, the ABC Company bonds had a fair value of $302,000, excluding accrued interest:

31. Investments—Bonds.....................................	2,000	
Revenue—Net Increase in Fair Value of Investments........		2,000

As of December 31, 2012, the books were closed for the Lee Cemetery Perpetual Care Fund:

	Debits	Credits
32. Revenues—Additions to Permanent Endowments	300,000	
Revenues—Investment Income—Interest	18,000	
Revenues—Investment Income—		
Net Increase in Fair Value of Investments.	2,000	
Expenditures—Cemetery.		11,000
Fund Balance		309,000

Financial statements for the Lee Cemetery Perpetual Care Fund are presented as part of the Governmental Funds Balance Sheet (Illustration 5–3) and the Governmental Funds Statement of Revenues, Expenditures, and Changes in Fund Balances (Illustration 5–4). Like other governmental funds, the fund balances of permanent funds are classified among the categories identified in GASB *Statement 54:* Nonspendable, Restricted, Committed, or Assigned. Since the principal (also called corpus) of permanent funds must be maintained, it is classified as *Nonspendable Fund Balance*. In most cases the remaining unexpended resources would typically be classified as *Assigned Fund Balance*.

FINANCIAL REPORTING FOR GOVERNMENTAL FUNDS

GASB *Statement 34* requires two financial statements for the General Fund and other governmental funds. Both report separate columns for major funds and a column for nonmajor funds, as well as a total column. The General Fund is always considered a major fund. Other governmental funds are considered major if both the following criteria exist:

1. Total assets, liabilities, revenues, *or* expenditures of that individual government fund are at least 10 percent of the corresponding total (assets, liabilities, and so forth) for all governmental funds.
2. Total assets, liabilities, revenues, *or* expenditures of the individual governmental fund are at least 5 percent of the corresponding total for all governmental and enterprise funds combined.

In addition, the government can *choose* to include any other governmental fund in these statements. Assume the Village of Elizabeth decides to include all governmental funds in the basic governmental funds statements.

Balance Sheet—Governmental Funds

Illustration 5–3 presents the Balance Sheet for the governmental funds for the Village of Elizabeth. This Balance Sheet includes the General Fund and special revenue fund illustrated in Chapter 4 as well as the debt service and permanent funds illustrated in this chapter. Note that the capital projects fund does not have a column because all accounts were closed when the project was completed. Major capital projects funds continuing into future periods would be included in this statement.

ILLUSTRATION 5–3   Governmental Funds Balance Sheet

VILLAGE OF ELIZABETH
Balance Sheet
Governmental Funds
As of December 31, 2012

	General	Motor Fuel Tax	Fire Station Addition Debt Service	Lee Cemetery Perpetual Care	Total Govern-mental Funds
Assets					
Cash	$ 443,000	$ 247,500	$ 36,500	$ 1,000	$ 728,000
Investments				302,000	302,000
Interest receivable, net	34,490			6,000	40,490
Taxes receivable, net	528,800				528,800
Due from state government	60,000	125,000			185,000
Total assets	$1,066,290	$372,500	$ 36,500	$309,000	$1,784,290
Liabilities and Fund Balances					
Liabilities:					
Accounts payable	$ 50,300	$135,000			$ 185,300
Due to other funds	135,000				135,000
Deferred revenues	40,000				40,000
Total liabilities	225,300	135,000	–0–	–0–	$ 360,300
Fund balances:					
Nonspendable:					
Permanent fund principal				300,000	300,000
Restricted for:					
Public works	75,000				75,000
Road repair and maintenance		237,500			237,500
Committed to:					
Capital projects	100,000				100,000
Assigned to:					
Debt service			36,500		36,500
Cemetery care				9,000	9,000
Other purposes	50,000				50,000
Unassigned	615,990				615,990
Total fund balances	840,990	237,500	36,500	309,000	1,423,990
Total liabilities and fund balances	$1,066,290	$372,500	$36,500	$309,000	$1,784,290

ILLUSTRATION 5–4 Governmental Funds Statement of Revenues, Expenditures, and Changes in Fund Balances

VILLAGE OF ELIZABETH
Statement of Revenues, Expenditures, and Changes in Fund Balances
Governmental Funds
For the Year Ended December 31, 2012

	General	Motor Fuel Tax	Fire Station Addition Debt Service	Fire Station Addition Capital Projects	Lee Cemetery Perpetual Care	Total Governmental Funds
Revenues						
Property Taxes	$3,178,800					$3,178,800
Motor fuel taxes		$650,000				650,000
Sales taxes	1,410,000					1,410,000
Interest and penalties on taxes	42,490					42,490
Licenses and permits	540,000					540,000
Fines and forfeits	430,000					430,000
Intergovernmental revenue	350,000	350,000		$600,000		1,300,000
Charges for services	100,000					100,000
Addition to permanent endowment					$300,000	300,000
Investment income—interest					18,000	18,000
Investment income—net increase in fair value of investments					2,000	2,000
Miscellaneous	30,000					30,000
Total revenues	$6,081,290	$1,000,000		$600,000	$320,000	$8,001,290

Expenditures

Current:						
General government	$810,000					$ 810,000
Public safety	2,139,500					2,139,500
Public works	630,000	$975,000				1,605,000
Health and welfare	480,100					480,100
Cemetery					$11,000	11,000
Parks and recreation	527,400					527,400
Contribution to retirement funds	423,000					423,000
Miscellaneous	20,300					20,300
Debt service						
Principal			$120,000			120,000
Interest			96,000			96,000
Capital outlay				$1,963,500		1,963,500
Total expenditures	5,030,300	975,000	216,000	1,963,500	11,000	8,195,800
Excess (deficiency) of revenues over expenditures	1,050,990	25,000	(216,000)	(1,363,500)	309,000	(194,510)
Other financing sources (uses)						
Proceeds of bonds				1,200,000		1,200,000
Premium on bonds				12,000		12,000
Transfers in			252,500	200,000		452,500
Transfers out	(800,000)			(48,500)		(848,500)
Total other financing sources (uses)	(800,000)	-0-	252,500	1,363,500	-0-	816,000
Special item						
Proceeds from sale of land	300,000	-0-	-0-	-0-	-0-	300,000
Net change in fund balances	550,990	25,000	36,500	-0-	309,000	921,490
Fund balances—beginning	290,000	212,500	-0-	-0-	-0-	502,500
Fund balances—ending	$ 840,990	$ 237,500	$ 36,500	$ -0-	$309,000	$1,423,990

143

Note that only current financial resources and obligations appear in the governmental funds Balance Sheet. The net position of each fund is displayed within the five categories of fund balances, but each fund balance has a separate line within those categories. Only the General Fund has an *Unassigned Fund Balance*. The government's decision to record resources in special revenue, capital projects, debt service, or permanent funds is an indication that the resources are at least assigned to a particular purpose. In this example, only the principal of the permanent fund appears as *Nonspendable Fund Balance*. If any of the funds had unused supplies or prepaid expenses, those resources would also have been classified as *Nonspendable Fund Balance*.

Statement of Revenues, Expenditures, and Changes in Fund Balances—Governmental Funds

Illustration 5–4 presents the Statement of Revenues, Expenditures, and Changes in Fund Balances. This statement includes the funds in Illustration 5–3 plus the capital project fund illustrated in this chapter. In the Village of Elizabeth example, students should be able to trace the transactions in the illustrative problems to this statement.

SUMMARY

This chapter illustrated representative transactions and the resulting financial statements for capital projects, debt service, and permanent funds. Like the General and special revenue funds, these governmental funds use the modified accrual basis and current financial resource measurement focus in the fund-basis financial statements. Unlike the General Fund, these funds do not typically record budgets and debt service and permanent funds do not record encumbrances. Characteristics of these funds are as follows:

• **Capital projects funds.** These funds commonly account for resources provided by long-term debt issues or dedicated taxes. The capital projects typically involve significant construction contracts which may take months or years to complete. Typically, the expenditures are for capital assets that appear in the government-wide (but not the fund basis) financial statements.

• **Debt service funds.** Typically resources are provided through transfers from the General or other funds. There are two types of debt service expenditures: interest and principal. In most cases, liabilities for interest and principal payments are not recorded until payment is due.

• **Permanent funds.** These funds are created when resources are provided to a government with the intent they be used to generate income to support a particular purpose. The trust agreement stipulates that the earnings are intended to benefit the government or citizens and the principal may not be expended. Principal of permanent funds is classified as *Nonspendable Fund Balance.*

Now that you have finished reading Chapter 5, complete the multiple choice questions provided on the text's Web site (www.mhhe.com/copley10e) to test your comprehension of the chapter.

Questions and Exercises

5–1. Using the annual financial report obtained for Exercise 1–1, answer the following questions:

  a. Examine the governmental fund financial statements. Are any major capital projects funds included? If so, list them. Attempt to find out the nature and purpose of the projects from the letter of transmittal, the notes, or MD&A. What are the major sources of funding, such as bond sales, intergovernmental grants, and transfers from other funds? Were the projects completed during the year?

  b. Again looking at the governmental fund financial statements, are any major debt service funds included? If so list them. What are the sources of funding for these debt service payments?

  c. Does your report include supplemental information including combining statements for nonmajor funds? If so, are any capital projects and debt service funds included? If so, list them. Indicate the major revenue and other financing source categories for these funds.

  d. Look at the governmental fund Statement of Revenues, Expenditures, and Changes in Fund Balances, specifically the expenditure classification. Compute a ratio of capital outlay/total expenditures. Again, compute a ratio of debt service/total expenditures. Compare those with your classmates' ratios. Comment on the possible meaning of these ratios.

  e. Look at the notes to the financial statements, specifically the note (in the summary of significant accounting policies) regarding the definition of modified accrual accounting. Does the note specifically indicate that modified accrual accounting is used for capital projects and debt service funds? Does the note indicate that debt service payments, both principal and interest, are recorded as an expenditure when due?

  f. Does your government report capital leases payable in the government-wide Statement of Net Assets? If so, can you determine if new capital leases were initiated during the year? Can you trace the payments related to capital leases?

  g. Does your government report any permanent funds, either major or nonmajor? If so, list them. What are the amounts of the permanent resources available for governmental purposes? What is/are the governmental purpose(s)?

5–2. A concerned citizen provides resources and establishes a trust with the local government. What factors should be considered in determining which fund to report the trust activities?

5–3. Assume a government leases equipment to be used in governmental activities under a noncancelable lease, meeting the requirements for classification as a capital lease. Where would the capital lease be reported in the government's financial statements?

5-4. The citizens of Spencer County approved the issuance of $2,000,000 in 6 percent general obligation bonds to finance the construction of a courthouse annex. A capital projects fund was established for that purpose. The preclosing trial balance of the courthouse annex capital project fund follows:

Trial Balance—December 31, 2012	Debits	Credits
Cash	$1,265,000	
Contract payable		$ 550,000
Due from state government	200,000	
Encumbrances	750,000	
Expenditures—capital	1,485,000	
Intergovernmental grant		400,000
OFS: premium on bonds		35,000
OFS: proceeds sale of bonds		2,000,000
Budgetary fund balance— Reserve for encumbrances		750,000
Transfer out	35,000	
	$3,735,000	$3,735,000

 a. Prepare any closing entries necessary at year-end.

 b. Prepare a Statement of Revenues, Expenditures, and Changes in Fund Balance for the courthouse annex capital project fund.

 c. Prepare a balance sheet for the Courthouse Annex Capital Project Fund, assuming all unexpended resources are restricted to construction of the courthouse annex.

5-5. A citizen group raised funds to establish an endowment for the Eastville City Library. Under the terms of the trust agreement, the principal must be maintained, but the earnings of the fund are to be used to purchase database and periodical subscriptions for the library. A preclosing trial balance of the library permanent fund follows:

Trial Balance—December 31, 2012	Debits	Credits
Cash	$ 8,500	
Investments	510,000	
Additions to permanent endowments		$500,000
Investment income		49,000
Expenditures—subscriptions	48,000	
Net increase in fair value of investments		10,000
Accrued interest receivable	1,500	
Accounts payable		9,000
	$568,000	$568,000

a. Prepare any closing entries necessary at year-end.

b. Prepare a Statement of Revenues, Expenditures, and Changes in Fund Balance for the library permanent fund.

c. Prepare a balance sheet for the Library Permanent Fund (Use *Assigned to Library* for any spendable fund balance).

5–6. *a.* Armstrong County established a County Office Building Construction Fund to account for a project that was expected to take less than one year to complete. The County's fiscal year ends on June 30.

(1) On July 1, 2011, bonds were sold at par in the amount of $8,750,000 for the project.

(2) On July 5, a contract was signed with the Sellers Construction Company in the amount of $8,650,000.

(3) On December 30, a progress bill was received from Sellers in the amount of $6,000,000. The bill was paid, except for a 5 percent retainage.

(4) On June 1, 2012, a final bill was received in the amount of $2,650,000 from Sellers, which was paid, except for the 5 percent retainage. An appointment was made between the County Engineer and Bill Sellers to inspect the building and to develop a list of items that needed to be corrected.

(5) On the day of the meeting, the County Engineer discovered that Sellers had filed for bankruptcy and moved to Florida. The City incurred a liability in the amount of $490,000 to have the defects corrected by the Baker Construction Company. (Charge the excess over the balance of Contracts Payable—Retained Percentage to Construction Expenditures.)

(6) All accounts (from 5 above) were paid; remaining cash was transferred to the Debt Service Fund.

(7) The accounts of the County Office Building Construction Fund were closed.

Record the transaction in the County Office Building Construction Fund.

b. Prepare a separate Statement of Revenues, Expenditures, and Changes in Fund Balances for the County Office Building Construction Fund for the year ended June 30, 2012.

5–7. The Village of Harris issued $5,000,000 in 6 percent general obligation, tax-supported bonds on July 1, 2011, at 101. A fiscal agent is not used. Resources for principal and interest payments are to come from the General Fund. Interest payment dates are December 31 and June 30. The first of 20 annual principal payments is to be made June 30, 2012. Harris has a calendar fiscal year.

1. A capital projects fund transferred the premium ($50,000) to the debt service fund. (5,000k x .06 x .05)

2. On December 31, 2011, funds in the amount of $150,000 were received from the General Fund and the first interest payment was made.

3. The books were closed for 2011.

4. On June 30, 2012, funds in the amount of $350,000 were received from the General Fund, and the second interest payment ($150,000) was made along with the first principal payment ($250,000).

5. On December 31, 2012, funds in the amount of $142,500 were received from the General Fund and the third interest payment was made ($142,500).

6. The books were closed for 2012.

   a. Prepare journal entries to record the events above in the debt service fund.

   b. Prepare a Statement of Revenues, Expenditures, and Changes in Fund Balance for the debt service fund for the year ended December 31, 2011.

   c. Prepare a Statement of Revenues, Expenditures, and Changes in Fund Balance for the debt service fund for the year ended December 31, 2012.

5–8. Beachfront property owners of the Village of Eden requested a seawall be constructed to protect their beach. The seawall was financed through a note payable, which was to be repaid from taxes raised through a special assessment on their properties. The Village guarantees the debt and accounts for the special assessment through a debt service fund. Assume the special assessments were levied in 2011, recording a special assessment receivable and deferred revenue in the amount of $600,000. One-third of the assessment is to be collected each year and used to pay the interest and principal on the note. Record the following transactions that occurred in 2012:

   1. June 30, $200,000 of the assessments became due and currently receivable. (*Hint:* The special assessment tax is recorded as revenue in the debt service fund when it becomes due.)

   2. July 31, the $200,000 were collected.

   3. September 30, interest of $40,000 and principal of $160,000 were paid.

   4. December 31, the books were closed.

5–9. The Village of Budekville, which has a fiscal year July 1 to June 30, sold $3,000,000 in 6 percent tax-supported bonds at par to construct an addition to its police station. The bonds were dated and issued on July 1, 2011. Interest is payable semiannually on January 1 and July 1, and the first of 10 equal annual principal payments will be made on July 1, 2012. The village used a capital projects fund to account for the project, and a debt service fund was created to make interest and principal payments.

   1. The bonds were sold on July 1, 2011.

   2. The General Fund transferred an amount equal to the first interest payment on December 31, 2011. The Debt Service Fund made the payment as of January 1, 2012.

3. The project was completed on June 15, 2012. Expenditures totaled $2,989,000. You may omit encumbrance entries.

4. The remaining balance was transferred to the Debt Service Fund from the Capital Projects Fund for the eventual payment of principal.

Required:

a. Prepare journal entries for the capital projects fund based on the afore-mentioned information. Include a closing entry.

b. Prepare journal entries for the debt service fund based on the information presented above. Include a closing entry.

c. Prepare a Statement of Revenues, Expenditures, and Changes in Fund Balance for the year ended June 30, 2012, for the governmental funds (i.e., use separate columns for the General, capital projects, and debt service funds). Assume the General Fund reports the following: property tax revenues $500,000, other revenues $200,000, public safety expenditures $450,000, general government expenditures $150,000, other financing sources—transfers out $125,000, and beginning fund balance $120,000.

5–10. On July 1, 2011, a five-year agreement is signed between the City of Genoa and the Computer Leasing Corporation for the use of computer equipment not associated with proprietary funds activity. The cost of the lease, exclud-ing executory costs, is $12,000 per year. The first payment is to be made by a capital projects fund at the inception of the lease. Subsequent payments, be-ginning July 1, 2012, are to be made by a debt service fund. The present value of the lease payments, including the first payment, is $54,552. The interest rate implicit in the lease is 5 percent.

a. Assuming the agreement meets the criteria for a capital lease under the pro-visions of *SFAS No. 13,* make the entries required in (1) the capital projects fund and (2) the debt service fund on July 1, 2011, and July 1, 2012.

b. Comment on where the fixed asset and long-term liability associated with this capital lease would be recorded and the impact of the journal entries recorded for *a.*

5–11. The Town of McHenry has $6,000,000 in general obligation bonds outstand-ing and maintains a single debt service fund for all debt service transactions. On July 1, 2012, a current refunding took place in which $6,000,000 in new general obligation bonds were issued. Record the transaction on the books of the debt service fund.

5–12. The City of Sharpesburg received a gift of $950,000 from a local resident on June 1, 2012, and signed an agreement that the funds would be invested perma-nently and that the income would be used to purchase books for the city library. The following transactions took place during the year ended December 31, 2012:

1. The gift was recorded on June 1.

2. On June 1, ABC Company bonds were purchased as investments in the amount of $950,000 (par value). The bonds carry an annual interest rate of 6 percent, payable semiannually on December 1 and June 1.

3. On December 1, the semiannual interest payment was received.

4. From December 1 through December 31, $27,700 in book purchases were made; full payment was made in cash.

5. On December 31, an accrual was made for interest.

6. Also, on December 31, a reading of the financial press indicated that the ABC bonds had a fair value of $966,000, exclusive of accrued interest.

7. The books were closed.

   Required:

   a. Record the transactions on the books of the Library Book Permanent Fund.

   b. Prepare a separate Statement of Revenues, Expenditures, and Changes in Fund Balances for the Library Book Permanent Fund for the Year Ended December 31, 2012.

Excel-Based Problems

5–13. Jefferson County established a capital project fund in 2011 to build low-income housing with the transfer of $100,000 from the General Fund. The following transactions occurred during 2012:

Capital Project Fund Trial Balance:
December 31, 2011

	Debits	Credits
Cash	$100,000	
Fund Balance		$100,000

1. April 1, 2012, 6 percent bonds with a face value of $700,000 were issued in the amount of $720,000. The bond premium was transferred to the debt service fund.

2. The County received notice that it had met eligibility requirements for a federal government grant intended to support the capital project in the amount of $250,000. The grant (cash) will be received when the project is completed in February 2013.

3. The County issued a contract for the construction in the amount of $1,000,000.

4. The contractor periodically bills the County for construction completed to date. During the year, bills totaling $390,000 were received. By year-end, a total of $350,000 had been paid.

Jefferson County established a debt service fund in 2012 to make interest and principle payments on the bonds issued in item 1 above. Bond payments are made on October 1 and April 1 of each year. Interest is based on an annual rate of 6 percent and principle payments are $17,500 each.

The following transactions occurred during 2012:

5. The bond premium was received through transfer from the capital project fund.

6. September 30, $38,500 was transferred from the General Fund for the October 1 bond payment.
7. The first debt service payment was made on October 1, 2012.

The Elwood Family Book Fund was established in December 2011, funded by a bequest with the legal restriction that only earnings, and not principal, can be used for the purchase of books for the James K. Polk Library in Jefferson County. The principal amount that must be maintained is $500,000. The following transactions occurred during 2012:

Permanent Fund Trial Balance:
December 31, 2011

	Debits	Credits
Receivable from Grantor	$500,000	
Nonspendable Fund Balance		
Library Purchases		$500,000

8. The Elwood family pledge of $500,000 was received in donated corporate bonds with a fair value of $370,000 and the balance in cash.
9. $130,000 was invested in U.S. Government Securities.
10. Interest in the amount of $17,000 was received in cash during the year.
11. During the year, books totaling $14,000 were ordered for the library.
12. During the year, the library reported receiving books with an invoice amount totaling $14,000. $13,900 of the amounts due for book purchases had been paid by year-end.
13. An additional $2,500 of interest had accrued on the investments at December 31 and will be received in January of next year.
14. The corporate bonds had a market value of $371,500 and the U.S. securities had a market value of $129,400 as of December 31.

   Required:

   Using the Excel template provided (a separate tab is provided for each of the requirements):

   a. Prepare journal entries recording the events 1 to 14 for the capital projects, debt service, and permanent funds.

   b. Post the journal entries to T-accounts.

   c. Prepare closing entries.

   d. Prepare a Statement of Revenues, Expenditures and Changes in Fund Balance for the Governmental Funds (The General Fund financial statements have already been prepared).

   e. Prepare a Balance Sheet for the Governmental Funds, assuming that unexpended spendable resources in the capital projects fund are classified as *restricted* and unexpended spendable resources in the debt service and permanent fund are classified as *assigned*.

5–14. The state government established a capital project fund in 2011 to build new highways. The fund is supported by a 5 percent tax on diesel fuel sales in the state. The tax is collected by private gas stations and remitted in the following month to the State. The following transactions occurred during 2012:

Capital Project Fund Trial Balance: December 31, 2011

	Debits	Credits
Cash	$12,200,000	
Taxes receivable	2,400,000	
Contracts payable		1,150,000
Budgetary Fund Balance— Reserve for Encumbrances		2,500,000
Fund Balance		10,950,000
Total	$14,600,000	$14,600,000

1. The encumbrances outstanding at December 31, 2011, were re-established.
2. During the year, fuel taxes were remitted to the State totaling $26,250,000, including the amount due at the end of the previous year. In addition, $2,990,000 is expected to be remitted in January of next year for fuel sales in December 2012.
3. The State awarded new contracts for road construction totaling $29,000,000.
4. During the year, contractors submitted invoices for payment totaling $30,790,000. These were all under the terms of contracts (i.e., same $ amounts) issued by the State.
5. The State made payments on outstanding accounts of $31,500,000.

The state government operates a debt service fund to service outstanding general obligation bonds. The following transactions occurred during 2012:

Debt Service Fund Trial Balance: December 31, 2011

	Debits	Credits
Cash	$310,000	
Fund Balance		$310,000
Total	$310,000	$310,000

6. The state general fund provided cash of $4,500,000 through transfer to the debt service fund.
7. Payments for matured interest totaled $3,200,000, and payments for matured principal totaled $1,600,000 during the year.

8. In December, the State refunded bonds to obtain a better interest rate. New bonds were issued providing proceeds of $20,000,000, which was immediately used to retire outstanding bonds in the same amount.

Required:

Use the Excel template provided. A separate tab is provided in Excel for each of the requirements:

a. Prepare journal entries recording the events 1 to 8 (above) for the capital projects, and debt service funds.

b. Post the journal entries to T-accounts.

c. Prepare closing entries.

d. Prepare a Statement of Revenues, Expenditures, and Changes in Fund Balance for the Governmental Funds (the General Fund and special revenue fund financial statements have already been prepared).

e. Prepare a Balance Sheet for the Governmental Fund assuming all unexpended spendable net resources in the capital projects fund are classified as *restricted* and in the debt service fund are classified as *assigned.*

Continuous Problem

Available on the text's Web site (www.mhhe.com/copley10e).

Proprietary Funds

The pride and presence of a professional football team is more important than 30 libraries. (Cleveland Browns owner Art Modell, who moved his team to Baltimore where a new stadium was built at public expense)

The packaging for a microwavable "microwave" dinner is programmed for a shelf life of maybe six months, a cook time of two minutes and a landfill dead-time of centuries. (David Wann, President of the Sustainable Futures Society. Wann is an author and videographer whose works focus on environmental sustainability)

Learning Objectives

- Apply the accrual basis of accounting in the recording of typical transactions of internal service and enterprise funds.
- Prepare the fund-basis financial statements for proprietary funds.
- Identify when an activity is required to be reported as an enterprise fund.
- Contrast statements of cash flow prepared under GASB guidelines with those prepared under FASB guidelines.

All of the funds discussed in previous chapters (General, special revenue, capital projects, debt service, and permanent) are classified as governmental funds, and owe their existence to constraints placed upon the raising of revenue and/or the use of resources for the provision of services to the public and the acquisition of facilities to aid in the provision of services. Funds discussed in previous chapters record only current financial resources and liabilities that will be settled with current financial resources. Fixed assets and long-term debt are not accounted for in governmental funds, but are presented in government-wide statements. Governmental funds recognize encumbrances and expenditures, not expenses.

A second fund classification, **proprietary funds,** describes funds that are used to account for activities similar to those often engaged in by profit-seeking businesses. That is, users of goods or services provided by a proprietary fund are charged amounts at least sufficient to cover the costs of providing the goods or services. Thus, in the pure case, proprietary funds are self-supporting. The accounting for proprietary funds is summarized in Illustration 6–1. Proprietary funds use the economic resources measurement focus and the accrual basis of accounting.

ILLUSTRATION 6–1 Summary of Proprietary Funds

Fund Name	Accrual Basis	Economic Resources Focus	Record Budgets	Encumbrances	Fund Description	Fund Term
Internal Service Fund	✓	✓			Funds used to report activities that provide goods and services to other funds, departments, or agencies on a cost-reimbursement basis. They are used when the government is the predominant user of the goods or services.	Indefinite life. Internal service funds are created by the government and exist at the discretion of the government.
Enterprise Fund	✓	✓			Funds used to report activities in which users are charged a fee for goods or services. They are appropriate when individuals or businesses external to the government are the predominant users.	Indefinite life. Enterprise funds must be maintained if debt is secured solely by user charges, laws require that costs be recovered through user charges, or government policy requires setting charges to cover the costs of providing the goods or service.

Because revenues and *expenses* (not expenditures) are recognized on the accrual basis, financial statements of proprietary funds are similar in many respects to those of business organizations. Fixed assets used in fund operations and long-term debt serviced from fund revenues are recorded in the accounts of each proprietary fund. Depreciation on fixed assets is recognized as an expense, and other accruals and deferrals common to business accounting are recorded in proprietary funds. Budgets should be prepared for proprietary funds to facilitate management of fund activities, but GASB standards do not require or encourage budget-actual reporting.

The use of accrual accounting permits financial statement users to observe whether proprietary funds are operated at a profit or a loss. The accrual basis of accounting requires revenues to be recognized when earned and expenses to be recognized when goods and services are used.

Two types of funds are classified as proprietary funds: internal service funds and enterprise funds. Internal service funds provide, on a user charge basis, services to other government departments. Enterprise funds provide, on a user charge basis, services to the public. Three financial statements are required for proprietary funds: a Statement of Net Assets (or Balance Sheet); a Statement of Revenues, Expenses, and Changes in Fund Net Assets; and a Statement of Cash Flows. As is true for governmental funds, enterprise funds are reported by major fund, with nonmajor funds presented in a separate column. However, internal service funds are reported in a single column. These statements will be discussed in more detail and illustrated later in this chapter.

GASB *Statement No. 20* provides guidance regarding the application of private sector accounting pronouncements to the accounting and reporting for proprietary funds. All FASB Statements and Interpretations, Accounting Principles Board Opinions, and Accounting Research Bulletins issued on or before November 30, 1989, that do not contradict GASB pronouncements are presumed to apply. In addition, for enterprise funds (but not for internal service funds), governments have the option to apply (or not apply) FASB Statements and Interpretations that are issued after November 30, 1989, and that apply to business organizations (FASB statements and interpretations applicable only to not-for-profit organizations do not apply to governments). The option chosen must be disclosed in the notes.

INTERNAL SERVICE FUNDS

As governments become more complex, efficiency can be improved if services used by several departments or funds or even by several governmental units are combined in a single department. Purchasing, computer services, garages, janitorial services, and risk management activities are common examples. Activities that produce goods or services to be provided to *other departments* or *other governmental units* on a cost-reimbursement basis are accounted for by internal service funds.

Internal service funds recognize revenues and expenses on the accrual basis. They account for fixed assets used in their operations and for long-term debt to be serviced from revenues generated from their operations, as well as for all current assets and current liabilities. Net assets (fund equity) are to be reported in three categories: (1) invested in capital assets, net of related debt; (2) restricted; and (3) unrestricted.

Establishment and Operation of Internal Service Funds

The establishment of an internal service fund is normally subject to legislative approval. The original allocation of resources to the fund may be derived from a transfer of assets of another fund, such as the General Fund or an enterprise fund, intended as a **transfer** not to be repaid or as a loan that is in the nature of a long-term **advance** to be repaid by the internal service fund over a period of years.

Because internal service funds are established to improve the management of resources, they should be operated and accounted for on a business basis. For example, assume that administrators request the establishment of a fund for the purchasing, warehousing, and issuing of supplies used by a number of funds and departments. A budget should be prepared for the internal service fund (but not recorded in the accounts) to demonstrate that fund management has realistic plans to generate sufficient revenues to cover the cost of goods issued and such other expenses, including depreciation, that the governing body intends fund operations to recover.

Departments and units expected to purchase goods and services from internal service funds should include in their budgets the anticipated outlays for goods and services. During the year, as supplies are issued or services are rendered, the internal service fund records operating revenues (Charges for Services is an account title commonly used instead of Sales). Since the customer is another department of the government, a journal entry to record the purchase is recorded at the same time the internal service fund records revenue. If the other fund is a governmental fund, the purchase is recorded as an expenditure. Periodically and at year-end, an operating statement should be prepared for each internal service fund to compare revenues and related expenses; these operating statements, called Statements of Revenues, Expenses, and Changes in Fund Net Assets, are similar to income statements prepared for investor-owned businesses.

Illustrative Case—Supplies Fund

Assume that the administrators of the Village of Elizabeth obtain approval from the Village Council in early 2012 to centralize the purchasing, storing, and issuing functions and to administer and account for these functions in a Supplies Fund. A payment of $596,000 cash is made from the General Fund which is not to be repaid by the Supplies Fund. Of the $596,000, $290,000 is to finance capital acquisitions and $306,000 is to finance noncapital acquisitions. Additionally, a long-term advance of $200,000 is made from the Water Utility Fund for the purpose of acquiring capital assets. The advance is to be repaid in 20 equal annual installments, with no interest. The receipt of the transfer in and the liability to the Water Utility Fund would be recorded in the Supplies Fund accounts in the following manner.[1]

---

[1] The corresponding entry in the General Fund is entry 22 in Chapter 4. The corresponding entry in the Water Utility Fund is entry 5 in the "Illustrative Case—Water Utility Fund" section later in this chapter.

	Debits	Credits
1. Cash	796,000	
Transfers In.		596,000
Advance from Water Utility Fund		200,000

To provide some revenue on funds not needed currently, $50,000 is invested in marketable securities:

	Debits	Credits
2. Investments	50,000	
Cash		50,000

Assume that early in 2012, a satisfactory warehouse building is purchased for $350,000; $80,000 of the purchase price is considered as the cost of the land. Necessary warehouse machinery and equipment is purchased for $100,000. Delivery equipment is purchased for $40,000. If the purchases are made for cash, the acquisition of the assets would be recorded in the books of the Supplies Fund as follows:

	Debits	Credits
3. Land	80,000	
Building	270,000 350K	
Machinery and Equipment—Warehouse	100,000	
Equipment—Delivery	40,000	
Cash		490,000

Supplies are ordered to maintain inventories at a level commensurate with expected usage. No entry is needed because proprietary funds are not required to record encumbrances. During 2012, it is assumed that supplies are received and related invoices are approved for payment in the amount of $523,500; the entry needed to record the asset and the liability is as follows:

	Debits	Credits
4. Inventory of Supplies.	523,500	
Accounts Payable		523,500

The Supplies Fund, accounts for its inventories on the perpetual inventory basis because the information is needed for proper performance of its primary function. Accordingly, when supplies are issued, the Inventory Account must be credited for the cost of the supplies issued. Because the using fund will be charged an amount in excess of the inventory carrying value, the Receivable and Revenue accounts reflect the selling price. The markup above cost should be determined on the basis of budgeted expenses and other items to be financed from net income. If the budget for the Village of Elizabeth's Supplies Fund indicates that a markup of 30 percent on cost is needed, issues to General Fund departments of supplies costing $290,000 would be recorded by the following entries:

	Debits	Credits
5a. Operating Expenses—Cost of Sales and Services	290,000	
Inventory of Supplies		290,000
5b. Due from General Fund	377,000	
Operating Revenues—Charges for Sales and Services		
($290,000 * 130%)		377,000

During the year, it is assumed that purchasing expenses totaling $19,000, warehousing expenses totaling $12,000, delivery expenses totaling $13,000, and administrative expenses totaling $11,000 are incurred. The government has chosen to separate operating expenses into three categories: (1) costs of sales and services, (2) administration, and (3) depreciation. If all liabilities are vouchered before payment, the entry would be as follows:

6. Operating Expenses—Costs of Sales and Services	44,000	
Operating Expenses—Administration	11,000	
Accounts Payable		55,000

If collections from the General Fund during 2012 total $322,000, the entry would be as follows (see Chapter 4, entries 20a and 20b for General Fund entries corresponding to entries 5b and 7):

7. Cash	322,000	
Due from General Fund		322,000

Assuming that payment of vouchers during the year totals the $567,500, the following entry is made:

8. Accounts Payable	567,500	
Cash		567,500

The advance from the Water Utility Fund is to be repaid in 20 equal annual installments; repayment of one installment at the end of 2012 is recorded as follows:

9. Advance from Water Utility Fund	10,000	
Cash		10,000

At the time depreciable assets are acquired, the warehouse building has an estimated useful life of 20 years; the warehouse machinery and equipment have an estimated useful life of 10 years; the delivery equipment has an estimated useful life of 10 years; and none of the assets is expected to have any salvage value at the expiration of its useful life.

Under these assumptions, straight-line depreciation of the building would be $13,500 per year; depreciation of machinery and equipment, $10,000 per year; and depreciation of delivery equipment, $4,000 per year. (Since governmental units are not subject to income taxes, there is no incentive to use any depreciation method other than straight-line.)

	Debits	Credits
10. Operating Expenses—Depreciation	27,500	
Accumulated Depreciation—Building		13,500
Accumulated Depreciation—Machinery and Equipment—		
Warehouse		10,000
Accumulated Depreciation—Equipment—Delivery		4,000

Organizations that keep perpetual inventory records must adjust the records periodically to reflect shortages, overages, and out-of-condition stock disclosed by physical inventories. Adjustments to the Inventory account are also considered to be adjustments to the warehousing expenses of the period. In this illustrative case, it is assumed that no adjustments are found to be necessary at year-end.

Interest income is earned and received in cash on the investments purchased at the beginning of the year:

11. Cash	3,000	
Nonoperating Revenues—Interest		3,000

Assuming that all revenues, expenses, and transfers applicable to 2012 have been properly recorded by the entries illustrated, the nominal accounts should be closed as of December 31:

12. Operating Revenues—Charges for Sales and Services	377,000	
Nonoperating Revenues—Interest	3,000	
Transfers In.	596,000	
Operating Expenses—Costs of Sales and Services		334,000
Operating Expenses—Administration		11,000
Operating Expenses—Depreciation		27,500
Net Assets.		603,500

Recall that the net position of governmental funds is termed *Fund Balance* and is classified within five categories. In contrast, the excess of assets over liabilities of proprietary funds is termed *Net Assets* and classified within three categories:

1. Net Assets Invested in Capital Assets, Net of Related Debt
2. Restricted Net Assets
3. Unrestricted Net Assets

Net Assets Invested in Capital Assets, Net of Related Debt is computed as capital assets less accumulated depreciation minus the balance of any debt associated with the acquisition of capital assets. **Restricted Net Assets** are defined as net resources whose use is restricted by external parties (creditors, grantors, or other governments) or by internally imposed laws. **Unrestricted Net Assets** is the residual account for any net resources that are not classified in either of the other two categories. For the Village of Elizabeth example, the net asset balances to be reported in the December 31, 2012, Statement of Net Assets are calculated as follows:

	Invested in Capital Assets, Net of Debt	Restricted	Unrestricted	Total
Invested in Capital Assets Net of Debt				
Capital Assets (Buildg , land ..)	$ 490,000			$ 490,000
Less Accumulated Depreciation	(27,500)			(27,500)
Less Advance to Enterprise Fund	(190,000)			(190,000)
Restricted		-0-		-0-
Unrestricted (plug)			$331,000	331,000
Total Net Assets	$ 272,500	-0-	$331,000	$ 603,500

The category *Invested in Capital Assets, Net of Related Debt* is calculated using end of period balances in capital assets, accumulated depreciation, and debt. Borrowings for operations (if any) would not be subtracted here. In most cases, internal service funds will not have *Restricted Net Assets. Unrestricted Net Assets* is the residual balance calculated after the other two categories. Similar to fund balances, some governments choose to allocate these amounts to individual net asset accounts through journal entry. Our approach will be to determine the components of net assets in the aforementioned manner and present the totals directly in the Statement of Net Assets. In this way we reduce the number of accounts necessary to record changes in overall fund net position. These amounts appear only in the Statement of Net Assets (Illustration 6–3, presented later in the chapter). In addition to the Statement of Net Assets, internal service funds report a Statement of Revenues, Expenses, and Changes in Fund Net Assets (Illustration 6–4) and a Statement of Cash Flows (Illustration 6–5).

OTHER ISSUES INVOLVING INTERNAL SERVICE FUNDS

Risk Management Activities

In recent years, governments have been turning to self-insurance for part or all of their risk financing activities. If a government decides to use a single fund to accumulate funds and make payments for claims, it must use either the General Fund or an internal service fund. Many use the internal service fund type.

When using internal service self-insurance funds, interfund premiums are treated as interfund services provided and used. Thus, revenues are recognized in the internal service fund for interfund charges, and an expenditure or expense, as appropriate, is recognized in the contributing fund. When claims are paid or accrued, an operating expense is recorded in the internal service fund.

Charges should be based on anticipated claims or on a long-range plan to break even over time, such as an actuarial method. Payments by contributing funds in excess of the amount required to break even are recorded as transfers. If an internal service fund has a material deficit at year-end, that deficit should be made up over a reasonable period of time and should be disclosed in the notes to the financial statements.

Implications for Other Funds

The operation of internal service funds has important implications for other funds. As we have seen, charges for services (i.e., revenues) of the internal service fund are recorded as expenditures in the governmental fund purchasing the services (or expenses if enterprise funds are the purchaser). Since the internal service fund records the costs of providing services as operating expenses, the costs of these services are recorded in two funds in the same set of fund-basis financial statements.

Additional problems arise if the internal service fund has significant positive (or negative) operating income. Operating income is the excess of service revenues over the costs of providing the service (i.e., operating expenses). Consider the case of an internal service fund servicing police, fire, and other vehicles used in departments reported in the General Fund. If the internal service fund has positive operating income, the expenditures reported in the General Fund exceed the true cost of operating the government. If these amounts are significant over periods of time, some of the accumulated surplus (fund balance) of the General Fund is effectively shifted to the internal service fund (net assets). The opposite is true if internal service funds have negative operating income: the General Fund understates the true cost of operating the government and net assets are effectively shifted from the internal service fund to the fund balance of the General Fund.

Compounding these problems is the fact that GASB Standards do not require the use of internal service funds. Some governments choose to use internal service funds and others choose to account for the same activities in other funds. This makes comparisons between governments difficult. The problems that internal service funds create in the fund-basis financial statements were a major consideration when the GASB designed the government-wide financial statements. As we will see in detail in Chapter 8, the problems of duplicate recording of costs, potential over- or understatement of governmental expenditures, and lack of comparability between governments are resolved in the government-wide financial statements.

ENTERPRISE FUNDS

Enterprise funds are used by governments to account for services provided *to the general public* on a user-charge basis. Under GASB *Statement 34,* enterprise funds *must* be used in the following circumstances:

- When debt is backed solely by fees and charges.
- When a legal requirement exists that the cost of providing services for an activity, including capital costs, be recovered through fees or charges.
- When a government has a policy to establish fees and charges to cover the cost of providing services for an activity.

The most common examples of governmental enterprises are public utilities, notably water and sewer utilities. Electric and gas utilities, transportation systems, airports, landfills, hospitals, toll bridges, municipal golf courses, parking lots, parking garages, lotteries, municipal sports stadiums, and public housing projects are other examples.

Enterprise funds are to be reported using the economic resources measurement focus and accrual basis of accounting. Fixed assets and long-term debt are included in the accounts. As indicated earlier in this chapter, enterprise funds are to use accounting and reporting standards provided for business enterprises issued on or before November 30, 1989 (unless that guidance conflicts with GASB guidance) and may use standards issued by the FASB for businesses issued after that date. As a result, accounting is similar to that for business enterprises and includes depreciation, accrual of interest payable, amortization of discounts and premiums on debt, and so on.

Governmental enterprises often issue debt, called **revenue bonds,** that is payable solely from the revenues of the enterprise. These bonds are recorded directly in the accounts of the enterprise fund. On the other hand, **general obligation bonds** are sometimes issued for governmental enterprises, in order to provide greater security by pledging the full faith and credit of the government in addition to enterprise revenues. If payment is to be paid from enterprise revenues, these general obligation bonds would also be reflected in the accounts of enterprise funds.

Budgetary accounts are used only if required by law. Debt service and construction activities of a governmental enterprise are accounted for within an enterprise fund, rather than by separate debt service and capital project funds. Thus, the reports of enterprise funds are self-contained; and creditors, legislators, or the general public can evaluate the performance of a governmental enterprise by the same criteria used to evaluate commercial businesses in the same industry.

Unlike internal service funds, it is frequently desirable for enterprise funds to operate at a profit (increase in net assets). Like commercial businesses, operating profits are necessary to establish adequate working capital, provide for expansion of physical facilities, and retire debt. Additionally, governments may find it desirable to use enterprise fund profits to support general government expenditures that would otherwise require increased taxes. State lotteries, for example, are established with the intent to operate at significant profits. The profits are then typically transferred from the lottery (enterprise fund) to the state General Fund in support of public education.

By far the most numerous and important enterprise services rendered by local governments are public utilities. In this chapter we examine typical transactions of a water utility fund.

Illustrative Case—Water Utility Fund

It is assumed that the Village of Elizabeth is located in a state that permits enterprise funds to operate without formal legal approval of their budgets. Accordingly, the budget is not recorded in enterprise accounts.

Assume that as of December 31, 2011, the accountants for the Village of Elizabeth prepared the postclosing trial balance shown here:

VILLAGE OF ELIZABETH Water Utility Fund Postclosing Trial Balance December 31, 2011		
	Debits	**Credits**
Cash	$ 467,130	
Customer Accounts Receivable	72,500	
Allowance for Uncollectible Accounts		$ 2,175
Materials and Supplies	37,500	
Restricted Assets	55,000	
Utility Plant in Service	4,125,140	
Accumulated Depreciation of Utility Plant		886,500
Construction Work in Progress	468,125	
Accounts Payable		73,700
Revenue Bonds Payable		2,700,000
Net Assets		1,563,020
Totals	$5,225,395	$5,225,395

It is common for governmental enterprises, especially utilities, to report "restricted assets." In this example, the restricted assets include $55,000 set aside for future debt service payments as required by a revenue bond indenture agreement.

When utility customers are billed during the year, appropriate revenue accounts are credited. Assuming that during 2012 the total bills to nongovernmental customers amounted to $975,300, bills to the Village of Elizabeth General Fund amounted to $80,000, and all revenue was from sales of water, the following entry summarizes the results: (see entry 19 in Chapter 4 for the corresponding entry in the General Fund).

	Debits	Credits
1. Customer Accounts Receivable.	975,300	
Due from General Fund	80,000	
Operating Revenues—Charges for Sales and Services		1,055,300

Assume collections from nongovernmental customers totaled $968,500 for water billings:

	Debits	Credits
2. Cash	968,500	
Customer Accounts Receivable		968,500

Customers owing bills totaling $1,980 left the Village and could not be located. The unpaid balances of their accounts receivable were written off to the allowance for uncollectible accounts as follows:

3. Allowance for Uncollectible Accounts	1,980	
Customer Accounts Receivable		1,980

Governments commonly impose impact fees on developers or builders to pay for capital improvements, such as increased water and sewer facilities, that are necessary to service new developments. Increasingly, governments are using impact fees to limit sprawl and to create incentives for developers to refurbish existing commercial properties rather than create new ones. Assume the Village of Elizabeth imposes impact fees on commercial developers in the amount of $12,500 and that these fees are not associated with specific projects or improvements.

4. Cash	12,500	
Capital Contributions		12,500

Note that Capital Contributions is a nominal account that will increase Net Assets but is reported separately in the Statement of Revenues, Expenses, and Changes in Fund Net Assets (see Illustration 6–4). Hook up fees for new customers are not capital contributions but are exchange transactions and are included in operating revenues. If the impact fees had been restricted to a specific project, the cash would have been reported as a restricted asset.

During 2012, the Village of Elizabeth established a Supplies Fund, and the Water Utility Fund advanced $200,000 to the Supplies Fund as a long-term receivable. The entry by the Supplies Fund is illustrated in entry 1 in the "Illustrative Case— Supplies Fund" section of this chapter. The following entry should be made by the Water Utility Fund:

5. Long-Term Advance to Supplies Fund	200,000	
Cash		200,000

Materials and supplies in the amount of $291,500 were purchased during the year by the Water Utility Fund, and vouchers in that amount were recorded as a liability:

6. Materials and Supplies.....................................	291,500	
Accounts Payable......................................		291,500

When materials and supplies are issued to the departments of the Water Utility Fund, operating expenses are charged for the cost of materials and supplies. Materials and supplies issued for use for construction projects are capitalized temporarily as Construction Work in Progress. (Entry 11 illustrates the entry required when a capital project is completed.)

	Debits	Credits
7. Operating Expenses—Costs of Sales and Services	110,400	
Operating Expenses—Administration	60,000	
Construction Work in Progress	127,600	
Materials and Supplies		298,000

Payrolls for the year were chargeable to the accounts in the following entry. Taxes were accrued and withheld in the amount of $90,200, and the remainder was paid in cash.

8. Operating Expenses—Costs of Sales and Services	253,600	
Operating Expenses—Administration	92,900	
Operating Expenses—Selling.	17,200	
Construction Work in Progress	58,900	
Payroll Taxes Payable		90,200
Cash		332,400

Bond interest in the amount of $189,000 was paid:

9. Nonoperating Expenses—Interest	189,000	
Cash		189,000

Included in the amount above was bond interest in the amount of $17,800 that was considered to be properly charged to construction:

10. Construction Work in Progress	17,800	
Nonoperating Expenses—Interest		17,800

Construction projects on which costs totaled $529,300 were completed and the assets placed in service. Utility Plant in Service summarizes the investment in fixed assets used for utility purposes.

11. Utility Plant in Service	529,300	
Construction Work in Progress		529,300

Payment of accounts totaled $275,600, and payments of payroll taxes amounted to $81,200.

	Debits	Credits
12. Accounts Payable..............................	275,600	
Payroll Taxes Payable	81,200	
Cash		356,800

Near the end of 2012, the Water Utility Fund received $10,000 cash from the Supplies Fund as partial payment of the long-term advance (see Supplies Fund, entry 9).

13. Cash	10,000	
Long-Term Advance to Supplies Fund		10,000

During the year, the Water Utility Fund made a transfer of $200,000 to the Fire Station Addition Capital Projects Fund (see entries 2 and 7 in Chapter 5):

14. Transfers Out	200,000	
Cash		200,000

At year-end, several adjustments are necessary. First, depreciation is recorded as an operating expense:

15. Operating Expenses—Depreciation.....................	122,800	
Accumulated Depreciation of Utility Plant		122,800

Provision is made for bad debts from utility customers. Consistent with guidance provided by a Question and Answer Guide issued by GASB, the bad debt provision is a revenue reduction not an expense:

16. Operating Revenues—Charges for Sales and Services	2,200	
Allowance for Uncollectible Accounts		2,200

Following a provision in the revenue bond indenture, $55,000 was transferred from operating cash to the Restricted Assets category.

17. Restricted Assets	55,000	
Cash		55,000

Illustration 6–2 presents the general ledger account balances after posting the Water Utility Fund journal entries.

Revenue, expense, transfers, and capital contributions accounts for the year were closed to the Net Assets account:

	Debits	Credits
18. Operating Revenues—Charges for Sales and Services	1,053,100	
Capital Contributions	12,500	
Operating Expenses—Costs of Sales and Services		364,000
Operating Expenses—Administration		152,900
Operating Expenses—Selling.		17,200
Operating Expenses—Depreciation		122,800
Transfers Out		200,000
Nonoperating Expenses—Interest		171,200
Net Assets.		37,500

After posting the closing entry, Net Assets has a balance of $1,600,520 ($1,563,020 beginning balance plus $37,500 from the closing entry). The net asset balances to be reported in the December 31, 2012, Statement of Net Assets are calculated as follows:

	Invested in Capital Assets, Net of Debt	Restricted	Unrestricted	Total
Invested in Capital Assets Net of Debt:				
Construction Work in Process	$ 143,125			$ 143,125
Utility Plant in Service	4,654,440			4,654,440
Less Accumulated Depreciation	(1,009,300)			(1,009,300)
Less Revenue Bonds Payable	(2,700,000)			(2,700,000)
Restricted: Restricted Assets		$110,000		110,000
Unrestricted (plug)			$402,255	402,255
Total Net Assets	$1,088,265	$110,000	$402,255	$1,600,520

Note that the capital assets included in Invested in Capital Assets, Net of Related Debt is comprised of both the Utility Plant in Service and the Construction Work in Process. Restricted Net Assets equals the balance of the Restricted Assets that are required to be maintained by debt covenant. Unrestricted Net Assets is the residual, computed as total net assets less the balance in the other two net asset categories ($1,600,520 − 1,088,265 − 110,000 = $402,255).

PROPRIETARY FUND FINANCIAL STATEMENTS

Governments are required to report the following proprietary fund financial statements: (1) Statement of Net Assets (or Balance Sheet), (2) Statement of Revenues, Expenses, and Changes in Fund Net Assets, and (3) Statement of Cash Flows. As was

ILLUSTRATION 6–2 Water Utility General Ledger

Cash

*bb	467,130	5	200,000
2	968,500	8	332,400
4	12,500	9	189,000
13	10,000	12	356,800
		14	200,000
		17	55,000
124,930			

Customer Accounts Receivable

bb	72,500	968,500	2	
1	975,300	1,980	3	
77,320				

Allowance for Uncollectible Accounts

3	1,980	2,175	bb
		2,200	16
		2,395	1

Due from General Fund

80,000	
80,000	

Materials & Supplies

bb	37,500	298,000	7
6	291,500		
31,000			

LT Advance to Other Funds

5	200,000	10,000	13

Restricted Assets

bb	55,000
17	55,000
110,000	

Utility Plant in Service

bb	4,125,140
11	529,300
4,654,440	

Accumulated Depreciation – Plant

	886,500	bb
	122,800	15
	1,009,300	

Construction Work in Process

bb	468,125	529,300	11
7	127,600		
8	58,900		
10	17,800		
143,125			

Accounts Payable

		73,700	bb
6	275,600	291,500	6
		89,600	

Payroll Taxes Payable

12	81,200	90,200	8
		9,000	

Revenue Bonds Payable

	2,700,000	bb
	2,700,000	

Net Assets

	1,563,020	bb
	1,563,020	

Cost of Sales & Services

7	110,400
8	253,600
364,000	

Administrative Expense

7	60,000
8	92,900
152,900	

Depreciation Expense

15	122,800
122,800	

Selling Expense

8	17,200
17,200	

Capital Contributions

		12,500	4
		12,500	

Transfers Out

14	200,000
200,000	

Operating Revenue Charges for Services

16	2,200	1,055,300	1
		1,053,100	

Nonoperating Expenses Interest

9	189,000	17,800	10
171,200			

* bb denotes beginning balance

169

true for governmental funds, *major* enterprise funds are to be presented, along with columns for nonmajor funds and total enterprise funds, where appropriate. On the other hand, a single column is to include all internal service funds. Illustrations 6–3, 6–4 and 6–5 reflect the proprietary funds statements for the Village of Elizabeth, which is assumed to have only one enterprise fund and one internal service fund.

Statement of Net Assets

The Statement of Net Assets for the proprietary funds for the Village of Elizabeth is presented as Illustration 6–3. GASB permits either this statement (Assets − Liabilities = Net Assets) or a Balance Sheet where Assets = Liabilities + Net Assets. GASB requires a classified format, where current assets, noncurrent assets, current liabilities, and noncurrent liabilities are presented separately. Net assets (fund equity accounts) are segregated into the same three categories used for the government-wide Statement of Net Assets. In the Village of Elizabeth example, the various fixed asset and accumulated depreciation accounts were combined to present a single net figure for each fund. It was assumed that all long-term debt was for capital assets.

Net assets that are restricted are presented separately. According to GASB *Statement 34*, restricted net assets are those that are the result of constraints either:

1. Externally imposed by creditors (such as through debt covenants), grantors, contributors, or laws or regulations of other governments.
2. Imposed by law through constitutional provisions or enabling legislation.

In the water utility fund of the Village of Elizabeth, it is assumed that the $110,000 was restricted through a bond covenant. GASB prohibits the display of designated, unrestricted net assets.

Statement of Revenues, Expenses, and Changes in Fund Net Assets

The Statement of Revenues, Expenses, and Changes in Fund Net Assets for the proprietary funds of the Village of Elizabeth is presented as Illustration 6–4. GASB requires that operating revenues and operating expenses be shown separately from and prior to nonoperating revenues and expenses. Operating income must be displayed. Operating revenues should be displayed by source. Operating expenses may be reported by function, as shown in Illustration 6–4, or may be reported by object classification, such as personal services, supplies, travel, and so forth.

Capital contributions, extraordinary and special items, and transfers should be shown separately, after nonoperating revenues and expenses. GASB requires the all-inclusive format, which reconciles to the ending net assets. Note that the ending net asset figure shown in Illustration 6–4 is the same as the total net assets shown in the Statement of Net Assets (Illustration 6–3).

Statement of Cash Flows

The Statement of Cash Flows for the proprietary funds for the Village of Elizabeth is presented as Illustration 6–5. Note that the figure for cash and cash equivalents includes the restricted assets, as is customary in practice. From Illustration 6–3,

ILLUSTRATION 6–3   Statement of Net Assets

VILLAGE OF ELIZABETH
Statement of Net Assets
Proprietary Funds
December 31, 2012

	Business-Type Activities— Enterprise Funds— Water Utility	Governmental Activities— Internal Service Funds
Assets		
Current assets:		
Cash	$ 124,930	$ 3,500
Investments		50,000
Accounts receivable (net)	74,925	
Due from general fund	80,000	55,000
Materials and supplies	31,000	233,500
Total current assets	310,855	342,000
Noncurrent assets:		
Restricted assets	110,000	
Long-term advance to supplies fund	190,000	
Capital assets, net of accumulated depreciation	3,788,265	462,500
Total noncurrent assets	4,088,265	462,500
Total assets	4,399,120	804,500
Liabilities		
Current liabilities:		
Accounts payable	89,600	11,000
Payroll taxes payable	9,000	
Total current liabilities	98,600	11,000
Noncurrent liabilities:		
Advance from water utility fund		190,000
Revenue bonds payable	2,700,000	
Total noncurrent liabilities	2,700,000	190,000
Total liabilities	2,798,600	201,000
Net Assets		
Invested in capital assets, net of related debt	1,088,265	272,500
Restricted for debt service	110,000	
Unrestricted	402,255	331,000
Total net assets	$1,600,520	$603,500

ILLUSTRATION 6–4 Statement of Revenues, Expenses, and Changes in Fund Net Assets

	VILLAGE OF ELIZABETH Statement of Revenues, Expenses, and Changes in Fund Net Assets Proprietary Funds For the Year Ended December 31, 2012	
	Business-Type Activities— Enterprise Funds— Water Utility	Governmental Activities— Internal Service Funds
Operating revenues:		
Charges for sales and services	$1,053,100	$377,000
Operating expenses:		
Cost of sales and services	364,000	334,000
Administration	152,900	11,000
Selling	17,200	
Depreciation	122,800	27,500
Total operating expenses	656,900	372,500
Operating income	396,200	4,500
Nonoperating revenues (expenses):		
Interest revenue		3,000
Interest expense	(171,200)	
Total nonoperating revenues (expenses)	(171,200)	3,000
Income before contributions and transfers	225,000	7,500
Capital contributions	12,500	
Transfers in		596,000
Transfers out	(200,000)	
Change in net assets	37,500	603,500
Net assets—January 1, 2012	1,563,020	–0–
Net assets—December 31, 2012	$1,600,520	$603,500

cash of $124,930 plus restricted assets of $110,000 equals the cash and cash equivalents of $234,930 (Illustration 6–5). GASB requires the direct method to report cash flows from operating activities. Other differences exist between GASB requirements and the requirements by FASB for businesses and nongovernmental, not-for-profit organizations.

First, cash flow statements for proprietary funds of government have four categories, rather than the three presented under FASB standards. The four categories are (1) operating, (2) noncapital financing activities, (3) capital and related financing activities, and (4) investing activities.

Cash flows from **operating activities** include receipts from customers, payments to suppliers, payments to employees, and receipt and payment of cash for quasi-external transactions (interfund services provided and used) with other funds. Cash flows from **noncapital financing activities** include proceeds and repayment

ILLUSTRATION 6–5   **Statement of Cash Flows**

VILLAGE OF ELIZABETH
Statement of Cash Flows
Proprietary Funds
For the Year Ended December 31, 2012

	Business-Type Activities— Enterprise Funds— Water Utility	Governmental Activities— Internal Service Funds
Cash flows from operating activities:		
Cash received from customers and departments	$968,500	$ 322,000
Cash paid to suppliers and employees	(502,700)	(567,500)
Net cash provided (used) by operating activities	465,800	(245,500)
Cash flows from noncapital financing activities:		
Transfer from general fund for working capital		306,000
Transfer to capital projects fund	(200,000)	
Net cash provided (used) by noncapital financing activities	(200,000)	306,000
Cash flows from capital and related financing activities:		
Advance from water utility fund		200,000
Transfer from general fund for capital assets		290,000
Acquisition and construction of capital assets	(204,300)*	(490,000)
Interest paid on long-term debt	(171,200)	
Contributed capital	12,500	
Partial repayment of advance from water utility fund		(10,000)
Net cash (used) by capital and related financing activities	(363,000)	(10,000)
Cash flows from investing activities:		
Advance to supplies fund	(200,000)	
Partial repayment of advance by supplies fund	10,000	
Purchase of investments		(50,000)
Interest received		3,000
Net cash (used) by investing activities	(190,000)	(47,000)
Net increase (decrease) in cash and cash equivalents	(287,200)	3,500
Cash and cash equivalents—beginning of year	522,130	0
Cash and cash equivalents—end of year	$234,930	$ 3,500
Reconciliation of operating income to net cash provided (used) by operating activities		
Operating income (loss)	396,200	4,500
Adjustments to reconcile operating income (loss) to net cash provided (used) by operating activities:		
Depreciation expense	122,800	27,500
Change in assets and liabilities:		
Increase in customer accounts receivable	(4,600)	
Increase in interfund receivables	(80,000)	(55,000)
(Increase) decrease in inventory	6,500	(233,500)
Increase (decrease) in accounts payable	15,900	11,000
Increase in accrued liabilities	9,000	
Net cash provided (used) by operating activities	$465,800	$(245,500)

* [$ 127,600 (entry 7) + 58,900 (entry 8) + 17,800 (entry 9)]

of debt not clearly related to capital outlay, grants received from and paid to other governments for noncapital purposes, transfers to and from other funds, and the payment of interest associated with noncapital debt. Illustration 6–5 makes the assumption that $306,000 of the initial contribution from the General Fund to the internal service fund was for working capital.

Cash flows from **capital and related financing activities** include proceeds and repayment of debt related to capital acquisition, the receipt of and payment of grants related to capital acquisition, the payment of interest on debt related to capital acquisition, and the purchase or construction of capital assets. Cash flows from **investing activities** include cash used to acquire investments, whether directly or through investment pools, the interest received on such investments, and cash received from the sale or redemption of investments. Note that cash flows from investing activities do not include acquisition of capital assets, as is the case with FASB requirements.

A reconciliation is required between the Statement of Revenues, Expenses, and Changes and Fund Net Assets and the Cash Flow Statement. The reconciliation should be between operating income and cash flows from operating activities. This also is different from FASB format cash flow statements, which reconcile overall net income (or total change in net assets) to cash flows from operations.

Governments are required to disclose noncash investing, capital-related financing and noncapital-related financing activities. These disclosures generally appear below the reconciliation of operating income and cash flows from operating activities at the bottom of the statement of cash flows. As the heading suggests, these are activities that do not affect cash but change the balance of nonoperating asset and liability accounts. A capital lease is an example of a transaction that affects a nonoperating asset (e.g., equipment) and a long-term liability. Capital leases entered during the year would be disclosed and the amount (present value of minimum lease payments) reported as part of the statement of cash flows. Sometimes developers contribute capital assets, such as water lines, to the local government. Since these do not involve cash, these contributions would also be disclosed as noncash items in a cash flow statement (see bottom of Illustration 2–11 for an example). A similar requirement exists for cash flow statements prepared for commercial businesses and private not-for-profit organizations.

Accounting for Municipal Solid Waste Landfills

Many of the solid waste landfills in the United States are operated by local governments. The GASB requires that certain postclosure costs be estimated and accrued during the period the landfills receive solid waste.

The federal government requires that owners and operators of solid waste landfills be responsible for the landfill after it closes. Governments must assume the cost of closure, including the cost of equipment used, the cost of the landfill cover, and the cost of caring for the site for a period of 30 years after closure, or whatever period is required by regulations. These costs are measured in current costs, in that the costs are estimated as if they were incurred at the time of estimate.

The GASB requires that a portion of those future estimated costs be charged as an expense and a liability of the landfill operation on a units-of-production method (based on capacity used divided by total capacity) as waste is accepted. For example, if the total estimated costs for closure and postclosure were $10 million, and the landfill accepted 10 percent of its anticipated capacity (cubic yards) in a given year, the charge and liability for that year would be $1 million. Each year, revisions would be made, if necessary, for changes in cost estimates, landfill capacity, and inflation.

If the landfill is operated as an enterprise fund, the entries would be made directly in the enterprise fund, following accrual accounting. If the landfill is operated as a governmental fund, then modified accrual principles would apply, and the fund expenditure and liability would be limited to the amount to be paid with available financial resources. The remainder would be reflected as a liability in the government-wide financial statements.

For example, assume a landfill is operated as an enterprise fund. The total estimated closure and postclosure costs are $30 million. Total estimated capacity of the landfill is 100 million tons. During 2012, the first year of operations, the landfill accepted 2 million tons, or 2 percent of its capacity. A $600,000 charge would be made during 2012:

	Debits	Credits
Operating Expenses—Estimated Landfill Closure and Postclosure Costs	600,000	
Accrued Liability for Estimated Landfill Closure and Postclosure Costs		600,000

The purpose of the charge is to match the estimated costs with the revenues during the period of time waste is accepted. Adjustments should be made yearly or whenever estimates for capacity or costs change. When the landfill is closed, and closure and postclosure costs are incurred, those costs will be charged to the liability account.

Pollution Remediation Costs

Increasingly, landfill and other waste storage sites are being identified by the U.S. Environmental Protection Agency or similar stage agencies as requiring pollution remediation (cleanup and control). In 1980, Congress passed the Comprehensive Environmental Response Compensation and Liability Act (generally referred to as the Superfund Act), which places responsibility for pollution remediation on current and past owners and users of waste sites.

State and local governments are increasingly finding they are responsible for the cleanup of sites found to not meet federal and state standards. Even in cases where they did not operate a site, but merely used the facility, local governments can be held responsible for the cleanup. In response, GASB issued *Statement 49, Accounting and Financial Reporting for Pollution Remediation Obligations,* which requires governments to accrue the cost of pollution remediation as a liability in the basic financial statements.

If the site is operated as an enterprise fund, the entries would be made in the enterprise fund, following accrual accounting. Otherwise, fund expenditures equal to the amount to be paid with available resources would appear in a governmental fund and the long-term portion of the liability in the government-wide Statement of Net Assets. In addition, note disclosure is required describing the nature and scope of the government's responsibility, the estimated liability, the methods and assumptions used to estimate the liability, and any estimates of recoveries that might reduce the liability.

SUMMARY

This chapter examines accounting and reporting for proprietary funds. These funds account for those activities of the government that are business-like in nature,—i.e. they charge other entities for goods and services with the purpose of measuring income. Enterprise funds provide goods and services to individuals and businesses and include water utilities, transit systems, airports, and recreational facilities. Internal service funds provide goods and services to other departments within the government and include centralized supplies, motor pools, printing centers, and risk management activities. These funds report using the accrual basis of accounting and the economic resource measurement focus. Significant aspects of proprietary fund accounting include the following:

- The required financial statements of proprietary funds include a Statement of Net Assets, a Statement of Revenues, Expenses, and Changes in Fund Net Assets, and a Statement of Cash Flows.
- The net position (i.e., fund equity) section of the Statement of Net Assets is displayed within three categories: (1) Invested in Capital Assets, Net of Related Debt, (2) Restricted Net Assets, and (3) Unrestricted Net Assets.
- The Statement of Cash Flows must be prepared using the direct method and includes cash flows from operating activities, investing activities, capital and related financing activities, and noncapital-related financing activities.

Now that you have finished reading Chapter 6, complete the multiple choice questions provided on the text's Web site (www.mhhe.com/copley10e) to test your comprehension of the chapter.

Questions and Exercises

6–1.   Using the annual financial report obtained for Exercise 1–1, answer the following questions:

   a. Find the Statement of Net Assets for the proprietary funds. Is the Net Asset or the Balance Sheet format used? List the major enterprise funds from that statement. Is the statement classified between current and non-current assets and liabilities? Are net assets broken down into the three classifications shown in your text? Is a separate column shown for internal service funds?

b. Find the Statement of Revenues, Expenses, and Changes in Net Assets for the proprietary funds. Is the "all-inclusive" format used? Are revenues reported by source? Are expenses (not expenditures) reported by function or by object classification? Is depreciation reported separately? Is operating income, or a similar title, displayed? Are nonoperating revenues and expenses shown separately after operating income? Are capital contributions, extraordinary and special items, and transfers shown separately? List any extraordinary and special items.

c. Find the Statement of Cash Flows for the proprietary funds. List the four categories of cash flows. Are they the same as shown in the text? Are interest receipts reported as cash flows from investing activities? Are interest payments shown as financing activities? Is the direct method used? Is a reconciliation shown from operating income to net cash provided by operations? Are capital assets acquired from financing activities shown as decreases in cash flows from financing activities? Does the ending cash balance agree with the cash balance shown in the Statement of Net Assets (note that restricted assets may be included)?

d. If your government has a CAFR, look to any combining statements and list the nonmajor enterprise funds. List the internal service funds.

e. Look at the financial statements from the point of view of a financial analyst. Write down the unrestricted net asset balances for each of the major enterprise funds, and (if you have a CAFR) the nonmajor enterprise funds and internal service funds. Look at the long-term debt of major enterprise funds. Can you tell from the statements or the notes whether the debt is general obligation or revenue in nature? Write down the income before contributions, extraordinary items, special items, and transfers for each of the funds. Compare these numbers with prior years, if the information is provided in your financial statements. Look at the transfers. Can you tell if the general government is subsidizing or is subsidized by enterprise funds?

6–2. What accounting problem arises if an internal service fund is operated at a significant profit? What accounting problem arises if an internal service fund is operated at a significant loss?

6–3. Why might it be desirable to operate enterprise funds at a profit?

6–4. The Village of Seaside Pines prepared the following enterprise fund Trial Balance as of December 31, 2012, the last day of its fiscal year. The enterprise fund was established this year through a transfer from the General Fund.

	Debits	Credits
Accounts payable		$ 210,000
Accounts receivable	$ 102,000	
Accrued interest payable		4,000
Accumulated depreciation		45,000
Administrative and selling expenses	75,000	
Allowance for uncollectible accounts		12,000
Capital assets	650,000	
Cash	95,000	
Charges for sales and services		505,000
Cost of sales and services	447,000	
Depreciation expense	45,000	
Due from General Fund	40,000	
Interest expense	18,000	
Interest revenue		28,000
Transfer In from General Fund		100,000
Revenue bonds payable		575,000
Supplies inventory	7,000	
Totals	$1,479,000	$1,479,000

a. Prepare the closing entries for December 31.

b. Prepare the Statement of Revenues, Expenses, and Changes in Fund Net Assets for the year ended December 31.

c. Prepare the Net Asset Section of the December 31 balance sheet. (Assume that the revenue bonds were issued to acquire capital assets and there are no restricted assets.)

6–5.   Using the information provided in exercise 6–4, prepare the reconciliation of operating income to net cash provided by operating activities that would appear at the bottom of the December 31 Statement of Cash Flows. Recall that the beginning balance of all asset and liabilities is zero.

6–6.   The Town of Wilson has a Water Utility Fund with the following trial balance as of July 1, 2011, the first day of the fiscal year:

	Debits	Credits
Cash	$ 130,000	
Customer accounts receivable	300,000	
Allowance for uncollectible accounts		$ 10,000
Materials and supplies	120,000	
Restricted assets	250,000	
Utility plant in service	7,100,000	
Accumulated depreciation—utility plant		2,600,000
Construction work in progress	100,000	
Accounts payable		130,000
Accrued expenses		80,000
Revenue bonds payable		3,500,000
Net assets		1,680,000
Totals	$8,000,000	$8,000,000

During the year ended June 30, 2012, the following transactions and events occurred in the Town of Wilson Water Utility Fund:

1. Accrued expenses at July 1, 2011, were paid in cash.
2. Billings to nongovernmental customers for water usage for the year amounted to $1,400,000; billings to the General Fund amounted to $57,000.
3. Liabilities for the following were recorded during the year:

Materials and supplies	$215,000
Costs of sales and services	354,000
Administrative expenses	200,000
Construction work in progress	212,200

4. Materials and supplies were used in the amount of $265,700, all for costs of sales and services.
5. $8,000 of old accounts receivable were written off.
6. Accounts receivable collections totaled $1,450,000 from nongovernmental customers and $48,400 from the General Fund.
7. $1,035,000 of accounts payable were paid in cash.
8. One year's interest in the amount of $175,000 was paid.
9. Construction was completed on plant assets costing $135,000; that amount was transferred to Utility Plant in Service.
10. Depreciation was recorded in the amount of $235,000.
11. Interest in the amount of $25,000 was charged to Construction Work in Progress. (This was previously paid in item 8.)
12. The Allowance for Uncollectible Accounts was increased by $13,100.
13. As required by the loan agreement, cash in the amount of $100,000 was transferred to Restricted Assets for eventual redemption of the bonds.
14. Accrued expenses, all related to costs of sales and services, amounted to $47,000.
15. Nominal accounts for the year were closed to Net Assets.

   Required:

   a. Record the transactions for the year in general journal form.

   b. Prepare a Statement of Revenues, Expenses, and Changes in Fund Net Assets.

   c. Prepare a Statement of Net Assets as of June 30, 2012.

   d. Prepare a Statement of Cash Flows for the Year Ended June 30, 2012. Assume all debt and interest are related to capital outlay. Assume the entire $212,200 construction work in progress liability (see item 3) was paid in entry 7. Include restricted assets as cash and cash equivalents.

6–7. The City of Sandwich purchased a swimming pool from a private operator as of April 1, 2012, for $500,000. Of the $500,000, $250,000 was provided by a one-time contribution from the General Fund, and $250,000 was provided by a loan from the First National Bank, secured by a note. The loan has an annual interest rate 6 percent, payable semiannually on October 1 and

April 1; principal payments of $100,000 are to be made annually, beginning on April 1, 2013. The city has a calendar year as its fiscal year. During the year ended December 31, 2012, the following transactions occurred, related to the City of Sandwich Swimming Pool:

1. The amounts were received from the City General Fund and the First National Bank.
2. A short-term loan was provided in the amount of $100,000 from the Water Utility Fund.
3. The purchase of the pool was recorded. Based on an appraisal, it was decided to allocate $100,000 to the land, $300,000 to improvements other than buildings (the pool), and $100,000 to the building. There is a 10-year life for both the pool and the building, and depreciation is to be recorded annually, based on monthly allocations (do not record depreciation until entry 10).
4. Charges to patrons during the season amounted to $340,000, all received in cash.
5. Salaries paid to employees amounted to $200,000, all paid in cash, of which $170,000 was cost of services, and $30,000 was administration.
6. Supplies purchased amounted to $40,000; all but $5,000 was used. Cash was paid for the supplies, all of which was for cost of sales and services.
7. Administrative expenses amounted to $12,000, paid in cash.
8. The first interest payment was made to the First National Bank.
9. The short-term loan was repaid to the Water Utility Fund.
10. Depreciation was accrued for the year. Record 9/12 of the annual amounts.
11. Interest was accrued for the year.
12. Closing entries were prepared.

    Required:

    a. Prepare entries to record the transactions.
    b. Prepare a Statement of Revenues, Expenses, and Changes in Fund Net Assets for the Year Ended December 31, 2012, for the City of Sandwich Swimming Pool Fund.
    c. Prepare a Statement of Net Assets as of December 31, 2012, for the City of Sandwich Swimming Pool Fund.
    d. Prepare a Statement of Cash Flows for the Year Ended December 31, 2012, for the City of Sandwich Swimming Pool Fund.

6–8. The Village of Parry reported the following for its Print Shop Fund for the year ended April 30, 2012.

VILLAGE OF PARRY—PRINT SHOP FUND
Statement of Revenues, Expenses, and Changes in Net Assets
For the Year Ended April 30, 2012

Operating revenues:		
Charges for services		$1,100,000
Operating expenses:		
Salaries and benefits	$500,000	
Depreciation	300,000	
Supplies used	200,000	
Utilities	70,000	1,070,000
Income from operations		30,000
Nonoperating income (expenses):		
Interest revenue	30,000	
Interest expense	(50,000)	(20,000)
Net income before transfers		10,000
Transfers in		180,000
Changes in net assets		190,000
Net assets—beginning		1,120,000
Net assets—ending		$1,310,000

The Print Shop Fund records also revealed the following:

1. Contribution from General Fund for working capital needs..... $ 80,000
2. Contribution from General Fund for purchase of equipment.... 100,000
3. Loan from Water Utility Fund for purchase of equipment 300,000
4. Purchase of equipment.................................. (500,000)
5. Purchase of one-year investments........................ (50,000)
6. Paid off a bank loan outstanding at May 1, 2011 .... (51,000)
   The loan was for short-term operating purposes. ....
7. Signed a capital lease on April 30, 2012................... $42,180

The following balances were observed in current asset and current liability accounts. ( ) denote credit balances:

	5/1/11	4/30/12
Cash	$151,000	$333,000
Accrued interest receivable	5,000	10,000
Due from other funds	40,000	50,000
Accrued salaries and benefits	(20,000)	(30,000)
Utility bills payable	(4,000)	(5,000)
Accounts payable	(30,000)	(25,000)
Accrued interest payable	(5,000)	(7,000)
Supplies inventory	0	0

Prepare a Statement of Cash Flows for the Village of Parry Print Shop Fund for the Year Ended April 30, 2012. Include the reconciliation of operating income to net cash provided by operating activities.

6–9.   The following is a statement of cash flows for the risk management internal service fund of the City of Wrightville. An inexperienced accountant prepared the statement using the FASB format rather than the format required by GASB. All long-term debt was issued to purchase capital assets. The transfer from the General Fund was to establish the internal service fund and provide the initial working capital necessary for operations.

CITY OF WRIGHTVILLE
Risk Management Internal Service Fund
Statement of Cash Flows
For the Year Ended June 30, 2012

Cash flows from operating activities:	
Cash received from other departments	$850,000
Cash paid for suppliers and employees	(120,000)
Cash paid on insurance claims	(360,000)
Transfer from General Fund	300,000
Investment income received	18,000
Interest paid on long-term debt	(15,000)
Cash flows from operating activities	673,000
Cash flows from investing activities:	
Acquisition of property, plant, and equipment	(290,000)
Purchase of investments	(370,000)
Sale of property, plant, and equipment	15,000
Cash flows from investing activities	(645,000)
Cash flows from financing activities:	
Proceeds from issuance of long-term debt	80,000
Payments on long-term debt	(12,000)
Cash flows from financing activities	68,000
Net decrease in cash and cash equivalents	96,000
Cash and cash equivalents, July 1, 2011	40,000
Cash and cash equivalents, June 30, 2012	$136,000

Prepare a statement of cash flows using the appropriate format as required by GASB. You do not need to prepare the reconciliation of operating income to cash flow from operations.

6–10.   The Town of Frostbite self-insures for some of its liability claims and purchases insurance for others. In an effort to consolidate its risk management activities, the Town recently decided to establish an internal service fund, the Risk Management Fund. The Risk Management Fund's purpose is to obtain liability coverage for the Town, to pay claims not covered by the insurance, and to charge individual departments in amounts sufficient to cover current-year costs and to establish a reserve for losses.

    The Town reports proprietary fund expenses by object classification using the following accounts: Personnel services (salaries), Contractual services (for the expired portion of prepaid service contracts), Depreciation, and

Insurance Claims. The following transactions relate to the year ended December 31, 2012, the first year of the Risk Management Fund's operations.

1. The Risk Management Fund is established through a transfer of $500,000 from the General Fund and a long-term advance from the water utility enterprise fund of $250,000.
2. The Risk Management Fund purchased (prepaid) insurance coverage through several commercial insurance companies for $200,000. The policies purchased require the Town to self-insure for $25,000 per incident.
3. Office Equipment is purchased for $10,000.
4. $450,000 is invested in marketable securities.
5. Actuarial estimates were made in the previous fiscal year to determine the amount necessary to attain the goal of accumulating sufficient funds to cover current-year claims and to establish a reserve for losses. It was determined that the General Fund and water utility be assessed a fee of 6 percent of total wages and salaries (Interfund premium). Wages and salaries by department are as follows:

Public Safety	5,000,000
General Administrative Operations	1,500,000
Education	1,500,000
Water Utility	2,500,000
Total	10,500,000

6. Cash received in payment of interfund premiums from the General Fund totaled $275,000 and cash received from the Water Utility totaled $100,000.
7. Interest and dividends received totaled $27,000.
8. Salaries for the Risk Management Fund amounted to $200,000 (all paid during the year).
9. Claims paid under self-insurance totaled $150,000 during the year.
10. The office equipment is depreciated on the straight-line basis over 5 years.
11. At year-end, $190,000 of the insurance policies purchased in January had expired.
12. The market value of investments at December 31 totaled $456,000 (*Hint:* credit *Net Increase in Fair Market Value of Investments*).
13. In addition to the claims paid in entry 9 above, estimates for the liability for the Town's portion of known claims since the inception of the Town's self-insurance program totaled $90,000.

    Required:
    a. Prepare the journal entries (including closing entries) to record the transactions.
    b. Prepare a Statement of Revenues, Expenses, and Changes in Fund Net Assets for the year ended December 31, 2012, for the Risk Management Fund.

    c. Prepare a Statement of Net Assets as of December 31, 2012, for the Risk Management Fund.

    d. Prepare a Statement of Cash Flows for the year ended December 31, 2012, for the Risk Management Fund. Assume $10,000 of the transfer from the General Fund was for the purchase of the equipment. Further, assume the remainder of the transfer from the General Fund and all of the advance from the enterprise fund are to establish working capital (noncapital related financing).

    e. Comment on whether the interfund premium of 6 percent of wages and salaries is adequate.

6–11. The City of Evansville operated a summer camp program for at-risk youth. Businesses and nonprofit organizations sponsor one or more youth by paying the registration fee for program participants. The following Statement of Cash Receipts and Disbursements summarizes the activity in the program's bank account for the year.

    1. At the beginning of 2012, the program had unrestricted cash of $12,000.

	Cash Basis
	12 months
Cash receipts:	
Registration fees	$127,000
Borrowing from bank	45,000
Total deposits	172,000
Cash disbursements:	
Payroll taxes	10,250
Labor	81,575
Insurance (paid monthly)	6,000
Purchase of bus	55,000
Interest on bank note	1,350
Total checks	154,175
Excess of receipts over disbursements	$ 17,825

    2. The loan from the bank is dated April 1 and is for a five-year period. Interest (6 percent annual rate) is paid on October 1 and April 1 of each year, beginning October 1, 2012.

    3. The bus was purchased on April 1 with the proceeds provided by the bank loan and has an estimated useful life of 5 years (straight line basis—use monthly depreciation).

    4. All invoices and salaries related to 2012 had been paid by close of business on December 31, except for the employer's portion of December payroll taxes, totaling $900.

        a. Prepare the journal entries, closing entries, and a Statement of Revenues, Expenses, and Changes in Fund Net Assets assuming the City intends to treat the summer camp program as an enterprise fund.

b. Prepare the journal entries, closing entries, and a Statement of Revenues, Expenditures, and Changes in Fund Balance assuming the City intends to treat the summer camp program as a special revenue fund.

6–12. The Town of Thomaston has a Solid Waste Landfill Enterprise Fund with the following trial balance as of January 1, 2012, the first day of the fiscal year.

	Debits	Credits
Cash	$2,380,000	
Supplies: diesel fuel	120,000	
Equipment	7,100,000	
Accumulated depreciation		2,600,000
Accounts payable		130,000
Accrued closure and postclosure care costs payable		2,080,000
Net assets		4,790,000
Totals	$9,600,000	$9,600,000

During the year, the following transactions and events occurred:

1. Citizens and trash companies dumped 500,000 tons of waste in the landfill, which charges $5.50 a ton payable in cash.
2. Diesel fuel purchases totaled $343,000 (on account).
3. Accounts payable totaling $430,000 were paid.
4. Diesel fuel used in operations amounted to $405,000.
5. Depreciation was recorded in the amount of $735,000.
6. Salaries totaling $75,000 were paid.
7. Future costs to close the landfill and postclosure care costs are expected to total $76,250,000. The total capacity of the landfill is expected to be 25,000,000 tons of waste.

Prepare the journal entries, closing entries, and a Statement of Revenues, Expenses, and Changes in Fund Net Assets for the year ended December 31, 2012.

Excel-Based Problems

6–13. Jefferson County operates a centralized motor pool to service county vehicles. At the end of 2011, the Motor Pool Internal Service Fund had the following account balances:

Due from General Fund	$ 9,500	
Cash	15,000	
Capital assets	35,000	
Supplies inventory	4,000	
Accounts payable		$ 5,500
Accrued wages payable		300
Accumulated depreciation		7,500
Advance from enterprise fund		25,000
Net assets		25,200
Total	$63,500	$63,500

The following events took place during 2012:

1. Additional supplies were purchased on account in the amount of $35,000.

2. Services provided to other departments on account totaled $95,000. A total of $65,000 was for departments in the General Fund and $30,000 for enterprise fund departments.

3. Supplies used amounted to $36,700.

4. Payments made on accounts payable amounted to $38,200.

5. Cash collected from the General Fund totaled $57,000 and cash collected from the enterprise fund totaled $30,000.

6. Salaries were paid in the amount of $47,000. Included in this amount is the accrued wages payable at the end of 2011. All of these are determined to be part of the cost of services provided.

7. In a previous year, the enterprise fund loaned the Motor Pool money under an advance for the purpose of purchasing garage equipment. In the current year, the Motor Pool repaid the enterprise fund $7,000 of this amount.

8. On July 1, 2012, the Motor Pool Fund borrowed $10,000 from the bank, signing a 12 percent note that is due on June 30, 2013. The borrowings are not related to capital asset purchases but were made to provide working capital.

Additional information includes:

9. Depreciation for the year amounted to $7,500.

10. The payment of interest on the note is payable on June 30, 2013.

11. Unpaid wages relating to the final week of the year totaled $420.

Using the Excel template provided; a separate tab is provided for each of the requirements:

a. Prepare journal entries.

b. Post entries to the T-accounts.

c. Prepare closing entries.

d. Prepare a Statement of Revenues, Expenses and Changes in Fund Net Assets.

e. Prepare a Statement of Net Assets.

f. Prepare a Statement of Cash Flows for the year ending December-31-2012.

6–14   Rural County is an agricultural community located hundreds of miles from any metropolitan center. The County established a *television reception improvement fund* to serve the public interest by constructing and operating television translator stations. TV translator stations serve communities that cannot receive the signals of free over-the-air TV stations because they are too far away from a broadcasting TV station. Because of the largest distances between customers, commercial cable TV providers are also not inclined to serve rural communities. The fund charges TV owners a monthly fee of $15. The fund was established on December 20, 2011, with a transfer of cash from the General Fund of $100,000. On December 31, 2011, the fund acquired land for its translator stations in the amount of $40,000. The remaining cash and the land are the only resources held by the fund at the beginning of 2012.

1. Other than beginning account balances, no entries have been made in the general ledger.

2. The county prepared a budget for 2012 with estimated customer fees of $30,000, operating costs of $30,000, capital costs of $65,000, and estimated loan proceeds of $55,000.

3. The following information was taken from the checkbook for the year ended December-31-2012.

	Cash Basis 12 months
Cash Receipts:	
Fees from customers	$28,875
Borrowing from bank	55,000
Total deposits	83,875
Cash Disbursements:	
Supplies	7,300
Labor	12,900
Utilities	7,500
Equipment	60,000
Interest on bank note	2,200
Total checks	89,900
Beginning Cash Balance	60,000
Ending Cash Balance	$53,975

4. The loan from the bank is dated April 1 and is for a five-year period. Interest (8 percent annual rate) is paid on October 1 and April 1 of each year, beginning October 1, 2012. The County has elected not to establish a debt service fund but will pay the interest on this note from the Television Reception Improvement Fund.

5. The machinery was purchased on April 1 with the proceeds provided by the bank loan and has an estimated useful life of 10 years (straight-line basis).

6. In January 2013, customers remitted fees totaling $2,500 for December 2012 service.

7. Supplies of $500 were received on December 29 and paid in January 2013.

8. Unused supplies on hand amounted to $760 at December 31, 2012.

9. Utilities are paid in the following month. The utility bill for December 2012 was received on January 4, 2013 in the amount of $620. (Utility bills are recorded through accounts payable.)

10. On December 21, the company placed an order for a new computer-ized control switch in the amount of $1,500 to be delivered and paid in January 2013.

   Required:

   You have been asked to provide financial statements for the upcoming County Board meeting for the Television Reception Improvement Fund.

   Part 1: Assume the County chooses to report the Television Reception Improvement Fund as a Special Revenue Fund following modified accrual basis statements. Using the Excel template provided,

   a. Prepare journal entries recording the events above for the year ending December 31, 2012.

   b. Post the journal entries to T-accounts.

   c. Prepare closing entries.

   d. Prepare a Statement of Revenues, Expenditures, and Changes in Fund Balance.

   e. Prepare a Balance Sheet, assuming there are no restricted or committed fund net resources.

   Part 2: Assume the County chooses to report the Television Reception Improvement Fund as an Enterprise Fund following accrual basis statements. Using the Excel template provided,

   a. Prepare journal entries recording the events above for the year ending December 31, 2012.

   b. Post the journal entries to T-accounts.

   c. Prepare closing entries.

   d. Prepare a Statement of Revenues, Expenses and Changes in Net Assets.

   e. Prepare a Statement of Net Assets, assuming the bank note is related to capital asset acquisitions.

   The Excel template contains separate tabs for (1) special revenue fund journal entries and T-accounts, (2) special revenue fund closing entries, (3) special revenue fund financial statements, (4) enterprise fund journal entries and T-accounts, (5) enterprise fund closing entries, and (6) enterprise fund financial statements. Both the T-accounts and financial statements contain accounts you will not need under either the modified accrual or accrual bases. Similarly, you may not need to record some of the events, depending on the basis of accounting.

Continuous Problem

Available on the text's Web site (www.mhhe.com/copley10e)

Fiduciary (Trust) Funds

Where large sums of money are concerned, it is advisable to trust nobody.
(Agatha Christie)

Always be nice to bankers. Always be nice to pension fund managers. Always be nice to the media. In that order. (John Gotti, onetime boss of the Gambino crime family)

Learning Objectives

- Identify the fiduciary funds and describe when each is appropriate.
- Apply the accrual basis of accounting in the recording of typical transactions of agency, private-purpose trust, investment trust, and pension trust funds.
- Prepare the fund-basis financial statements for fiduciary funds.
- Apply GASB standards for the measurement and reporting of investments.

Fiduciary funds are used to account for assets held by a government acting as a trustee or agent for entities external to the governmental unit: including individuals, organizations, and other governmental units. (Assets held in trust for other governmental funds or for purposes of the governmental unit would be reported as special revenue funds, if expendable, and as permanent funds, if nonexpendable.) For this reason, fiduciary funds are often identified in governmental financial reports as Trust and Agency Funds. Trust relationships are generally established through formal trust agreements, while agency relationships are not. Generally, governments have more of a degree of involvement in decision-making for trust agreements than for agency relationships.

GASB pronouncements distinguish four types of fiduciary funds: (1) agency funds, (2) private-purpose trust funds, (3) investment trust funds, and (4) pension (and other employee benefit) trust funds. An **agency fund** accounts for assets held by a government temporarily as agent for individuals, organizations, or other governmental units. A **private-purpose trust fund** results when a contributor and a government agree that the principal and/or income of trust assets is for the benefit of individuals, organizations, or other governments. An **investment trust fund** exists when the government is the sponsor of a multigovernment investment pool and accounts for the external portion of those trust assets. Finally, a **pension (or other employee benefit) trust fund** exists when the government is the trustee for a defined benefit pension plan, defined contribution pension plan, other postemployment benefit plan, or other employee benefit plan.

Fiduciary funds use the economic resources measurement focus and accrual basis of accounting, with two exceptions. First, agency funds do not report revenues, expenses, or net assets; however, changes in assets and liabilities are recognized on the accrual basis. Second, certain liabilities of defined benefit pension plans and certain postemployment health care plans are recognized following the requirements of GASB *Statements 25* and *43*. We describe these later in the chapter. The terms **additions** and **deductions** are used in trust fund reporting in lieu of revenues and expenses. However, additions and deductions are measured on the accrual basis. The accounting for fiduciary funds is summarized in Illustration 7–1.

Fiduciary funds are reported by fund type: pension (and other employee benefit) trust funds, investment trust funds, private-purpose trust funds, and agency funds. Two statements are required: the **Statement of Fiduciary Net Assets** and the **Statement of Changes in Fiduciary Net Assets.** Agency funds are not included in the Statement of Changes in Net Assets because they have no revenues (additions) or expenses (deductions). In addition, two schedules are required for pension (and other employee benefit) trust funds as Required Supplementary Information (RSI): the **Schedule of Funding Progress** and the **Schedule of Employer Contributions.** Fiduciary funds are *not* included in the government-wide financial statements.

This chapter discusses and illustrates agency, private-purpose trust, investment trust, and pension (and other employee benefit) trust funds. In addition, employer accounting for pensions is presented. Village of Elizabeth examples are provided for private-purpose and pension (and other employee benefit) trust funds.

AGENCY FUNDS

Agency funds are used to account for assets held by a government acting as agent for one or more other governmental units or for individuals or private organizations. Assets accounted for in an agency fund belong to the party or parties for which the government acts as agent. Therefore, *agency fund assets are offset by liabilities equal in amount; no fund equity exists.* Agency fund assets and liabilities are to be recognized at the time the government becomes responsible for the assets. Additions (revenues) and deductions (expenses) are not recognized in the accounts of agency funds.

Unless use of an agency fund is mandated by law, by GASB standards, or by decision of the governing board, an agency relationship may be accounted for within governmental and/or proprietary funds. For example, local governments must act as agents of the federal and state governments in the collection of employees' withholding taxes and Social Security taxes. However, it is perfectly acceptable to account for the withholdings and the remittance to federal and state governments within the same funds that account for the gross pay of the employees.

ILLUSTRATION 7–1   Summary of Fiduciary-Type Funds

Fund Name	Accrual Basis	Economic Resource Focus	Record Budgets	Encumbrances	Fund Description	Fund Term
Agency Fund	✓*	✓			Accounts for assets held temporarily for individuals, organizations, or other governments.	Indefinite term: While assets continue to be collected or held for others.
Private-Purpose Trust Fund	✓	✓			Accounts for assets contributed to a government in which the trust agreement stipulates that the income (or principal) be used to benefit individuals, organizations, or other governments.	Indefinite term: While assets continue to be held in trust.
Investment Trust Fund	✓	✓			Accounts for assets held and invested on behalf of other governments in a multigovernment investment pool in which the reporting government is the sponsor.	Indefinite term: While other parties (e.g., governments) continue to participate in the investment pool.
Pension (or other employee benefit) Trust Fund	✓†	✓			Accounts for assets held and invested on behalf of government employee pension (or other benefit) plans in which the reporting government acts as trustee.	Indefinite term.

* Agency funds do not record revenues, expenses, or net assets.

† Pension trust funds do not report the unfunded actuarial liability in the Statement of Plan Net Assets. However, this information is provided in the required supplementary information.

r22ok2

Only rarely is the use of a certain fund type mandated by GASB standards, rather than by law or by decision of the governing board of a government. However, GASB standards mandate that a government should account for special assessment activities in an agency fund if the government has no obligation to assume responsibility for debt payments, even if the property owners default. GASB determined that only an agency relationship exists, even though the government may perform the functions of billing property owners for the assessments, collecting installments from the property owners, and making the principal and interest payments. (On the other hand, if the government *is* liable for payment of special assessment debt in the event of default by the property owners, the transactions are handled as any other general government debt, normally through a debt service fund.)

Tax Agency Funds

An activity that often results in the creation of an agency fund is the collection of taxes or other revenues by an official of one government for other governmental units. State governments commonly collect sales taxes, gasoline taxes, and many other taxes that are apportioned between state agencies and local governments within the state. At the local government level, it is common for an elected county official to serve as collector for all property taxes within the county. Taxes levied by all funds and units within the county are certified to the county collector for collection. The county collector is required by law to make periodic distributions of tax collections for each year to each fund or unit in the proportion the levy for that fund or unit bears to the total levy for the year.

Accounting for Tax Agency Funds

Assume that, for a given year, a county government levies for its General Fund the amount of $2,000,000 in property taxes, from which it expects to realize $1,960,000. The levy also includes $3,000,000 in property taxes for the consolidated school district and $1,000,000 in property taxes for a village within the county. The county General Fund levy would be recorded in the accounts of the county General Fund in the same manner as in Chapter 4:

(General Fund)	Debits	Credits
Taxes Receivable—Current	2,000,000	
Estimated Uncollectible Current Taxes		40,000
Revenues Control		1,960,000

Each unit using the Tax Agency Fund (i.e., the school district and the village) would record its own levy in the manner just illustrated.

The Tax Agency Fund entry for recording levies of other governments certified to it, in this example totaling $4,000,000, would be as follows:

1. Taxes Receivable for Other Governments—Current	4,000,000	
Due to Other Governments		4,000,000

Note that the *gross* amount of the tax levy for all funds and units, not the net amount expected to be collected, should be recorded in the Tax Agency Fund as a receivable, because the county collector is responsible for attempting to collect all taxes as billed. Note also that the receivable is offset in total by the liability.

If collections of taxes during a certain portion of the year amounted to $2,400,000 for other governments and $1,800,000 for the County, the entry for the Tax Agency Fund would be:

	Debits	Credits
2. Cash	2,400,000	
Taxes Receivable for Other Governments—Current		2,400,000

The County General Fund would make the following journal entry:

(General Fund)		
Cash.	1,800,000	
Taxes Receivable—Current		1,800,000

In an actual case the tax collections must be identified with the parcels of property against which the taxes are levied, because the location of each parcel determines the governmental units and funds that should receive the tax collections. Assume that the County General Fund is given 1 percent of all collections for other governments as reimbursement for the cost of operating the Tax Agency Fund:

	Taxes Collected		Collection Fee (Charged) Received	Cash to Be Distributed
County	$1,800,000		$24,000 $(6 + 18)$	$1,824,000
Village	600,000	$\times 1\%$ =	(6,000)	594,000
School District	1,800,000	$\times 1\%$ =	(18,000)	1,782,000
	$4,200,000		$ -0-	$4,200,000

If cash is not distributed as soon as the previous computation is made, the entry by the Tax Agency Fund to record the liability to other governments would be as follows:

3. Due to Other Governments.	2,400,000	
Due to County General Fund		24,000
Due to Village		594,000
Due to Consolidated School District		1,782,000

The entry made by the County General Fund to record the 1 percent fee would be:

(General Fund)	Debits	Credits
Due from County Tax Agency Fund.	24,000	
Revenues Control		24,000

An entry would be made by the Village General Fund and the General Fund of the consolidated school district to record an expenditure for the amount of the collection fee. When cash was transferred, the *due to* and *due from* accounts would be extinguished.

Financial Reporting for Agency Funds

The assets and liabilities of agency funds should be included in the fiduciary funds Statement of Fiduciary Net Assets. However, since agency relationships do not generate revenues or expenses for the reporting entity, the operations of agency funds are not included in the Statement of Changes in Fiduciary Net Assets. The Comprehensive Annual Financial Report should include a Combining Statement of Changes in Assets and Liabilities—All Agency Funds. This statement is shown as Illustration 7–2.

PRIVATE-PURPOSE TRUST FUNDS

Private-purpose trust funds are created to account for trust agreements where principal and/or income benefit individuals, private organizations, or other governments. The distinguishing characteristic of a private-purpose trust fund is that the benefit is limited to specific private, rather than general public, purposes (see Illustration 5–2 for a summary of trust types). In some cases, these trusts are created when individuals or organizations contribute resources with the agreement that principal and/or income will be used to benefit others. For example, a government may agree to be trustee for a community foundation, where awards are made to not-for-profit organizations. In some cases, the principal of those gifts may be *nonexpendable,* in which case an **endowment** has been created. In other cases, the principal of those gifts may be expendable. In either case, management of the trust may involve significant investments.

Accounting for Investments

GASB *Statement 31, Accounting and Financial Reporting for Certain Investments and for External Investment Pools,* applies to (1) interest-earning investment contracts (CDs, time deposits, etc.), (2) external investment pools, (3) open-end mutual funds, (4) debt securities, and (5) equity securities that have readily determinable fair values. These investments are to be reported in the balance sheet at fair value, which is defined as the "amount at which an investment could be exchanged in a current transaction between willing parties, other than in a forced or liquidation sale." When a quoted market price is available, that price should be used.

ILLUSTRATION 7–2   Combining Statement of Changes in Assets and Liabilities—
All Agency funds

Example County Government Combining Statement of Changes in Assets and Liabilities—All Agency Funds For the Fiscal Year Ended December 31, 2012				
(Amounts assumed for illustration)	Balance January 1	Additions	Deductions	Balance December 31
Property tax collection				
Assets:				
Cash	$ 90,000	$ 3,900,000	$ 3,750,000	$ 240,000
Taxes receivable	180,000	4,000,000	3,900,000	280,000
	270,000	7,900,000	7,650,000	520,000
Liabilities:				
Due to school district	60,000	3,000,000	2,990,000	70,000
Due to town	210,000	1,000,000	760,000	450,000
	270,000	4,000,000	3,750,000	520,000
Special assessment collection				
Assets:				
Cash	90,000	800,000	790,000	100,000
	90,000	800,000	790,000	100,000
Liabilities:				
Due to property owners	90,000	800,000	790,000	100,000
	90,000	800,000	790,000	100,000
Total all agency funds				
Assets:				
Cash	180,000	4,700,000	4,540,000	340,000
Taxes receivable	180,000	4,000,000	3,900,000	280,000
	360,000	8,700,000	8,440,000	620,000
Liabilities:				
Due to school district	60,000	3,000,000	2,990,000	70,000
Due to town	210,000	1,000,000	760,000	450,000
Due to property owners	90,000	800,000	790,000	100,000
	$360,000	$4,800,000	$4,540,000	$620,000

Source: Adapted from GASB *Codification* Sec. 2200.922.

Statement 31 does not apply to investments of pension funds, which have similar requirements. Fair value, then, is to be reported for investments in all funds of state and local governmental units. Investments not covered by *Statement 31* are to follow other accounting principles currently in effect. For example, investments in bonds without determinable fair values would be reported at amortized cost. Also, if a government has sufficient investments in a company to justify the equity method of accounting (see an intermediate accounting text), then the equity method of accounting would be followed.

As a result, according to *Statement 31,* "all investment income, including changes in the fair value of investments, should be recognized as revenue in the operating statement (or other statement of activities). When identified separately as an element of investment income, the change in the fair value of investments should be captioned *net increase (decrease) in the fair value of investments.*" GASB does not permit separate display of the realized and unrealized components of the change in fair value, with the exception of external investment pools. However, GASB does permit note disclosure of the amount of realized gains. Other major disclosures include (1) methods and assumptions used to determine fair value, if other than quoted market prices and (2) the policy for determining which investments would be accounted for at amortized cost.

The GASB recently issued two additional standards dealing with the reporting of investments. GASB *Statement 52*[1] requires that endowments with investments in real estate report those assets at fair value rather than historical cost. Any resulting changes in fair value (e.g., gains or losses) are to be reported as investment income. The standard applies to land and other real estate held in endowments for investment purposes, including investments held in permanent funds. The standard ensures similar accounting treatment for real estate investments between endowments and other investment activities (e.g., pensions or external investment pools).

GASB *Statement 53*[2] establishes reporting requirements for governments entering into derivative instruments. Derivative instruments are financial contracts the prices of which are derived from the price of an underlying asset or obligation. For example, a government may enter into a derivative contract to protect against increases in natural gas costs or interest rates. Derivatives include swaps, options, forward contracts, and futures contracts. The key provision of *Statement 53* is that derivative instruments are to be reported in the Statement of Net Assets at fair value. However, the reporting of the change in value (i.e., gains or losses) depends on the type of derivative.

• **Hedging derivatives** Governments can enter derivative contracts to mitigate the risk of economic loss arising from changes in the underlying asset or obligation. This activity is known as *hedging.* For example, a government purchasing equipment from a Japanese manufacturer enters a forward (currency) exchange contract to protect against an unfavorable change in exchange rates. If the derivative is effective in reducing a government's exposure to identifiable risks, then the changes in the value of that derivative are deferred. This means the changes in value are reported in the Statement of Net Assets, not the activity statement. The deferred gains or losses typically continue to be reported as assets or liabilities until the hedged transaction occurs (e.g., when payment is made for the equipment).

---

[1] GASB *Statement 52: Land and Other Real Estate Held as Investments by Endowments* is effective for fiscal years ending in June 2009 and later.

[2] GASB *Statement 53: Accounting and Financial Reporting for Derivative Instruments* is effective for fiscal years ending in June 2010 and later.

• **Investment derivatives** Alternatively, governments can enter derivative contracts for the purpose of earning a return. Changes in the value of derivatives classified as investment purpose are reflected as investment gains or losses in the period that the value changes.

Much of *Statement 53* describes various tests to determine a hedge's effectiveness. These are beyond the scope of this text. However, derivative instruments that are deemed to be ineffective hedges are classified as investment purpose and the gains and losses are recognized in each period's activity statement. The provisions of *Statement 53* apply to government financial statements prepared using the accrual basis of accounting, including government-wide statements, proprietary funds, and fiduciary funds. In the case of governmental funds engaged in derivative activities, the provisions of *Statement 53* apply only to reporting at the government-wide level, not the fund-basis statements.

Illustrative Case—Private-Purpose Trust Funds

In the example that follows, we examine the accounting for investments (specifically, GASB *Statement 31*) in the context of a private-purpose trust fund. However, it should be noted that the concepts apply to accounting and reporting for all fund types.

Assume that, on January 2, 2012, a wealthy individual contributed $500,000 to the Village of Elizabeth and signed a trust agreement specifying that the principal amount be held intact and invested. The income is to be used to provide selected graduates from the Village's two high schools scholarships to the colleges of their choice. On January 2, the gift was recorded in the newly created Scholarship Fund:

	Debits	Credits
1. Cash	500,000	
Additions—Contributions		500,000

On the same day, Village administrators purchased AB Company bonds, as an investment, in the amount of $480,000 plus accrued interest. The bonds carry an annual rate of interest of 6 percent, payable semiannually on May 1 and November 1. As of that date, accrued interest amounted to $4,800 ($480,000 $\times$ .06 $\times$ $^2/_{12}$):

2. Investment in AB Bonds	480,000	
Accrued Interest Receivable	4,800	
Cash		484,800

On May 1, the Scholarship Fund received interest in the amount of $14,400, of which $4,800 was accrued at the time of purchase (item 2 above).

	Debits	Credits
3. Cash	14,400	
Accrued Interest Receivable............................		4,800
Additions—Investment Earnings—Interest.................		9,600

On May 31, $9,000 in scholarships were awarded:

	Debits	Credits
4. Deductions—Scholarship Awards	9,000	
Cash		9,000

On November 1, interest in the amount of $14,400 was received:

	Debits	Credits
5. Cash	14,400	
Additions—Investment Earnings—Interest.................		14,400

As of December 31, an interest accrual was made for November and December:

	Debits	Credits
6. Accrued Interest Receivable..............................	4,800	
Additions—Investment Earnings—Interest.................		4,800

GASB *Statement 31* requires that investments with determinable fair values be reported at fair value. It was determined that the AB Company bonds had a fair value of $482,000 on December 31, exclusive of accrued interest:

	Debits	Credits
7. Investment in AB Bonds	2,000	
Additions—Investment Earnings—Net Increase in Fair Value of Investments		2,000

Finally, a closing entry was prepared for the Scholarship Fund:

	Debits	Credits
8. Additions—Contributions	500,000	
Additions—Investment Earnings—Interest..................	28,800	
Additions—Investment Earnings—Net Increase in the Fair Value of Investments	2,000	
Deductions—Scholarship Awards		9,000
Net Assets Held in Trust for Scholarship Benefits..........		521,800

Financial statements for the Scholarship Private—Purpose Trust Fund are included in the Village of Elizabeth Statement of Fiduciary Net Assets (Illustration 7–4, page 205) and Statement of Changes in Fiduciary Net Assets (Illustration 7–5, page 206).

A Note about Escheat Property

In many cases, state governments obtain property in the absence of legal claimants or heirs. For example, if property is abandoned or if legal owners cannot be found, the property is turned over to state governments until the legal owners can be found. This property is known as **escheat property.** Some escheat property is ultimately claimed by rightful owners; other escheat property never is claimed and is eventually used by the government in some way.

GASB standards for the recording of escheat property are included in *Statement 37, Basic Financial Statements—and Management's Discussion and Analysis—for State and Local Governments: Omnibus. Statement 37,* paragraph 4, states in part, "Escheat property generally should be reported as an asset in the governmental or proprietary fund to which the property ultimately escheats." For example, a state might have legislation that requires the residual value of unclaimed property be dedicated to the state education fund. In this case, the resources might be reported in a special revenue fund dedicated to education. The value of unclaimed property expected to be paid out to claimants would either be reported as a liability in that fund or in an agency or private-purpose trust fund. If the second option is chosen, amounts ultimately payable to other governments would be reported in an agency fund (offset by liabilities), and amounts expected to be paid to individuals would be reported in a private-purpose trust fund (offset by Net Assets).

INVESTMENT TRUST FUNDS

GASB *Statement 31, Accounting and Financial Reporting for Certain Investments and for External Investment Pools,* provides requirements for investment pools. Internal investment pools, which account for investments of the reporting entity, are to be reported by the funds providing the resources. For example, if a reporting government has $900 million in investments, which are pooled for management purposes, and those investments came one-third each from the General, an enterprise, and a private-purpose trust fund, then each fund would report $300 million of investments in the Balance Sheet or Statement of Net Assets. Likewise, income earned on the investments would be reported directly in those funds.

On the other hand, many governments participate in external investment pools, where investments for several governments are maintained. For example, a county government might, through the County Treasurer, maintain an investment pool for all governments situated within the county. For governments that maintain the multigovernment investment pool, the *external portion* is to be maintained in an *investment trust fund,* a fiduciary fund. The external portion includes assets held for any government other than the County government and may include independent school districts, villages, and towns. The internal portion is to be reported in the County's funds, (i.e., the county's portion) as described in the preceding paragraph.

Investment trust funds are to be reported, as fiduciary funds, using the economic resources measurement focus and accrual basis of accounting. Investment trust funds are reported in the fiduciary funds Statement of Fiduciary Net Assets and Statement of Changes in Fiduciary Net Assets. Investments are to be reported at fair value, as described earlier in this chapter. In addition, a number of note disclosures are required for investment trust funds.

PUBLIC EMPLOYEE RETIREMENT SYSTEMS (PENSION TRUST FUNDS)

State and local governments commonly provide pension plans for their employees. Statewide plans often exist for teachers, state government employees, local government general employees, local government police and fire department employees, and legislators. In addition, many local governments maintain their own pension plans.

For local governments, a statewide multiemployer plan may be either an **agency plan** or a **cost-sharing plan.** An agency plan is one in which each contributing employer, such as a local government, has a separate account and each local government is required to keep its own contributions up to date. A cost-sharing plan is a statewide plan in which separate accounts are not kept for each employer. In this plan, unfunded actuarial liabilities are made up on a statewide basis; that is, the state applies extra charges to all participating governments to eliminate the actuarial deficiency. Employer disclosure requirements are more extensive for single-employer and agency plans than for cost-sharing plans.

A pension plan may be either *contributory* or *noncontributory,* depending on whether employees are required to contribute. A plan also may be defined benefit or defined contribution. A **defined benefit** plan is one in which the plan is required to pay out a certain level of benefit (for example, 2 percent times the average salary over the past four years times the number of years worked), regardless of the amount available in the plan. A **defined contribution plan** is required only to pay out the amount that has been accumulated for each employee. As a result, defined benefit plans may have unfunded actuarial liabilities, whereas defined contribution plans do not.

Pension plans for governments are often called **Public Employee Retirement Systems (PERS).** When a PERS is a part of the reporting entity of a government, whether state or local, a pension trust fund is created and included in the Comprehensive Annual Financial Report. The pension trust fund data will be included in the fiduciary fund statements—the Statement of Fiduciary Net Assets and Statement of Changes in Fiduciary Net Assets. The fiduciary fund type is actually called *pension and other employee benefit trust funds* and includes other postemployment plans and any other employment benefit plans, including any IRS 457 Deferred Compensation plans (see section page 209).

Whether or not the PERS is a part of the reporting entity, certain employer disclosures are required in the notes to the statements. Full treatment of accounting and reporting requirements for both governmental employers and PERS is beyond the scope of this book. This section introduces the topic and presents a general overview of current standards.

Accounting and Reporting for Defined Benefit Pension Plans

The material in this section applies to stand-alone pension plans (for example, statewide pension plans for teachers) and to pension trust funds that are found in Comprehensive Annual Financial Reports (CAFRs) of state or local governmental units (for example, a local government police retirement system). This material applies to single-employer plans, agent multiemployer plans, and cost-sharing multiemployer plans.

Financial reporting requirements include two statements and two schedules. The schedules are reported as **Required Supplementary Information** immediately after the notes to the financial statements:

1. Statement of Plan Net Assets. This statement provides information about the fair value of plan assets, liabilities, and the net assets held in trust for benefits. This statement does *not* provide information about the actuarial status of the plan. In the CAFR of a government with a single employer plan reported as a trust fund, this information would be included in the fiduciary funds Statement of Net Assets.
2. Statement of Changes in Plan Net Assets. This statement provides information about additions to and deductions from net assets. It would be included in the fiduciary funds Statement of Changes in Net Assets.
3. Schedule of Funding Progress. This schedule provides information about the actuarial status of the plan from an ongoing long-term perspective.
4. Schedule of Employer Contributions. This schedule provides historical trend information about the **annual required contributions (ARC)** and the actual contributions made by employers.

In addition, certain note disclosures are required. The statements, schedules, and notes will be illustrated through an example of financial reporting for the Village of Elizabeth Public Employees Retirement Fund, assuming the reporting is made only through a pension trust fund section of a CAFR.

Assume that the Public Employees Retirement Fund had the Statement of Plan Net Assets as of December 31, 2011, shown in Illustration 7–3. During the year ended December 31, 2012, the following events and transactions that affected the Village of Elizabeth's Public Employees Retirement Fund took place:

Accrued interest receivable as of January 1, 2012, was collected:

	Debits	Credits
1. Cash	50,000	
Accrued Interest Receivable.		50,000

ILLUSTRATION 7–3   Statement of Plan Net Assets

VILLAGE OF ELIZABETH
Public Employees Retirement Fund
Statement of Plan Net Assets
December 31, 2011

Assets	
Cash	$ 30,500
Accrued Interest Receivable	50,000
Investments, at Fair Value:	
Bonds	3,200,000
Common Stocks	2,100,000
Commercial Paper and Repurchase Agreements	500,000
Total Assets	5,880,500
Liabilities	
Accounts Payable and Accrued Expenses	30,000
Net Assets Held in Trust for Pension Benefits	$5,850,500

Member contributions in the amount of $210,000 and employer contributions in the amount of $210,000 were received in cash:

	Debits	Credits
2. Cash	420,000	
Additions—Contributions—Plan Members		210,000
Additions—Contributions—Employer		210,000

Annuity benefits in the amount of $110,000 and disability benefits in the amount of $15,000 were recorded as liabilities:

3. Deductions—Annuity Benefits	110,000	
Deductions—Disability Benefits	15,000	
Accounts Payable and Accrued Expenses		125,000

Accounts payable and accrued expenses paid in cash amounted to $140,000:

4. Accounts Payable and Accrued Expenses	140,000	
Cash		140,000

Terminated employees whose benefits were not vested were refunded $50,000 in cash:

	Debits	Credits
5. Deductions—Refunds to Terminated Employees	50,000	
Cash		50,000

Investment income received in cash amounted to $410,000, of which $210,000 was dividends and $200,000 was interest; additionally, $70,000 interest income was accrued at year-end:

6. Cash	410,000	
Accrued Interest Receivable.	70,000	
Additions—Investment Earnings—Interest		270,000
Additions—Investment Earnings—Dividends		210,000

Commercial paper and repurchase agreements carried at a cost of $200,000 matured, and cash in that amount was received:

7. Cash	200,000	
Commercial Paper and Repurchase Agreements		200,000

Common stock carried at a fair value of $1,250,000 was sold for $1,300,000. New investments included $500,000 in common stock and $1,600,000 bonds.

8a. Cash	1,300,000	
Investments in Common Stock.		1,250,000
Additions—Investment Earnings—Net Increase in Fair Value of Investments		50,000
8b. Investments in Bonds	1,600,000	
Investments in Common Stock.	500,000	
Cash		2,100,000

Administrative expenses for the year totaled $80,000, all paid in cash:

9. Deductions—Administrative Expenses	80,000	
Cash		80,000

During the year, the fair value of common stock increased $40,000; the fair value of bonds decreased $30,000:

	Debits	Credits
10. Investments in Common Stock.	40,000	
Investments in Bonds		30,000
Additions—Investment Earnings—Net Increase in Fair Value of Investments		10,000

Nominal accounts for the year were closed:

	Debits	Credits
11. Additions—Contributions—Plan Members	210,000	
Additions—Contributions—Employer.	210,000	
Additions—Investment Earnings—Interest	270,000	
Additions—Investment Earnings—Dividends	210,000	
Additions—Investment Earnings—Net Increase in Fair Value of Investments	60,000	
Deductions—Annuity Benefits		110,000
Deductions—Disability Benefits		15,000
Deductions—Refunds to Terminated Employees		50,000
Deductions—Administrative Expenses		80,000
Net Assets Held in Trust for Pension Benefits.		705,000

Illustration 7–4 reflects the Statement of Fiduciary Net Assets for the fiduciary funds, including the private-purpose trust fund and the Public Employees Retirement Fund as of December 31, 2012.

Illustration 7–5 (page 206) presents the Statement of Changes in Net Assets for the fiduciary funds, including the private-purpose trust fund and the Public Employee Retirement System for the Year Ended December 31, 2012. It should be noted that the GASB standards do not allow the realized and unrealized gains on investments to be reported separately.

A Schedule of Funding Progress is required for all defined benefit pension plans. It presents, for at least the past six fiscal years, the actuarial valuation date, the actuarial value of plan assets, the actuarial liability, the total unfunded actuarial liability, the funded ratio, the annual covered payroll, and the ratio of the unfunded actuarial liability to the annual covered payroll. Illustration 7–6 (page 207) reflects a Schedule of Funding Progress using assumed figures for the Village of Elizabeth.

A Schedule of Employer Contributions is also required to present six-year information. For each of the past six fiscal years, the Schedule should present the annual required employer contribution and the percentage contributed. Illustration 7–7 (page 207) reflects the information for the Village of Elizabeth.

ILLUSTRATION 7–4   Statement of Fiduciary Net Assets

	Public Employee Retirement Fund	Private-Purpose Trust
VILLAGE OF ELIZABETH **Statement of Fiduciary Net Assets** **Fiduciary Funds** **December 31, 2012**		
Assets		
Cash	$ 40,500	$ 35,000
Accrued interest receivable	70,000	4,800
Investments, at fair value:		
Bonds	4,770,000	482,000
Common stocks	1,390,000	
Commercial paper and repurchase agreements	300,000	
Total investments	6,460,000	482,000
Total assets	6,570,500	521,800
Liabilities		
Accounts payable and accrued expenses	15,000	–0–
Net Assets		
Held in trust for pension benefits and other purposes	$6,555,500	$521,800

A Note about Other Postemployment Benefits

Many governments offer benefits to their retired employees (e.g., life insurance). The most significant of these is health care benefits. GASB *Statement 43, Financial Reporting for Postemployment Benefit Plans Other Than Pension Plans* is very similar to *Statement 25,* which establishes reporting guidelines for pension plans. As with pensions, governments are required to present two financial statements related to other postemployment benefits (OPEB):

1. The Statement of Plan Net Assets reports the fair value of assets (and liabilities) available for payment of retiree benefits. Although prudent financial management would advocate early funding of these benefits, most governments have operated on a pay-as-you-go basis and the assets appearing in this statement are frequently small relative to the benefits promised.
2. The Statement of Changes in Plan Net Assets reports additions from the employer-government, members (employees and retirees), and investment income and deductions for benefits payable and administrative expenses.

These statements would be shown as additional columns in Illustrations 7–4 and 7–5. *Statement 43* also requires that a schedule of funding progress and a schedule of employer contributions be included as Required Supplementary Information.

ILLUSTRATION 7–5   Statement of Changes in Fiduciary Net Assets

VILLAGE OF ELIZABETH Statement of Changes in Fiduciary Net Assets Fiduciary Funds For the Year Ended December 31, 2012		
	Public Employee Retirement Fund	Private-Purpose Trust
Additions		
Contributions:		
Employer	$ 210,000	
Plan members	210,000	
Individuals		$500,000
Total contributions	420,000	500,000
Investment earnings:		
Interest	270,000	28,800
Dividends	210,000	
Net increase in fair value of investments	60,000	2,000
Total investment earnings	540,000	30,800
Total additions	960,000	530,800
Deductions		
Annuity benefits	110,000	
Refunds to terminated employees	50,000	
Administrative expenses	80,000	
Disability benefits	15,000	
Scholarship awards		9,000
Total deductions	255,000	9,000
Change in net assets	705,000	521,800
Net assets—beginning of the year	5,850,500	–0–
Net assets—end of the year	$6,555,500	$521,800

1. The Schedule of Funding Progress is similar to Illustration 7–6 and shows the funded status of the plan and the government's progress in accumulating assets to pay retiree benefits as they come due.
2. The Schedule of Employer Contributions is similar to Illustration 7–7 and shows the actuarially determined contributions required to adequately fund the plan and what percentage of these required contributions have actually been made by the government.

Summary of Employer Reporting

Pension or other employee benefit trust funds exist when a government acts as trustee for its retirement plans (pension or OPEB). What we have discussed to this point is termed "reporting for the plan" and is guided by GASB *Statement 25* for pension plans and *Statement 43* for OPEB plans. The other form of reporting is

ILLUSTRATION 7–6 Schedule of Funding Progress

VILLAGE OF ELIZABETH Public Employee Retirement Fund Schedule of Funding Progress Six Years Ending November 30, 2012 ($ amounts in thousands)						
Actuarial Valuation Date	Actuarial Value of Assets	Actuarial Accrued Liability— Entry Age	Unfunded Accrued Liability	Funded Ratio	Covered Payroll	Unfunded Accrued Liability as a Percentage of Covered Payroll
11/30/07	4,500	7,200	2,700	62.5%	2,000	135.0%
11/30/08	4,700	7,500	2,800	62.7	2,150	130.2
11/30/09	4,900	7,900	3,000	62.0	2,300	130.4
11/30/10	5,400	8,200	2,800	65.9	2,500	112.0
11/30/11	5,800	8,400	2,600	69.0	2,800	92.9
11/30/12	6,500	8,900	2,400	73.0	3,000	80.0

ILLUSTRATION 7–7 Schedule of Employer Contributions

VILLAGE OF ELIZABETH Public Employee Retirement Fund Schedule of Employer Contributions Six Years Ended December 31, 2012		
Year Ended December 31	Annual Required Contribution	Percentage Contributed
2007	$160,000	100%
2008	168,000	100
2009	173,000	100
2010	182,000	100
2011	196,000	100
2012	210,000	100

termed "employer reporting" and is guided by GASB *Statements 27* and *50* for pension plans and *Statements 45* for OPEB plans. Among other things, employer reporting determines the amount and timing of the recognition of pension expenditure for governmental funds or pension expense for proprietary funds.

Regardless of whether an employer government is trustee for a given pension plan, certain accounting, financial reporting, note disclosure, and required supplementary schedules are required. The nature and extent of GASB requirements for employer reporting depend upon whether plans are single employer, agent multiple-employer, cost-sharing multiple-employer, or defined contribution.

Governments that contribute to single employer and agent multiple-employer plans compute annual pension cost as the **annual required contributions (ARC),** which are actuarially determined as the employer's **normal cost** plus a provision for amortizing the **unfunded actuarial liability.** If the government has a **net pension obligation (NPO)** (the cumulative difference between the employers' required and actual contributions), the annual pension cost will include the ARC, interest on the NPO, and an adjustment to the ARC. Any one of several generally accepted actuarial methods can be used to determine the ARC as long as it meets certain parameters defined by the GASB. Actual contributions by governmental funds are recorded as expenditures using modified accrual accounting. Unfunded amounts (the NPO) are recorded in the government-wide statements. Contributions by proprietary funds are recorded as expenses on the accrual basis in the proprietary funds, and the NPO is recorded as a fund liability.

Governments that contribute to cost-sharing multiple-employer plans should record expenditures (for governmental funds) and expenses (for proprietary funds) equal to the annual contractually required contributions to the plans. By definition, individual amounts cannot be computed for each employer, for cost-sharing plans.

Note disclosures for all defined benefit plans include plan descriptions and funding policies. In addition, note disclosures for single-employer and agent multiple-employer plans include the annual pension cost compared with the actual contributions made. Three-year schedules list the annual pension cost, the percentage of annual pension cost contributed, and the NPO at the end of the year. Contributors to single-employer and agent multiple-employer plans are also required to provide supplementary schedules listing additional three-year information. Keep in mind that these disclosures are required of all employers, even when they are not trustees of the pension plans.

Defined contribution plans are simple, because the government is only promising to contribute a set amount to the employee's retirement savings. Pension contributions to defined contribution plans should be measured as an expenditure or expense equal to the amount required in accordance with the terms of the plan. Assets and liabilities arise only if the required and actual contributions differ.

The purpose of GASB *Statement 45, Accounting and Financial Reporting by Employers for Postemployment Benefits Other Than Pensions* is to recognize OPEB costs over the period of time that employees earn the benefits—that is, over the employees' years of service to the government. As with pensions, governments are required to compute an actuarially determined ARC. The ARC is an estimate of the amount of contribution needed to cover the normal cost of the plan and amortize the unfunded liability. The cumulative difference between the amount funded and the ARC is termed the **OPEB obligation.**

Actual contributions (amounts that were or will soon be provided by available resources) by governmental funds are recorded as expenditures using modified accrual accounting. Unfunded amounts (the OPEB obligation) are reported in the government-wide statements, but not the fund-basis statements. Proprietary funds record an expense equivalent to the required contribution and the OPEB obligation is reported as a fund liability.

A Note about IRS 457 Deferred Compensation Plans

Many governments have established **IRS 457 Deferred Compensation Plans** for their employees. If legal requirements are met, these represent tax-deferred compensation plans in which employees are not required to pay taxes on the amounts withheld until distributed to them after retirement. If the plans are administered by an entity outside a government, which is the most common case, then no accounting is required by the government, other than to account for funds withheld and distributed. If a government administers the plan, the resources are held in trust and accounted for as a pension (and other employee benefit) trust fund.

A FINAL COMMENT ON FUND ACCOUNTING AND REPORTING

Chapters 4 to 7 presented accounting and fund-basis financial reporting requirements for governmental, proprietary, and fiduciary fund types. These are summarized for the Village of Elizabeth example in Illustration. 7–8. Governmental fund reports for the General and major governmental funds include the Balance Sheet and

ILLUSTRATION 7–8 Summary of Fund-Basis Reporting for Village of Elizabeth

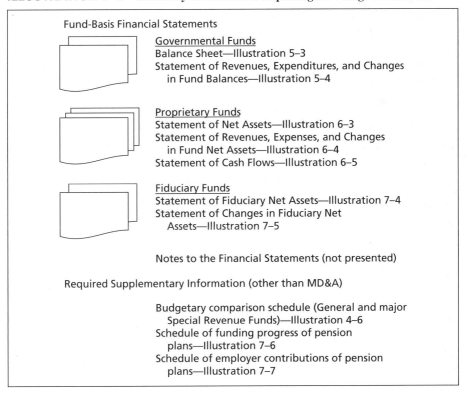

Fund-Basis Financial Statements

Governmental Funds
Balance Sheet—Illustration 5–3
Statement of Revenues, Expenditures, and Changes
  in Fund Balances—Illustration 5–4

Proprietary Funds
Statement of Net Assets—Illustration 6–3
Statement of Revenues, Expenses, and Changes
  in Fund Net Assets—Illustration 6–4
Statement of Cash Flows—Illustration 6–5

Fiduciary Funds
Statement of Fiduciary Net Assets—Illustration 7–4
Statement of Changes in Fiduciary Net
  Assets—Illustration 7–5

Notes to the Financial Statements (not presented)

Required Supplementary Information (other than MD&A)

Budgetary comparison schedule (General and major
  Special Revenue Funds)—Illustration 4–6
Schedule of funding progress of pension
  plans—Illustration 7–6
Schedule of employer contributions of pension
  plans—Illustration 7–7

the Statement of Revenues, Expenditures, and Changes in Fund Balances. Finally, a Budgetary Comparison Schedule is required as an RSI schedule and is presented in Illustration 4–6. Proprietary fund reports for major enterprise funds and the internal service fund type include the Statement of Net Assets; the Statement of Revenues, Expenses, and Changes in Fund Net Assets; and the Statement of Cash Flows.

Fiduciary fund reporting, by fund type, includes the Statement of Fiduciary Net Assets and the Statement of Changes in Fiduciary Net Assets. In addition, GAAP require two RSI schedules for governments with defined benefit pension and other employee benefit trust plans: a Schedule of Funding Progress and a Schedule of Employer Contributions.

As indicated in Chapter 2, GAAP require the presentation of government-wide financial statements: a Statement of Net Assets and a Statement of Activities. These are *consolidated* statements, presented using the economic resources measurement focus and accrual basis of accounting. Fiduciary funds are not included in the government-wide statements because governments merely have custody, not ownership, of fiduciary resources. The process of converting the fund-basis statements to government-wide statements is described in Chapter 8. The fund-basis statements prepared in Chapters 5 and 6 serve as inputs to the government-wide statements. Our approach will be similar to the approach most commonly taken in practice. That is, governments record events on a day-to-day basis in a manner that leads directly to preparation of the fund-basis statements. At year-end, worksheet adjustments are made to those balances to comply with the requirements for government-wide statements.

Now that you have finished reading Chapter 7, complete the multiple choice questions provided on the text's Web site (www.mhhe.com/copley10e) to test your comprehension of the chapter.

Questions and Exercises

7–1. Using the annual report obtained for Exercise 1–1, answer the following questions:

 a. Look at the Statement of Fiduciary Net Assets. Which fund types are included? Is the Statement prepared in a format in which Assets − Liabilities = Net Assets? Are net assets shown as being held in trust for employee benefits and other purposes? Look at the Statement of Changes in Fiduciary Net Assets. Has the government refrained from including agency funds in that statement? Are increases and decreases shown as additions and deductions, rather than revenues and expenses? What are the main additions? What are the main deductions?

 b. Are agency funds included in the Statement of Fiduciary Net Assets? If so, look to the notes or combining schedules and list the individual agency funds. Has the government limited itself to agency funds that are held for individuals, organizations, or other governments—not for other government funds? Do agency funds report only assets and liabilities, not net assets? Does the government report a Statement or Schedule of Changes in Assets and Liabilities for agency funds?

c. Does the government have private-purpose funds? If so, list them. Describe the purposes for which they exist. Can you tell if any of those funds are endowments, and have resources permanently restricted? How much income was generated by each of the private-purpose funds, and how much was released for use? Does the government report escheat property as private-purpose funds? If so, indicate the nature of the process by which property is released and for what purposes.

d. Does the government report investment trust funds? If so, describe the nature of the external investment pool. Which other governments are included? Has your government refrained from including its own investments in the investment trust funds?

e. List the pension funds included in the financial statements. From the notes, list the other pension plans that are available to employees of your governmental unit. Are those plans agent plans or cost-sharing plans? Defined contribution or defined benefit? Are required disclosures made in the notes for all pension plans, whether or not the plans are included as trust funds? Are the two RSI schedules included in your report (when defined benefit plans are reported)? Look at the actuarial status of the plans and comment about the potential impact of pensions on the financial condition of the government.

f. Look at the note disclosures regarding investments. Are investments reported at fair value? Do the notes disclose the realized gains or losses on investments? Do the notes categorize investments based on risk? When the government creates internal investment pools for management purposes, does the government report the individual investments and income from those investments in the funds that provided the resources?

Agency Funds

7–2. Residents of a neighborhood financed the installation of sidewalks through a note payable. The note was to be repaid through a special assessment tax on their properties. When is it appropriate to account for special assessment activities in an agency fund? In which fund should the special assessment tax receipts be reported if they do not meet the criteria for an agency fund?

7–3. Benton County maintains a tax agency fund for use by the County Treasurer to record receivables, collections, and disbursements of all property tax collections to all other units of government in the county. For FY 2011–2012, the following taxes were assessed:

Benton County General Fund	$10,500,000
Town of Thomas	7,400,000
Town of Hart	3,200,000
Benton County School District	23,900,000
Various Special Districts	6,300,000
Total	$51,300,000

During the first six months of the fiscal year, the following transactions took place:

1. The tax levy became effective. All units of government provided for an estimated 3 percent in uncollectible taxes.
2. Cash collections of the first installment of taxes amounted to $5,080,000 for the County General Fund and $19,544,000 for the other governments.
3. It was determined that the cash collections pertained to the funds and governmental units in the following amounts. Record the liability to the county General Fund and to the other governmental units, assuming that the county General Fund charges other governments 1½ percent of all tax collected because the county General Fund incurs all costs of billing, recording, and collecting taxes.

Benton County General Fund	$ 5,080,000
Town of Thomas	4,070,000
Town of Hart	1,018,000
Benton County School District	11,472,000
Various Special Districts	2,984,000
Total	$24,624,000

4. Cash was paid to the various governmental units.
   Required:
   Record the transactions on the books of the:
   a. Benton County Tax Agency Fund.
   b. Benton County General Fund.
   c. Town of Thomas.

Private-purpose Trust Funds

7–4. A concerned citizen provides resources and establishes a trust with the local government. What factors should be considered in determining which fund to report the trust activities?

7–5. Presented below is the preclosing trial balance for the Scholarship Fund, a private-purpose trust fund, of the Algonquin School District.

Trial Balance—December 31, 2012	Debits	Credits
Accounts Payable		$ 8,000
Accrued Interest Receivable	$ 2,000	
Administrative Expense	6,000	
Cash	42,000	
Decrease in Fair Value of Investments	10,000	
Distributions—Scholarships	35,000	
Interest Income		53,600
Investment in Bonds	1,240,000	
Net Assets Held in Trust		1,273,400
	$1,335,000	$1,335,000

Prepare the year-end closing entries and a Statement of Changes in Fiduciary Net Assets for the year ended December 31, 2012.

7–6. On July 1, 2011, the City of Belvedere accepted a gift of cash in the amount of $3,000,000 from a number of individuals and foundations and signed an agreement to establish a private-purpose trust. The $3,000,000 and any additional gifts are to be invested and retained as principal. Income from the trust is to be distributed to community nonprofit groups as directed by a Board consisting of city officials and other community leaders. The agreement provides that any increases in the market value of the principal investments are to be held in trust; if the investments fall below the gift amounts, then earnings are to be withheld until the principal amount is reestablished.

a. The following events and transactions occurred during the fiscal year ended June 30, 2012. Record them in the Belvedere Community Trust Fund.

(1) On July 1, the original gift of cash was received.

(2) On July 1, $2,000,000 in XYZ Company bonds were purchased at par plus accrued interest. The bonds pay an annual rate of 6 percent interest semiannually on April 1 and October 1.

(3) On July 2, $950,000 in ABC Company common stock was purchased. ABC normally declares and pays dividends semiannually, on January 31 and July 31.

(4) On October 1, the first semiannual interest payment was received from XYZ Company. Note that part of this is for accrued interest due at the time of purchase; the remaining part is an addition that may be used for distribution.

(5) On January 31, a cash dividend was received from ABC Company in the amount of $38,000.

(6) On March 1, the ABC stock was sold for $960,000. On the same day, DEF Company stock was purchased for $965,000.

(7) On April 1, the second semiannual interest payment was received from XYZ Company.

(8) During the month of June, distributions were approved by the Board and paid in cash in the amount of $104,000.

(9) Administrative expenses were recorded and paid in the amount of $7,500.

(10) An accrual for interest on the XYZ bonds was made as of June 30, 2012.

(11) As of June 30, 2012, the fair value of the XYZ bonds, exclusive of accrued interest, was determined to be $2,002,000. The fair value of the DEF stock was determined to be $960,000.

(12) Closing entries were prepared.

b. Prepare, in good form, (1) a Statement of Changes in Fiduciary Net Assets for the Belvedere Community Trust Fund and (2) a Statement of Fiduciary Net Assets.

7–7. On July 1, 2011, the Morgan County School District received a $30,000 gift from a local civic organization with the stipulation that, on June 30 of each year, $2,000 plus any interest earnings on the unspent principal be awarded as a college scholarship to the high school graduate with the highest academic average. A private-purpose trust fund, the Civic Scholarship Fund, was created.

a. Record the following transactions on the books of the Civic Scholarship Fund:

(1) On July 1, 2011, the gift was received and immediately invested.

(2) On June 30, 2012, $3,000 of the principal was converted into cash. In addition, $1,800 of interest was received.

(3) On June 30, the $4,800 was awarded to Ann Korner, who had maintained a 4.0 grade point average throughout each of her four years.

(4) The nominal accounts were closed.

b. Prepare a Statement of Changes in Fiduciary Net Assets for the Civic Scholarship Fund for the Year Ended June 30, 2012.

Investment Trust Funds

7–8. Describe GASB requirements for accounting for Investment Trust Funds. Include (a) a discussion of when the use of investment trust funds is appropriate; (b) the investments to be included and excluded; (c) the basis at which investments are to be reported; (d) reporting of realized and unrealized gains and losses on investments; and (e) financial reporting (i.e., financial statements).

7–9. Baird County maintains an investment trust fund for the School District and the Town of Bairdville (separate governments). Presented below is the preclosing trial balance for the investment trust fund, a private-purpose trust fund.

Trial Balance—December 31, 2012	Debits	Credits
Accrued Interest Receivable	$ 5,000	
Cash	14,000	
Deposits—School District		$ 242,000
Deposits—Town of Bairdville		121,000
Decrease in Fair Value of Investments (bonds)	12,000	
Interest Income		33,000
Investments—Corporate Bonds	1,220,000	
Investments—U.S. Treasury Securities	645,000	
Net assets held in trust—School District (Jan. 1)		1,000,000
Net assets held in trust—Town of Bairdville (Jan. 1)		500,000
	$1,896,000	$1,896,000

Prepare the year-end closing entries and a Statement of Changes in Fiduciary Net Assets for the year ended December 31, 2012. Investment earnings are distributed among the School District and Town in proportion to the amounts contributed (two-thirds to the School District and one-third to the Town).

Pension Trust Funds

7–10. What are the required financial statements for a pension trust fund? What are the required supplementary information schedules?

7–11. With regard to current GASB standards for pension reporting do the following:

    a. Distinguish between (1) defined contribution plans and (2) defined benefit plans.

    b. Distinguish between (1) agent and (2) cost-sharing multiemployer plans.

    c. Define the following terms: (1) annual required contribution and (2) net pension obligation.

    d. Distinguish between expenditure/expense reporting for (1) agent multi-employer plans and (2) cost-sharing multiemployer plans.

    e. Distinguish between reporting for employers for (1) general government employees and for (2) enterprise fund employees.

7–12. Assume that a local government is the trustee for the pension assets for its police and fire department employees and participates in a statewide plan for all of its other employees. Individual accounts are maintained for all local governments in the statewide plan. Discuss the financial reporting requirements related to pensions for (*a*) police and fire department employees and (*b*) all other employees.

7–13. The City of Sweetwater maintains an Employees' Retirement Fund, a single-employer, defined benefit plan that provides annuity and disability benefits. The fund is financed by actuarially determined contributions from the city's General Fund and by contributions from employees. Administration of the retirement fund is handled by General Fund employees, and the retirement fund does not bear any administrative expenses. The Statement of Net Assets for the Employees' Retirement Fund as of July 1, 2011, is shown here:

CITY OF SWEETWATER
Employees' Retirement Fund
Statement of Net Assets
As of July 1, 2011

Assets

Cash	$ 50,000
Accrued Interest Receivable	135,000
Investments, at Fair Value:	
Bonds	4,500,000
Common Stocks	1,300,000
Total Assets	5,985,000

Liabilities

Accounts Payable and Accrued Expenses	350,000
Net Assets Held in Trust for Pension for Benefits	$5,635,000

During the year ended June 30, 2012, the following transactions occurred:

1. The interest receivable on investments was collected in cash.
2. Member contributions in the amount of $400,000 were received in cash. The city's General Fund also contributed $600,000 in cash.
3. Annuity benefits of $700,000 and disability benefits of $150,000 were recorded as liabilities.
4. Accounts payable and accrued expenses in the amount of $900,000 were paid in cash.
5. Interest income of $240,000 and dividends in the amount of $40,000 were received in cash. In addition, bond interest income of $140,000 was accrued at year-end.
6. Refunds of $130,000 were made in cash to terminated, nonvested participants.
7. Common stocks, carried at a fair value of $500,000, were sold for $480,000. That $480,000, plus an additional $300,000, was invested in stocks.
8. At year-end, it was determined that the fair value of stocks held by the pension plan had decreased by $50,000; the fair value of bonds had increased by $30,000.
9. Nominal accounts for the year were closed.

   a. Record the transactions on the books of the Employees' Retirement Fund.

   b. Prepare a Statement of Changes in Net Assets for the Employees' Retirement Fund for the Year Ended June 30, 2012.

    c. Prepare a Statement of Net Assets for the Employees' Retirement Fund as of June 30, 2012.

Other Postemployment Benefits

7–14. Presented below is the pre-closing trial balance for the Retiree Health Benefit Plan of the Alger County School District.

Trial Balance—December 31, 2012	Debits	Credits
Accrued Interest Receivable	$ 10,200	
Cash	15,500	
Accounts Payable		$ 1,500
Contributions—Employee		328,000
Contributions—Employer		659,000
Deductions: Benefit Payments	272,000	
Deductions: Administrative Expense	2,300	
Increase in Fair Value of Investments		375,000
Investment Income—Dividends		55,000
Investment Income—Interest Income		127,300
Investments—Corporate Bonds	1,227,000	
Investments—Corporate Stocks	2,523,000	
Investments—U.S. Treasury Securities	650,000	
Net assets held in trust—for other post employment benefits		3,454,200
Receivables—Employee	100,000	
Receivables—Employer	200,000	
	$5,000,000	$5,000,000

Prepare (1) the year-end closing entries, (2) a Statement of Changes in Plan Net Assets, and (3) a Statement of Plan Net Assets for the year ended December 31, 2012.

Excel-Based Problems

7–15. In December 2011, the Hamilton County Board of Commissioners established the Hamilton County OPEB Trust Fund. Retired employees of Hamilton County can participate in post-employment benefits through the Trust. The Trust is a single-employer defined benefit plan. The benefits provided are health insurance and life insurance.

In December 2011, the County made a one-time contribution to the fund of $23,890,000. No other events took place in 2011.

Fiscal Year 2012 transactions were as follows:

1. The County paid its actuarially determined annual contribution of $18,335,000.

2. Member (employee) contributions totaled $4,061,000. Of this, $4,020,000 was collected by December 31st and the remainder will be collected in January 2013.

3. Cash totaling $31,000,000 was invested in U.S. government securities.

4. Interest totaling $1,438,000 was earned on these securities. Of this amount, $1,431,000 was collected during the year.

5. Because the County offers a drug plan to retired employees, the federal government Medicare program provides a subsidy to the County. The County received $498,000 from this subsidy.

6. Benefit claims from employees totaled $10,903,000 for the year. By year-end, $9,575,000 had been paid to employees.

7. Administrative expenses totaled $552,000 (all paid in the current year).

Hamilton County operates the Domestic Relations Agency Fund. The fund works with the State Government's Domestic Relations Court the purpose of which is to establish child support, enforce child support obligations, and locate absent parents to assure noncustodial parents contribute toward the support of their children. The Domestic Relations Agency Fund is used to account for receipts and disbursements of support payments collected by the County, which are ultimately owed to the State Government's Domestic Relations Court. The County ended the year 2011 with $40,000 of cash.

Fiscal Year 2012 transactions were as follows:

8. The County collected $475,000 from noncustodial parents.

9. The County remitted $477,500 to the State Government's Domestic Relations Court.

Required:

Use the Excel template provided to complete the following requirements; a separate tab is provided in Excel for each of these steps.

a. Prepare journal entries to record the information described in items 1 to 9.

b. Post these entries to T-accounts.

c. Prepare closing journal entries. Post to the T-account provided.

d. Prepare a Statement of Changes in Fiduciary Net Assets for the year ending 2012.

e. Prepare a Statement of Fiduciary Net Assets as of December 31, 2012.

7–16. A successful businessman in the community has contacted the Moose County Board of Commissioners about donating income producing securities to the County to support a particular activity. Under the agreement, the County would be required to maintain the principal amount of the gift but could use the resulting earnings. The following events occurred in 2012:

1. Securities, which had an original cost of $4,250,000 were donated to the County on January 1. The fair value of the securities at that date was $5,790,000, including:

   • Corporate equities of $2,700,000.

- Corporate bonds of $3,000,000.
- Accrued interest receivable on the bonds of $90,000.

2. During the year the fund received $240,000 in interest payments on the bonds. At the end of the year, accrued interest on the bonds totaled $85,000.

3. During the year the fund received dividends on the corporate equities of $108,000.

4. During the year the fund paid $297,000 supporting activities identified in the trust agreement and had outstanding bills to be paid of $2,500.

5. The fair value of the securities at December 31 was:

- Corporate equities of $2,550,000.
- Corporate bonds of $3,190,000.

Required:

You are to prepare financial statements for the fund. In Part 1 the activities supported by the fund benefit the citizenry in general. In Part 2, the activities benefit only selected individuals.

Part 1 Assume it is appropriate to report the gift and related transactions in a Permanent Fund following modified accrual basis statements. Using the Excel template provided:

a. Prepare journal entries recording the events above.

b. Post the journal entries to T-accounts.

c. Prepare closing entries.

d. Prepare a Statement of Revenues, Expenditures, and Changes in Fund Balance and a Balance Sheet (assume spendable net resources are to be classified as *restricted for other purposes*).

Part 2 Assume it is appropriate to report the gift and related transactions in a Private Purpose Trust Fund following the accrual basis. Using the Excel template provided:

a. Prepare journal entries recording the events above.

b. Post the journal entries to T-accounts.

c. Prepare closing entries.

d. Prepare a Statement of Changes in Fiduciary Net Assets and a Statement of Fiduciary Net Assets.

The Excel template contains separate tabs for (1) permanent fund journal entries and T-accounts, (2) private-purpose trust fund journal entries and T-accounts, (3) closing entries, (4) permanent fund financial statements, and (5) private-purpose trust fund financial statements. Both the T-accounts and financial statements may contain accounts you will not need.

Continuous Problem

Available on the text's Web site (www.mhhe.com/copley10e).

Chapter Eight

Government-wide Statements, Fixed Assets, Long-Term Debt

Christmas is the time when kids tell Santa what they want and adults pay for it. Deficits are when adults tell government what they want and their kids pay for it. (Richard Lamm, Governor of Colorado, 1975–1987)

Deficits mean future tax increases, pure and simple. Deficit spending should be viewed as a tax on future generations, and politicians who create deficits should be exposed as tax hikers. (Ron Paul, M.D., U.S. House of Representatives from Texas's 14th district)

Learning Objectives

- Perform the steps necessary to prepare government-wide financial statements, including:
- Prepare worksheet entries to convert the governmental fund records to the economic resources measurement focus and the accrual basis of accounting.
- Prepare worksheet entries to include internal service funds with governmental activities.
- Prepare required schedules reconciling the government-wide and fund-basis financial statements.
- Record events and transactions related to general fixed assets and general long-term debt and describe required schedules related to long-term debt.

The focus of Chapters 3 through 7 has been the preparation of fund-basis financial statements. The focus of this chapter is the preparation of the government-wide statements (i.e., Statement of Net Assets and Statement of Activities) and required schedules that reconcile the government-wide and fund-basis financial statements. Our approach is consistent with the practice of most governments. That is, we assume the initial recording of transactions is done at the fund level, using the measurement focus and basis of accounting used for each fund's statements (current financial resources focus and modified accrual basis for governmental funds and economic resources focus and accrual basis for all others). At the end of the reporting period, governments adjust governmental fund records to the economic resources focus and accrual basis required in the government-wide statements. This is accomplished through worksheet entries. Worksheet entries differ from other journal entries, in that they are not posted to the general ledger—in effect, they are never "booked."[1]

Illustration 8–1 summarizes this process. The government-wide statements are separated into governmental activities and business-type activities (discretely presented component units are also separately displayed). The governmental-type funds' Balance Sheet and Statement of Revenues, Expenditures, and Changes in Fund Balances serve as inputs to the governmental activities sections of the government-wide statements. However, because the fund-basis statements reflect modified accrual accounting, they must be adjusted to the accrual basis. In contrast, balances from the enterprise funds' Statement of Net Assets and Statement of Revenues, Expenses, and Changes in Fund Net Assets are entered directly to the business-type activities sections of the government-wide statements. No adjustment is necessary because enterprise funds use the accrual basis.

As Illustration 8–1 suggests, internal service funds are typically reported in the governmental activities sections of the government-wide statements, while fiduciary activities are not included in the government-wide statements at all. Finally, preparation of the government-wide statements requires information on the balances and changes in general fixed assets and general long-term debt. As the illustration shows, these amounts are not included in the fund-basis statements but must be recorded in the government's accounting records if they are to be available at the time the government-wide statements are prepared. Entries to record events affecting general fixed assets and general long-term debt are illustrated later in the chapter. Like earlier chapters, the Village of Elizabeth example is extended in this chapter to illustrate the preparation of government-wide statements and certain required schedules.

CONVERSION FROM FUND FINANCIAL RECORDS TO GOVERNMENT-WIDE FINANCIAL STATEMENTS

The conversion worksheet is illustrated within the shaded area of Illustration 8–1. The fund-basis financial statements for the governmental funds are entered directly into the left-hand column of the worksheet. General fixed assets, general long-term debt, and internal service funds are added through worksheet journal entries. In addition, worksheet entries eliminate elements of the modified accrual basis fund statements that do not conform to accrual accounting, such as expenditures for capital assets and principal repayments. Expenditures that are not eliminated become

---

[1] Worksheet entries are commonly used by corporations in the process of consolidating subsidiary companies.

ILLUSTRATION 8–1   Information Flow to the Government-Wide Statements

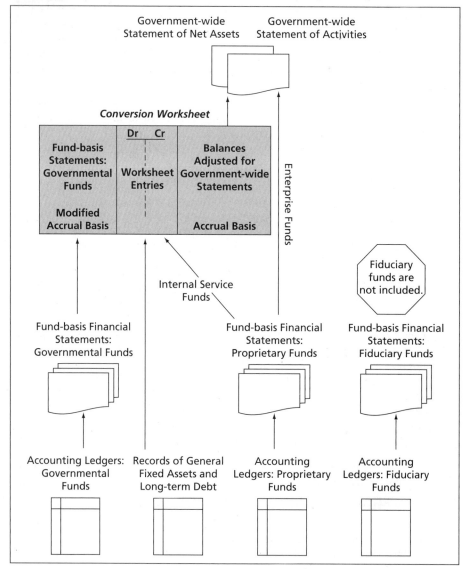

expenses in the right-hand column. Additional entries are necessary to adjust revenues to the accrual basis, record expenses not recognized under the modified accrual basis, and eliminate interfund transfers and balances. The resulting balances appearing in the far right column are entered into the governmental activities sections of the government-wide statements. No entries are necessary to eliminate fiduciary funds; they are simply left out of the worksheet and therefore never appear in the government-wide statements.

A process similar to Illustration 8–1 is followed in the event a government has a discretely presented component unit. Component units are displayed as a separate column in the Statement of Net Assets (see Illustration 2–5) and as separate rows in the Statement of Activities (see Illustration 2–6). Many component units use the accrual basis of accounting and the balances of assets, liabilities, and net assets may be entered directly into the component unit column in the Statement of Net Assets. Similarly, the revenues and expenses are entered directly into the component unit rows of the Statement of Activities. Other component units use the modified accrual basis in their accounting records and must be converted to the accrual basis for presentation in the government-wide statements. If this is the case, the component unit's information flow is similar to that of governmental funds. Worksheet entries are needed to convert the component unit to the accrual basis and economic resources measurement focus. Component units that are fiduciary in nature are not included in the government-wide statements.

The next section of the text discusses and presents, for the Village of Elizabeth, example adjustments necessary to convert from fund financial statements to government-wide statements. These examples are not exhaustive but contain the major changes and include:

1. Capital Asset–Related Entries: Recording capital assets, removing expenditures for capital outlays, recording depreciation, and converting sales of capital assets to the accrual basis.
2. Long-term Debt–Related Entries: Changing "proceeds of bonds" to debt liabilities, changing expenditures for debt service principal to reduction of liabilities, amortizing bond premiums, and adjusting for interest accruals.
3. Adjusting to convert revenue recognition to the accrual basis.
4. Adjusting expenses to the accrual basis.
5. Adding internal service funds to governmental activities.
6. Eliminating interfund activities and balances within governmental activities.

Each of these is discussed and illustrated in turn, using the information in the governmental funds Balance Sheet (Illustration 5–3) and Statement of Revenues, Expenditures, and Changes in Fund Balances (Illustration 5–4) as the starting point.

CAPITAL ASSET–RELATED ENTRIES

GASB requires that general fixed assets be included in the government-wide financial statements. General fixed assets include fixed assets other than those used by proprietary or fiduciary funds and are usually acquired through General, special revenue, or capital projects funds. Fixed assets acquired through proprietary and fiduciary funds are reported in the Statement of Net Assets of those funds. Assume that the Village of Elizabeth maintains fixed asset records for general fixed assets, including the original cost and accumulated depreciation. Categories include land, buildings, improvements other than buildings (infrastructure), and equipment. The first worksheet entry is needed to record the capital assets and related accumulated depreciation as of the beginning of the year:

	Debits	Credits
1. Land	3,100,000	
Buildings	38,300,000	
Improvements Other Than Buildings...................	15,400,000	
Equipment	5,600,000	
Accumulated Depreciation—Buildings		15,100,000
Accumulated Depreciation—Improvements Other Than Buildings............................		6,300,000
Accumulated Depreciation—Equipment		3,700,000
Net Assets......................................		37,300,000

The amount of detail necessary in this journal entry depends on whether a government intends to report individual capital asset balances (e.g., land, buildings, etc.). Assuming the Village of Elizabeth only reports capital assets in total, the journal entry could be condensed to a debit to Capital Assets of $62,400,000, a credit to Accumulated Depreciation of $25,100,000, and a credit to Net Assets of $37,300,000. Because worksheet entries are not posted to the fund general ledger, an entry to record beginning balances will be required each year. Note that the account, Net Assets, is credited for the difference. The difference between assets and liabilities in the government-wide statements is called net assets.

A second adjustment is required to eliminate the charge to expenditures for capital outlay and to record those expenditures as capital assets, as is required for accrual accounting. In practice, this would require a review of all governmental fund expenditures, to determine which should be capitalized. In the Village of Elizabeth example, it is assumed that the only capital assets acquired this year were reflected in the capital projects fund example in Chapter 5. Note that the amount of expenditures, including interest, closed out in entry 17 of the capital projects fund example in Chapter 5, is $1,963,500.

GASB *Statement 37* specifically prohibits interest during construction in governmental funds from being capitalized in the government-wide statements. As a result, the $2,500 in interest is charged to interest expense, and the $1,961,000 is capitalized. The following adjustment is required.

2. Buildings	1,961,000	
Interest Expense	2,500	
Expenditures—Capital Outlay . Ɓ੩ɑ੩ᴇᴅ . . ੩ɼ੩ᴉ		1,963,500

Remember that these entries are only worksheet entries used to prepare the government-wide statements and would not be posted to the general ledgers of the governmental funds.

A third adjustment is necessary to record depreciation expense. Assume that the Village of Elizabeth uses straight-line depreciation with no salvage value and that buildings have a 40-year life, improvements other than buildings have a 20-year life, and equipment has a 10-year life. Also assume the building capitalized this year was acquired late in the year, and that no depreciation is charged. The adjustment would be:

	Debits	Credits
3. Depreciation Expense.	2,287,500	
Accumulated Depreciation—Buildings ($38,300,000/40). . .		957,500
Accumulated Depreciation—Improvements Other Than Buildings ($15,400,000/20)		770,000
Accumulated Depreciation—Equipment ($5,600,000/10). . .		560,000

Additional information regarding fixed asset accounting and reporting is discussed in the appendix of this chapter.

If a government sold or disposed of fixed assets during the year, an additional entry is required. Entry 28 in the General Fund example in Chapter 4 reflects proceeds in the amount of $300,000 on the sale of land. That amount was properly reported as an other financing source in the Governmental Fund Statement of Revenues, Expenditures, and Changes in Fund Balances (Illustration 5–4). Assume now that the cost of that land was $225,000, which is included in the land amount reported in entry 1 above. It is necessary to convert this to an accrual basis so that the gain on the sale is reflected in the Statement of Activities and land removed from the Statement of Net Assets.

4. Special Item—Proceeds from the Sale of Land	300,000	
Land		225,000
Special Item—Gain on Sale of Land		75,000

Panel A of Illustration 8–2 demonstrates how the worksheet entries act with the existing modified accrual outcomes to produce accrual basis results. The first column of the illustration displays the journal entry that took place during the year under the modified accrual basis of accounting and the second column displays the related worksheet entry. The final (shaded) column is the net effect of the previous two entries and is the entry that *would have* been made had the government recorded the events using the accrual basis. Note that the entry appearing in the "accrual basis" column is never made, either during the year or at year-end. It is simply the outcome of the previous two entries. This illustration summarizes for capital asset transactions the process we will use throughout this chapter. We begin the process with the results for the year computed using the modified accrual basis, then apply worksheet entries, and end the process with results "as if" we had kept the records on the accrual basis.

ILLUSTRATION 8–2 Panel A: How Worksheet Entries Produce Accrual Basis Outcomes: Capital Assets

Entry Under Modified Accrual (entry made sometime during the year)	Worksheet Entry for Preparation of Government-wide Statements	Net Effect after Worksheet Entry (Same as Accrual Basis)
1. Capital Asset Acquisitions		
Expenditures – Capital Outlay .... Dr	Capital Assets – Buildings ----- Dr	Capital Assets – Buildings Dr
Cash .... Cr	Expenditures – Capital Outlay Cr	*account eliminated* –
		Cash Cr
2. Annual Depreciation		
No entry	Depreciation Expense ----- Dr	Depreciation Expense Dr
	Accumulated Depreciation ----- Cr	Accumulated Depreciation Cr
3. Sale of Capital Assets		
Cash ----- Dr	Proceeds sale of capital asset Dr	Cash Dr
Proceeds sale of capital asset ----- Cr	Capital asset – equipment (net) Cr	*account eliminated* –
	Gain on sale of capital asset Cr	Capital asset – equipment (net) Cr
		Gain on sale of capital asset Cr

ILLUSTRATION 8–2   Panel B: How Worksheet Entries Produce Accrual Basis Outcomes: Long-term Debt

Entry Under Modified Accrual (entry made sometime during the year)		Worksheet Entry for Preparation of Government-wide Statements		Net Effect after Worksheet Entry (Same as Accrual Basis)	
1. Sale of Bonds					
Cash	Dr	OFS: Proceeds of bonds	Dr	Cash	Dr
OFS: Proceeds of bonds	Cr	OFS: Premium on bonds	Dr	account eliminated	–
OFS: Premium on bonds	Cr	Bonds Payable	Cr	account eliminated	–
		Premium on Bonds	Cr	Bonds Payable	Cr
				Premium on Bonds	Cr
2. Amortization of Bond Premium					
No entry		Premium on Bonds	Dr	Premium on Bonds	Dr
		Interest Expense	Cr	Interest Expense	Cr
3. Principal Payment					
Expenditure: Bond Principal	Dr	Bonds Payable	Dr	Bonds Payable	Dr
Cash	Cr	Expenditure: Bond Principal	Cr	account eliminated	–
				Cash	Cr

Handwritten annotations (top):
Principal 1200k 10yr serial bond
Sold on 01/2 @ $1212k 1st principal payment=120k
i=8% semi 06/30 & 12/31 paid on 12/31

LONG-TERM DEBT–RELATED ENTRIES

In this section we examine typical worksheet entries related to long-term debt. Under accrual accounting, debt principal is recorded as a liability, interest expense is accrued at year-end, and premiums and discounts are amortized over the life of bonds. In the Village of Elizabeth example, 10-year serial bonds, with a principal amount of $1,200,000 were sold on January 2, for $1,212,000. Annual interest of 8 percent was paid semiannually on June 30 and December 31, and the first principal payment of $120,000 was paid on December 31. The $1,212,000 was recorded as another financing source in the capital projects fund (entries 8a and 8b in Chapter 5). To convert to accrual accounting, the following entry would be required:

	Debits	Credits
5. Other Financing Sources—Proceeds of Bonds	1,200,000	
Other Financing Sources—Premium on Bonds	12,000	
Bonds Payable		1,200,000
Premium on Bonds Payable		12,000

(margin note: governmental fund)

The account, Premium on Bonds Payable, is an addition to the liability, as would be the case in business accounting. In subsequent years the debit in this entry (equal to the beginning balance of the bonds) will be to Net Assets. To adjust the principal payment (entry 22b, debt service funds, Chapter 5), the following would be required:

6. Bonds Payable	120,000	
Expenditures—Bond Principal		120,000

(margin note: 12/31 1st payment)

Normally, an adjustment would be required to accrue interest at year-end. In the Village of Elizabeth example, the last interest payment is the final day of the fiscal year, so an accrual is not necessary. If there had been an interval of time between the last interest payment and the end of the fiscal year, the entry to accrue the interest would take the following form:

2012		
Interest Expense (2012)	$ XXX	
Accrued Interest Payable		$ XXX

It is important to recognize that accruals such as interest require entries in two years. The interest accrued above for the 2012 fiscal year would have been paid and recorded as an expenditure in 2013 under modified accrual accounting. Therefore, in 2013 we have too much interest and an additional worksheet entry would be required to move the accrued interest expense out of 2013, as follows:

	Debits	Credits
2013		
Net Assets	$ XXX	
Interest Expense (2013).		$ XXX

Why is the debit in 2013 to Net Assets rather than to Accrued Interest Payable? Recall that the 2012 entry was a worksheet entry—never booked to the General Ledger. Therefore, there is no Accrued Interest Payable to remove in 2013. However, the net assets (at the government-wide level) at the beginning of 2013 would have been smaller as a result of the 2012 accrual and the debit in 2013 reflects that effect.

Although interest accruals are not required in the Village of Elizabeth example, the bond premium must be amortized. Assume, for simplicity, that the straight-line method of amortization is considered not materially different from the effective interest method. As a result, the amortization would be $1,200. An adjusting entry to provide for the amortization would be as follows:

	Debits	Credits
7. Premium on Bonds Payable ($12,000/10)	1,200	
Interest Expense		1,200

The adjusted balance of interest ($96,000 + $2,500 − $1,200) will be reported as "interest expense" in the government-wide statement of activity.

Panel B of Illustration 8–2 demonstrates how the worksheet entries act with the existing modified accrual outcomes to produce accrual basis results for long-term debt. Again, the first column of the illustration displays the journal entry that took place during the year under the modified accrual basis of accounting and the second column displays the related worksheet entry. The final (shaded) column is the net effect of the previous two entries and is the entry that *would have been made* had the government recorded transactions affecting long-term debt on the accrual basis. Accounts that exist only under the modified accrual basis, such as *Other Financing Sources,* are eliminated and long-term liability balances are recorded and adjusted.

Again, no entries would be required for debt issued by proprietary funds because those funds already report on the accrual basis.

Adjusting to Convert Revenue Recognition to the Accrual Basis

Chapter 3 introduced the concept of revenue recognition under modified accrual accounting. We observed that revenues are recognized when available and measurable. Revenues are deemed to be *available* if they are collectible within the current fiscal year or soon enough after the year-end that they could be used to settle current period liabilities. A special rule applied to property taxes—the sixty day rule. Under modified accrual, property taxes expected to be collected more than 60 days following year-end are deferred and recognized as revenue in the following year.

Chapter 3 also introduced the four classes of nonexchange transactions and described how they are reported in the modified accrual basis financial statements (Illustration 3–5). The government-wide statements are prepared using accrual accounting. GASB *Statement 33, Accounting and Financial Reporting for Nonexchange Transactions,* describes how nonexchange transactions should be reported in the government-wide financial statements under the accrual basis. Whenever revenue is recognized in a different time period under the modified accrual basis than under the accrual basis, worksheet entries will be required.

Illustration 8–3 presents the four classes of nonexchange transactions. Panel A describes and contrasts revenue recognition under the modified accrual and accrual bases. Panel B illustrates the journal entries to record the revenue under the modified accrual basis in the governmental fund basis financial statements. The final column of panel B illustrates the journal entry to convert the governmental fund basis financial statements to the accrual basis used in the government-wide statements. Generally government-mandated and voluntary nonexchange transactions recognize revenue in the same time periods and no worksheet entries are needed. Property, sales, and income taxes deferred under the *available* criteria will require worksheet entries to convert to the accrual basis.

When converting to government-wide statements, governments need to examine all revenue sources to see which should be accrued. Assume, for the Village of Elizabeth, the only revenue that needs adjustment is property taxes. Chapter 4 reflected property tax revenue of $3,178,800 (See Illustration 4–5). Entry 27 of the General Fund example in Chapter 4 indicated that the Village deferred $40,000 in property tax revenues because that amount was not considered "available." Assume it is determined that the property tax levy is for 2012 and should be entirely recognized in that year in the government-wide statements. An adjustment would be required to convert to the accrual basis:

	Debits	Credits
8a. Deferred Revenues—Property Taxes..................	40,000	
Revenues—Property Taxes		40,000

Because the deferred revenue at December 31, 2011, is recognized in the 2012 fund-basis statements (see entry 3 in Chapter 4) but would have been recognized through a journal entry similar to 8a in last year's government-wide statements, an additional worksheet entry is required. That entry debits property tax revenues and credits net assets for the $20,000 recognized as revenue under modified accrual accounting.

8b. Revenues—Property Taxes	20,000	
Net Assets.......................................		20,000

Generally speaking, *Net Assets* will be the offset to worksheet entries that affect revenues or expenses recognized in a prior year, as well as worksheet entries affecting beginning asset and liability balances (for example, worksheet entries 1 and 9). In this case, property tax revenue of $20,000 was recognized in the previous year's government-wide Statement of Activity. The revenue had the effect of increasing the net assets at the end of 2011. However, because worksheet entries are not posted, beginning net assets (i.e., fund balance) computed under the modified accrual basis will not reflect the increase. Entry 8b has the effect of correcting the current year's revenues as well as restating the beginning net asset balance. Note that the Net Asset account appearing in these worksheet entries is the *beginning* of year net assets. End of year net assets will only be determined once all revenues and expenses have been adjusted.

Adjusting Expenses to the Accrual Basis

Under modified accrual, most expenditures are recorded when current obligations exist. A major exception is interest on long-term debt, which is recorded when due. As indicated earlier, interest payments on the general obligation long-term debt for the Village of Elizabeth were paid on the last day of the fiscal year; as a result, no accrual is necessary. Another exception, to recording expenditures on the accrual basis, is that expenditures for compensated absences are recognized only to the extent they will be liquidated with available resources. Assume the Village of Elizabeth had memorandum records indicating accumulated compensated absences payable at the first of the year in the amount of $300,000 and that an additional accrual of $25,000 is necessary in 2012. The following memorandum adjusting entries would be necessary to convert to government-wide statements:

	Debits	Credits
9. Net Assets..	300,000	
Compensated Absences Payable		300,000
10. Compensated Absences Expense.....................	25,000	
Compensated Absences Payable		25,000

A worksheet entry similar to entry 9 would be used to record any long-term liabilities outstanding at the beginning of the year, including bonds, notes, and capital leases payable.

Adding Internal Service Funds to Governmental Activities

Internal service funds are not included in the governmental fund statements as they are considered to be proprietary funds. However, most internal service funds serve primarily governmental departments. Four steps are necessary to incorporate internal service funds into the governmental fund category, keeping in mind that the starting point is the governmental fund statements illustrated in Chapter 4. The first step is to bring in the balance sheet accounts from the Statement of Net Assets. For

ILLUSTRATION 8–3   Panel A: Classes and Timing of Recognition of Revenue from Nonexchange Transactions

Type	Description and Examples	Modified Accrual Basis (Governmental Fund Basis Reporting)	Accrual Basis (Government-wide Reporting)
Imposed Nonexchange Revenues	Taxes and other assessments that do not result from an underlying transaction. Examples include property taxes and special assessments imposed on property owners. Also includes fines and forfeits	Record the receivable (and an allowance for uncollectibles) when an enforceable claim exits. Revenues should be recognized in the period for which the taxes are levied (i.e., budgeted), but are also subject to the 60 day rule. Revenues expected to be collected > 60 days after year-end are deferred.	Record the receivable (and allowance) when an enforceable claim exits. Revenues should be recognized in the period for which the taxes are levied—not subject to the 60 day rule.
Derived Tax Revenues	These are taxes assessed on exchange transactions conducted by businesses or citizens. Examples include sales, income, and excise taxes.	Record the receivable when the taxpayer's underlying transaction takes place. Revenues should be recognized when available and measurable. Revenues not expected to be collected in time to settle current liabilities are deferred (i.e., available and measurable criteria).	Record the receivable when the underlying transaction takes place. Revenues should be recognized when the taxpayer's underlying transaction takes place, regardless of when it is to be collected.
Government-mandated Nonexchange Transactions	Grants from higher levels of government (federal or state) given to support a program. Since the program is required, the lower-level government has no choice but to accept. For example, a state may require schools to mainstream certain students and provide funds to carry out this mandate.	Record the receivable and the revenue when all eligibility requirements have been met. Many of these are reimbursement grants. In this case, revenue is recognized only when qualified expenditures have been incurred. Advance receipts are deferred until expenditures are incurred. Revenue recognition is subject to the available and measurable criteria.	The recognition criteria for grants under accrual accounting are generally the same as modified accrual. However, recognition in the government-wide statements does not require revenues to be collected in time to settle current liabilities (i.e., available and measurable criteria do not apply).
Voluntary Nonexchange Transactions	Donations and grants given to support a program. Since the program is not required, the receiving government voluntarily agrees to participate.	The recognition rules are the same as mandated grants.	The recognition rules are the same as mandated grants.

ILLUSTRATION 8–3   Panel B: Representative Nonexchange Transactions and Example Journal Entries

Type	Representative Transaction	Modified Accrual Basis (Governmental Fund Basis Reporting)	Adjustment to Accrual Basis (Government-wide Reporting)
Imposed Nonexchange Revenues	1. Property taxes levied	1. Taxes Receivable ....Dr Estimated Uncollectible Taxes.............Cr Revenues Control.............Cr	1. No adjustment needed for current year levy.
	2. Deferral of portion expected to be collected > 60 days after year-end	2. Revenues Control ....Dr Deferred Revenues—Property Taxes.......Cr	2. Deferrals resulting from the 60 day rule would be reversed. Deferred Revenues ......Dr Revenues – Property Tax.......Cr
Derived Tax Revenues	1. Income tax withholdings are received.	1. Cash.....................................Dr Revenues Control........................Cr	1. No adjustment needed for collections resulting from taxable income earned in the current year.
	2. Additional income taxes expected to be received after year-end. Part of this will not be received in time to be available to settle current liabilities.	2. Taxes Receivable ....Dr Revenues Control.............Cr Deferred Revenues—Income Taxes ....Cr	2. Deferrals resulting from applying the "available criterion" would be reversed. Deferred Revenues ......Dr Revenues – Income Taxes ......Cr
Government-mandated Nonexchange Transactions & Voluntary Nonexchange Transactions	Reimbursement-type grant: 1. Incur qualified expenditures	1. Expenditures Control ....Dr Accounts Payable/Cash....................Cr	Generally no adjustment needed for government-wide reporting.
	2. Recognize revenue.	2. Due from grantor ....Dr Revenues Control.............Cr	
	Advance funded grant: 1. Receipt of advance funding.	1. Cash.....................................Dr Deferred Revenues—Grants ....Cr	Generally no adjustment needed for government-wide reporting.
	2. Incur qualified expenditures and recognize revenue.	2a. Expenditures Control.............Dr Accounts Payable/Cash.......Cr 2b. Deferred Revenues—Grants .....Dr Revenues Control.............Cr	

the Village of Elizabeth, these are found in the Internal Service Fund column of the proprietary funds Statement of Net Assets (Illustration 6–3). To be consistent with entry 1 in this section, the same detail of the capital assets is posted:

	Debits	Credits
11. Cash	3,500	
Investments.	50,000	
Due from Other Funds	55,000	
Inventory of Materials and Supplies	233,500	
Land	80,000	
Buildings	270,000	
Equipment	140,000	
Accumulated Depreciation—Capital Assets		27,500
Accounts Payable.		11,000
Advance from Water Utility Fund		190,000
Net Assets.		603,500

The remaining steps relate to the current period changes in the internal service fund's assets and liabilities. Changes in net assets are reflected in the Statement of Revenues, Expenses, and Changes in Fund Net Assets, reproduced in Illustration 8–4. It is important to identify the sources of those changes, including exchange transactions with external parties, exchange transactions with other government departments, and interfund transfers.

Transactions between the government and external parties should be reflected in the government-wide Statement of Activities. In this case the only such transaction

ILLUSTRATION 8–4   **Sources of Change in Internal Fund Net Assets**

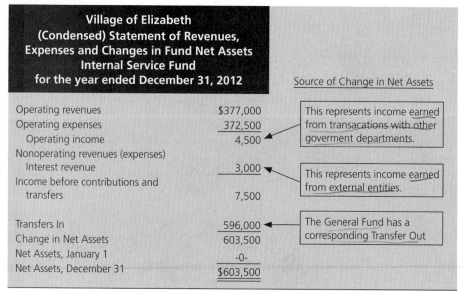

Village of Elizabeth (Condensed) Statement of Revenues, Expenses and Changes in Fund Net Assets Internal Service Fund for the year ended December 31, 2012		Source of Change in Net Assets
Operating revenues	$377,000	This represents income earned from transacations with other goverment departments.
Operating expenses	372,500	
Operating income	4,500	
Nonoperating revenues (expenses)		
Interest revenue	3,000	This represents income earned from external entities.
Income before contributions and transfers	7,500	
Transfers In	596,000	The General Fund has a corresponding Transfer Out
Change in Net Assets	603,500	
Net Assets, January 1	-0-	
Net Assets, December 31	$603,500	

is investment income of $3,000. This income is added to the Statement of Activities through the following journal entry:

	Debits	Credits
12. Net Assets...	3,000	
Investment Income................................		3,000

The third step is to eliminate the effect of exchange transactions between the internal service fund and other departments accounted for within the General Fund. The net effect of these transactions (revenues less expenses) is reflected in the $4,500 of operating income. Recall from our discussion in Chapter 6 that if an internal service fund has positive operating income, the expenditures reported in the General Fund overstate the true cost of running the government. To correct for this overstatement of expenditures in the General Fund, the operating income of $4,500 is deducted from the appropriate expense function categories. If the operating income was large, an effort would be made to determine which functions contributed to that profit and deduct the profit on a proportionate basis. In this case the amount is small and the Village chooses to credit Expenditures—General Government:

13. Net Assets...	3,000	
Expenditures—General Government.................		3,000

Finally, an entry is made to incorporate the internal service fund's Transfer In from the General Fund in the amount of $596,000. (This transfer is recorded in entry 22 of the General Fund example in Chapter 4 and entry 1 of the internal service fund example in Chapter 6.) The transfer that is established here will be eliminated in the next section.

14. Net Assets...	596,000	
Transfers In...		596,000

The previous three entries have all debited Net Assets. The purpose here is to establish the beginning balance of the internal service fund's net assets. Recall that entry 11 recorded the end-of-year balances of assets, liabilities, and net assets. Beginning-of-year net assets can be determined by subtracting the change in net assets from the end-of-year balance, as follows:

End-of-Year Net Assets (Entry 11)	$603,500
Less: Entry 12	(3,000)
Entry 13	(4,500)
Entry 14	(596,000)
Beginning-of-Year Net Assets	$ -0-

Because the internal service fund was established this year, the beginning net assets balance is zero. Next year these journal entries should combine to reflect a beginning net assets balance of $603,500, this year's ending balance.

Eliminating Interfund Activities and Balances within Governmental Activities

The final set of worksheet entries serves to eliminate transactions and balances between governmental funds (including internal service funds). After considering entry 14, the governmental funds report Transfers In of $1,048,500 and Transfers Out of $848,500, comprised of the following:

Transfers In—Governmental Funds		Transfers Out—Governmental Funds	
Fire Station Debt Service Fund	$ 204,000	General Fund	$204,000
Fire Station Debt Service Fund	48,500	Fire Station Capital Projects Fund	48,500
Supplies, Internal Service Fund	596,000	General Fund	596,000
Fire Station Capital Projects Fund	200,000		
	$1,048,500		$848,500

Because enterprise funds are reported in the business-type activities column of the government-wide statements, the transfer of $200,000 from the Water Utility Enterprise Fund (entry 14, Chapter 6) to help finance the construction of a new fire station cannot be eliminated through worksheet entry. Therefore the smaller of the two amounts (Transfers In or Transfers Out) is eliminated as follows:

	Debits	Credits
15. Transfers In..	848,500	
Transfers Out		848,500

This leaves a $200,000 transfer in from the enterprise fund to the Fire Station Capital Projects Fund, which should be reported as a transfer between governmental activities and business-type activities.

When looking at the governmental funds Balance Sheet (Illustration 5–3), note the liability account, Due to Other Funds in the amount of $135,000. This consists of $55,000 due to internal service funds, now incorporated into the governmental funds through entry 11 recording the internal service fund's assets and $80,000 due to the Water Utility Fund, an enterprise fund (see Illustration 6–2 for the detail). The $55,000 must be eliminated; the $80,000 should remain, as it is a liability from governmental activities to business-type activities and will be reported as internal balances in the Statement of Net Assets:

16. Due to Other Funds	55,000	
Due from Other Funds		55,000

Worksheet to Illustrate the Adjustments

Illustration 8–5 presents a worksheet incorporating the adjustments listed above. The worksheet begins by reproducing the accounts from the governmental funds Balance Sheet (Illustration 5–3) and Statement of Revenues, Expenditures, and Changes in Fund Balances (Illustration 5–4). The worksheet uses a trial balance format with accounts classified as to whether they are debits or credits. Items appearing in parentheses represent credit balances.

Because the balances of revenues and expenditures appear in this worksheet, it represents a preclosing trial balance. Like all preclosing trial balances, equity accounts (fund balances or net assets) represent beginning balances and (as a starting point) have been grouped into one Net Assets account. The $502,500 entry appearing at the bottom of the first column of numbers is the *beginning* of the year balance and is in agreement with *"Fund Balances—Beginning"* found on the second line from the bottom of the Statement of Revenues, Expenditures, and Changes in Fund Balance from Illustration 5–4. The worksheet entries are then incorporated into the worksheet, and ending account balances are produced. The ending balances are measured on the economic resources measurement focus and accrual basis of accounting. Items previously labeled as expenditures are now expenses. These ending account balances would be, in effect, a preclosing trial balance for the governmental activities section of the government-wide statements.

To take full advantage of the presentation in this chapter, trace the beginning balances from the governmental funds statements (Illustrations 5–3 and 5–4) to the worksheet. Then, trace the entries discussed previously in this chapter to the worksheet by number. Finally, trace the ending balances in the worksheet to the statements presented in the next section.

GOVERNMENT-WIDE FINANCIAL STATEMENTS

The GASB requires two government-wide financial statements: the Statement of Net Assets and the Statement of Activities. These two statements are presented in this section, using the Village of Elizabeth example presented in Chapters 4 to 7 and continued in the first section of this chapter.

Statement of Net Assets

The Statement of Net Assets for the Village of Elizabeth is presented as Illustration 8–6. Assets, liabilities, and net assets are separately displayed for governmental activities and business-type activities. In the case of the Village of Elizabeth, governmental activities include those activities accounted for by the governmental funds (General, special revenue, debt service, capital projects, and permanent) and internal service funds. Business-type activities include activities of enterprise funds. The Village of Elizabeth has no component units; if it had component units, they would be displayed in a separate column as shown in Illustration 2–5. Previous sections of this chapter reflected how the governmental funds statements were adjusted to prepare this Statement.

ILLUSTRATION 8–5 Worksheet to Convert to Government-Wide Statement

	Governmental Fund Balances	ref.	Adjustments & Eliminations Debits	Adjustments & Eliminations Credits	ref.	ref.	Internal Service Funds Debits	Internal Service Funds Credits	ref.	Balances for Government-wide Statements
DEBITS:										
Cash	728,000					(11)	3,500			731,500
Investments	302,000					(11)	50,000			352,000
Due from Other Funds						(11)	55,000	(55,000)	(16)	—
Interest Receivable, net	40,490									40,490
Taxes Receivable, net	528,800									528,800
Due from State Govt.	185,000									185,000
Inventories						(11)	233,500			233,500
Capital Assets		(1)	62,400,000	(225,000)	(4)	(11)	490,000			64,626,000
		(2)	1,961,000							
Expenditures (expenses) Current										
General Govt.	810,000							(4,500)	(13)	805,500
Public Safety	2,139,500									2,139,500
Public Works	1,605,000									1,605,000
Health & Welfare	480,100									480,100
Cemetery	11,000									11,000
Parks and Recreation	527,400									527,400
Contribution to Retirement Funds	423,000									423,000
Miscellaneous	20,300									20,300
Compensated Absences		(10)	25,000							25,000
Other Expenditures (expenses)										
Debt Service Principal	120,000			(120,000)	(6)					—
Debt Service Interest	96,000	(2)	2,500	(1,200)	(7)					97,300
Capital Outlay	1,963,500			(1,963,500)	(2)	-				—
Depreciation		(3)	2,287,500							2,287,500
Other Financial Uses—Transfers Out	848,500							(848,500)	(15)	—
Total Debits	10,828,590									75,118,890

CREDITS:

CREDITS:										
Accounts Payable	(185,300)							(11,000)	(11)	(196,300)
Due to Other Funds	(135,000)					(16)	55,000			(80,000)
Deferred Revenues	(40,000)	(8a)	40,000							—
Bonds Payable		(6)	120,000	(1,200,000)	(5)					(1,080,000)
Premium on Bonds		(7)	1,200	(12,000)	(5)					(10,800)
Compensated Absence Payable				(300,000) (25,000)	(9) (10)					(325,000)
Advances from Water Utility Fund								(190,000)	(11)	(190,000)
Accumulated Depreciation				(25,100,000) (2,287,500)	(1) (3)			(27,500)	(11)	(27,415,000)
Revenues										
Property Taxes	(3,178,800)	(8b)	20,000	(40,000)	(8a)					(3,198,800)
Motor Fuel Taxes	(650,000)									(650,000)
Sales Taxes	(1,410,000)									(1,410,000)
Interest & Penalties on Taxes	(42,490)									(42,490)
Licenses & Permits	(540,000)									(540,000)
Fines & Forfeits	(430,000)									(430,000)
Investment Income	(20,000)							(3,000)	(12)	(23,000)
Miscellaneous	(30,000)									(30,000)
State Grant for Road Repairs	(350,000)									(350,000)
Capital Grant for Fire Station	(600,000)									(600,000)
Capital Contributions—Endowment	(300,000)									(300,000)
Grant for Law Enforcement	(350,000)									(350,000)
Charges for Services	(100,000)									(100,000)
Other Financing Sources										
Proceeds of Bonds	(1,200,000)	(5)	1,200,000							—
Premium on Bonds	(12,000)	(5)	12,000							—
Transfers In	(452,500)					(15)	848,500	(596,000)	(14)	(200,000)
Special Items										
Proceeds of Sale of Land	(300,000)	(4)	300,000							—
Gain on Sale of Land				(75,000)	(4)					(75,000)
Net Assets at beginning of year	(502,500)	(9)	300,000	(20,000) (37,300,000)	(8b) (1)	(14) (12) (13)	596,000 3,000 4,500	(603,500)	(11)	(37,522,500)
Total Credits	(10,828,590)									(75,118,890)

Note: Amounts in parentheses represent credits.

ILLUSTRATION 8–6 Statement of Net Assets

	VILLAGE OF ELIZABETH Statement of Net Assets December 31, 2012		
	Governmental Activities	Business-Type Activities	Total
Assets			
Cash	$731,500	$124,930	$856,430
Investments	352,000	——	352,000
Interest receivable	40,490	——	40,490
Taxes receivable, net	528,800	——	528,800
Accounts receivable	——	74,925	74,925
Due from state government	185,000	——	185,000
Due from governmental activities	——	80,000	80,000
Inventories	233,500	31,000	264,500
Restricted cash and cash equivalents	——	110,000	110,000
Long-term advance to governmental activities	——	190,000	190,000
Capital assets, net of depreciation	37,211,000	3,788,265	40,999,265
Total assets	39,282,290	4,399,120	43,681,410
Liabilities			
Accounts payable	196,300	89,600	285,900
Due to business-type activities	80,000	——	80,000
Payroll taxes payable	——	9,000	9,000
Long-term advance from business-type activities	190,000	——	190,000
Revenue bonds payable	——	2,700,000	2,700,000
General obligation bonds payable	1,090,800	——	1,090,800
Compensated absences payable	325,000	——	325,000
Total liabilities	1,882,100	2,798,600	4,680,700
Net assets			
Invested in capital assets, net of related debt	35,930,200	1,088,265	37,018,465
Restricted	612,500	110,000	722,500
Unrestricted	857,490	402,255	1,259,745
Total net assets	$37,400,190	$1,600,520	$39,000,710

Assets and liabilities are reported in order of liquidity or GASB standards permit reporting a classified statement with subtotals for current assets and liabilities. It is also permissible to use a balance sheet format, where Assets = Liabilities + Net Assets.

The governmental activities column reflects total assets of $39,282,290 and liabilities of $1,882,100, resulting in net assets of $37,400,190. The net asset balances to be reported in the December 31, 2012, Statement of Net Assets are calculated as follows:

	Invested in Capital Assets, Net of Debt	Restricted	Unrestricted	Total
Invested in Capital Assets, Net of Debt:				
Capital Assets	$64,626,000			$64,626,000
Less Accumulated Depreciation	(27,415,000)			(27,415,000)
Less Bonds Payable + Premium	(1,090,800)			(1,090,800)
Less Long-term Advance	(190,000)			(190,000)
Restricted:				
Permanent fund principal		$300,000		300,000
Restricted for public works		75,000		75,000
Restricted for road repair		237,500		237,500
Unrestricted (plug)			$857,490	857,490
Total Net Assets	$35,930,200	$612,500	$857,490	$37,400,190

Note that the long-term advance from the enterprise fund ($190,000) was for the purchase of capital assets by the internal service fund and is subtracted in calculating the balance of Invested in Capital Assets, Net of Related Debt. Restricted Net Assets include the balances of the *Restricted Fund Balances* appearing in the governmental funds balance sheet (Illustration 5–3) plus the *Nonspendable Fund Balance,* representing the nonexpendable principal of the permanent fund. Unrestricted net assets is a "plug" figure ($37,400,190 − 35,930,200 − 612,500 = 857,490) calculated as the difference between total net assets and the balances of the two previously determined net asset components. The net asset amounts appearing in the business-type activities column correspond with those reported in the enterprise fund Statement of Net Assets (Illustration 6–3).

Although interfund receivables and payables were eliminated for funds appearing within the governmental activities column (entry 16), receivables and payables between governmental and business-type funds remain. In particular, Due from Governmental Activities ($80,000) and Long-term Advance to Governmental Activities ($190,000) appear as assets in the business-type activities column with liabilities in equal amounts appearing in the governmental activities column. GASB standards also permit offsetting these accounts by displaying them together in rows titled *Internal Balances*. In this case there would be two rows with negative balances in the governmental activities column offset by positive amounts in the business-type activities column as follows:

	Governmental Activities	Business-Type Activities	Total
(Asset Section)			
Internal Balances—Current	(80,000)	80,000	0
Internal Balances—Long-term	(190,000)	190,000	0

Statement of Activities

Illustration 8–7 reflects the Statement of Activities for the Village of Elizabeth. This is the same format as Illustration 2–6, although GASB does permit different formats.

ILLUSTRATION 8–7   Statement of Activities

VILLAGE OF ELIZABETH
Statement of Activities
For the Year Ended December 31, 2012

| Functions/Programs | Expenses | Program Revenues | | | Net (Expense) Revenue and Changes in Net Assets | | |
		Charges for Services	Operating Grants and Contributions	Capital Grants and Contributions	Governmental Activities	Business-type Activities	Total
Governmental activities:							
General government	$ 805,500	——			$ (805,500)	——	$ (805,500)
Public safety	2,139,500	——	$350,000	$600,000	(1,189,500)	——	(1,189,500)
Public works	1,605,000	——	350,000		(1,255,000)	——	(1,255,000)
Health and welfare	480,100	——			(480,100)	——	(480,100)
Cemetery	11,000	——		300,000	289,000	——	289,000
Parks and recreation	527,400	$ 100,000			(427,400)	——	(427,400)
Contribution to retirement funds	423,000	——			(423,000)	——	(423,000)
Compensated absences	25,000	——			(25,000)	——	(25,000)
Depreciation expense	2,287,500	——			(2,287,500)	——	(2,287,500)
Interest expense	97,300	——			(97,300)	——	(97,300)
Miscellaneous	20,300	——			(20,300)	——	(20,300)
Total governmental activities	8,421,600	100,000	700,000	900,000	(6,721,600)	——	(6,721,600)
Business-type activities:							
Water utility	828,100	1,053,100	——	12,500		$237,500	237,500
Total government	$9,249,700	$1,153,100	$700,000	$912,500	$ (6,721,600)	$237,500	$ (6,484,100)

Functions/Programs	Expenses	Program Revenues			Net (Expense) Revenue and Changes in Net Assets		
		Charges for Services	Operating Grants and Contributions	Capital Grants and Contributions	Governmental Activities	Business-type Activities	Total
General revenues:							
Taxes:							
Property taxes					3,198,800	——	3,198,800
Motor fuel taxes					650,000	——	650,000
Sales taxes					1,410,000	——	1,410,000
Interest and penalties on taxes					42,490	——	42,490
Licenses and permits					540,000	——	540,000
Fines and forfeits					430,000	——	430,000
Investment income					23,000	——	23,000
Miscellaneous					30,000	——	30,000
Special item—gain on sale of park land					75,000	——	75,000
Transfers					200,000	(200,000)	——
Total general revenues, special items, and transfers					6,599,290	(200,000)	6,399,290
Change in net assets					(122,310)	37,500	(84,810)
Net assets—beginning					37,522,500	1,563,020	39,085,520
Net assets—ending					$37,400,190	$1,600,520	$39,000,710

The general concept is that expenses less program revenues equal net expenses; general revenues are subtracted from net expenses in the lower right-hand corner to get the change in net assets. Information is available separately for governmental and business-type activities. Information would also be presented for component units if the Village of Elizabeth had component units.

Expenses for governmental activities are taken from the governmental funds Statement of Revenues, Expenditures, and Changes in Fund Balances (Illustration 5–4) as modified by the worksheet developed in this chapter (Illustration 8–5). The program revenues were identified as follows:

- $350,000 of General Fund intergovernmental revenues were considered a grant for law enforcement.
- $600,000 was received, through capital projects funds, as a grant for the construction of the police station addition.
- $350,000 was received, through a special revenue fund, as a state reimbursement grant for road repairs.
- $300,000 was received as a gift for establishment of a permanent fund for the maintenance of the city cemetery.
- $100,000 in charges for services was assumed to be for charges for city parks and recreation.

These revenues were deducted directly from related expenses to arrive at net expenses. All other revenues were considered to be general. GASB has determined that all taxes, including motor fuel taxes, are general revenues.

Transfers, special items, and extraordinary items are to be reported separately. In the case of the Village of Elizabeth a transfer is shown in the amount of $200,000 from business-type activities to governmental activities. This represents a transfer from the Water Utility Enterprise Fund to the Fire Station Addition Capital Projects Fund (see entry 2 in the capital projects section of Chapter 5 and entry 14 in the enterprise fund section of Chapter 6). All other transfers were eliminated through the worksheet entries, as those transfers were between funds that are reported as governmental activities.

Required Reconciliation to Government-wide Statements

GASB requires a reconciliation from the fund financial statements to the government-wide financial statements. Normally no reconciliation is required when going from the proprietary fund financial statements to the government-wide statements' business-activities columns because enterprise funds use accrual accounting. On the other hand, reconciliations are required from the governmental fund Balance Sheet to the Statement of Net Assets and from the governmental fund Statement of Revenues, Expenditures, and Changes in Fund Balances to the Statement of Activities.

ILLUSTRATION 8–8   Reconciliation of the Balance Sheet of Governmental Funds
to the Statement of Net Assets

VILLAGE OF ELIZABETH Reconciliation of the Balance Sheet of Governmental Funds to the Statement of Net Assets December 31, 2012	
Fund balances reported in governmental funds Balance Sheet (Illustration 5–3)	$ 1,423,990
Amounts reported for *governmental activities* in the Statement of Net Assets are different because:	
Capital assets used in governmental activities are not financial resources and, therefore, are not reported in the funds.	36,748,500*
Internal service funds are used by management to charge the costs of certain activities (stores and services) to individual funds. The assets and liabilities of internal service funds are included in governmental funds in the Statement of Net Assets.	603,500
Deferred revenue for property taxes is reported in the funds but accrued as revenue in the governmentwide statements and added to net assets.	40,000
Long-term liabilities, including bonds payable, are not due and payable in the current period and, therefore, are not reported in the funds.	(1,415,800)
Net assets of governmental activities (Illustration 8–6).	$37,400,190

*This number does not include the capital assets of internal service funds, which are included in the $603,500.

These reconciliations are required to be presented on the face of the governmental fund financial statements or in separate schedules immediately after the fund financial statements.

Illustration 8–8 reflects a reconciliation between the governmental fund Balance Sheet (Illustration 5–3) and the governmental activities column in the Statement of Net Assets (Illustration 8–6) for the Village of Elizabeth. The elements in this reconciliation can be traced through earlier sections of this chapter.

Illustration 8–9 presents a reconciliation between the changes in fund balances in the governmental fund Statement of Revenues, Expenditures, and Changes in Fund Balances (Illustration 5–4) and the governmental activities change in net assets in the Statement of Activities (Illustration 8–7). Again, the elements in the reconciliation are generated in earlier sections of this chapter.

ILLUSTRATION 8–9   Reconciliation of the Statement of Revenues, Expenditures, and
Changes in Fund Balances of Governmental Funds to
the Statement of Activities

VILLAGE OF ELIZABETH
Reconciliation of the Statement of Revenues, Expenditures, and Changes
in Fund Balances of Governmental Funds to the Statement of Activities
For the Year Ended December 31, 2012

Net change in fund balances—total governmental funds. (Illustration 5–4)	$ 921,490
Amounts reported for *governmental activities* in the Statement of Activities are different because:	
Governmental funds report capital outlays as expenditures. However, in the Statement of Activities, the cost of those assets is allocated over their estimated useful lives as depreciation expense. This is the amount by which depreciation exceeded capital outlays in the current period. (See entries 2 and 3.)	(326,500)
In the Statement of Activities, only the *gain* on the sale of land is reported, whereas in the governmental funds, the proceeds from the sale increase financial resources. Thus, the change in net assets differs from the change in fund balance by the cost of the land sold. (See entry 4.)	(225,000)
Revenues in the Statement of Activities that do not provide current financial resources are not reported as revenues in the funds. (See entries 8a and 8b.)	20,000
Bond proceeds provide current financial resources to governmental funds, but issuing debt increases long-term liabilities in the Statement of Net Assets. Repayment of bond principal is an expenditure in the governmental funds, but the repayment reduces long-term liabilities in the Statement of Net Assets. This is the amount by which proceeds exceeded repayments. (See entries 5 and 6.)	(1,080,000)
Some expenses reported in the Statement of Activities do not require the use of current financial resources and therefore are not reported as expenditures in governmental funds. (See entry 10.)	(25,000)
Internal service funds are used by management to charge the costs of certain activities, such as stores and services. The net revenue of the internal service funds is reported with governmental activities.	7,500
A transfer was made from the General Fund to an Internal Service Fund; that transfer reduced the changes in fund balance of governmental funds but not the change in net assets of governmental activities. (See entry 14.)	596,000
Bond premium was reported as another financing source in the governmental funds. The amortization of bond premium was reported as an expense reduction in the Statement of Activities. This is the amount by which the bond premium exceeded the amortization for the period. (See entries 5 and 7.)	(10,800)
Change in net assets of governmental activities (Illustration 8–7)	$ (122,310)

SUMMARY

In addition to the fund basis statements, GASB *Statement 34* requires government-wide statements that are prepared on the accrual basis using the economic resources measurement focus. The statements separately present information on component units, business-type activities (generally enterprise funds), and governmental activities. Fiduciary activities are not reported in the government-wide statements.

Government-wide information may be taken directly from the fund-basis financial statements of enterprise funds and component units using the accrual basis. However, governmental funds are prepared using the modified accrual basis and current financial resources measurement focus and must be adjusted to meet the requirements for government-wide reporting. Our approach is similar to that used by most governments. Specifically, we use the modified accrual–based governmental fund financial statements as a starting point. These are adjusted for:

- Capital asset related events.
- Long-term debt-related events.
- Differences in timing of the recognition of revenue and expenses between accrual and modified accrual accounting.
- Internal service fund activities.
- Interfund activities and balances.

The adjusted amounts are then presented in the Governmental Activities sections of the government-wide Statement of Activities and Statement of Net Assets.

Many of the differences that arise between accrual and modified accrual accounting relate to the capital assets and long-term debt of governmental funds. These are often termed **General Capital (or Fixed) Assets** and **General Long-term Debt.** Although GASB standards require these capital assets and long-term liabilities to be reported in the government-wide statements, the day-to-day accounting for these items is not prescribed. In the appendix to this chapter, we demonstrate a common method for recording capital asset and long-term debt transactions so that the information is available for preparation of government-wide financial statements. Reporting requirements for capital assets and long-term liabilities are also described.

Now that you have finished reading Chapter 8, complete the multiple choice questions provided on the text's Web site (www.mhhe.com/copley10e) to test your comprehension of the chapter.

APPENDIX: ACCOUNTING FOR CAPITAL ASSETS AND LONG-TERM DEBT IN GOVERNMENTAL ACTIVITIES

ACCOUNTING FOR GENERAL CAPITAL ASSETS, INCLUDING INFRASTRUCTURE

GASB *Statement 34,* paragraph 80, states:

> General capital assets are capital assets of the government that are not specifically related to activities reported in proprietary or fiduciary funds. General capital assets are associated with and generally arise from governmental activities. Most often, they result from the expenditure of governmental fund financial resources. They should not be reported as assets in governmental funds but should be reported in the governmental activities column of the government-wide statement of net assets.

As a result, the fund financial statements for proprietary and fiduciary funds report fixed assets used in operations; those of governmental funds do not. However, both are included and depreciated in the government-wide statements. Even though general capital assets are not reported in fund financial statements, it is necessary to maintain fixed asset records to support the reporting that is done in the government-wide statements. Prior to the adoption of GASB *Statement 34,* government accounting principles required the use and reporting of a General Fixed Asset Group that reflected fixed assets by category (land, buildings, equipment, etc.). Account groups were merely an accounting mechanism for recording the balances of fixed assets and long-term liabilities that were not otherwise recorded. Because most accounting systems will not accept an unbalanced journal entry (i.e., debits must equal credits), an offset account was often used termed *Investment in General Fixed Assets.* Entries to record changes in fixed asset balances would be reflected as follows:

	Debits	Credits
To record asset acquisitions		
Capital Assets—Buildings	1,961,000	
Investment in General Fixed Assets		1,961,000
To record depreciation		
Investment in General Fixed Assets	2,287,500	
Accumulated Depreciation—Buildings		957,500
—Improvements		770,000
—Equipment		560,000
To record asset sales/disposals		
Investment in General Fixed Assets	225,000	
Land		225,000

The *Investment in General Fixed Assets* account has no significance and does *not* appear in any financial statements.

GASB *Statement 34* provides guidance regarding depreciation. Any of the generally recognized methods might be used, such as straight-line, sum-of-the-years digits, or declining-balance methods. Most governments use the straight-line method. GASB indicates that useful lives for fixed assets may be estimated from (1) general guidelines obtained from professional or industry organizations, (2) information for comparable assets of other governments, or (3) internal information.

GASB *Statement 34* requires significant disclosures in the notes to financial statements regarding capital assets. These disclosures should be by major classes of capital assets (land, buildings, improvements other than buildings, equipment, etc.) and separated between capital assets associated with governmental activities and business-type activities. Disclosure must be made of the beginning balances, capital acquisitions, sales and other dispositions, ending balances, and current period depreciation expense. In addition to note disclosures, GASB requires that summary information be presented in the Management's Discussion and Analysis.

Governments are required to include infrastructure assets in the statement of Net Assets and note disclosures. Infrastructure assets are "long-lived capital assets that normally are stationary in nature and normally can be preserved for a significantly greater number of years than most capital assets. Examples of infrastructure assets include roads, bridges, tunnels, drainage systems, water and sewer systems, dams, and lighting systems" (GASB *Statement 34,* paragraph 19).

Governments are permitted a choice regarding depreciation of infrastructure. Governments can record depreciation in the same manner as for other depreciable fixed assets. This is the method assumed in the Village of Elizabeth example, where a 20-year life was assumed. Alternatively, governments can use the modified approach.

The Modified Approach for Reporting Infrastructure

Infrastructure assets are characterized by long useful lives, if properly maintained. For example, it is not uncommon to find aquaducts, bridges, and roads constructed by the Roman Empire that are still in use today. Because of the long life of these assets, it may be argued that infrastructure assets have an indefinite life. For this reason, GASB permits governments to choose an alternative to depreciation that expenses costs incurred to extend the life of infrastructure assets. Governments electing to use the modified approach must meet two conditions. First, the government must have an asset management system that (1) keeps an up-to-date inventory of eligible infrastructure assets; (2) performs condition assessments of those eligible infrastructure assets at least every three years, using a consistent measurement scale; and (3) estimates each year the annual amount to maintain and preserve those assets at the condition level established and disclosed by the government. Second, the government must document that the eligible infrastructure assets are being maintained at a level at or above the condition level established and disclosed by the government.

These requirements are documented by a government in two RSI schedules reflecting (1) the assessed condition of eligible infrastructure assets and (2) the estimated annual amount to maintain and preserve eligible infrastructure assets compared with the amount actually expended for each of the preceding five fiscal periods. An example is provided in Illustration 2–15. Certain note disclosures are also required.

When using the modified approach, expenditures *to extend the life* of infrastructure assets are charged to expense; if governments choose to depreciate infrastructure assets rather than use the modified approach, expenditures to extend the life of infrastructure assets would be capitalized in the government-wide statements. In either case, expenditures to add to or improve infrastructure assets would be capitalized.

For example, assume a government expends the following for infrastructure: $2,000,000 for general repairs (always expensed); $2,500,000 for improvements that extend the life (but not the quality) of existing infrastructure; and $3,000,000 to add to and improve existing infrastructure. If the government chooses to simply depreciate infrastructure, the current year provision would be $2,750,000. The accounting treatment of these costs under the traditional depreciation approach and the modified approach are as follows:

	Added to Capital Assets	Expensed
Depreciation Approach		
General repairs		$2,000,000
Improvements to extend life	$2,500,000	
Additions to existing infrastructure	3,000,000	
Provision for depreciation		2,750,000
Total	$5,500,000	$4,750,000
Modified Approach		
General repairs		$2,000,000
Improvements to extend life		2,500,000
Additions to existing infrastructure	$3,000,000	
Depreciation: *The modified approach does not depreciate infrastructure.*		
Total	$3,000,000	$4,500,000

Collections

Governments are encouraged, but not required, to capitalize collections. To qualify as a **collection,** a donated or purchased item must meet all of the following conditions (from paragraph 27 of *Statement 34*):

- Held for public exhibition, education, or research in furtherance of public service, rather than for financial gain.
- Protected, kept unencumbered, cared for, and preserved.
- Subject to an organizational policy that requires the proceeds from sales of collection items to be used to acquire other items for collections.

Disclosures are required for collections. Donated collections would be reported as revenues; if donated collections are not capitalized, the amount would be charged to the proper expense category; the revenue and expense would be equal. Collections are especially important for public colleges and universities and for governmental museums reported as special entities, discussed in Chapter 9. It should be noted that the same criteria exist for private sector not-for-profit organizations to choose not to capitalize collections (Chapter 10).

Asset Impairment

Because GASB *Statement 34* required reporting and depreciation of capital assets, an additional GASB standard was deemed necessary to determine what governments should do in the event of an unexpected decline in the usable capacity of a capital asset. GASB *Statement 42, Accounting and Financial Reporting for Impairment of Capital Assets and for Insurance Recoveries,* establishes guidance for the reporting of impairment of capital assets. *Statement 42* provides a two-step process for determining whether an asset is impaired.

Step 1: Identify Potential Impairment Events Examples include physical damage through fire or flood, changes in regulation, technological changes, construction stoppage, and discontinued use of a capital asset. However, a decrease in the demand for a particular service does not (in and of itself) indicate impairment.

Step 2: Test for Impairment Impairment is deemed to exist if both of the following factors are present:

1. The decline in the service utility is unexpected (not part of the normal life cycle of an asset).
2. The amount of the decline in service utility is large.

For example, the following might be determined to result in asset impairments:

- A bridge is damaged by an earthquake.
- Congress enacts new water quality standards and it is not economical to modify an existing water treatment plant to meet the new standards.
- A costly piece of diagnostic equipment at a city hospital is no longer used because new technology exists that does a better job.
- An expansion project at the city airport is halted because a major airline stops service to the city.

Capital assets that are determined to be permanently impaired are written-down with a resulting expense or loss in the government-wide Statement of Activities and the Statement of Revenues, Expenses, and Changes in Fund Net Assets (proprietary funds only). The expense or loss is reported net of any insurance recovery in these accrual basis statements. Insurance proceeds received by modified accrual basis funds are generally classified as Other Financing Sources in the Statement of Revenues, Expenditures, and Changes in Fund Balances. Since the governmental funds do not report capital assets, it is not necessary to record a loss in the fund-basis statements.

ACCOUNTING FOR LONG-TERM DEBT

As is the case for capital assets, long-term liabilities associated with proprietary funds and fiduciary funds are reported with those funds. However, long-term liabilities associated with governmental funds are not reported in the governmental fund financial statements. These long-term liabilities are referred to as **general long-term debt** and are reported in the government-wide statements only. General

long-term debt includes all debt that is to be paid with general governmental resources. Sometimes this is called **general obligation debt.** General obligation
debt has as backing the **full faith and credit** of the governmental unit, including
its taxing power. However, it should be noted that in some cases, general obligation
debt will be paid with enterprise fund resources and would properly be reported in
the enterprise funds. The term "general long-term debt" represents debt that is to be
paid out of general government resources.

Types of General Long-Term Debt

General long-term debt includes the principal of unmatured bonds, the noncurrent
portion of capital lease agreements, compensated absences, claims and judgments,
pensions (the net pension obligation, not the actuarial liability), OPEB liabilities,
special termination benefits, operating leases with scheduled rent increases, pollution remediation costs, and landfill closure and postclosure care liabilities (when
paid out of general government resources).

As is the case with general fixed assets, governments need detailed records of
long-term debt. Historically, this has been accomplished through the General Long-
term Debt Account Group. Again, since most accounting systems will not accept
an unbalanced journal entry, an offset account was often used termed *Amount to
be Provided.* Entries to record changes in long-term liability balances would be
reflected as follows:

	Debits	Credits
To record bond issue		
Amount to be Provided...	1,212,000	
Bonds Payable..		1,200,000
Bond Premium		12,000
To premium amortization		
Bond Premium	1,200	
Amount to be Provided...		1,200
To record payment of principal		
Bonds Payable..	120,000	
Amount to be Provided		120,000

The Amount to be Provided account has no significance and does *not* appear in any
financial statements.

Debt Disclosures and Schedules

Governments are required to prepare a number of note disclosures related to long-
term debt. Among these are:

- **Schedule of Changes in Long-term Debt.** This schedule lists the long-term
  debt obligations (including enterprise fund debt) and displays the beginning
  balance, additions, reductions, and ending balance of each.

- **Schedule of Debt Service Requirements.** This schedule displays the amount of principal and interest due on debt issues by year.
- **Schedule of Legal Debt Margin.** This schedule displays a government's debt margin, that is, how much of the government's legal debt limit has been used.
- ***Debt Limit*** is the total amount of indebtedness allowed by law and is generally determined as a proportion of the assessed value of property.
- ***Debt Margin*** is the difference between the amount of debt outstanding and the debt limit. If the debt margin is small, a government may be unable to issue additional debt in periods of financial need.
- **Schedule of Direct and Overlapping Debt.** This schedule reflects the fact that taxpayers often reside simultaneously within multiple jurisdictions. For example, a resident could live in a county and an independent school district with identical geographic boundaries. This schedule displays the total debt burden placed on residents of a government from these multiple sources.

Questions and Exercises

8–1. Using the annual financial report obtained for Exercise 1–1, answer the following questions:

a. Find the reconciliation between the governmental fund balances and the governmental-type activities net assets. This might be on the governmental fund Balance Sheet or in a separate schedule in the basic financial statements. List the major differences. What is the amount shown for capital assets? How much is due to the incorporation of internal service funds? Was an adjustment made for deferred property taxes or any other revenue? What is the adjustment due to the inclusion of long-term liabilities? What other adjustments are made?

b. Find the reconciliation between the governmental fund changes in fund balances and the governmental-type activities changes in net assets. This might be on the governmental Statement of Revenues, Expenditures, and Changes in Fund Balances or in a separate schedule. List the major differences. How much is due to the difference between depreciation reported on the Statement of Activities and the reported expenditures for capital outlays on the Statement of Revenues, Expenditures, and Changes in Fund Balances? How much is due to differences in reporting expenditures versus expenses for debt service? How much is due to the incorporation of internal service funds? How much is due to differences in reporting proceeds versus gains on sale of capital assets? How much is due to additional revenue accruals? How much is due to additional expense accruals? What other items are listed?

    c. Look at the Statement of Net Assets, especially the net asset section. Attempt to prove the Net Assets Invested in Capital Assets, Net of Related Debt figure from the information in the statement or the notes. List the individual items of net assets that are restricted; this might require examination of the notes to the financial statements.

    d. Look at the Statement of Activities. List the net expenses (revenues) for governmental activities, business-type activities, and component units. List the change in net assets for governmental activities, business-type activities, and component units. Attempt to find from the notes the component units that are discretely presented.

    e. Look throughout the annual report for disclosures related to capital assets. This would include the notes to the financial statements, any schedules, and information in the Management's Discussion and Analysis (MD&A). Summarize what is included. What depreciation method is used? Are lives of major classes of capital assets disclosed?

    f. Look throughout the annual report for disclosures related to long-term debt. This would include the notes to the financial statements, any schedules in the financial and statistical sections, and the MD&A. Summarize what is included. Are the schedules listed in this chapter included? What is the debt limit and margin? What is the direct debt per capita? The direct and overlapping debt per capita?

8–2. Identify the types of nonexchange revenues that are most likely to result in differences in the timing of recognition between the accrual and modified accrual bases of accounting.

8–3. The government-wide Statement of Net Assets separately displays governmental activities and business activities. Why are internal service funds most commonly displayed as governmental activities?

8–4. Answer the following questions with regard to infrastructure:

    a. What is infrastructure?

    b. What are the two methods that might be used to record infrastructure expense from year to year? How is the accounting different under the two methods?

    c. What conditions must exist in order to use the modified approach to record and report infrastructure?

    d. What are the disclosure requirements if the modified approach is used?

8–5. Under the reporting model required by GASB *Statement 34,* fund statements are required for governmental, proprietary, and fiduciary funds. Government-wide statements include the Statement of Net Assets and Statement of Activities. Answer the following questions related to the reporting model:

    1. What is the measurement focus and basis of accounting for: governmental fund statements; proprietary fund statements; fiduciary fund statements; and government-wide statements?

2. Indicate differences between fund financial statements and government-wide statements with regard to: component units; fiduciary funds; and location of internal service funds.

3. Indicate what should be included in the Statement of Net Assets categories: Invested in Capital Assets, Net of Related Debt; Restricted; and Unrestricted.

8–6. List some of the major adjustments required when converting from fund financial statements to government-wide statements.

8–7. The following information is available for the preparation of the government-wide financial statements for the City of Southern Springs as of April 30, 2012:

Cash and cash equivalents, governmental activities	$1,880,000
Cash and cash equivalents, business-type activities	850,000
Receivables, governmental activities	459,000
Receivables, business-type activities	1,330,000
Inventories, business-type activities	520,000
Capital assets, net, governmental activities	12,500,000
Capital assets, net, business-type activities	10,340,000
Accounts payable, governmental activities	650,000
Accounts payable, business-type activities	559,000
General obligation bonds, governmental activities	5,000,000
Revenue bonds, business-type activities	3,210,000
Long-term liability for compensated absences, governmental activities	350,000

From the preceding information, prepare (in good form) a Statement of Net Assets for the City of Southern Springs as of April 30, 2012. Assume that outstanding bonds were issued to acquire capital assets and restricted net assets total $554,000 for governmental activities and $215,000 for business-type activities. Include a *Total* column.

8–8. The following information is available for the preparation of the government-wide financial statements for the City of Northern Pines for the year ended June 30, 2012:

Expenses:

General government	$10,300,000
Public safety	23,900,000
Public works	11,290,000
Health and sanitation	6,210,000
Culture and recreation	4,198,000
Interest on long-term debt, governmental type	721,000
Water and sewer system	9,550,000
Parking system	419,000

Revenues:

Charges for services, general government	1,110,000
Charges for services, public safety	210,000
Operating grant, public safety	798,000
Charges for services, health and sanitation	2,555,000
Operating grant, health and sanitation	1,210,000
Charges for services, culture and recreation	2,198,000
Charges for services, water and sewer	11,578,000
Charges for services, parking system	398,000
Property taxes	27,112,000
Sales taxes	20,698,000
Investment earnings, business-type	319,000
Special item—gain on sale of unused land, governmental type	1,250,000
Transfer from business-type activities to governmental activities	700,000
Net assets, July 1, 2011, governmental activities	13,222,000
Net assets, July 1, 2011, business-type activities	22,333,000

From the previous information, prepare, in good form, a Statement of Activities for the City of Northern Pines for the year ended June 30, 2012. Northern Pines has no component units.

8–9. The City of Grinders Switch maintains its books so as to prepare fund accounting statements and records worksheet adjustments in order to prepare government-wide statements. You are to prepare, in journal form, worksheet adjustments for each of the following situations.

1. General fixed assets as of the beginning of the year, which had not been recorded, were as follows:

Land	$ 7,250,000
Buildings	32,355,000
Improvements Other Than Buildings	16,111,000
Equipment	11,554,000
Accumulated Depreciation, Capital Assets	14,167,000

2. During the year, expenditures for capital outlays amounted to $6,113,000. Of that amount, $4,321,000 was for buildings; the remainder was for improvements other than buildings.

3. The capital outlay expenditures outlined in (2) were completed at the end of the year (and will begin to be depreciated next year). For purposes of financial statement presentation, all capital assets are depreciated using the straight-line method, with no estimated salvage value. Estimated lives are as follows: buildings, 40 years; improvements other than buildings, 20 years; and equipment, 10 years.

4. In the governmental funds Statement of Revenues, Expenditures, and Changes in Fund Balances, the City reported proceeds from the sale of land in the amount of $600,000. The land originally cost $535,000.

5. At the beginning of the year, general obligation bonds were outstanding in the amount of $4,000,000. Unamortized bond premium amounted to $40,000. Note: This entry is not covered in the text, but is similar to entry 9 in the chapter.

6. During the year, debt service expenditures for the year amounted to: interest, $580,000; principal, $400,000. For purposes of government-wide statements, $4,000 of the bond premium should be amortized. No adjustment is necessary for interest accrual.

7. At year-end, additional general obligation bonds were issued in the amount of $1,200,000, at par.

8–10. The City of South Pittsburgh maintains its books so as to prepare fund accounting statements and records worksheet adjustments in order to prepare government-wide statements. You are to prepare, in journal form, worksheet adjustments for each of the following situations:

1. Deferred property taxes of $89,000 at the end of the previous fiscal year were recognized as property tax revenue in the current year's Statement of Revenues, Expenditures, and Changes in Fund Balance.

2. The City levied property taxes for the current fiscal year in the amount of $10,000,000. When making the entries, it was estimated that 2 percent of the taxes would not be collected. At year-end, $600,000 of the taxes had not been collected. It was estimated that $300,000 of that amount would be collected during the 60-day period after the end of the fiscal year and that $100,000 would be collected after that time. The City had recognized the maximum of property taxes allowable under modified accrual accounting.

3. In addition to the expenditures recognized under modified accrual accounting, the City computed that $250,000 should be accrued for compensated absences and charged to public safety.

4. The City's actuary estimated that the annual required contribution (ARC) under the City's public safety employees pension plan is $229,000 for the current year. The City, however, only provided $207,000 to the pension plan during the current year.

5. In the Statement of Revenues, Expenditures, and Changes in Fund Balances, General Fund transfers out included $500,000 to a debt service fund, $600,000 to a special revenue fund, and $900,000 to an enterprise fund.

8–11. The City of Southern Pines maintains its books so as to prepare fund accounting statements and records worksheet adjustments in order to prepare government-wide statements. As such, the City's internal service fund, a motor pool fund, is included in the proprietary funds statements. Prepare necessary adjustments in order to incorporate the internal service fund in the government-wide statements as a part of governmental activities.

1. Balance sheet asset accounts include: Cash, $150,000; Investments, $125,000; Due from the General Fund, $15,000; Inventories, $325,000; and Capital Assets (net), $1,340,000. Liability accounts include: Accounts Payable, $50,000; Long-Term Advance from Enterprise Fund, $800,000.

2. The only transaction in the internal service fund that is external to the government is interest revenue in the amount of $5,300.

3. Exclusive of the interest revenue, the internal service fund reported net income in the amount of $36,000. An examination of the records indicates that services were provided as follows: one-third to general government, one-third to public safety, and one-third to public works.

8–12. Presented on the following pages are partial financial statements for the City of Shenandoah, including:

Fiscal year 2012:
  A. Total Governmental Funds:
     Balance Sheet
     Statement of Revenues, Expenditures, and Changes in Fund Balances
  B. Internal Service Fund:
     Statement of Net Assets
     Statement of Revenues, Expenses, and Changes in Net Assets

Fiscal year 2011:
  A. Total Governmental Funds:
     Balance Sheet
  B. Government-wide—Governmental Activities:
     Statement of Net Assets

CITY OF SHENANDOAH
Balance Sheet
Governmental Funds
December 31, 2012 and 2011

	December 31, 2012 Total Governmental Funds	December 31, 2011 Total Governmental Funds
Assets		
Cash and cash equivalents	$1,372,900	$1,029,675
Investments	136,450	102,338
Receivables:		
Taxes	97,522	73,142
Interest	28,768	31,325
Due from state government	513,000	384,750
Total assets	2,148,640	1,621,230

Liabilities

Accounts payable	74,600	55,950
Due to other funds	10,200	10,400
Deferred property taxes	50,000	27,000
Total liabilities	134,800	93,350

Fund balances

Reserved for:

Encumbrances	259,300	124,248
Debt service	1,009,450	807,560
Unreserved, reported in:		——
General Fund	438,390	350,712
Other Funds	306,700	245,360
Total fund balances	2,013,840	1,527,880
Total liabilities and fund balances	$2,148,640	$1,621,230

CITY OF SHENANDOAH

**Statement of Revenues, Expenditures and Changes
in Fund Balances—Governmental Funds
For the Year Ended December 31, 2012**

	Total Governmental Funds
Revenues	
Property taxes	$6,469,000
Sales taxes	3,115,000
Interest	32,000
Licenses and permits	800,000
Intergovernmental	1,763,000
Miscellaneous	270,000
Total revenues	12,449,000
Expenditures	
Current	
General government	1,692,300
Public safety	3,258,700
Landfill operations	2,337,400
Cultural and recreational	2,605,600
Capital outlay	4,914,150
Debt service	
Principal	400,000
Interest	508,000
Total expenditures	15,716,150
Revenues over (under) expenditures	(3,267,150)

(Continued)

Other financing sources (uses)

Proceeds of bonds	4,000,000
Premium on bonds	50,000
Transfers from other funds	137,450
Transfers (to) other funds	(137,450)
	4,050,000
Excess of revenues and other sources over (under) expenditures and other uses	782,850
Fund balance—beginning of year	1,230,990
Fund balance—end of year	$2,013,840

CITY OF SHENANDOAH
Statement of Net Assets
Proprietary Funds
December 31, 2012

	December 31, 2012 Governmental Activities: Internal Service Fund
Current assets	
Cash and cash equivalents	$37,000
Receivables:	
Due from General Fund	10,200
Due from Enterprise Fund	11,000
Inventories	15,000
Total current assets	73,200
Noncurrent assets	
Land	25,000
Buildings	44,000
Accumulated depreciation buildings	(13,200)
Equipment	21,000
Accumulated depreciation equipment	(12,600)
	64,200
Total assets	$137,400
Liabilities	
Accounts payable	$18,400
Total current liabilities	18,400
Noncurrent liabilities	
Advance from Enterprise Fund	10,000
Total noncurrent liabilities	10,000
Total liabilities	28,400

Net assets

Invested in capital assets net of related debt	$54,200
Unrestricted	54,800
Total net assets	$109,000

CITY OF SHENANDOAH
Statement of Revenues, Expenses, and Changes
in Net Assets Proprietary Funds
For the Year Ended December 31, 2012

	Governmental Activities: Internal Service Fund
Revenues	
Charges for sales and services	$371,200
Total revenues	371,200
Operating expenses	
Cost of sales and services	358,600
Administration	10,300
Depreciation	4,300
Total expenditures	373,200
Operating (loss)	(2,000)
Nonoperating income	
Investment income	5,000
	5,000
Change in net assets	3,000
Net assets—beginning of year	106,000
Net assets—end of year	$109,000

CITY OF SHENANDOAH
Statement of Net Assets
Government-wide Statements
December 31, 2011

	December 31, 2011 Governmental Activities
Current assets	
Cash and cash equivalents	$1,230,000
Investments	95,500
Receivables (net)	
Taxes receivable	69,500
Due from business activities	23,000
Due from state government	156,000
Total current assets	1,574,000

(Continued)

Noncurrent assets

Land	7,230,000
Buildings	25,600,000
Accumulated depreciation buildings	(13,000,000)
Infrastructure	24,500,000
Accumulated depreciation buildings	(9,000,000)
Equipment	6,370,000
Accumulated depreciation equipment	(3,100,000)
Total capital assets	38,600,000
Total assets	$40,174,000

Liabilities

Accrued interest on bonds	$180,000
Accounts payable	96,500
Total current liabilities	276,500

Noncurrent liabilities

General obligation bonds payable	6,000,000
Accrued costs for landfill closure and postclosure care	29,500
Total noncurrent liabilities	6,029,500
Total liabilities	6,306,000

Net assets

Invested in capital assets net of related debt	32,600,000
Unrestricted	1,268,000
Total net assets	$33,868,000

Additional Information

1. $445,600 of the capital assets purchased in fiscal year 2012 was equipment. All remaining capital acquisitions were for a new building.
2. Depreciation of general fixed assets: buildings $1,100,000, infrastructure $975,000, and equipment $537,500.
3. The City had $6,000,000 of 6 percent general obligation bonds (issued at par) outstanding at December 31, 2011. In addition, the City issued $4,000,000 of 8 percent bonds on January 2, 2012 (sold at a premium). Interest payments on both bond issues are due on January 1 and July 1. Principal payments are made on January 1. Interest and principal payments for the current year include:

	6 percent General Obligation Bonds	8 percent General Obligation Bonds
Interest Payment—January 1	$180,000	—
Interest Payment—July 1	168,000	$160,000
Principal Payment—January 1	$400,000	—

The January interest payments are accrued for purposes of the government-wide statements but not the fund-basis statements. The bond premium is to be amortized in the amount of $2,500 per year.

4. Property taxes expected to be collected more than 60 days after year-end are deferred in the fund basis statements.

5. At the end of 2012, the accumulated liability for landfill closure and post-closure care costs is estimated to be $37,000. Landfill operations are reported in the General Fund—Public Works.

6. The internal service fund serves several departments of the General Fund, all within the category of "General Government." The internal service fund was created at the end of 2011 and had no capital assets or long-term liabilities at the end of 2011.

Prepare all worksheet journal entries necessary for fiscal year 2012 to convert the governmental fund basis amounts to the economic resources measurement focus and accrual basis required for the governmental activities sections of the government-wide statements.

Excel-Based Problems

8–13. The fund-basis financial statements of Jefferson County have been completed for the year 2012 and appear in the first tab of the Excel spreadsheet provided with this exercise. The following information is also available:

a. Capital Assets
- Capital assets purchased in previous years through governmental type funds totaled $752,000 (net of accumulated depreciation) as of January 1, 2012.
- Depreciation on capital assets used in governmental-type activities amounted to $79,500 for 2012.
- No capital assets were sold or disposed of in 2012 and all purchases are properly reflected in the fund-basis statements as capital expenditures.

b. Long-term Debt
- There was no outstanding long-term debt associated with governmental-type funds as of January 1, 2012.
- April 1, 2012, 6 percent bonds with a face value of $700,000 were issued in the amount of $720,000. Bond payments are made on October 1 and April 1 of each year. Interest is based on an annual rate of 6 percent and principal payments are $17,500 each. The first payment (interest and principal) was made on October 1.
- Amortization of the bond premium for the current year is $1,000.

c. Deferred Revenues
- Deferred revenues (comprised solely of property taxes) are expected to be collected more than 60 days after year-end. The balance of deferred taxes at the end of 2011 was $18,200.

    d. Transfers

- Transfers were between governmental-type funds.

    e. Internal Service Fund

- The (motor pool) internal service fund's revenue is predominantly derived from departments classified as governmental-type activities.
- There were no amounts due to the internal service fund from the General Fund. The outstanding balance of "due to other funds" was with the Enterprise Fund and is not capital related.
- The enterprise fund provided a long-term advance to the internal service fund (not capital related).

Required:

Use the Excel template provided to complete the following requirements; a separate tab is provided in Excel for each of these steps.

1. Prepare the journal entries necessary to convert the governmental fund financial statements to the accrual basis of accounting.
2. Post the journal entries to the conversion worksheet provided.
3. Prepare a government-wide Statement of Activities and Statement of Net Assets for the year 2012. All of the governmental fund revenues are "general revenues."

This is an involved problem, requiring many steps. Here are some hints.

    a. Tab 1 is information to be used in the problem. You do not enter anything here.

    b. After you make the journal entries (Tab 2), post these to the worksheet to convert to the accrual basis. This worksheet is set up so that you enter **debits as positive** numbers and **credits as negative.** After you post your entries, look at the numbers below the total credit column to see that debits equal credits. If not, you probably entered a credit as a positive number.

    c. Make sure that total debits equal total credits in the last column (balances for government-wide statements).

    d. When calculating Restricted Net Assets, recall that permanent fund principal is added to restricted fund balances.

8–14. The fund-basis financial statements of the City of Cottonwood have been completed for the year 2012 and appear in the first tab of the Excel spreadsheet provided with this exercise. In addition, the Statement of Net Assets from the previous fiscal year is provided and should be used to determine beginning balances for accounts not appearing in the fund-basis statements. The following information is also available:

    a. Capital Assets:

- Capital assets purchased by governmental funds are charged to capital expenditure and do not appear as assets in the fund-basis balance sheet. However, the balance is reflected in the statement of net assets in the government-wide financial statements.

- Depreciation on capital assets used in governmental-type activities amounted to $2,450,000 for 2012.
- No capital assets were sold or disposed of in 2012, and all purchases are properly reflected in the fund-basis statements as capital expenditures.

b. Long-term debt

- Proceeds from bonds issued by governmental funds are reflected in other financing sources and do not appear as liabilities in the fund-basis balance sheet. Payments of principal are recognized as expenditures when due. The balance of outstanding bonds balance is reflected in the statement of net assets in the government-wide financial statements.
- Interest is recognized in the fund-basis statements only when payment is due. Interest accrued but not yet payable amounted to $107,500 at December 31, 2012. Interest accrued for purposes of the government-wide statements in 2011 has been paid and is reflected in interest expenditure in 2012.
- There are no bond discounts or premiums.

c. Deferred Revenues

- Deferred revenues are comprised solely of property taxes expected to be collected more than 60 days after year-end. The balance of deferred taxes at the end of 2011 was $128,200 and was recognized as revenue in the fund-basis statements in 2012.

d. The City accounts for its solid waste landfill in the General Fund (public works department). The estimated liability for closure and post-closure care costs as of December 31, 2012, is $1,580,900 and appears only in the government-wide statements.

e. Transfers

- During the year, the General Fund transferred cash to the courthouse renovation, debt service, and enterprise funds.

f. The City does not operate any Internal Service Funds.

g. When entering amounts in the Statement of Activities, *Charges for Services Revenue* in the governmental funds is attributable to the following functions:

General Government	$1,144,018
Judicial Administration	56,497
Public Safety	275,492
Parks and Recreation	604,359
Community Development	51,611
Total	$2,131,977

Required:

Use the Excel template provided to complete the following requirements; a separate tab is provided in Excel for each of these steps.

1. Prepare the journal entries necessary to convert the governmental fund financial statements to the accrual basis of accounting.
2. Post the journal entries to the conversion worksheet provided.
3. Prepare a government-wide Statement of Activities and Statement of Net Assets for the year 2012.

This is an involved problem, requiring many steps. Here are some hints.

a. Tab 1 is information to be used in the problem. You do not enter anything here.
b. After you make the journal entries (Tab 2), post these to the worksheet to convert to the accrual basis. This worksheet is set up so that you enter **debits as positive** numbers and **credits as negative.** After you post your entries, look at the numbers below the total credit column to see that debits equal credits. If not, you probably entered a credit as a positive number.
c. Make sure that total debits equal total credits in the last column (Balances for government-wide statements).
d. When calculating Restricted Net Assets, recall that permanent fund principal is added to restricted fund balances.

Continuous Problem

Available on the text's Web site (www.mhhe.com/copley10e).

Chapter Nine

Accounting for Special-Purpose Entities, Including Public Colleges and Universities

Be thankful we're not getting all the government we're paying for. (Will Rogers, American humorist, 1879–1935)

The best way to find yourself is to lose yourself in the service of others. (Mahatma Gandhi, 1869–1948)

Learning Objectives

- Describe characteristics of special-purpose entities and identify the required financial statements of varying types of special-purpose entities.
- Prepare combined fund-basis/government-wide financial statements for a special-purpose entity engaged in a single governmental activity.
- Apply the accrual basis of accounting in the recording of typical transactions of a public college or university.
- Prepare the financial statements for a public college or university.

This chapter describes GASB reporting standards for special-purpose entities. These standards are then applied to an important class of special-purpose entities, public colleges and universities.

GASB *STATEMENT 34* REPORTING RULES FOR SPECIAL-PURPOSE ENTITIES

Chapters 2 through 8 provide accounting and financial reporting guidance for **general-purpose** state and local governments. General-purpose local governments include states, counties, cities, towns, and villages. Other governments are called

special-purpose local governments and include governments such as fire protection districts, park districts, library districts, tollway authorities, and transit authorities. Special-purpose governments may be stand-alone local governments or may be component units of other governments that are issuing separate reports. GASB does not give a clear definition of either general-purpose or special-purpose governments. The distinction is not always between types of governments, as one government (say, a township) may be either a general-purpose or special-purpose government, for purposes of financial reporting.

However, the *Implementation Guide for GASB Statement 34* provides a distinction by indicating that "General-purpose governments are thought to be those that offer more than one type of *basic governmental services*—for example, general government, public safety, transportation, health and welfare. Special-purpose governments generally provide a limited (or sometimes a single) set of services or programs—for example, fire protection, library services, mosquito abatement, and drainage." Governmental health care entities, public school systems, other not-for-profit entities (e.g., museums), and public colleges and universities may be considered special-purpose entities for financial reporting purposes.

Chapter 2 of this text provides an introduction to financial reporting for special-purpose local governments. This chapter provides more detail and a few examples. Financial reporting for a special-purpose local government depends upon whether that government is engaged in governmental-type activities, business-type activities only, or fiduciary-type activities only. The reporting requirements of special purpose entities are summarized in Illustration 9–1.

Reporting by Special-purpose Local Governments Engaged in Governmental Activities

According to GASB *Statement 34,* governmental activities "generally are financed through taxes, intergovernmental revenues, and other nonexchange revenues. These activities are usually reported in governmental funds and internal service funds." This would include general government, public safety, general public works, and other activities such as public health, culture and recreation, and community development when paid for through general governmental revenues. A special-purpose local government may be engaged in (1) both governmental activities and business-type activities, (2) more than one governmental activity, or (3) a single governmental activity.

Special-purpose governments that are engaged in both governmental and business-type activities or in more than one governmental activity are required to follow the reporting outlined in Chapters 2 through 8 of this text. That is, the full reporting model is required, including MD&A, government-wide and fund-basis financial statements, notes to the financial statements, and Required Supplementary Information (RSI).

Some special-purpose governments are engaged in only one governmental-type activity. Examples might include fire protection, sanitation, or cemetery districts. Special-purpose governments that are engaged in only one governmental-type

ILLUSTRATION 9–1   Summary of Reporting Requirements for Special-purpose Entities

Description of Special-purpose Entity	Management's Discussion & Analysis	Government-wide Statements	Fund-Basis Statements	Notes to the Financial Statements	RSI Other Than MD&A	Financial Statements
Entities engaged in both governmental and business-type activities	✓	✓	✓	✓	✓	Statement of Net Assets (government-wide) Statement of Activities Balance Sheet (governmental funds) Statement of Revenues, Expenditures, and Changes in Fund Balances Statement of Net Assets (proprietary funds) Statement of Revenues, Expenses, and Changes in Fund Net Assets Statement of Cash Flows
Entities engaged in more than one governmental activity	✓	✓	✓	✓	✓	Statement of Net Assets (government-wide) Statement of Activities Balance Sheet (governmental funds) Statement of Revenues, Expenditures, and Changes in Fund Balances
Entities engaged in a single governmental activity	✓	✓*	✓*	✓	✓	Governmental Funds Balance Sheet/Statement of Net Assets Statement of Governmental Fund Revenues, Expenditures, and Changes in Fund Balances/Statement of Activities
Entities engaged in only business-type activities	✓		✓	✓	✓	Statement of Net Assets (proprietary funds) Statement of Revenues, Expenses, and Changes in Fund Net Assets Statement of Cash Flows
Entities engage in only fiduciary activities	✓		✓	✓	✓	Statement of Fiduciary Net Assets Statement of Changes in Fiduciary Net Assets

* Government-wide and fund-basis statements may be combined.

activity are permitted to combine the fund and government-wide financial statements. This could be done by showing reconciliations between governmental fund accounting policies (modified accrual) and government-wide statements (accrual) on the face of the statements. Thus, a government might present only one Balance Sheet and one Statement of Revenues, Expenditures, and Changes in Fund Balances. Other information, including Management's Discussion & Analysis, notes and RSI, would also be included.

Illustration 9–2 presents a (combined) Balance Sheet/Statement of Net Assets for the Salem Independent Fire District, a special-purpose entity engaged in a single governmental activity. The first three columns of numbers reflect the fund-basis statements prepared using the current financial resources measurement focus and the modified accrual basis of accounting. An adjustment column is added to convert to the economic resource measurement focus and accrual basis of accounting as required in the government-wide statements. This format is not required; the Fire District could have prepared separate fund-basis and government-wide statements.

Illustration 9–3 presents a (combined) Statement of Governmental Fund Revenues, Expenditures, and Changes in Fund Balances/Statement of Activities for the same independent fire district. Again, an adjustment column is added to convert to the economic resource measurement focus and accrual basis of accounting as required in the government-wide statements. As with all activity statements, fund balance or net assets is reconciled at the bottom of this statement to the balances appearing in Illustration 9–2. GASB stresses that only governments that have a single program should use the formats shown in Illustrations 9–2 and 9–3.

Examine the adjustments column in the two statements. Adjustments have been made for the following items:

1. Interfund receivables/payables are eliminated in the amount of $23,747.
2. Interfund transfers are eliminated in the amount of $25,395.
3. Capital expenditures are reclassified as capital assets in the amount of $23,589.
4. Depreciation expense is recorded in the amount of $26,805.
5. Capital assets (net of depreciation) are recorded in the amount of $247,380.
6. Expenditures for payments of principal are reclassified as a reduction in long-term liabilities in the amount of $15,000.
7. Long-term notes payable of $161,000 are included (beginning balance of $176,000 less expenditures for principal of $15,000).

These adjustments are similar to those prepared in the worksheets in Chapter 8. Additional items can include reversing entries made to defer tax revenues not collectible within 60 days or accruals of interest on long-term debt not recorded in the governmental funds.

Reporting by Special-purpose Local Governments Engaged Only in Business-type Activities

Paragraph 15 of GASB *Statement 34* indicates that "Business-type activities are financed in whole or in part by fees charged to external parties for goods or services.

ILLUSTRATION 9–2 Governmental Funds Balance Sheet/Statement of Net Assets (Special-purpose Entity Engaged in a Single Governmental Activity)

				Adjustments to	
Assets	General Fund	Special Revenue Fund	Total	Government-wide	Statement of Net Assets
SALEM FIRE PROTECTION DISTRICT Governmental Funds Balance Sheet/Statement of Net Assets As of December 31, 2012					
Cash and cash equivalents	$140,821	$15,280	$156,101		$156,101
Inventories	5,784	—	5,784		5,784
Receivables (net)	—	—	—		—
Taxes receivable	195,860	—	195,860		195,860
Due from other governments	85,184	6,589	91,773		91,773
Due from other funds	—	23,747	23,747	(23,747)	—
Capital assets	—	—	—	238,379	238,379
Total assets	427,649	45,616	473,265	214,632	687,897
Liabilities					
Accounts payable	185,378	43,458	228,836		228,836
Due to other funds	23,747	—	23,747	(23,747)	—
Notes due in more than one year	—	—	—	161,000	161,000
Total liabilities	209,125	43,458	252,583	137,253	389,836
Fund balance					
Nonspendable (inventories)	5,785	—	5,785		
Assigned for other purposes	—	2,158	2,158		
Unassigned	212,739	—	212,739		
Total fund balance	218,524	2,158	220,682		
Total liabilities and fund balance	$427,649	$45,616	$473,265		
Net assets:					
Invested in capital assets net of related debt					77,379
Unrestricted					220,682
Total					$298,061

These activities are usually reported in enterprise funds." This would include water and sewer utilities, airports, transit systems, and other authorities. GASB *Statement 35* indicates that public higher education institutions may choose to report as business-type activities, as will be described later. It should be noted that these

ILLUSTRATION 9–3   Governmental Funds Statement of Revenues, Expenditures, and Changes in Fund Balance/Statement of Activities (Special-purpose Entity Engaged in a Single Governmental Activity)

SALEM FIRE PROTECTION DISTRICT
Governmental Funds: Statement of Revenues, Expenditures, and Changes in Fund Balances / Statement of Activities
For the Year Ended December 31, 2012

Revenues	General Fund	Special Revenue Fund	Total	Adjustments to Government-wide	Statement of Activities
Property taxes	$361,830	——	$361,830		$361,830
Charges for services	1,435	——	1,435		1,435
Intergovernmental	23,589	$209,143	232,732		232,732
Miscellaneous	2,549	——	2,549		2,549
Total revenues	389,403	209,143	598,546		598,546
Expenditures/expenses					
Current					
Personnel services	153,250	235,492	388,742		388,742
Supplies	56,735	——	56,735		56,735
Depreciation				26,805	26,805
Capital outlay	23,589	——	23,589	(23,589)	——
Debt service					
Principal	15,000	——	15,000	(15,000)	——
Interest	18,500	——	18,500		18,500
Total expenditures	267,074	235,492	502,566	(11,784)	490,782
Revenues over (under) expenditures	122,329	(26,349)	95,980		
Other financing sources (uses)					
Transfers from other funds	——	25,395	25,395	(25,395)	——
Transfers (to) other funds	(25,395)	——	(25,395)	25,395	——
Total	(25,395)	25,395	——		
Excess of revenues and other sources over (under) expenditures and other uses	96,934	(954)	95,980		
Change in net assets					107,764
Fund balance / net assets— Beginning of year	121,590	2,212	123,802		190,297
Fund balance / net assets— End of year	$218,524	$1,258	$219,782		$298,061

entities may have more than one program but must be involved only in business-type activities.

Special-purpose local governments engaged only in business-type activities are required to include the following in their financial statements:

- Management's Discussion and Analysis (MD&A).
- Enterprise Fund Financial Statements, including:
    Statement of Net Assets or Balance Sheet.
    Statement of Revenues, Expenses, and Changes in Net Assets.
    Statement of Cash Flows.
- Notes to the Financial Statements.
- Required Supplementary Information (RSI), other than MD&A, if applicable.

These financial statements are illustrated in Chapter 6, related to enterprise funds. All of the requirements for enterprise financial statements described in Chapter 6, such as using an operating income figure, are required for the separate financial statements for single-purpose governments engaged only in business-type activities. In other words, the basic financial statements for a stand-alone utility would appear the same as the enterprise fund columns of Illustrations 6–3, 6–4, and 6–5. Governmental health care entities generally report as special-purpose entities engaged only in business-type activities. Certain extensions of reporting requirements for these organizations are contained in the *AICPA Audit and Accounting Guide: Health Care Organizations*. These extensions are described in Chapter 12.

Reporting by Special-purpose Local Governments Engaged Only in Fiduciary-type Activities

Public Employee Retirement Systems (PERS) are special-purpose governments that manage one or more retirement plans. Some of these are defined benefit plans; others include defined contribution plans, deferred compensation, and health care plans.

Many states have special-purpose local governments that exist solely to manage retirement systems for state and/or local government employees. These are often statewide systems. They prepare separate financial statements as special-purpose local governments that are engaged only in fiduciary-type activities.

These governments are required to prepare the following financial reports:

- MD&A.
- Statement of Fiduciary Net Assets.
- Statement of Changes in Fiduciary Net Assets.
- Notes to the Financial Statements.
- Required Supplementary Information (RSI), other than MD&A, if applicable.

ACCOUNTING AND FINANCIAL REPORTING FOR PUBLIC COLLEGES AND UNIVERSITIES

Public colleges and universities are those educational institutions owned or controlled by a government, generally the state. Roughly three out of four college students attend public institutions. It is important to distinguish between public and private colleges and universities because public institutions follow GASB guidelines while private institutions follow FASB guidelines. Private colleges and universities are the topic of Chapter 11 and public colleges and universities are the topic of the remainder of this chapter. GASB *Statement 35, Basic Financial Statements—and Management's Discussion and Analysis—for Public Colleges and Universities* was an amendment to *Statement 34* that incorporated public institutions of higher education into the basic governmental reporting model. Public colleges and universities are allowed to choose, as special-purpose entities, to report as entities: (1) engaged in only business-type activities; (2) engaged in both governmental- and business-type activities; or (3) engaged in only governmental-type activities. Most institutions choose to report as engaged in only business-type activities, although some community colleges report as engaged in both governmental- and business-type activities if they are significantly supported by a property tax.

The Environment of Public Higher Education

Each state has established unique arrangements for the governance of public higher education. Public four-year higher education institutions (hereafter, public colleges) are often (but not always) in systems of higher education, with several institutions under the same governing board. Governing board members are appointed by state officials, often the governor. Institutions have varying degrees of autonomy from their state government officials and regulations. Often, a coordinating council (say, a Board of Higher Education) exists to provide oversight and to coordinate budget requests. Sometimes, but not always, public colleges and universities are included as component units in the state CAFR. However, nearly all issue separate financial reports.

Community colleges, in some states, are distinct governmental entities, with independently elected board members, with the power to tax, to prepare budgets, and to hire administrators. In other states, community colleges are more like four-year colleges, in effect, state agencies.

Revenue sources include tuition and fees, state appropriations, specific state and federal grants, revenues from auxiliary enterprise activities (dormitories, etc.), alumni and other donations, and endowment income. Public colleges often create separate foundations, legally separate not-for-profit organizations, to receive and administer some or all of the following: contributions, research, and athletics. These foundations are commonly included as component units in the institutions' annual reports. Many public colleges have the power to issue debt; however, that debt is often for revenue-producing activities only, such as dormitories, student centers, food service activities, and athletics. Debt for academic facilities may be issued for the institution but is often issued as state general obligation debt.

Accounting and Financial Reporting for Public Institutions of Higher Education

Colleges and universities that choose to report as special-purpose entities engaged in governmental- and business-type activities prepare reports similar to those of general government, as described in Chapters 2 through 8. Few choose to report as special-purpose entities engaged only in governmental-type activities. This text focuses on institutions that choose to report as special-purpose entities engaged only in business-type activities. These institutions will be required to prepare the following:

- Management's Discussion and Analysis (MD&A).
- Statement of Net Assets (or Balance Sheet).
- Statement of Revenues, Expenses, and Changes in Net Assets.
- Statement of Cash Flows.
- Notes to the Financial Statements.
- Required Supplementary Information Other Than MD&A.

The basic requirements for the statements are the same as outlined for proprietary funds in Chapter 6 of this text. However, due to the scope and importance of public higher education, separate coverage is given.

Prior to the adoption of *Statement 35,* public colleges used a form of fund accounting. Fund groups included: current unrestricted, current restricted, loan, endowment and similar, annuity and life income, plant, and agency. Many institutions continue to use some form of fund accounting to manage their operations. However, fund accounting is not illustrated in this text, which is concerned primarily with external reporting.

Public colleges and universities receive many grants and contributions. The net assets for these grants and contributions are often, but not always, restricted. The business-type activity model provides for a separation of net assets that are restricted. As indicated earlier, many institutions have most of their restricted resources sent to and managed by related entities, called *foundations.* In addition, net assets may be restricted by external parties for debt reserves and for resources restricted by state legislation and regulation.

With respect to public college foundations, GASB issued *Statement 39: Determining Whether Certain Organizations Are Component Units.* The effect of *Statement 39* is to require that most public college foundations be reported as discretely presented component units in the college's financial reports. Specifically, foundations are to be reported if they meet all three of the following criteria:

- The economic resources received or held by the separate organization are entirely or almost entirely for the direct benefit of the primary government, its component units, or its constituents.

- The primary government, or its component units, is entitled to, or has the ability to otherwise access, a majority of the economic resources received or held by the separate organization.
- The economic resources received or held by an individual organization that the specific primary government is entitled to, or has the ability to otherwise access, are significant to that primary government.

GASB *Statement 39* applies to foundations of all types of governments, including general governments, public colleges, public schools, museums, and health care entities. The last criterion effectively rules out organizations that are insignificant financially, such as most PTA organizations and booster clubs.

Public colleges and universities often have extensive capital assets, including infrastructure. Included are land, buildings for academic and auxiliary enterprise purposes, research and other equipment, improvements other than buildings (infrastructure), library books, and collections and other works of art. GASB standards require that capital assets be recorded and depreciated. As with general-purpose governments, infrastructure may be reported using the modified approach.

As indicated earlier, many educational institutions have the power to issue debt. This debt is often revenue bonds that are backed by revenue-producing facilities such as dormitories, bookstores, and food service operations. GASB requirements for business-type activities call for accrual accounting for debt, including accrual of interest and amortization of debt discount and premium.

Colleges often issue tuition discounts and other forms of financial aid. Some of this financial aid comes from institutional funds, and some comes from the outside, including the federal government, specific state appropriations, and grants from individuals and businesses. Responding to GASB *Statement 35,* the National Association of College and Business Officers issued Advisory Report 00–5, *Accounting and Reporting Scholarship Discounts and Allowances to Tuition and Other Fee Revenues by Public Higher Education.* Public institutions are to report all tuition and fee revenue net of any scholarship discounts and allowances. Only amounts that are to be paid by students and third-party payers can be shown as tuition fee income. The amounts paid by institutional funds and other sources must be deducted from student fee income (normally using contra-revenue accounts). On the other hand, fees waived by the institution in return for services provided by employees and student assistants are shown as expenses, and tuition and fee revenue is reported at the gross amount.

Illustrative Case—Northern State University— Beginning Trial Balance

This section presents a beginning trial balance, journal entries, and financial statements for Northern State University, a hypothetical state four-year institution choosing to report as a special-purpose entity engaged only in business-type activities. The fiscal year is the year ended June 30, 2012.

Assume the following trial balance as of July 1, 2011, the first day of the new fiscal year:

NORTHERN STATE UNIVERSITY
Post-closing Trial Balance
June 30, 2011

	Debits	Credits
Cash and cash equivalents	$ 2,500,000	
Accounts receivable—net	1,250,000	
Short-term investments	12,520,000	
Interest receivable—unrestricted	25,000	
Inventories	1,560,000	
Deposits with bond trustee	2,100,000	
Restricted cash and cash equivalents	135,000	
Endowment investments	11,300,000	
Interest receivable—restricted	185,000	
Land	6,300,000	
Buildings	56,100,000	
Accumulated depreciation—buildings		$ 22,000,000
Equipment	31,400,000	
Accumulated depreciation—equipment		16,200,000
Improvements other than buildings	8,900,000	
Accumulated depreciation—improvements other than buildings . . .		4,800,000
Accounts payable and accrued liabilities		1,725,000
Deferred revenue		830,000
Long-term liabilities—current portion		1,525,000
Revenue bonds payable		25,000,000
Compensated absences payable		3,200,000
Net assets—invested in capital assets, net of related debt		33,175,000
Net assets—restricted, nonexpendable—scholarships and fellowships		9,000,000
Net assets—restricted, nonexpendable—research		2,300,000
Net assets—restricted, expendable—scholarships and fellowships .		6,300,000
Net assets—restricted, expendable—research		5,040,000
Net assets—restricted, expendable—capital projects		1,500,000
Net assets—restricted, expendable—debt service		2,100,000
Net assets—unrestricted	420,000	
Totals	$134,695,000	$134,695,000

The University maintains separate Net Asset accounts for each of the restricted revenue sources (scholarships and fellowships, research, and capital projects). Net assets labeled as *restricted, nonexpendable* are used to record endowment principal that must be maintained. The restricted net asset account labeled *debt service* is a sinking fund required by debt covenant. In the example that follows, restricted revenues (and the associated cash received) are designated through account titles that reflect these categories of restricted net assets. At year-end, restricted revenues (endowment income, grants, and contributions) are closed along with any expenses incurred from restricted resources to reflect the ending balance in each restricted net asset category.

Illustrative Case—Journal Entries

Student tuition and fees, exclusive of summer session, were assessed in the amount of $21,500,000. Scholarship allowances were made, for which no services were required, in the amount of $800,000. Graduate and other assistantships awarded, for which services were required, amounted to $1,500,000 of unrestricted resources. Collections were made on student fees in the amount of $19,100,000.

	Debits	Credits
1. Accounts Receivable	21,500,000	
Operating Revenue—Student Tuition and Fees.........		21,500,000
2. Operating Revenue Deduction—Scholarship Allowances ...	800,000	
Accounts Receivable		800,000
3. Scholarships and Fellowships Expense	1,500,000	
Accounts Receivable		1,500,000
4. Cash and Cash Equivalents	19,100,000	
Accounts Receivable		19,100,000

Note that the $800,000 is recorded as a revenue reduction and the $1,500,000 is recorded as an expense. This is due to the requirement that scholarships for which no services are required are to be recorded as a revenue deduction, and scholarships for which services are required are to be recorded as an expense.

The $830,000 Deferred Revenue in the beginning trial balance represents tuition and fees that applied to the summer school term running from June to August 2011. As of June 30, services had not been provided for much of that summer school session. The $830,000 is recognized as a revenue for the year ended June 30, 2012. In June 2012, $1,150,000 was assessed for the summer term that takes place June through August. Of that amount, $300,000 applied to the year ending June 30, 2012, the remainder is deferred until the following year. No scholarships or fellowships were involved.

5. Deferred Revenues................................	830,000	
Operating Revenues—Student Tuition and Fees.........		830,000
6. Cash and Cash Equivalents	1,150,000	
Operating Revenues—Student Tuition and Fees.........		300,000
Deferred Revenues................................		850,000

State appropriations were received in cash as follows: $22,500,000 for unrestricted general purposes and $1,300,000 for capital outlay, set aside for specific projects.

7. Cash and Cash Equivalents	22,500,000	
Restricted Cash and Cash Equivalents.................	1,300,000	
Nonoperating Revenues—State Appropriations		22,500,000
Capital Appropriations............................		1,300,000

It should be noted that GASB made a deliberate decision to categorize the general state appropriation as a nonoperating revenue of public colleges and universities, even though similar items, such as those shown in the next entry, are considered operating revenues.

Federal grants and contracts were awarded and received in cash in the amount of $4,250,000. State grants and contracts were awarded and also received in cash in the amount of $1,690,000. All of these grants and contracts were restricted for specific purposes, as the following entries show (amounts assumed):

	Debits	Credits
8. Restricted Cash and Cash Equivalents.................	5,940,000	
Operating Revenues—Restricted—Federal Grants and Contracts—Research.......................		2,250,000
Operating Revenues—Restricted—Federal Grants and Contracts—Scholarships and Fellowships		2,000,000
Operating Revenues—Restricted—State Grants and Contracts—Research.......................		890,000
Operating Revenues—Restricted—State Grants and Contracts—Scholarships and Fellowships		800,000

In practice, many grants are reimbursement grants, which are reimbursed after expenditures take place. If this is the case, GASB *Statement 33* requires that revenues be recognized only after the expenditure takes place. Assume that expenditures for these grants are included in entry 18.

Revenues from bookstore, dormitory, food service, and other auxiliary enterprise operations are received in cash in the amount of $15,200,000.

9. Cash and Cash Equivalents	15,200,000	
Operating Revenues—Auxiliary Enterprises............		15,200,000

Contributions were received as follows, all in cash: unrestricted, $870,000; restricted for scholarships and fellowships, $500,000; restricted for research, $620,000; restricted for building projects, $600,000:

10. Cash and Cash Equivalents	870,000	
Restricted Cash and Cash Equivalents..................	1,720,000	
Nonoperating Revenues—Gifts.....................		870,000
Nonoperating Revenues—Restricted—Gifts— Scholarships and Fellowships		500,000
Nonoperating Revenues—Restricted—Gifts—Research ..		620,000
Capital grants and gifts..............................		600,000

GASB *Statement 33* contains provisions regarding the recognition of voluntary nonexchange transactions, including contributions. Generally speaking, pledges or contributions receivable are recognized as assets and revenues when eligibility requirements are met. In order to be recognized in advance of collection, the contribution must be unconditional and must not contain a provision that funds are to be used in future years. Chapter 3 contains more detail on revenue recognition from nonexchange transactions.

Donors contributed $1,200,000 for endowments, the principal of which may not be expended. Of this amount, $700,000 was to support scholarships and fellowships; the remainder was to support research. The cash was immediately invested.

	Debits	Credits
11. Restricted Cash and Cash Equivalents.....................	1,200,000	
Additions to Permanent Endowments—		
Income Restricted for Scholarships and Fellowships		700,000
Additions to Permanent Endowments—		
Income Restricted for Research.....................		500,000
12. Endowment Investments	1,200,000	
Restricted Cash and Cash Equivalents..................		1,200,000

Interest receivable at the beginning of the year was collected in the amount of $210,000. Note that, of that amount, $185,000 was restricted:

	Debits	Credits
13. Cash and Cash Equivalents	25,000	
Restricted Cash and Cash Equivalents...................	185,000	
Interest Receivable—Unrestricted.....................		25,000
Interest Receivable—Restricted.......................		185,000

During the year, investment income was earned on investments whose income is unrestricted in the amount of $430,000, of which $30,000 was accrued interest at year-end. Investment income was earned on investments for which income is restricted amounted to $1,970,000, of which $200,000 was accrued interest at year-end. Of the $1,970,000, $1,260,000 is for scholarships and fellowships and $710,000 is for research:

	Debits	Credits
14. Cash and Cash Equivalents	400,000	
Interest Receivable—Unrestricted......................	30,000	
Nonoperating Revenues—Investment Income............		430,000

	Debits	Credits
15. Restricted Cash and Cash Equivalents.................	1,770,000	
Interest Receivable—Restricted.......................	200,000	
Nonoperating Revenues—Restricted—		
Investment Income—Scholarships and Fellowships		1,260,000
Nonoperating Revenues—Restricted—		
Investment Income—Research		710,000

All accounts payable and accrued liabilities existing at the beginning of the year were paid. Of the $1,725,000, $1,234,000 was paid with unrestricted cash and $491,000 was paid with restricted cash:

	Debits	Credits
16. Accounts Payable and Accrued Liabilities..............	1,725,000	
Cash and Cash Equivalents		1,234,000
Restricted Cash and Cash Equivalents................		491,000

Unrestricted expenses amounted to: salaries—faculty, $17,432,000; salaries—exempt staff, $14,143,000; wages—nonexempt employees, $6,212,000; benefits, $4,567,000; utilities, $5,515,000; supplies and other services, $4,753,000. All beginning inventories ($1,560,000) were consumed in the process of incurring those expenses, cash was paid in the amount of $50,000,000; accounts payable and accrued liabilities increased by $1,062,000:

	Debits	Credits
17. Operating Expenses—Salaries—Faculty................	17,432,000	
Operating Expenses—Salaries—Exempt Staff	14,143,000	
Operating Expenses—Wages—Nonexempt	6,212,000	
Operating Expenses—Benefits	4,567,000	
Operating Expenses—Utilities.......................	5,515,000	
Operating Expenses—Supplies and Other Services........	4,753,000	
Inventories		1,560,000
Cash and Cash Equivalents		50,000,000
Accounts Payable and Accrued Liabilities.............		1,062,000

Note that the expenses are reported by object classification rather than by functions such as instruction and research. Past accounting principles required the reporting of expenditures by function; public colleges and universities normally budget by departments, which can be combined into functions. Colleges may wish to report by function in lieu of (or in addition to) reporting by object classification; however, the GASB *Statement 35* illustrative statements reflect reporting by object classification.

Restricted operating expenses included salaries—faculty, $1,899,000; salaries—exempt staff, $644,000; wages—nonexempt staff, $499,000; benefits, $634,000; utilities, $253,000; supplies and other services, $142,000; scholarships and fellowships, $4,000,000. Restricted cash was paid in the amount of $7,872,000; accounts payable and accrued liabilities increased by $199,000:

	Debits	Credits
18. Operating Expenses—Restricted—Salaries—Faculty........	1,899,000	
Operating Expenses—Restricted—Salaries—Exempt Staff ...	644,000	
Operating Expenses—Restricted—Wages—Nonexempt	499,000	
Operating Expenses—Restricted—Benefits	634,000	
Operating Expenses—Restricted—Utilities...............	253,000	
Operating Expenses—Restricted—Supplies and Other Services.....................	142,000	
Operating Expenses—Restricted—Scholarships and Fellowships	4,000,000	
Restricted Cash and Cash Equivalents................		7,872,000
Accounts Payable and Accrued Liabilities.............		199,000

During the year, depreciation was recorded in the following amounts: buildings, $1,402,000; equipment, $3,140,000; improvements other than buildings, $600,000. Northern State depreciates infrastructure (improvements other than buildings) rather than using the modified approach:

	Debits	Credits
19. Operating Expenses—Depreciation....................	5,142,000	
Accumulated Depreciation—Buildings................		1,402,000
Accumulated Depreciation—Equipment...............		3,140,000
Accumulated Depreciation—Improvements Other Than Buildings............................		600,000

During the year, the following capital expenditures were made: land, $2,125,000; buildings, $1,600,000; equipment, $2,400,000; improvements other than buildings, $400,000. Restricted cash was decreased in the amount of $2,600,000; unrestricted cash was decreased in the amount of $3,825,000; accounts payable and accrued liabilities increased by $100,000:

	Debits	Credits
20. Land..	2,125,000	
Buildings	1,600,000	
Equipment	2,400,000	
Improvements Other Than Buildings....................	400,000	
Restricted Cash and Cash Equivalents................		2,600,000
Cash and Cash Equivalents		3,825,000
Accounts Payable and Accrued Liabilities.............		100,000

Inventories were purchased in the amount of $1,355,000; unrestricted cash was paid:

	Debits	Credits
21. Inventories	1,355,000	
Cash and Cash Equivalents		1,355,000

Interest on revenue bonds, all related to capital outlay purchases, amounted to $1,500,000; all but $120,000 was paid in cash. In addition, revenue bonds were paid in the amount of $1,525,000; no new revenue bonds were issued. Next year, revenue bonds in the amount of $1,475,000 will be payable. Additional cash was sent to the bond trustee, as required by the bond indenture, in the amount of $200,000. Unrestricted cash was used for all these transactions:

	Debits	Credits
22. Nonoperating Expenses—Interest on		
Capital-Asset-Related Debt	1,500,000	
Cash and Cash Equivalents		1,380,000
Accounts Payable and Accrued Liabilities.		120,000
23. Long-Term Liabilities—Current Portion	1,525,000	
Cash and Cash Equivalents		1,525,000
24. Revenue Bonds Payable.............................	1,475,000	
Long-Term Liabilities—Current Portion		1,475,000
25. Deposits with Bond Trustee.........................	200,000	
Cash and Cash Equivalents		200,000
Net Assets—Unrestricted...........................	200,000	
Net Assets—Restricted—Debt Service		200,000

It was determined that the accrued liability for compensated absences increased by $412,000 during the year:

	Debits	Credits
26. Operating Expenses—Benefits	412,000	
Compensated Absences Payable		412,000

All short-term investments existing at the beginning of the year, in the amount of $12,520,000, were sold for $12,770,000. New short-term investments were purchased in the amount of $13,550,000. Unrealized gains on short-term investments at year-end amounted to $166,000. The value of endowment investments remained unchanged.

	Debits	Credits
27. Cash and Cash Equivalents	12,770,000	
Short-Term Investments...........................		12,520,000
Investment Income...............................		250,000
28. Short-Term Investments............................	13,550,000	
Cash and Cash Equivalents		13,550,000
29. Short-Term Investments............................	166,000	
Investment Income...............................		166,000

The same account, Investment Income, is credited in entries 27 and 29, as GASB *Statement 31* does not allow realized and unrealized gains to be reported separately.

Illustrative Case—Closing Entries

A number of closing entries are required to place the correct amounts in the appropriate net asset classifications. The first is to close all unrestricted revenues and expenses to Net Assets—Unrestricted:

30. Operating Revenues—Student Tuition and Fees.............	22,630,000	
Nonoperating Revenues—State Appropriations	22,500,000	
Operating Revenues—Auxiliary Enterprises...............	15,200,000	
Nonoperating Revenues—Gifts.........................	870,000	
Nonoperating Revenues—Investment Income	846,000	
Operating Revenue Deduction—Scholarship Allowances ...		800,000
Operating Expenses—Scholarships and Fellowships		1,500,000
Operating Expenses—Salaries—Faculty.................		17,432,000
Operating Expenses—Salaries—Exempt Staff		14,143,000
Operating Expenses—Wages—Nonexempt		6,212,000
Operating Expenses—Benefits		4,979,000
Operating Expenses—Utilities.........................		5,515,000
Operating Expenses—Supplies and Other Services		4,753,000
Operating Expenses—Depreciation.....................		5,142,000
Nonoperating Expenses—Interest on Capital-Related Debt...		1,500,000
Net Assets—Unrestricted............................		70,000

The restricted revenues and expenses are closed out to the related restricted net asset accounts. First, the nonexpendable additions are closed out:

	Debits	Credits
31. Addition to Permanent Endowment—		
Scholarships and Fellowships	700,000	
Addition to Permanent Endowment—Research	500,000	
Net Assets—Restricted—Nonexpendable—		
Scholarships and Fellowships		700,000
Net Assets—Restricted—Nonexpendable—Research		500,000

Next, the grants for scholarships and fellowships are closed out against the restricted expenses:

	Debits	Credits
32. Operating Revenues—Restricted—Federal Grants		
and Contracts—Scholarships and Fellowships	2,000,000	
Operating Revenues—Restricted—State Grants		
and Contracts—Scholarships and Fellowships	800,000	
Nonoperating Revenues—Restricted—Gifts—		
Scholarships and Fellowships	500,000	
Nonoperating Revenues—Restricted—Investment Income—		
Scholarships and Fellowships	1,260,000	
Operating Expenses—Scholarships and Fellowships		4,000,000
Net Assets—Restricted—Expendable—		
Scholarships and Fellowships		560,000

The grants for research are closed out against the related expenses, with the difference going to the appropriate net asset category:

	Debits	Credits
33. Operating Revenues—Restricted—Federal Grants		
and Contracts—Research	2,250,000	
Operating Revenues—Restricted—State Grants		
and Contracts—Research	890,000	
Nonoperating Revenues—Restricted—Gifts—Research	620,000	
Nonoperating Revenues—Restricted—		
Investment Income—Research	710,000	
Operating Expenses—Restricted—Salaries—Faculty		1,899,000
Operating Expenses—Restricted—Salaries—Exempt Staff . . .		644,000
Operating Expenses—Restricted—Wages—Nonexempt		499,000
Operating Expenses—Restricted—Benefits		634,000
Operating Expenses—Restricted—Utilities		253,000
Operating Expenses—Restricted—Supplies and Other Services		142,000
Net Assets—Restricted—Expendable—Research		399,000

The capital appropriations and gifts restricted for capital acquisition are closed to the Net Assets—Restricted—Expendable—Capital Projects:

	Debits	Credits
34. Capital Appropriations	1,300,000	
Capital Gifts and Grants	600,000	
Net Assets—Restricted—Expendable—Capital Projects		1,900,000

An examination of entry 20 reveals that $2,600,000 of restricted resources were used to acquire plant; this amount should be taken from the account Net Assets—Expendable—Capital Projects classification and transferred to the Net Assets—Invested in Capital Assets, Net of Related Debt classification:

35. Net Assets—Restricted—Expendable—Capital Projects	2,600,000	
Net Assets—Invested in Capital Assets, Net of Related Debt .		2,600,000

Finally, it is necessary to adjust the Net Assets—Invested in Capital Assets, Net of Related Debt to reflect the balance of the fixed assets, less depreciation, less debt. The balance of the capital assets accounts (land, buildings, equipment, improvements other than buildings) is $109,225,000. The balance of the accumulated depreciation accounts is $48,142,000. The accounts for capital related debt (Revenue Bonds Payable plus Long-Term Liabilities—Current Portion) is $25,000,000. The balance in the Net Assets—Invested in Capital Assets, Net of Related Debt, should be $36,083,000. As the balance reflects $35,775,000 (after entry 35), an adjusting entry is needed to increase the account by $308,000:

36. Net Assets—Unrestricted	308,000	
Net Assets—Invested in Capital Assets, Net of Related Debt . .		308,000

An examination of related journal entries explains the $308,000:

Entry 20, purchase of capital assets	$ 6,525,000
Entry 19, depreciation.	(5,142,000)
Entry 23, debt payment.	1,525,000
Less adjustment for entry 35	(2,600,000)
Entry 35	$ 308,000

Illustrative Case—Financial Statements

Colleges reporting as special-purpose entities engaged only in business-type activities are required to prepare three statements. These are (1) the Statement of Net Assets, (2) the Statement of Revenues, Expenses, and Changes in Net Assets, and (3) the Statement of Cash Flows. Illustrations 9–4, 9–5, and 9–6 present these

ILLUSTRATION 9–4   Statement of Net Assets

NORTHERN STATE UNIVERSITY Statement of Net Assets June 30, 2012	
Assets	
Current assets:	
Cash and cash equivalents	$ 1,446,000
Short-term investments	13,716,000
Accounts receivable, net	1,350,000
Interest receivable, unrestricted	30,000
Inventories	1,355,000
Deposits with bond trustee	2,300,000
Total current assets	20,197,000
Noncurrent assets:	
Restricted cash and cash equivalents	87,000
Endowment investments	12,500,000
Interest receivable, restricted	200,000
Capital assets, net	61,083,000
Total noncurrent assets	73,870,000
Total assets	94,067,000
Liabilities	
Current liabilities:	
Accounts payable and accrued liabilities	1,481,000
Deferred revenues	850,000
Long-term liabilities—current portion	1,475,000
Total current liabilities	3,806,000
Noncurrent liabilities:	
Revenue bonds payable	23,525,000
Compensated absences payable	3,612,000
Total noncurrent liabilities	27,137,000
Total liabilities	30,943,000
Net Assets	
Invested in capital assets, net of related debt	36,083,000
Restricted for:	
Nonexpendable:	
Scholarships and fellowships	9,700,000
Research	2,800,000
Expendable:	
Scholarships and fellowships	6,860,000
Research	5,439,000
Capital projects	800,000
Debt service	2,300,000
Unrestricted	(858,000)
Total net assets	$63,124,000

statements for Northern State University. These statements incorporate the beginning trial balance and journal entries shown above and follow the illustrative statements in GASB *Statement 35*.

Illustration 9–4 reports the Statement of Net Assets for Northern State University. Northern State does not have a discretely presented component unit: if it did, then a column would be prepared for this and the other two statements for the component unit. As mentioned earlier, many public universities have related foundations that hold resources, some of which are nonexpendable (endowments) and some of which are expendable for restricted and unrestricted purposes. Such foundations normally meet the requirements for presentation as component units.

Illustration 9–5 reports the Statement of Revenues, Expenses, and Changes in Net Assets for Northern State University. This is in the same general format as presented for the enterprise fund for the Village of Elizabeth in Chapter 6 (Illustration 6–4) and follows the GASB illustrative statement in *Statement 35*. Note that an operating income figure is presented; this is required. GASB specifically requires that state appropriations for operating purposes be shown as nonoperating revenue. As is true with all GASB operating statements, an "all-inclusive" format is used, reconciling to the ending net asset balance. The net asset balance in this statement is the same as the total net assets in Illustration 9–4.

Illustration 9–6 presents the Statement of Cash Flows for Northern State University. This statement follows the rules outlined in Chapter 6 for cash flows for enterprise funds. GASB specifically requires that cash received for the state appropriation for operations be reported under cash flows from noncapital financing activities rather than cash flows for operating activities. The direct method is required by GASB, and a reconciliation is provided between the operating income (loss) in Illustration 9–5 and the cash flow from operations in this illustration. Note, as was the case in Chapter 6, that cash received for interest is shown as cash flows received from investing activities, cash paid for interest is shown as cash used for financing activities, and capital asset acquisitions are shown as financing activities.

The numbers in the Statement of Cash Flows can be traced from the trial balance, journal entries, and other statements, with one exception. In the reconciliation section, Accounts Payable and Accrued Liabilities includes liabilities for accrued interest payable and for plant acquisition, both of which are not related to cash flows from operations. If $180,000 of the $1,725,000 balance in the beginning trial balance is related to debt service and plant acquisition and $220,000 of the ending balance of $1,481,000 in the Statement of Net Assets (Illustration 9–4) is related to debt service and plant acquisition (see entries 20 and 22), then the decrease in cash caused by a decrease in accounts payable and accrued liabilities from operations would be $244,000 ($1,525,000 − $1,281,000).

ILLUSTRATION 9–5   Statement of Revenues, Expenses, and Changes in Net Assets

NORTHERN STATE UNIVERSITY Statement of Revenues, Expenses, and Changes in Net Assets For the Year Ended June 30, 2012	
Revenues	
Operating revenues:	
Student tuition and fees (net of scholarship allowances of $800)	$21,830,000
Federal grants and contracts	4,250,000
State grants and contracts	1,690,000
Auxiliary enterprises	15,200,000
Total operating revenues	42,970,000
Expenses	
Operating expenses:	
Salaries:	
Faculty	19,331,000
Exempt staff	14,787,000
Nonexempt wages	6,711,000
Benefits	5,613,000
Scholarships and fellowships	5,500,000
Utilities	5,768,000
Supplies and other services	4,895,000
Depreciation	5,142,000
Total operating expenses	67,747,000
Operating income (loss)	(24,777,000)
Nonoperating Revenues (Expenses)	
State appropriations	22,500,000
Gifts	1,990,000
Investment income	2,816,000
Interest on capital-related debt	(1,500,000)
Total nonoperating revenues (expenses)	25,806,000
Income before other revenues expenses, gains, or losses	1,029,000
Capital appropriations	1,300,000
Capital gifts and grants	600,000
Additions to permanent endowments	1,200,000
Increase in net assets	4,129,000
Net Assets	
Net assets—beginning of year	58,995,000
Net assets—end of year	$63,124,000

ILLUSTRATION 9–6   Statement of Cash Flows

NORTHERN STATE UNIVERSITY Statement of Cash Flows For the Year Ended June 30, 2012	
Cash Flows from Operating Activities	
Tuition and fees	$ 20,250,000
Federal grants and contracts	4,250,000
State grants and contracts	1,690,000
Auxiliary enterprises	15,200,000
Payments to employees, including benefits	(46,030,000)
Payment to suppliers	(10,922,000)
Payment of scholarships to students	(4,000,000)
Net cash provided (used) by operating activities	(19,562,000)
Cash Flows from Noncapital Financing Activities	
State appropriations	22,500,000
Gifts, other than for endowment purposes	1,990,000
Gifts for endowment purposes	1,200,000
Net cash flows provided by noncapital financing activities	25,690,000
Cash Flows from Capital and Related Financing Activities	
Capital appropriations	1,300,000
Capital grants and gifts	600,000
Purchases of capital assets	(6,425,000)
Interest on capital-related debt	(1,380,000)
Principal on capital-related debt	(1,525,000)
Cash deposited with bond trustee	(200,000)
Net cash provided (used) by capital and related financing activities	(7,630,000)
Cash Flows from Investing Activities	
Purchase of endowment investments	(1,200,000)
Interest on investments	2,380,000
Proceeds from sales of investments	12,770,000
Purchase of investments other than endowments	(13,550,000)
Net cash provided by investing activities	400,000
Net increase (decrease) in cash	(1,102,000)
Cash—beginning of year	2,635,000
Cash—end of year	$ 1,533,000
Reconciliation of net operating revenues (expenses) to net cash **provided (used) by operating activities:**	
Operating income (loss)	$(24,777,000)
Adjustments to reconcile operating income (loss) to net cash provided (used) by operating activities:	
Depreciation expense	5,142,000
Changes in assets and liabilities:	
Receivables, net	(100,000)
Inventories	205,000
Deposit with bond trustee	(200,000)
Accounts payable and accrued liabilities	(264,000)
Deferred revenue	20,000
Compensated absences	412,000
Net cash provided (used) by operating activities	$(19,562,000)

SUMMARY

This chapter presents reporting by special-purpose entities, including accounting and financial reporting by public colleges and universities.

Financial reporting by a special-purpose governmental entity depends upon whether that entity is engaged in governmental and business-type activities, multiple governmental activities, a single governmental activity, business-type activities only, or fiduciary activities only. Special-purpose entities that are engaged only in one governmental activity are allowed to combine fund and government-wide statements. Special-purpose governments that are engaged in business-type or fiduciary activities only are permitted to report only fund information.

Accounting and financial reporting by public colleges and universities follows GASB *Statement 35,* which incorporated public educational institutions into GASB *Statement 34* as special-purpose entities. Many public colleges and universities follow the provisions outlined in *Statement 34* for reporting as special-purpose entities engaged in business-type activities only. GASB *Statement 35* includes nonauthoritative financial statement presentations which serve as the basis for the presentation in this text.

Now that you have finished reading Chapter 9, complete the multiple choice questions provided on the text's Web site (www.mhhe.com/copley10e) to test your comprehension of the chapter.

Questions and Exercises

9–1. Obtain an annual report from a public college or university and answer the following questions:

    a. Does the institution report as a special-purpose entity engaged in (1) governmental- and business-type activities or (2) business-type activities only? Are the financial statements appropriate, based on the choice made by the institution? (The remaining questions assume the institution reports as a special-purpose entity engaged only in business-type activities.)

    b. Does the institution report a Statement of Net Assets? Are net assets separated between (1) invested in capital assets, net of related debt, (2) restricted, and (3) unrestricted? List the major restrictions. Is the statement reported in a classified format? Does the institution report component units? What are they? Note the balance of unrestricted net assets. Is the number negative? Look at the number shown for compensated absences. Would that change your opinion of the financial status of the institution?

    c. Does the institution report a Statement of Revenues, Expenses, and Changes in Net Assets? If so, is a measure of operations (such as operating income) reported? Are scholarships and fellowships, for which no service is provided, deducted from student tuition and fees? Is the state appropriation for operations shown as a nonoperating revenue? Are operating expenses reported by object classification or by function? Are capital appropriations, capital gifts and grants, additions to permanent endowments, and any special or extraordinary items shown after non-operating revenues (expenses)? Does the statement reconcile to the ending net assets figure?

d. Does the institution report a Statement of Cash Flows? Is the direct method used, as required by GASB? Are the four categories required by GASB shown? If not, which is not shown? Are interest receipts shown as cash provided by investing activities and interest payments shown as cash used for financing activities? Are capital assets acquired shown as cash used for financing activities? Is a reconciliation schedule prepared, reconciling operating income to cash provided (used) for operations? Is the state appropriation for operations shown as cash provided by financing activities?

Special-Purpose Entities

9–2. GASB *Statement 34, Basic Financial Statements—and Management's Discussion and Analysis—for State and Local Governments,* provides guidance for reporting by special-purpose entities. That guidance depends upon whether special-purpose entities are engaged in activities that are governmental-type, business-type only, or fiduciary-type only. Discuss the guidance and list required basic financial statements for:

  a. Governments engaged in governmental-type activities. Include those that are engaged in governmental- and business-type activities, more than one governmental activity, and only one governmental activity.

  b. Governments engaged in business-type activities only.

  c. Governments engaged in fiduciary-type activities only.

9–3. Presented below is the governmental funds balance sheet for the Warrenton Library District, a special-purpose entity engaged in a single governmental activity. Prepare a combined Governmental Funds Balance Sheet/Statement of Net Assets in the format presented in Illustration 9–2.

WARRENTON LIBRARY DISTRICT
Governmental Funds Balance Sheet
As of December 31, 2012

Assets	General Fund	Special Revenue Fund	Total
Cash and cash equivalents	$125,000	$12,000	$137,000
Inventories	6,000		6,000
Receivables (net)			
Taxes receivable	95,000		95,000
Due from General Fund		7,500	7,500
Total assets	226,000	19,500	245,500

Liabilities

Accounts payable	85,000	3,500	88,500
Due to Special Revenue Fund	7,500		7,500
Total liabilities	92,500	3,500	96,000
Fund balance			
Nonspendable (inventories)	6,000		6,000
Restricted for other purposes		16,000	16,000
Unassigned	127,500		127,500
Total fund balance	133,500	16,000	149,500
Total liabilities and fund balance	$226,000	$19,500	$245,500

Additional information:

a. Capital assets (net of accumulated depreciation) amounted to $300,000 at year-end.

b. The liability for long-term compensated absences is estimated to be $86,000 at year-end.

c. Long-term notes payable amounted to $250,000 at year-end.

9–4. Presented below is the governmental funds Statement of Revenues, Expenditures, and Changes in Fund Balance the Trinity Parish Fire District, a special-purpose entity engaged in a single governmental activity. Prepare a combined Governmental Funds Balance Sheet/Statement of Net Assets in the format presented in Illustration 9–3.

TRINITY PARISH FIRE DISTRICT
Governmental Funds: Statement of Revenues, Expenditures and
Changes in Fund Balances
For The Year Ended December 31, 2012

	General Fund	Special Revenue Fund	Total
Revenues			
Property taxes	$300,000	—	$300,000
Intergovernmental	28,000	$19,500	47,500
Miscellaneous	5,000	—	5,000
Total revenues	333,000	19,500	352,500
Expenditures			
Current			
Personnel services	150,000	15,000	165,000
Supplies	25,000	—	25,000
Capital outlay	128,000	—	128,000
Debt service			
Principal	2,000	—	2,000
Interest	8,000	—	8,000
Total expenditures	313,000	15,000	328,000

Revenues over expenditures	20,000	4,500	24,500
Other financing sources (uses):			
Issuance of debt	15,000	—	15,000
Transfers from other funds		5,000	5,000
Transfers (to) other funds	(5,000)	—	(5,000)
	10,000	5,000	15,000
Excess of revenues and other sources over			
(under) expenditures and other uses	30,000	9,500	39,500
Fund balance—beginning of year	22,000	(8,000)	14,000
Fund balance—end of year	$52,000	$1,500	$53,500

Additional information:

a. Property taxes expected to be collected more than 60 days following year-end are deferred in the fund-basis statements. Deferred taxes totaled $22,000 at the end of 2011 and $36,000 at the end of 2012.

b. The current year provision for depreciation totaled $52,000.

c. Interest on long-term notes payable is paid monthly (no accrual is necessary).

d. Total Net Assets on the December 31, 2011, Statement of Net Assets totaled $140,000.

Public Colleges and Universities

9–5. Southern State University had the following account balances as of June 30, 2012. Debits are not distinguished from credits, so assume all accounts have a "normal" balance:

Accounts receivable	$ 325,000
Accounts payable	265,000
Cash and cash equivalents	154,000
Deferred revenue—current	220,000
Endowment investments	6,123,000
General obligation bonds payable (related to capital acquisition)	1,250,000
Inventories	333,000
Short-term investments—unrestricted	1,444,000
Net assets—restricted—nonexpendable	6,123,000
Restricted cash and cash equivalents	92,000
Capital assets, net of depreciation	7,226,000
Revenue bonds payable (related to capital acquisition)	2,200,000
Long-term investments	1,683,000
Long-term liabilities—current portion (related to capital acquisition)	200,000
Net assets—restricted—expendable	1,775,000
Net assets—invested in capital assets, net of related debt	?
Net assets—unrestricted	?

Required:

Prepare, in good form, a Statement of Net Assets for Southern State University as of June 30, 2012.

9–6. Western State University had the following account balances for the year ended and as of June 30, 2012. Debits are not distinguished from credits, so assume all accounts have a "normal" balance.

Student tuition and fee revenue	$ 9,045,000
Scholarship tuition and fee contra revenue	920,000
Scholarships and fellowships expense	988,000
State appropriation for operations	10,000,000
Auxiliary enterprise revenue	9,321,000
Salaries—faculty	8,312,000
Capital appropriations	2,100,000
Depreciation expense	3,276,000
Salaries—exempt staff	5,432,000
Capital grants and gifts	1,110,000
Benefits	3,582,000
Federal grants and contracts revenue	1,221,000
Nonexempt wages	4,729,000
State and local grants and contracts revenue	898,000
Gifts	1,345,000
Additions to permanent endowments	900,000
Investment income	873,000
Other operating expenses	2,982,000
Interest on capital-related debt	1,984,000
Net assets, beginning of year	4,680,000

Required:

Prepare, in good form, a Statement of Revenues, Expenses, and Changes in Net Assets for Western State University for the year ended June 30, 2012.

9–7. The New City College reported deferred revenues of $607,000 as of July 1, 2011, the first day of its fiscal year. Record the following transactions related to student tuition and fees and related scholarship allowances for New City College for the year ended June 30, 2012.

a. The deferred revenues related to unearned revenues for the summer session, which ended in August.

b. During the fiscal year ended June 30, 2012, student tuition and fees were assessed in the amount of $12,000,000. Of that amount $9,600,000 was collected in cash. Also of that amount, $650,000 pertained to that portion of the summer session that took place after June 30.

c. Student scholarships, for which no services were required, amounted to $930,000. Students applied these scholarships to their tuition bills at the beginning of each semester.

d. Student scholarships and fellowships, for which services were required, such as graduate assistantships, amounted to $760,000. These students also applied their scholarship and fellowship awards to their tuition bills at the beginning of each semester.

9–8. Eastern State College had the following trial balance as of July 1, 2011, the first day of its fiscal year (in thousands):

	Debits	Credits
Cash and cash equivalents	$ 330	
Accounts receivable—net	1,100	
Short-term investments	2,400	
Interest receivable—unrestricted	50	
Deposits with bond trustee	1,800	
Restricted cash and cash equivalents	210	
Endowment investments	9,100	
Long-term investments	8,400	
Interest receivable—restricted	200	
Capital assets	22,300	
Accumulated depreciation—capital assets		$ 9,210
Accounts payable and accrued liabilities		800
Deferred revenues		500
Long-term liabilities—current portion		800
Bonds payable (related to capital outlay)		5,000
Compensated absences payable		900
Net assets—invested in capital assets, net of related debt		7,290
Net assets—restricted—nonexpendable		9,100
Net assets—restricted—expendable—debt service		1,800
Net assets—restricted—expendable—capital outlay		500
Net assets—restricted—expendable—other		8,100
Net assets—unrestricted		1,890
Totals	$45,890	$45,890

During the fiscal year ended June 30, 2012, the following transactions occurred (amounts are in thousands):

1. Student tuition and fees were assessed in the amount of $18,350. Scholarship allowances were made, for which no services were required, in the amount of $1,260. Graduate and other assistantships were awarded, for which services were required, in the amount of $1,420. All scholarship and assistantship allowances were credited against student's bills. Collections were made on account in the amount of $15,700.

2. The $500 in deferred revenues relate to cash collected prior to June 30, 2011, and to tuition revenue that should be recognized in the current year. Also $550 of the $18,300 assumed in (1) above applies to fees that should be recognized as revenue in the year ended June 30, 2013 (i.e., next year).

3. State appropriations were received in cash as follows: $13,020 for general operations and $800 for capital outlay, set aside for specific projects.

4. Federal grants and contracts, for restricted purposes, were received in cash in the amount of $2,310. State and local grants and contracts, also for restricted purposes, were received in cash in the amount of $930.

5. Revenues from auxiliary enterprise operations amounted to $12,300, of which $12,100 was received in cash.

6. Contributions were received in cash as follows: unrestricted, $650; restricted for capital projects, $300; restricted for other purposes, $500.

7. Donors contributed $600 for endowments, the principal of which may not be expended. The income from these endowments is all restricted for operating purposes. The cash was immediately invested.

8. Interest receivable at the beginning of the year was collected.

9. During the year, investment income was earned on investments whose income is unrestricted in the amount of $200, of which $175 was received in cash. Investment income was earned on investments whose income is restricted in the amount of $1,500, of which $1,250 was received in cash.

10. All accounts payable and accrued liabilities as of the end of the previous year were paid in cash at year-end, using unrestricted cash.

11. Unrestricted expenses amounted to: salaries—faculty, $14,123; salaries—exempt staff, $10,111; nonexempt wages, $6,532; benefits, $6,112; other operating expenses, $1,100. Cash was paid in the amount of $36,878; the remainder was payable at year-end.

12. Restricted expenses amounted to: salaries—faculty, $2,256; salaries—exempt staff, $745; nonexempt wages, $213; benefits, $656; other operations, $1,100. Cash was paid in the amount of $4,612; the remainder was payable at year-end.

13. Depreciation was recorded in the amount of $1,410, all charged as unrestricted expense.

14. During the year, expenditures were made for property, plant, and equipment in the amount of $3,265, of which $1,050 was from resources restricted for capital outlay and the remainder was from unrestricted cash.

15. Interest on bonds payable, all related to capital outlay purchases, amounted to $348; all but $22 was paid in cash. Bonds were paid in the amount of $800; next year, $300 will be payable. No new revenue bonds were issued during the year. Unrestricted cash was used for all these transactions.

16. An additional $100 was deposited with the bond trustee, in accord with legal requirements.

17. The accrued liability for compensated absences increased by $100 during the year.

18. All short-term investments existing at the beginning of the year were sold for $2,450. New short-term investments were purchased for $2,650.

Unrealized gains were recorded at year-end as follows: short-term investments (unrestricted), $40; long-term investments (restricted) $120; endowment investments, $61.

19. Closing entries were prepared, separately, for each net asset class.

Required:

a. Prepare journal entries for each of the above transactions.

b. (Optional) Prepare a ledger. Enter beginning balances from the trial balance and all transactions.

c. Prepare, in good form, a Statement of Net Assets for Eastern State College as of June 30, 2012.

d. Prepare, in good form, a Statement of Revenues, Expenses, and Changes in Net Assets for Eastern State College for the year ended June 30, 2012.

Excel-Based Problem

9–9. The fund-basis financial statements of Cherokee Library District (a special-purpose government engaged only in governmental activities) have been completed for the year 2012 and appear in the second and third tabs of the Excel spreadsheet provided with this exercise. The following information is also available:

a. Capital assets

- Capital assets purchased in previous years through governmental-type funds totaled $17,000,000 and had accumulated depreciation of $2,250,000.

- Depreciation on capital assets used in governmental-type activities amounted to $300,000 for 2012.

- No capital assets were sold or disposed of in 2012, and all purchases are properly reflected in the fund-basis statements as capital expenditures.

b. Long-term debt

- There was $12,600,000 of outstanding long-term notes associated with governmental-type funds as of January 1, 2012. Interest is paid monthly.

- December 31, 2012, notes with a face value of $4,370,000 were issued at par. In addition, principal payments totaled $1,340,000.

- The notes, and any retained percentage on construction contracts, are associated with the purchase of capital assets.

c. Deferred revenues

- Deferred revenues are comprised solely of property taxes expected to be collected more than 60 days after year-end. The balance of deferred taxes at the end of 2011 was $65,000.

d. Transfers: Transfers were between governmental-type funds.

e. Beginning net assets for the government-wide statements totaled $17,589,321 as of January 1, 2012. This amount has already been entered in the Statement of Activities.

Required:

Use the Excel template provided to complete the following requirements; a separate tab is provided for each requirement.

a. Prepare the journal entries necessary to convert the governmental fund financial statements to the accrual basis of accounting.

b. Post the journal entries to the (shaded) Adjustments column to produce a Statement of Activities. You do not have to post amounts debited or credited to "(beginning) net assets." These have been reflected in item *e* above.

c. Post the journal entries to the (shaded) Adjustments column to produce a Statement of Net Assets. Calculate the appropriate amounts for the Net Assets accounts, assuming there are no restricted net assets.

Accounting for Private Not-for-Profit Organizations

As I started getting rich, I started thinking, "what the hell am I going to do with all this money?" . . . You have to learn to give. —Over a three year period, I gave away half of what I had. To be honest, my hands shook as I signed it away. I knew I was taking myself out of the race to be the richest man in the world. (Ted Turner, founder of CNN)

We need to motivate Americans to donate their time and their treasure, which is never easy, but always comes down to whether they trust an organization and believe in its work. (Marsha Johnson Evans, Red Cross President and CEO)

Learning Objectives

- Describe characteristics of private not-for-profit organizations and the accounting for contributions.
- Apply the accrual basis of accounting in the recording of typical transactions of private not-for-profit organizations.
- Prepare the financial statements for private not-for-profit organizations.

Chapter 1 indicated that the authority to set GAAP is split between the Financial Accounting Standards Board (FASB), the Governmental Accounting Standards Board (GASB), and the Federal Accounting Standards Advisory Board (FASAB). The FASB has standards-setting authority over business organizations and private not-for-profit organizations. The GASB has standards-setting authority over state and local governments, including governmentally related not-for-profit organizations such as hospitals and colleges and universities. Chapters 2 through 8 described accounting for state and local governmental units as outlined by the GASB. Chapter 9 outlined accounting for special-purpose entities and public colleges and universities. This chapter describes the accounting and reporting practices of private (nongovernmental) not-for-profit organizations.

Like governments, these organizations do not have an identifiable individual or group of individuals who hold a legally enforceable residual claim to the net assets of the organization. A distinguishing characteristic of the organizations described in this chapter is that they are not owned or controlled by a government. The activities of private not-for-profits are commonly financed through voluntary contributions. In 2008, Americans contributed more than $307 billion (about 2 percent of gross domestic product) to not-for-profit organizations.[1] Although these organizations may have creditors, the financial statements are intended primarily for use by present and potential donors. As was the case with governments, donors to private not-for-profit organizations often impose restrictions on the use of contributed resources.

Private not-for-profits must follow all applicable FASB standards in recording trans-actions.[2] For example, FASB standards regarding contingencies, capital leases, pensions, foreign exchange, and compensated absences all apply to not-for-profits engaged in those types of transactions. In addition, the FASB issues some standards that apply only to not-for-profit organizations. Typically these are in response to transactions or practices unique to not-for-profit organizations. Examples include contributions, donor-imposed restrictions, and gifts that are to be directed to another beneficiary.

The FASB's direct involvement in standard setting for private not-for-profits effectively began in 1993 with the issuance of two standards. FASB *Statement 116, Accounting for Contributions Received and Contributions Made,* and *Statement 117, Financial Statements of Not-for-Profit Organizations.* Prior to this, the financial reporting practices of not-for-profits had been established primarily through audit and accounting guides issued by the American Institute of Certified Public Accountants (AICPA). Under the old AICPA guides, different types of not-for-profit organizations (e.g., colleges, hospitals, or charities) followed very different accounting practices. Because all not-for-profits must now follow FASB *Statement 117,* not-for-profit financial statements are standardized across industries. While the AICPA still issues audit and accounting guides, these provide additional guidance in applying FASB standards to a particular industry.

The FASB, in Appendix D of *Statement 116,* distinguished a not-for-profit organization from a business as follows:

> an entity that possesses the following characteristics that distinguish it from a business enterprise: (a) contributions of significant amounts of resources from resource providers who do not expect commensurate or proportionate pecuniary return, (b) operating purposes other than to provide goods or services at a profit, and (c) absence of ownership interests like those of business enterprises.

As a result, private-sector not-for-profit organizations are to be distinguished both from business organizations, as indicated, and from governmental units. While the FASB has primary standard-setting authority, accounting practices are also influenced by two AICPA audit and accounting guides: *Not-for-Profit Organizations*

---

[1] American Association of Fund-Raising Counsel Trust for Philanthropy, *Giving USA* 2009, Glenview. IL (www.aafrc.org).

[2] Not all FASB statements are applicable to not-for-profit organizations (e.g., earnings per share would not be applicable since not-for-profits don't issue shares of stock).

(Not-for-Profit Guide)[3] and *Health Care Organizations* (Health-Care Guide).[4] The Health-Care Guide is discussed extensively in Chapter 12. The Not-for-Profit Guide applies only to nongovernmental not-for-profits, including voluntary health and welfare (i.e., social service) organizations and other (nonhealth care) organizations. This latter group include civic, political and religious associations, museums and schools, visual and performing arts groups, as well as professional, trade, and union organizations.

This chapter introduces the FASB and AICPA standards as applied to voluntary health and welfare organizations and other not-for-profit organizations. Chapters 11 and 12 cover nongovernmental colleges and universities and health care entities, respectively.

ORGANIZATIONS COVERED IN THIS CHAPTER

A **voluntary health and welfare organization** receives most of its support from voluntary contributions and is engaged in activities that promote the general health and well-being of the public. Typically, these organizations generate some revenues through user charges but receive most of their support from others who do not receive direct benefits. For example, a community mental health center may charge patients a fee based on their ability to pay, receive allocations from a United Way drive and direct gifts, get federal and state grants, and receive donated services and materials. Other examples of voluntary health and welfare organizations are charities such as the American Heart Association and the American Cancer Society, Meals on Wheels, senior citizen centers, Girl and Boy Scouts, and Big Brothers/Big Sisters.

Other not-for-profit organizations include cemetery associations, civic organizations, fraternal organizations, labor unions, libraries, museums, other cultural institutions, performing arts organizations, political parties, private schools, professional and trade associations, social and country clubs, research and scientific organizations, and religious organizations. Not-for-profit entities that operate essentially as commercial businesses for the direct economic benefit of members or stockholders (such as employee benefit and pension plans, mutual insurance companies, mutual banks, trusts, and farm cooperatives) are specifically excluded, as are governmental units.

OVERVIEW OF NOT-FOR-PROFIT ACCOUNTING

Three Classes of Net Assets

Private not-for-profits report both current and long-term assets and liabilities and measure revenues and expenses using the accrual basis of accounting. The financial statements of these organizations do not report by fund and the excess of assets

---

[3] American Institute of Certified Public Accountants, *AICPA Audit and Accounting Guide: Not-for-Profit Organizations* (New York: AICPA, 2009).

[4] *AICPA Audit and Accounting Guide: Health Care Organizations* (New York: AICPA, 2008).

over liabilities is termed *net assets,* not fund balance. The FASB has identified three classes of net assets: unrestricted, temporarily restricted, and permanently restricted. To be restricted, resources must be restricted by donors or grantors; internally (Board) designated resources are considered unrestricted.

Permanently restricted net assets include permanent endowments (resources that must be invested permanently) and certain assets such as land or artwork that must be maintained or used in a certain way. As the term indicates, these resources are expected to be restricted as long as the organization has custody.

Temporarily restricted net assets include unexpended resources that are to be used for a particular purpose or at a time in the future and resources that are to be invested for a period of time (under a term endowment). Temporarily restricted resources might also be used for the acquisition of a fixed asset. Temporarily restricted net assets come from contributions with donor-imposed restrictions and are released from restriction at some point in the future either through the passage of time or as a result of the organization using the resources according to the donor's wishes.

Unrestricted net assets include all other resources such as unrestricted contributions, revenues from providing services, and unrestricted income from investments. Resources are presumed to be unrestricted unless there is evidence of donor-imposed restrictions. Donor-restricted contributions whose restrictions are satisfied in the same accounting period that the contribution is received may also be reported as unrestricted.

Financial Reporting

Statements required are (1) Statement of Financial Position, (2) Statement of Activities, and (3) Statement of Cash Flows. Certain note disclosures are also required and others are recommended. In addition, voluntary health and welfare organizations are required to report a Statement of Functional Expenses that shows expenses by both function and natural classification. A great deal of flexibility is permitted in statement preparation, as long as certain requirements are met.

The **Statement of Financial Position** reports assets, liabilities, and net assets. Assets and liabilities are reported in order of liquidity, or a classified statement may be prepared. Net assets must be broken down into unrestricted, temporarily restricted, and permanently restricted classes. It is not necessary to identify which assets and liabilities are restricted.

The **Statement of Activities** reports revenues, expenses, gains, losses, and reclassifications (between classes of net assets). Organizationwide totals must be provided. Separate revenues, expenses, gains, losses, and reclassifications are also provided for each class of net assets. (Expenses are reported as decreases in unrestricted net assets.)

The **Statement of Cash Flows** uses the standard FASB categories (operating, investing, and financing). Either the indirect or the direct method may be used. The indirect method (or the reconciliation schedule for the direct method) reconciles the change in *total* net assets to the net cash used or provided by operating activities. Restricted contributions or restricted investment proceeds that will be used for long-term purposes (endowments or plant) are reported as financing activities.

A **Statement of Functional Expenses** is required for voluntary health and welfare organizations. It presents a matrix of expenses classified, on the one hand, by function (various programs, fund-raising, etc.) and, on the other hand, by object or natural classification (salaries, supplies, travel, etc.).

Note Disclosures

Note disclosures are required for all the standard FASB items that are relevant to nonprofit organizations. Additional specific requirements are: (1) policy disclosures related to choices made regarding whether temporarily restricted gifts received and expended in the same period and donated plant are reported first as temporarily restricted or unrestricted; (2) detailed information regarding the nature of temporarily and permanently restricted resources; (3) the amount of unconditional promises receivable in less than one year, one to five years, and more than five years; (4) the amount of the allowance for uncollectible promises receivable; (5) the total of conditional amounts promised; and (6) a description and amount for each group of conditional promises having similar characteristics.

Note disclosures are encouraged for (1) detail of reclassifications, (2) detail of investments, and (3) breakdown of expenses by function and natural classifications.

Accounting for Contributions, Including Reclassifications of Net Assets

Not-for-profit organizations record revenues, expenses, gains, and losses on the accrual basis. Expenditures, encumbrances, and budgetary accounts are not used. Although many not-for-profit organizations use funds for internal purposes, the financial statements do not report separate funds. Like commercial enterprises, revenues and expenses should be reported at gross amounts; gains and losses may be reported net; and investment gains and losses (realized and unrealized) may be reported net.

Generally speaking, not-for-profit organizations record and measure transactions and events in the same manner as commercial enterprises. They do, however, differ from commercial enterprises in two important ways: (1) not-for-profit organizations receive considerable amounts of resources in the form of donations and (2) donors frequently impose restrictions on the use of these resources.

FASB *Statement 116* requires contributions, including unconditional promises to give, to be recorded as revenues when the promise is made. Conditional promises to give are not recognized as revenues until the conditions are met. If a condition is not met, the potential donor is not bound by the promise. However, conditions are carefully distinguished from restrictions. Conditions require some action on the part of the donee before the gift is given. Restrictions are created when the donor indicates that contributions are to be expended for a particular purpose or in a certain time period. Specifically, contributions may be restricted as to purpose or time or for plant acquisition.

Revenues, including contributions, are considered to be unrestricted unless donor-imposed restrictions apply. In the case of contributions restricted for purpose or plant acquisition, a presumption is made that subsequent disbursements are made first from restricted resources and any additional disbursements are made from unrestricted resources. If a not-for-profit fails to comply with donor restrictions, the organization must accrue and disclose a contingent liability following FASB *Statement 5, Accounting for Contingencies.* In evaluating the failure to comply with donor restrictions, the organization should consider both whether the noncompliance could result in a liability to refund the contributions and whether the noncompliance is likely to result in a loss of future revenues.

All contributions are to be recorded at fair market value at the date of receipt. Pledges or promises to contribute in the future are recorded as receivables. The contribution revenue is recorded at the time of the pledge, net of an allowance for estimated uncollectibles. It is important to estimate the expected time period of the collection of pledged contributions for two reasons. First, there may be an implied time restriction. That is, a donation expected to be received in a future period could not be expected to be available to support current operations. Therefore, there is an implied time restriction and the contribution would be recorded as temporarily restricted. Second, FASB *Statement 116* requires multiyear pledges to be recorded at the present value of the future collections. As time passes, the present value of the pledge receivable will increase. At the end of each accounting period the difference between the previously recorded revenue and the new present value is recorded as additional contribution revenue, not interest.

If temporarily restricted resources are used, a reclassification is made from temporarily restricted net assets to unrestricted net assets. Reclassifications are made for (1) satisfaction of program restrictions (a purpose restriction by a donor), (2) satisfaction of equipment acquisition restrictions (depreciation of assets classified as temporarily restricted and/or use of temporarily restricted assets to purchase plant), and (3) satisfaction of time restrictions (donor actual or implied restrictions as to when funds should be used).

Reporting of Expenses and Assets

All expenses are reported in the unrestricted net asset class. Expenses are to be reported by function in the Statement of Activities or in the notes. The FASB does not prescribe functional classifications but does describe functions as either *program* or *supporting.* Major program classifications should be shown. Supporting activities include management and general, fund-raising, and membership development. Other classifications, such as operating income, may be included, but they are not required.

Collections, such as artwork in a museum, may or may not be recorded. To be classified as collections, the items must be held for public display and be protected and preserved. In the event of sale, the proceeds must be reinvested in other collections. If recorded, collections are recorded as permanently restricted assets. If not recorded, note disclosures are required.

With the exception of collections, fixed assets may be recorded as either temporarily restricted or unrestricted, depending on the policy of the organization. This is true both when an asset is acquired with temporarily restricted resources and when it is acquired with unrestricted resources. All fixed assets other than land and museum collections are depreciated. If fixed assets are recorded as temporarily restricted assets, then a reclassification is made each accounting period to unrestricted resources in an amount equal to the depreciation or an allocation based on the time the asset is restricted, whichever is shorter.

FASB *Statement 124, Accounting for Certain Investments of Not-for-Profit Organizations,* requires that investments in equity securities with determinable fair values and investments in debt securities be carried at fair value. Income from these investments is recorded as increases in unrestricted, temporarily restricted, or permanently restricted net assets, depending upon the presence or absence of donor restrictions or legal requirements. Unrealized gains and losses and realized gains and losses on investments are reported together in the Statement of Activities as unrestricted, temporarily restricted, or permanently restricted gains or losses, again depending on the presence or absence of donor instructions or legal requirements. *Statement 124* does not apply to investments that are accounted for under the equity method or investments in consolidated subsidiaries (in which a not-for-profit owns the majority of the voting stock of a corporation).

FASB *Statement 133, Accounting for Derivative Instruments and Hedging Activities,* requires that investments in derivative instruments be recorded as either assets or liabilities and be measured at fair value. Additionally, Statement of Position 94–3, *Reporting of Related Entities by Not-for-Profit Organizations,* requires consolidation of entities controlled through majority stock ownership or if there is an economic interest or control and the not-for-profit appoints a majority of the related entity's governing board. Some investments (interest in trusts, oil and gas properties, real estate ventures, and closely held companies and partnerships) are not covered by *Statement 124*. In such case, not-for-profits would follow the reporting rules in effect for commercial businesses with similar investments.

Special Topics: Accounting for Contributions

Contributed Services   Contributed services are recognized as revenue only when the service (1) creates or enhances nonfinancial assets or (2) requires specialized skills, is provided by someone possessing those skills, and typically would be purchased if not provided by donation. The journal entry to record donated services would debit a fixed asset if the service created or enhanced a nonfinancial asset (e.g., carpenter) or an expense if the service required specialized skills and would have been purchased if not donated (e.g., lawyer). In both cases the credit would be to Contribution Revenue—Unrestricted (donated services) and the amount would be the fair value of the services contributed.

Exchange Transaction   It is sometimes difficult to determine whether a transaction is a nonreciprocal gift (i.e., contribution) or an exchange of goods and services. Exchange transactions do not meet the definition of a contribution; therefore, they should be accounted for following accrual basis accounting where revenues are recognized when earned. In contrast to contributions, payments received in advance of exchange transactions are recorded as deferred revenue, a liability, rather than as a revenue. Some payments may be partially exchange transactions and partially contributions. If significant, the two parts should be separately accounted for.

This sometimes becomes an issue in evaluating how to record dues or memberships. Assume that an organization with a June 30 year-end collects annual dues in January. At fiscal year-end, six months remain on these memberships. How these amounts are recorded depends on whether the memberships are deemed to be contributions or exchange transactions.

Assume that the organization is a public radio station, there are no gifts exchanged at the time of membership, and membership provides little direct benefit (e.g., a monthly schedule of programming). Since the benefits of public radio are not restricted to members, the dues have the characteristic of a contribution and would be recorded as follows:

		Debits	Credits
Jan. 1	Cash	5,000	
	Contribution Revenue—Unrestricted.		5,000

Assume instead that the organization is a YMCA and that members have access to a gym, pool, and other facilities that nonmembers do not enjoy. In this case the dues have the characteristic of an exchange transaction and would be recorded as follows:

		Debits	Credits
Jan. 1	Cash	5,000	
	Deferred Revenue.		5,000
June 30	Deferred Revenue.	2,500	
	Membership Revenue Unrestricted		2,500

Intentions to Give Assume that a parishioner informs her church that she has named the church in her will and provides a written copy of the will to the church. At what point should the church record this as a contribution? FASB *Statement 116* explains that an intention to give is not the same thing as an unconditional promise to give. Therefore, the church would make no entry to record a contribution until the individual dies and the probate court declares the will valid.

Transfers to a Not-for-Profit Organization That Holds Contributions for Others It is common for a not-for-profit organization to accept cash or other assets that are intended to be redirected to other organizations or individuals. For example, an individual transfers cash to a seminary and instructs the seminary to grant a scholarship to a specified student. Under most circumstances, the recipient organization (i.e., the seminary) records the asset. The central issue is whether the recipient organization should record a liability or a contribution as the other half of the journal entry.

FASB *Statement 136, Transfer of Assets to a Not-for-Profit Organization or Charitable Trust That Raises or Holds Contributions for Others,* provides guidance on how the original donor, intermediary recipient organization, and final beneficiary should record the transaction. Generally, if the recipient organization agrees to transfer the assets to a specified beneficiary, the recipient organization is deemed to be merely an agent; therefore, a liability, rather than a contribution, is recorded. If the recipient organization has the ability to redirect the assets to another beneficiary, or if the recipient organization and beneficiary are financially interrelated, the transfer is recorded as a contribution.

ILLUSTRATIVE TRANSACTIONS AND FINANCIAL STATEMENTS

In the following section, a beginning trial balance, journal entries, and financial statements for a performing arts organization are provided as an example of the accounting practices described on the preceding pages.

Beginning Trial Balance

Assume that the Performing Arts Organization has the following balances as of July 1, 2011.

PERFORMING ARTS ORGANIZATION Trial Balance July 1, 2011		
	Debits	**Credits**
Cash	$ 1,128	
Accounts receivable	240	
Interest receivable	744	
Contributions receivable	996	
Supplies inventories	264	
Investments: Current	4,344	
Investments: Endowment	42,000	
Land	6,000	
Buildings	14,400	
Accumulated depreciation: Buildings		$ 4,800
Equipment	15,000	
Accumulated depreciation: Equipment		3,600
Accounts payable		64
Grants payable		360
Notes payable		2,400
Deferred revenue		2,400
Long-term debt		9,600
Net assets—unrestricted		11,900
Net assets—temporarily restricted		7,992
Net assets—permanently restricted		42,000
Totals	$85,116	$85,116

Assume that the $7,992 in temporarily restricted net assets is restricted for the following: (1) restricted as to providing continuing professional education for instructors in particular programs, $3,480; (2) restricted for future time periods, $4,272; and (3) restricted for future musical instrument acquisitions, $240. The organization maintains an endowment. Endowment principal is permanently restricted. Income from this endowment is unrestricted. Also assume the Performing Arts Organization reports expenses by function and has Program (performance, ballet school, neighborhood productions, and grants), Management and General, Fund-Raising, and Membership Development as functional categories. Fixed assets are recorded as unrestricted when acquired.

Transactions

During the fiscal year ended June 30, 2012, unrestricted cash receipts included: $240 accounts receivable at the beginning of the year (for tuition), $2,640 in contributions, $1,440 in single ticket admission charges, $600 in tuition, $480 in concessions, and $960 in interest revenue.

	Debits	Credits
1. Cash	6,360	
Accounts Receivable		240
Contributions—Unrestricted		2,640
Admission Revenue—Unrestricted		1,440
Tuition Revenue—Unrestricted		600
Concession Revenue—Unrestricted.......................		480
Interest Revenue—Unrestricted...........................		960

Note that revenue accounts are identified as unrestricted, temporarily restricted, or permanently restricted. It is not necessary to label asset and liability accounts in this manner.

A receivable of $360 was recorded for tuition related to the current fiscal year:

2. Accounts Receivable	360	
Tuition Revenue—Unrestricted		360

The deferred revenue liability at the end of the previous year represented the unexpired portion of season tickets. The related performances were completed in the current fiscal year.

3. Deferred Revenue..	2,400	
Admission Revenue—Unrestricted		2,400

Season tickets totaling $6,240 were sold in the current year. In addition, 60 memberships were sold at $200 each. Members receive a season ticket ($80 value), but no other direct benefit.

	Debits	Credits
4. Cash	6,240	
Deferred Revenue.		6,240
5. Cash	12,000	
Deferred Revenue ($80 × 60)		4,800
Contributions—Unrestricted ($120 × 60).		7,200

Notice that part of the membership ($120) is deemed to be a contribution and recognized as revenue immediately. The other part ($80) is deemed to be an exchange transaction and deferred until earned. Half of the performances were completed by year-end. (($6,240 + $4,800)/2).

	Debits	Credits
6. Deferred Revenue.	5,520	
Admission Revenue—Unrestricted		5,520

Interest received on the endowment investments amounted to $2,280. This included $744 accrued at the end of the previous year. Accrued interest at the end of the current year was $240. By agreement with donors, endowment income is unrestricted.

	Debits	Credits
7. Cash	2,280	
Interest Receivable	240	
Interest Receivable		744
Interest Revenue—Unrestricted		1,776

Note: In some instances the trust agreement governing permanently restricted resources may specify that the principal must grow by a certain percentage or by the excess of earnings over a specified annual draw. In such cases, the income that is required to remain in the endowment would be credited to Interest Revenue—Permanently Restricted.

Pledges are received for the following: $1,080 promise to give for current unrestricted purposes, $2,280 to support specific programs, and a promise to provide $600 in each of the next five years to support an educational program in those years (the present value of five payments discounted at 6 percent is $2,527). Assume the five-year pledge was made on January 1, 2012. Entry 8b records interest from January 1 to June 30 ($2,527 × 6% × 6/12 = $76).

		Debits	Credits
8a.	Contributions Receivable	5,887	
	Contributions—Temporarily Restricted.		4,807
	Contributions—Unrestricted		1,080
8b.	Contributions Receivable	76	
	Contributions—Temporarily Restricted.		76

No additional contribution revenue is recorded upon collection of the pledge. The journal entry would debit Cash and credit Contributions Receivable.

Cash of $996 pledged in the prior year for unrestricted use in the current year was received.

9.	Cash	996	
	Contributions Receivable		996

Cash of $3,360 was received on the pledges recorded in journal entry 8a, including the $1,080 for current unrestricted purposes.

10.	Cash	3,360	
	Contributions Receivable		3,360

Continuing professional education expenses for instructors were incurred and paid. These were supported by restricted gifts as follows: $1,920 performance assistance, $600 ballet school, and $960 neighborhood productions.

11a.	Performance Expense—CPE	1,920	
	Ballet School Expense—CPE.	600	
	Neighborhood Productions Expenses—CPE	960	
	Cash		3,480
11b.	Reclassification from temporarily restricted net assets—		
	Satisfaction of Program Restrictions	3,480	
	Reclassification to Unrestricted Net Assets—		
	Satisfaction of Program Restrictions		3,480
	(To record expiration of program restrictions)		

A new harp was donated to the organization. It had a fair value of $22,500.

12.	Equipment.	22,500	
	Contributions—Unrestricted		22,500

The $240 received in a prior year for musical instrument acquisitions, together with an additional $90, was used to acquire percussion instruments.

	Debits	Credits
13a. Equipment...	330	
Cash		330
13b. Reclassification from Temporarily Restricted Net Assets— Satisfaction of Plant Acquisition Restrictions	240	
Reclassification to Unrestricted Net Assets— Satisfaction of Plant Acquisition Restrictions		240
(To record expiration of plant acquisition restrictions)		

Note that the amount of the reclassification is limited to the amount of the restricted contribution, even though the cost of the equipment exceeds that amount.

At the beginning of this year, Temporarily Restricted Net Assets included $4,272 restricted for future time periods. Of this total, $2,100 collected in the prior year plus the $996 received in entry 9 relates to the current year. The time restriction has now expired and these assets are released from restriction.

14. Reclassification from Temporarily Restricted Net Assets— Expiration of Time Restrictions	3,096	
Reclassification to Unrestricted Net Assets— Expiration of Time Restrictions		3,096
(To record expiration of time restrictions)		

A gift of securities with a fair market value of $12,000 is received for the endowment. The principal of the gift is to be maintained indefinitely with interest to be used for unrestricted purposes.

15. Investments—Endowment	12,000	
Contributions—Permanently Restricted.................		12,000

At year-end, all of the investments had determinable market values. FASB *Statement 124, Accounting for Certain Investments Held by Not-for-Profit Organizations,* requires that investments in equity securities with readily determinable values and all debt investments be reported at fair market value. The resulting gains or losses are recorded as increases or decreases in unrestricted net assets, unless unrealized gains or losses are explicitly restricted by donor or by law. It was determined that the endowment investments had a fair value of $2,100 in excess of recorded amounts.

16. Investments—Endowment	2,100	
Gains on Investments—Unrestricted		2,100

Salaries were paid in the following amounts: $2,400 performance, $4,800 ballet school, $600 neighborhood productions, $4,200 management and general, $500 fund-raising, and $700 membership development.

	Debits	Credits
17. Performance Expense—Salaries.	2,400	
Ballet School Expense—Salaries	4,800	
Neighborhood Productions Expense—Salaries	600	
Management and General Expense—Salaries	4,200	
Fund-Raising Expense—Salaries	500	
Membership Development Expense—Salaries	700	
Cash		13,200

During the year, depreciation is recorded as follows: $720 buildings and $3,330 equipment. The depreciation was allocated to functional categories in the following amounts: $1,610 performance, $840 ballet school, $60 neighborhood productions, $720 management and general, $520 fund-raising, and $300 membership development.

	Debits	Credits
18. Performance Expense—Depreciation.	1,610	
Ballet School Expense—Depreciation	840	
Neighborhood Productions Expense—Depreciation	60	
Management and General Expense—Depreciation	720	
Fund-Raising Expense—Depreciation	520	
Membership Development Expense—Depreciation	300	
Accumulated Depreciation—Buildings		720
Accumulated Depreciation—Equipment		3,300

3,330

To assist in school productions, $960 in grants was awarded to local schools. A total of $1,200, including the $360 beginning grants payable, was paid during the year.

	Debits	Credits
19a. Grant Expense.	960	
Grants Payable		960
19b. Grants Payable	1,200	
Cash		1,200

Supplies were purchased on account in the amount of $2,280. A total of $2,316, including $64 of beginning accounts payable, was paid during the year.

	Debits	Credits
20a. Supplies	2,280	
Accounts Payable		2,280
20b. Accounts Payable	2,316	
Cash		2,316

Supplies were used for the following activities: $720 performance, $600 ballet school, $120 neighborhood productions, $564 management and general, $240 fund-raising, and $120 membership development.

21. Performance Expense—Supplies	720	
Ballet School Expense—Supplies	600	
Neighborhood Productions Expense—Supplies.............	120	
Management and General Expense—Supplies...............	564	
Fund-Raising Expense—Supplies	240	
Membership Development Expense—Supplies.............	120	
Supplies		2,364

Interest expense in the amount of $720 was paid during the year, along with $500 of the principal of the notes payable and $400 of the long-term debt. Interest expense was allocated to functional categories in the following amounts: $256 performance, $180 ballet school, $20 neighborhood productions, $200 management and general, $32 fund-raising, and $32 membership development.

22. Performance Expense—Interest	256	
Ballet School Expense—Interest	180	
Neighborhood Productions Expense—Interest	20	
Management and General Expense—Interest	200	
Fund-Raising Expense—Interest	32	
Membership Development Expense—Interest...............	32	
Notes Payable.....................................	500	
Long-Term Debt...................................	400	
Cash		1,620

Note that revenues are identified as unrestricted, temporarily restricted, or permanently restricted. All expenses appear in the financial statements as unrestricted and entries 11b, 13b, and 14 have been made in response to temporarily restricted net assets being released from restriction due to the expiration of time restrictions or the satisfaction of program restrictions.

Closing entries for the three categories of net assets are as follows:

	Debits	Credits
23. Contributions—Unrestricted	33,420	
Admission Revenue—Unrestricted	9,360	
Interest Revenue—Unrestricted	2,736	
Concession Revenue—Unrestricted.	480	
Tuition Revenue—Unrestricted	960	
Gains on Investments—Unrestricted	2,100	
Reclassification to Unrestricted Net Assets— Expiration of Time Restrictions	3,096	
Reclassification to Unrestricted Net Assets— Satisfaction of Plant Acquisition Restrictions	240	
Reclassification to Unrestricted Net Assets— Satisfaction of Program Restrictions	3,480	
Performance Expense—Total.		6,906
Ballet School Expense—Total		7,020
Neighborhood Productions Expense—Total		1,760
Management and General Expense—Total		5,684
Grant Expense		960
Fund-Raising Expense—Total		1,292
Membership Development Expense—Total		1,152
Net Assets—Unrestricted		31,098
24. Contributions—Temporarily Restricted.	4,883	
Net Assets—Temporarily Restricted	1,993	
Reclassification from Temporarily Restricted Net Assets— Expiration of Time Restrictions		3,096
Reclassification from Temporarily Restricted Net Assets— Satisfaction of Plant Acquisition Restrictions		240
Reclassification from Temporarily Restricted Net Assets— Satisfaction of Program Restrictions		3,480
25. Contributions—Permanently Restricted.	12,000	
Net Assets—Permanently Restricted		12,000

Financial Statements

FASB *Statement 117* requires three basic statements for nonprofit organizations: (1) Statement of Activities, (2) Statement of Financial Position, and (3) Statement of Cash Flows. Voluntary health and welfare organizations are required also to present a Statement of Functional Expenses, and other not-for-profits are encouraged to provide the information included in that statement.

Statement of Activities FASB *Statement 117* provides flexibility in this statement and illustrates a variety of formats. Requirements are to provide totals for revenues, expenses, gains, losses, the amounts of assets released from restriction, and the change in net assets for each of the three classes (unrestricted, temporarily restricted, and permanently restricted). Generally, revenues and expenses are

ILLUSTRATION 10–1   Statement of Activities

PERFORMING ARTS ORGANIZATION Statement of Activities For the Year Ended June 30, 2012				
	Unrestricted	**Temporarily Restricted**	**Permanently Restricted**	**Total**
Revenues, gains, and other support:				
Contributions	$33,420	$4,883	$12,000	$ 50,303
Admission revenues	9,360			9,360
Tuition	960			960
Concessions	480			480
Interest	2,736			2,736
Net gains on endowment investments	2,100			2,100
Net assets released from restrictions:				
Satisfaction of program/use restrictions	3,480	(3,480)		
Satisfaction of plant acquisition restrictions	240	(240)		
Expiration of time restrictions	3,096	(3,096)		
Total revenues, gains, and other support	55,872	(1,933)	12,000	65,939
Expenses:				
Performance	6,906			6,906
Ballet school	7,020			7,020
Neighborhood productions	1,760			1,760
Grant expense	960			960
Management and general	5,684			5,684
Fund-raising	1,292			1,292
Membership development	1,152			1,152
Total expenses	24,774			24,774
Change in net assets	31,098	(1,933)	12,000	41,165
Net assets beginning	11,900	7,992	42,000	61,892
Net assets ending	$42,998	$6,059	$54,000	$103,057

reported gross, and gains and losses may be reported net. Expenses must be reported by functional classifications, either in the statements or the notes. The functional expense categories include Programs, Management and General, Fund-Raising, and Membership Development.

Illustration 10–1 presents a Statement of Activities for the Performing Arts Organization. Note that all expenses appear in the unrestricted category and that the net assets released from restrictions (i.e., the effects of entries 11b, 13b, and 14) appear at the bottom of the revenue section as increases in unrestricted net assets and decreases in temporarily restricted net assets. Because permanently restricted net assets result from permanent donor-imposed restrictions, no such reclassification should occur for these resources.

ILLUSTRATION 10–2 Statement of Financial Position *b/s*

PERFORMING ARTS ORGANIZATION Statement of Financial Position June 30, 2012 and 2011		
	2012	**2011**
Assets		
Cash	$ 10,218	$ 1,128
Short-term investments	4,344	4,344
Accounts receivable	360	240
Interest receivable	240	744
Supplies inventories	180	264
Contributions receivable	2,603	996
Land, buildings and equipment, net of		
accumulated depreciation of 5,520 and 6,930	45,780	27,000
Long-term investments	56,100	42,000
Total assets	119,825	76,716
Liabilities		
Accounts payable	28	64
Grants payable	120	360
Deferred revenues	5,520	2,400
Notes payable	1,900	2,400
Long-term debt	9,200	9,600
Total liabilities	16,768	14,824
Net Assets		
Unrestricted	42,998	11,900
Temporarily restricted	6,059	7,992
Permanently restricted	54,000	42,000
Total net assets	103,057	61,892
Total liabilities and net assets	$119,825	$76,716

Statement of Financial Position   Again, more than one format is possible for this statement. However, *Statement 117* illustrates a comparative statement showing organization-wide totals, with assets organized according to liquidity and liabilities according to term. In place of an equity section, the statement presents separate totals for unrestricted, temporarily restricted, and permanently restricted net assets. Some organizations present additional details of unrestricted net assets, such as net assets internally designated for some purpose or unrestricted assets invested in property, plant, and equipment net of related debt. Illustration 10–2 presents the Statement of Financial Position for the Performing Arts Organization.

Statement of Cash Flows   The third required statement is the Statement of Cash Flows. Either the direct or indirect method may be used. The indirect method is presented in Illustration 10–3. Illustration 11–5 presents a cash flow statement using the direct method for a private not-for-profit college. Either method is permitted under

ILLUSTRATION 10–3 Statement of Cash Flows

PERFORMING ARTS ORGANIZATION Statement of Cash Flows For the Year Ended June 30, 2012		
Cash flows from operating activities:		
Change in net assets	$ 41,165	
Depreciation expense	4,050	
Noncash contributions	(34,500)	
Gains on endowment investments	(2,100)	
Increase in accounts receivable	(120)	
Decrease in interest receivable	504	
Decrease in supplies inventories	84	
Increase in contributions receivable	(1,607)	
Decrease in accounts payable	(36)	
Decrease in grants payable	(240)	
Increase in deferred revenues	3,120	
Net cash provided by operating activities		$10,320
Cash flows from investing activities.		
Purchase of equipment	(330)	
Net cash provided by investing activities		(330)
Cash flows from financing activities.		
Payment of notes payable	(500)	
Payment of long-term debt	(400)	
Net cash provided by financing activities		(900)
Net increase in cash		9,090
Cash balance—beginning		1,128
Cash balance—ending		$10,218
Noncash investing and financing activities:		
Gift of investments	$ 12,000	
Gift of equipment	22,500	
Supplemental disclosure of cash flow information:		
Cash paid during the year for interest	$ 720	

Statement 117. Generally, classification of cash flows follows the format for business entities (operating, investing, and financing activities). However, *Statement 117* requires that donor-restricted cash that must be used for long-term purposes is classified as cash flows from financing activities. Noncash investing and financing activities must also be disclosed; typically at the bottom of the statement.

Statement of Functional Expenses   Voluntary health and welfare organizations are required to prepare a Statement of Functional Expenses that shows expenses detailed by both function (program, management and general, etc.) and object (salaries, supplies, etc.). The FASB also recommends that other not-for-profit organizations disclose this information. Illustration 10–4 presents a Statement of Functional Expenses for the Performing Arts Organization. Note that the total

ILLUSTRATION 10–4   Statement of Functional Expenses

PERFORMING ARTS ORGANIZATION
Statement of Functional Expenses
For the Year Ended June 30, 2012

	Program Services					Supporting Services				Total Expenses
	Performance	Ballet School	Neighbor-hood Productions	Grants	Total	Manage-ment	Fund-Raising	Member-ship	Total	
Salaries	$2,400	$4,800	$ 600		$ 7,800	$4,200	$ 500	$ 700	$5,400	$13,200
Continuing education	1,920	600	960		3,480					3,480
Supplies	720	600	120		1,440	564	240	120	924	2,364
Grants				$960	960					960
Interest	256	180	20		456	200	32	32	264	720
Depreciation	1,610	840	60		2,510	720	520	300	1,540	4,050
Total expenses	$6,906	$7,020	$1,760	$960	$16,646	$5,684	$1,292	$1,152	$8,128	$24,774

expenses reported in the bottom right-hand corner ($24,774) agrees with the total expenses reported in the Statement of Activities (Illustration 10–1).

Alternative Procedure for Recording Fixed Assets

As indicated earlier, the FASB gives not-for-profit organizations the option of (1) recording all fixed assets as unrestricted and reclassifying resources donated to purchase fixed assets to unrestricted net assets (entries 13a and 13b) or (2) recording fixed assets as temporarily restricted and reclassifying net assets to unrestricted as the asset is depreciated or over the term of the restriction, if shorter. If the latter method were followed, entries 13a and 13b would be as follows:

(Alternative entries)	Debits	Credits
13a. Equipment.	330	
Cash		330
13b. Reclassification from Unrestricted Net Assets—		
Use of Unrestricted Assets to Acquire Fixed Assets	90	
Reclassification to Temporarily Restricted Net Assets—		
Use of Unrestricted Assets to Acquire Fixed Assets		90

Similar entries would be made for all acquisitions of fixed assets using unrestricted resources (e.g., entry 12). Entry 18, to record depreciation, would be followed by an additional entry to reclassify the depreciated portion of the assets:

(Alternative entry)		
18b. Reclassification from Temporarily Restricted Net Assets—		
Satisfaction of Fixed Asset Restrictions.	4,050	
Reclassification to Unrestricted Net Assets—		
Satisfaction of Fixed Asset Restrictions.		4,050

PERFORMANCE EVALUATION

The not-for-profit organizations described in this chapter apply accrual accounting concepts and measure revenues and expenses in much the same manner as business enterprises. In the Statement of Activities, change in net assets is computationally equivalent to net income reported on the financial statements of business enterprises (i.e., revenues–expenses). However, change in net assets is not as effective a performance measure for not-for-profits as net income is for businesses. This is not surprising since not-for-profit organizations are established for purposes other than generating net income.

It is commonly perceived that not-for-profit organizations should not generate surpluses. However, there are a number of reasons why a not-for-profit organization would need to generate a surplus (positive change in net assets). These include:

- Establishing working capital.
- Expanding or replacing physical facilities.
- Retiring debt.
- Continuing a program beyond the period that initial funding is provided.

If these needs are satisfied, a not-for-profit organization may also find it desirable to draw upon earlier surpluses and operate at a deficit for a period of time. For these reasons, a positive change in net assets is not inherently either a good or a bad condition.

The financial measure of greatest interest in evaluating not-for-profit organizations is the ratio of program service expenses to total expenses (commonly called the "program expense ratio"). The ratio is readily calculated from the financial statements. For example, Illustration 10–4 reports program expenses totaling $16,646 and total expenses of $24,774 for a ratio of approximately 67 percent. The ratio is a measure of the efficiency of a not-for-profit organization in utilizing resources to fulfill its mission, rather than for fund-raising and administration. The ratio is commonly reported in rankings of charitable organizations. For example, *Money* magazine does an annual ranking of charitable organizations. The Better Business Bureau recommends a minimum ratio of 60 percent.

Because of the importance of this ratio, care is taken in the allocation of costs between program and supporting expense categories. Not-for-profits frequently require employees to keep detailed records of their time for purposes of allocating salary and benefit costs. Additionally, depreciation is commonly allocated on the basis of square feet dedicated to program versus administrative functions.

The American Institute of CPAs issued Statement of Position 98–02 which establishes guidance for allocation of costs that involve fund-raising. Examples of the activities covered by the statement are mass mailings, annual dinners, and TV or radio commercials. The statement indicates that it is appropriate to allocate costs from fund-raising to another function when the activity meets three conditions:

1. *Purpose:* The purpose of the joint activity includes accomplishing program functions. (Merely asking the audience to make contributions is not an activity that fulfills the organization's mission.)
2. *Audience:* The audience is selected based on characteristics other than ability or likelihood to make contributions.
3. *Content:* The activity calls for specific action by the recipient that will help accomplish the organization's mission.

If any of the conditions are not met, all costs of the joint activity should be reported as fund-raising.

Mergers and Acquisitions

The AICPA Audit and Accounting Guide, *Not-for-Profit Organizations,* requires consolidation of entities in which a not-for-profit organization has a controlling financial interest. Control may be determined by a majority ownership interest or by holding a majority voting interest in the governing board of an entity in which the not-for-profit has an economic interest through contractual or affiliation agreements. This is similar to practices followed in the public sector with component unit reporting.

Until recently, the FASB had excluded not-for-profit entities from its guidance on how to account for business combinations. Similar to commercial businesses, not-for-profit organizations occasionally merge or acquire a controlling interest in other organizations. This may be done voluntarily to leverage the comparative advantages of two organizations. For example, the *American Federation of Labor* and *Congress of Industrial Organizations* merged to form the AFL-CIO, becoming the most influential federation of labor unions in the United States. Alternatively, mergers can be forced upon organizations. Recently, the *Girl Scouts of America* required the merger of many of its independently incorporated councils, reducing the number of chartered councils to approximately one-third.

FASB *Statement 141, Business Combinations,* establishes that mergers and acquisitions among commercial enterprises should all be accounted for as purchase transactions. In contrast, FASB *Statement 164, Not-for Profit Entities: Mergers and Acquisitions,* permits two different accounting treatments for combinations by not-for-profit organizations. The central issue is whether the combination is a merger or an acquisition.

Mergers   A *merger* is a transaction in which the governing bodies of two or more not-for-profit entities relinquish control of those entities to create a new not-for-profit entity. To qualify as a new entity, the combined entity must have a newly formed governing body. Although commonly there will be a new legal entity, that is not a requirement. The resulting not-for-profit entity will account for the merger using the **carryover method.** Under the carryover method:

- The new entity recognizes the assets and liabilities of the separate merging entities in the amounts (and classifications) reported in the financial statements of the merging entities.
- No internally developed intangible assets (such as goodwill) are recognized.
- The entity resulting from the merger is a new reporting entity, with no activity before the date of the merger.

The essential element of the carryover method is that the entity does not recognize either additional assets (intangibles) or changes in the fair value of recognized assets and liabilities. The two merging organizations' asset and liability book balances are "carried over" to the new reporting entity.

Acquisitions   Combinations not meeting the definition of a merger are reported as acquisitions. In an acquisition, a not-for-profit may acquire control of either business enterprises or other not-for-profit organizations. Under the *acquisition method:*

- The not-for-profit entity recognizes the identifiable assets acquired and liabilities assumed at their fair values at the date of acquisition. Noncontrolling interest (if any) is reported at fair value at the acquisition date and is adjusted in subsequent periods in a manner similar to business organizations.

- Goodwill can be reported.
- The financial statements of the acquirer report the acquisition as activity of the period in which it occurs. Contribution revenue is recognized if the acquired entity is donated (i.e., no purchase price) or if the price paid is less than the fair value of the net assets acquired.

The essential element of the acquisition method is that the entity records the acquired assets and liabilities at their fair values, not at the acquired entity's book values. In this manner, the acquisition method is similar to purchase accounting. However, in many cases the treatment of goodwill is substantially different from that of business enterprises.

FASB *Statement 164* recognizes that there are varying types of not-for-profit organizations. Some derive their revenues principally from contributions (or earnings of investments from previously contributed resources). Other not-for-profit organizations (such as hospitals) receive most of their revenues from the sale of goods and services. This distinction determines how the not-for-profit reports goodwill resulting from an acquisition. Not-for-profit entities that derive their revenues from businesslike activities are required to measure and report goodwill as an asset in a similar manner as businesses. However, entities that derive their revenues primarily from contributions are to charge (i.e., expense) the goodwill at the date of acquisition. In making this distinction, the FASB recognizes that goodwill can be useful in evaluating the activities of entities engaged in business activities, but is of limited usefulness to donors in deciding whether to contribute resources to a not-for-profit entity. Since donated acquisitions commonly result in the not-for-profit entity reporting contribution revenue, the charge for goodwill has the effect of reducing what might otherwise be a large reported increase in the Statement of Activities.

SUMMARY OF NOT-FOR-PROFIT ACCOUNTING AND REPORTING

Not-for-profit organizations in the private sector are required to follow FASB standards. The FASB requires three statements: (1) Statement of Financial Position, (2) Statement of Activities, and (3) Statement of Cash Flows. A Statement of Functional Expenses is required for voluntary health and welfare organizations and encouraged for all not-for-profit organizations.

Accrual accounting is required, and depreciation is recorded on fixed assets. Net assets are classified as (1) unrestricted, (2) temporarily restricted, or (3) permanently restricted. Contributions are recorded as revenue in the appropriate net asset class when unconditional. This means that unconditional pledges, even multiyear pledges, are recorded as revenue when pledged. Temporarily restricted net assets are restricted as to (1) purpose, (2) time period, or (3) plant acquisition. All expenses are recorded and reported as unrestricted expenses. As temporarily restricted resources are released from restrictions, reclassification entries are made, increasing unrestricted net assets.

Now that you have finished reading Chapter 10, complete the multiple choice questions provided on the text's Web site (www.mhhe.com/copley10e) to test your comprehension of the chapter.

Questions and Exercises

10–1. Obtain a copy of the annual report of a private not-for-profit organization. Answer the following questions from the report (if obtaining a report online, use the site search or the "about us" button to locate the annual report). For examples, try the following:

The American Accounting Association	www.aaahq.org
U.S. Olympic Committee	www.usoc.org
Habitat for Humanity	www.habitat.org
American Diabetes Association	www.diabetes.org
Save the Children	www.savethechildren.org

    a. What financial statements are presented?

    b. How are the contribution revenues recognized?

    c. Does the organization have temporarily restricted net assets? What is the nature of the restrictions?

    d. Does the organization have permanently restricted net assets?

    e. Compute the ratio of program expenses to total expenses.

10–2. Consider FASB standards for reporting by private not-for-profit organizations and answer the following:

    a. What are the financial reports required of all not-for-profits? What additional report is required for voluntary health and welfare organizations?

    b. List the three classes of net assets.

    c. Outline the accounting required for property, plant, and equipment. Include accounting for plant acquired with both unrestricted and restricted revenues.

    d. Outline accounting and reporting for investments.

10–3. Consider FASB standards for accounting for contributions and answer the following:

    a. Outline revenue recognition criteria for resources restricted for (1) time and (2) purpose.

    b. Describe the difference in accounting for contributions with a condition and a restriction.

    c. Outline the requirements for recognizing contributed services as revenue.

    d. Outline accounting for multiyear pledges.

10–4. Consider FASB standards for mergers and acquisitions by not-for-profit organizations. Answer the following questions:

a. What is the difference between a merger and an acquisition?

b. What is the principal difference in the accounting treatment of assets and liabilities under mergers and acquisitions?

c. Under what circumstances may a not-for-profit organization record goodwill?

10–5. For the following transactions and events, indicate what effect each will have on the three classes of net assets using this format. Put an X in the appropriate column. If the net assets are unaffected, leave the column blank.

	Unrestricted Net Assets		Temporarily Restricted Net Assets		Permanently Restricted Net Assets	
	Increase	Decrease	Increase	Decrease	Increase	Decrease
Ex1			X			
Ex2	X			X		

Ex1: Received a pledge from a donor to provide $1,000 a year to support summer educational programs to be held each July for five years.

Ex2: A time restriction on cash received in a prior year expired in the current period.

1. A capital campaign in support of a new building brought in pledges of $150,000.

2. Cash collections on the pledges described in (1) totaled $97,000 in the current year.

3. $25,000 was expended from the capital campaign on architects' fees. The organization records all fixed assets in the unrestricted class of net assets.

4. Interest income on the unexpended capital campaign funds amounted to $560. No restriction exists as to how the income may be used.

5. Operating revenues (admission fees and gift shop sales) amounted to $80,000.

6. Salaries, utilities, and operating supplies totaled $76,000.

7. Depreciation on plant and equipment amounted to $25,000.

8. Volunteers staffing the gift shop contributed 500 hours. The services did not require specialized skills but are estimated at a value of $8.50 per hour.

9. Securities valued at $100,000 are received for permanent endowment. Income earned on the endowment is to be used to sponsor visiting speakers.

10. Interest and dividends received on the endowment totaled $2,000.

10–6. Presented below is a partially completed Statement of Activities for a homeless shelter. Complete the Statement of Activities by filling in the amounts that would appear in each of the shaded areas. (Include zero amounts.)

CENTERVILLE AREA HOMELESS SHELTER
Statement of Activities
For the Year Ended December 31, 2012

	Unrestricted	Temporarily Restricted	Permanently Restricted	Total
Revenues				
Contribution revenues				$1,564,310
Net assets released from restriction		(25,000)		0
Total Revenues				1,564,310
Expenses				
Temporary shelter program				1,030,500
Self-sufficiency program				353,000
Fund-raising				12,600
Administration				78,900
Total Expenses				1,475,000
Increase in net assets	81,000	2,060	6,250	89,310
Net assets January 1	18,000	1,200	12,650	31,850
Net assets December 31	$ 99,000	$3,260	$18,900	$ 121,160

10–7. On January 1, the Voluntary Action Agency received a cash contribution of $300,000 restricted to the purchase of buses to be used in transporting senior citizens. On January 2 of that same year, buses were purchased with the $300,000 cash. The buses are expected to be used for five years and have no salvage value at the end of that time.

1. Record the journal entries on January 1, January 2, and December 31 for the receipt of cash, the purchase of buses, and one year's depreciation, assuming that plant assets are recorded as unrestricted assets at the time of purchase.

2. Record the journal entries on January 1, January 2, and December 31 for the receipt of cash, the purchase of buses, and one year's depreciation, assuming that plant assets purchased with restricted resources are recorded as temporarily restricted assets at the time of purchase and reclassified in accord with the depreciation schedule.

3. Compute the amount that would be included in net assets (after closing the books on December 31) for (a) unrestricted net assets and (b) temporarily restricted net assets under requirements 1 and 2. What incentives might exist for the Voluntary Action Agency to choose either alternative?

10–8. On January 1, 2012, a foundation made a pledge to pay $30,000 per year at the end of each of the next five years to the Cancer Research Center, a non-profit voluntary health and welfare organization as a salary supplement for a well-known researcher. On December 31, 2012, the first payment of $30,000 was received and paid to the researcher.

1. On the books of the Cancer Research Center, record the pledge on January 1 in the temporarily restricted asset class, assuming the appropriate discount rate is 5 percent on an annual basis. The appropriate discount factor is 4.33.

PV ordinary annuity

2. Record the increase in the present value of the receivable in the temporarily restricted net asset class as of December 31.

3. Record the receipt of the first $30,000 on December 31 and the payment to the researcher. Indicate in which asset class (unrestricted, temporarily restricted) each account is recorded.

10–9. The Evangelical Private School follows FASB standards of accounting and reporting. Record the following transactions during the year ended June 30, 2012.

1. Cash contributions were received as follows: (*a*) $1,200,000 for any purpose desired by the school, (*b*) $500,000 for salary supplements for school faculty, (*c*) $300,000 to be used during the next fiscal year in any manner desired by the school, (*d*) $600,000 for the construction of a new auditorium, and (*e*) $700,000 to be invested permanently, with the income to be used as desired by the school. The school's policy is to record all restricted gifts as temporarily restricted and then reclassify when the restriction is lifted.

2. The school expended $400,000 of the $1,200,000 mentioned in 1(*a*) for school furniture. Record the plant as unrestricted.

3. The school expended the $470,000 for salary supplements as directed by the donor in 1(*b*).

4. The $300,000 in 1(*c*) was retained for use next year, as directed by the donor.

5. $650,000 was expended for the construction of the new auditorium. School policy is to record all plant as unrestricted.

6. The $700,000 mentioned in 1(*e*) was invested permanently, as directed by the donor, and in the year ended June 30, 2012, earned $16,000, none of which was expended.

10–10. The Ombudsman Foundation is a private not-for-profit organization providing training in dispute resolution and conflict management. The Foundation had the following preclosing trial balance at December 31, 2012, the end of its fiscal year:

Account:	Debits	Credits
Accounts payable		$78,000
Accounts receivable (net)	$79,000	
Accrued interest receivable	15,500	
Accumulated depreciation		2,300,000
Cash	105,000	
Contributed services—unrestricted		77,000
Contributions—unrestricted		2,250,500
Contributions—temporarily restricted		725,000
Contributions—permanently restricted		2,650,000
Current pledges receivable (net)	45,000	

(Continued)

Account:	Debits	Credits
Education program expenses	505,000	
Fund-raising expense	16,000	
Grant revenue—temporarily restricted		96,000
Training seminar expenses	5,456,000	
Land, buildings, and equipment	5,600,000	
Long-term investments	2,690,000	
Management and general expense	750,000	
Net assets:		
Unrestricted (January 1)		358,000
Temporarily restricted (January 1)		759,000
Permanently restricted (January 1)		1,250,000
Net gains on endowment investments—unrestricted		17,500
Noncurrent pledge receivables (net)	365,000	
Program service revenue—unrestricted		6,595,000
Post employment benefits payable (noncurrent)		123,500
Reclassifications:		
Satisfaction of program restrictions	150,000	
Satisfaction of time restrictions	325,000	
Satisfaction of program restrictions		150,000
Satisfaction of time restrictions		325,000
Research program expenses	1,256,000	
Short-term investments	365,000	
Supplies inventory	32,000	
Totals	$17,754,500	$17,754,500

a. Prepare closing entries for the year-end, using separate entries for each net asset classification.

b. Prepare a Statement of Activities for the year ended December 31, 2012.

c. Prepare a Statement of Financial Position as of December 31, 2012. Use a classified approach, providing separate totals for current and noncurrent items.

10–11. The Folpe Museum Association, a nonprofit organization, had the following transactions for the year ended December 31, 2012.

1. Cash contributions to the Association for the year included (a) unrestricted, $1,100,000; (b) restricted for traveling displays, $350,000; (c) restricted by the donor for endowment purposes, $1,400,000; and (d) restricted by the donor for equipment, $500,000.

2. Additional unrestricted cash receipts included (a) admission charges, $300,000; (b) interest income, $210,000; and (c) tuition for museum school, $50,000.

3. Donors made pledges in 2012 in a pledge drive specifically for funds to be used in 2013. The amount was $400,000.

4. A multiyear pledge (temporarily restricted) was made at the end of the year by a private foundation. The foundation pledged $50,000 per year for

the next five years (at the end of each year). The present value (rounded) of those future payments is $211,000, using a 6 percent discount rate.

5. $195,000 in funds restricted for traveling displays was expended during 2012.

6. The Museum Association had $150,000 in pledges in 2011 that was intended by the donors to be expended in 2012. The cash was received in 2012. (Expenses are included in transaction 8.)

7. $575,000 in cash previously restricted for equipment purchases was expended in 2012. The Museum Association records all equipment in the unrestricted class of net assets.

8. In addition to the amount expended in transaction 5, expenses (paid in cash) amounted to (*a*) museum displays, $1,300,000; (*b*) museum school, $90,000; (*c*) management and general, $350,000; (*d*) fundraising, $250,000; and (*e*) membership development, $200,000.

9. Depreciation on museum fixed assets amounted to: (*a*) $40,000 for museum displays, (*b*) $7,000 for museum school, (*c*) $12,000 for management and general, (*d*) $4,000 for fund-raising, and (*e*) $4,000 for membership development.

Required:

a. Prepare journal entries to record these transactions, including closing entries. Prepare a Statement of Activities for the Folpe Museum Association for the year ended December 31, 2012. Use the format in the text. The beginning net asset balances were unrestricted, $400,000; temporarily (time) restricted, $150,000; and permanently restricted, $3,500,000.

b. The Museum School program expenses are substantially larger than its revenues. Do you recommend that the program be discontinued?

10–12. The Grant Wood Arts Association had the following trial balance as of January 1, 2012, the first day of the year:

	Debits	Credits
Cash	$ 420,000	
Temporary investments	1,550,000	
Equipment	1,500,000	
Accumulated depreciation		$1,130,000
Contributions receivable	500,000	
Long-term investments	3,000,000	
Accounts payable		340,000
Unrestricted net assets		800,000
Temporarily restricted net assets		1,700,000
Permanently restricted net assets		3,000,000
	$6,970,000	$6,970,000

During the year ended December 31, 2012, the following transactions occurred:

1. Cash contributions during the year included (*a*) unrestricted, $2,000,000; (*b*) restricted for neighborhood productions, $500,000; (*c*) restricted by

the donor for endowment purposes, $1,000,000; and (d) restricted by the donor for equipment purchases, $450,000.

2. Additional unrestricted cash receipts included (a) admission charges, $300,000; (b) interest income, $200,000; and (c) tuition, $500,000, and (d) $100,000 borrowed from the bank for working capital purposes.

3. Donors made pledges late in 2012 in a pledge drive that indicated the funds were to be used in 2013; the amount was $400,000.

4. A multiyear pledge (temporarily restricted) was made at the end of the year by a private foundation. The foundation pledged $100,000 per year for the next five years (at the end of the year) for unrestricted purposes. The applicable discount rate is 6 percent, and the present value of the pledge is $421,236.

5. $200,000 in funds restricted for neighborhood productions was recorded in accounts payable and paid.

6. The Arts Association had $500,000 in pledges in 2011 that were intended by the donors to be expended in 2012 for unrestricted purposes. The cash was received in 2012.

7. $350,000 in cash restricted for equipment purchases was expended. The Arts Association records all fixed assets in the Unrestricted class of net assets.

8. In addition to the $200,000 in transaction 5, expenses incurred through Accounts Payable and Depreciation amounted to:

	Accounts Payable	Depreciation	Total
Performances	$1,320,000	$ 80,000	$1,400,000
Ballet school	570,000	80,000	650,000
Management and general	400,000	100,000	500,000
Fund-raising	280,000	20,000	300,000
Membership development	180,000	20,000	200,000
Total	$2,750,000	$300,000	$3,050,00

9. Cash of $2,800,000 was paid on accounts payable during the year.

10. At year-end, temporary investments were purchased with cash as follows: (a) unrestricted, $750,000; and (b) temporarily restricted, $300,000. In addition, investments in the amount of $1,000,000 were purchased with permanently restricted cash.

11. At year-end, the recorded value of temporary investments was the same as fair value. However, the fair value of the investments recorded as permanently restricted amounted to $4,200,000. Gains and losses of permanent endowments are required by the donor to be maintained in the endowment.

12. Interest, an administrative expense, is accrued on the outstanding bank note in the amount of $4,000.

Required:

a. Prepare journal entries to reflect the transactions. Prepare closing entries.

b. Prepare a Statement of Activities for the Arts Association for the year ending December 31, 2012.

c. Prepare a Statement of Financial Position for the Arts Association as of December 31, 2012. Use the format in the text; combine assets but show net assets by class.

d. Prepare a Statement of Cash Flows for the Arts Association for the year ending December 31, 2012. Use the direct method. Assume the temporary investments are *not* cash equivalents. (*Hint:* The $400,000 for plant expansion in transaction 1 is a financing transaction.)

Excel-based Problem

10–13. Jefferson Animal Rescue is a private not-for-profit clinic and shelter for abandoned domesticated animals, chiefly dogs and cats. At the end of 2011, the organization had the following account balances:

	Debits	Credits
Pledges receivable	$ 1,500	
Cash	23,000	
Land buildings & equipment	45,000	
Supplies inventory	4,000	
Accounts payable		$ 5,500
Accrued wages payable		300
Accumulated depreciation		17,500
Note payable to bank		25,000
Net assets—temporarily restricted:		
for use in KDAC program		2,500
for purchase of capital assets		9,500
Unrestricted net assets		13,200
Total	$ 73,500	$73,500

The following took place during 2012:

1. Additional supplies were purchased on account in the amount of $15,000.

2. Unconditional (and unrestricted) pledges of support were received totaling $95,000. In light of a declining economy, 5 percent is expected to be uncollectible. The remainder is expected to be collected in 2012.

3. Supplies used for animal care amounted to $16,700.

4. Payments made on accounts payable amounted to $18,200.

5. Cash collected from pledges totaled $91,000.

6. Salaries were paid in the amount of $47,000. Included in this amount is the accrued wages payable at the end of 2011. (The portion of wages expense attributable to administrative expense is $15,000 and fund-raising expense is $2,000. The remainder is for animal care.)

7. Jefferson Animal Rescue entered an agreement with KDAC, Channel 7 News, to find more homes for shelter pets. This special adoption program highlights a shelter animal in need of a home on the evening news the first Thursday of each month. The program was initially funded by a restricted gift received in 2011. During 2012, Jefferson Animal Rescue paid $1,800 ($150 per month) for the production of the monthly videos. In December 2012, the original donor unconditionally pledged to support the project for an additional 24 months by promising to pay $3,600 in January 2013 (all of this is expected to be collectible).

8. The shelter's building was partially financed by a bank note with an annual interest rate of 6 percent. Interest totaling $1,500 was paid during 2012. Interest is displayed as *Other Changes* in the Statement of Activities.

9. Animal medical equipment was purchased during the year in the amount of $3,000. Funding came from a special capital campaign conducted in 2011.

Additional information includes:

10. Depreciation for the year amounted to $7,500. (The portion of depreciation expense attributable to administrative is $2,000, and the remainder is related to animal care.)

11. Unpaid wages relating to the final week of the year totaled $420 (all animal care).

Using the information above and the Excel template provided:

a. Prepare journal entries and post entries to the T-accounts.

b. Prepare closing entries.

c. Prepare a Statement of Activities, Statement of Financial Position, and Statement of Cash Flows for the year ending December 31, 2012.

10–14. The Association of Women in Government established an Educational Foundation to raise money to support scholarship and other education initiatives. The Educational Foundation is a private not-for-profit. Members of the Association of Women in Government periodically make donations to the Educational Foundation. With the exception of the gift described below, these are unrestricted.

In December 2011, a donor established a permanent endowment with an initial payment of $100,000 and a pledge to provide $10,000 per year for 3 years, beginning in December 2012. At the time, the pledge was recorded at the present value ($ 27,232), discounted at 5 percent. Earnings of the endowment (interest and investment gains) are derived from investment in AAA-rated corporate bonds and are restricted for the payment of scholarships.

At the end of 2011, the organization had the following account balances:

	Debits	Credits
Cash	$ 23,000	
Interest receivable	600	
Investments in bonds	100,000	
Pledges receivable	27,232	
Supplies inventory	400	
Scholarships payable		$ 5,500
Permanently restricted net assets		127,232
Net assets—temporarily restricted:		
for scholarships		2,500
Unrestricted net assets		16,000
Total	$151,232	$151,232

The following took place during 2012:

1. The Educational Foundation has no employees. Administrative costs are limited to supplies, postage, and photocopying. Postage and photocopying expenses (paid in cash) totaled $2,800 for the year. The Foundation purchased supplies of $1,900 on account and made payments of $1,200. Unused supplies at year-end totaled $600.

2. Unrestricted donations received totaled $5,000.

3. Interest received on the bonds totaled $7,800, which included amounts receivable at the end of 2011. Accrued interest receivable at December 31, 2012, totaled $750.

4. The fair value of the bonds at year-end was determined to be $102,300. Income, including increases in the value of endowment investments, may be used for scholarships in the year earned.

5. The donor who established the permanent endowment made the scheduled payment of $10,000 at the end of 2012. (*Hint:* First record the increase in the present value of the pledge and then record the receipt of the $10,000.)

6. New scholarships were awarded in the amount of $18,000. Payments of scholarships (including those amounts accrued at the end of the previous year) totaled $22,000 during the year. Consistent with FASB standards, scholarships are assumed to be awarded first from resources provided

from restricted revenues. (*Hint:* add beginning temporarily restricted net assets to endowment earnings to determine the amount to reclassify from temporarily restricted net assets.)

Using the information above and the Excel template provided:

a. Prepare journal entries and post entries to the T-accounts.

b. Prepare closing entries.

c. Prepare a Statement of Activities, Statement of Financial Position, and Statement of Cash Flows for the year ending December 31, 2012.

College and University Accounting—Private Institutions

Our progress as a nation can be no swifter than our progress in education. The human mind is our fundamental resource. (John F. Kennedy, 35th president of the United States)

The function of education is to teach one to think intensively and to think critically . . . Intelligence plus character—that is the goal of true education. (Martin Luther King, Jr., orator and civil rights icon, 1929–1968)

Learning Objectives

- Apply the accrual basis of accounting in the recording of typical transactions for private not-for-profit colleges and universities.
- Prepare the financial statements for private not-for-profit colleges and universities.
- Identify the various types of split-interest agreements and describe accounting practices for each.

As indicated in Chapters 1 and 10, authority to establish accounting and financial reporting principles for certain organizations is split between the Financial Accounting Standards Board (FASB) and the Governmental Accounting Standards Board (GASB). This split is especially significant for colleges and universities. Private institutions, such as Northwestern University and Notre Dame, are subject to the standards issued by the FASB, and public institutions, such as James Madison University and Northern Illinois University, are subject to the standards issued by the GASB.

Illustration 11–1 identifies the authoritative standards-setting body, basis of accounting, and required financial statements for the three types of colleges and universities. Because all three types use the economic resources measurement focus and accrual basis of accounting, most transactions are recorded similarly in the three types of organizations. The most obvious distinction between the ownership

ILLUSTRATION 11–1   College and University Reporting—Ownership Forms

Type of Entity	Authoritative Standards	Accrual Basis of Accounting	Components of Financial Report	Equity Section of Balance Sheet/Statement of Net Assets
Private, Not-for-Profit Colleges and Universities (Chapter 11)	FASB	✓	Statement of Financial Position/Balance Sheet Statement of Activities Statement of Cash Flows Notes to the Financial Statements	Unrestricted Net Assets Temporarily Restricted Net Assets Permanently Restricted Net Assets
Investor-Owned: "Proprietary Schools"	FASB	✓	Balance Sheet Income Statement Statement of Changes in Retained Earnings (or Equity) Statement of Cash Flows Notes to the Financial Statements	Paid in Capital Retained Earnings
Public Colleges and Universities* (Chapter 9)	GASB	✓	MD&A Statement of Net Assets Statement of Revenues, Expenses and Changes in Net Assets Statement of Cash Flows Notes to the Financial Statements RSI Other Than MD&A	Net Assets Invested in Capital Assets, Net of Related Debt Restricted Net Assets Unrestricted Net Assets

*Typically these are special-purpose entities engaged in business-type activities.

forms is in the equity section of the balance sheet. This chapter describes and illustrates FASB and AICPA (American Institute of Certified Public Accountants) requirements for private not-for-profit colleges and universities. Chapter 9 illustrates GASB standards for public institutions. Proprietary (for profit) schools follow FASB standards for commercial businesses and are not illustrated in this text.

Accounting standards for colleges and universities evolved through the efforts of the **National Association of College and University Business Officers (NACUBO),** an industry group composed of university financial vice presidents, comptrollers, and other finance officers. In 1973, AICPA issued *Audits of Colleges and Universities,* which incorporated and modified the principles issued by NACUBO. With respect to private colleges and universities, the 1973 *Audit Guide* is now superceded by *Accounting and Audit Guide: Not-for-Profit Organizations,* issued in 2009 for all private not-for-profit organizations except for health care entities (described in Chapter 12).

As mentioned in Chapter 10, the FASB has issued a number of pronouncements that relate to all private-sector not-for-profit organizations, including colleges and universities. These include *SFAS 93,* which requires depreciation; *SFAS 116,* which provides regulations for accounting for contributions; *SFAS 117,* which provides guidelines for display in financial statements of not-for-profit organizations; and *SFAS 124,* which requires that investments in equity securities with determinable fair values and all investments in debt securities be reported at fair value and that unrealized gains and losses be reported with realized gains and losses in the Statement of Activities. Additionally, FASB issued *Statement 136, Transfers of Assets to a Not-for-Profit Organization That Raises or Holds Contributions for Others.* This statement was also described in Chapter 10.

OVERVIEW OF PRIVATE COLLEGE AND UNIVERSITY ACCOUNTING

Financial Statements

As is true for all not-for-profit organizations under the jurisdiction of the FASB, private colleges and universities are to prepare a Statement of Financial Position, a Statement of Activities, and a Statement of Cash Flows. Considerable flexibility is allowed for colleges and universities as well as for other not-for-profit organizations. For example, the NACUBO *Financial Accounting and Reporting Manual for Higher Education* (Section 500) illustrates Statements of Financial Position using (1) single-column, "corporate" style, (2) FASB Net Asset Class Disaggregation, (3) Operating/Capital Disaggregation, (4) Managed Asset Group Disaggregation, and (5) AICPA Audit Guide Fund Groups Disaggregation. All are acceptable, and similar flexibility is allowed for the Statement of Activities and Statement of Cash Flows. This text uses the more common single-column "corporate" model for the Statement of Financial Position and for the Statement of Cash Flows and presents an illustrative Statement of Unrestricted Revenues, Expenses, and Changes in Unrestricted Net Assets and an illustrative Statement of Changes in Net Assets. These latter two statements are acceptable alternatives to the Statement of Activities illustrated in Chapter 10.

Net Asset Classification

Private colleges and universities are required to report net assets in the same manner as other not-for-profits within three categories: **unrestricted, temporarily restricted,** and **permanently restricted.** As is the case for other not-for-profit organizations, donors or grantors must establish the restrictions; resources subject to designations by the governing board would be considered unrestricted.

Unrestricted inflows include tuition and fees, governmental appropriations (some states provide per student grants to private institutions), unrestricted contributions, unrestricted income on endowments and other investments, gains on investments, and sales and services of **auxiliary enterprises.** Auxiliary enterprises are college operations that are generally intended to be self-supporting, such as bookstores, dormitories, food service operations, and (for some institutions) college athletics. Unrestricted outflows are generally reported in categories of Educational and General, Auxiliary Enterprises, and Other Gains and Losses. Educational and General is often classified functionally as instruction, research, public service, academic support, student services, institutional support, operation and maintenance of physical plant, and scholarships and fellowships.

Temporarily restricted inflows include contributions temporarily restricted for time, purpose, plant acquisition, and term endowments. Temporarily restricted inflows include split interest agreements such as annuity agreements, in which donors contribute funds that are to be invested, with a certain portion going to the donors or other outside parties and the rest going to the institution. Life income agreements, also temporarily restricted, pay investment income in total to the donor during the donor's lifetime, with the institution receiving the proceeds upon the death of the donor. Also in this category are temporarily restricted investment income and gains and losses on investments. All expenses are reported in the unrestricted net asset section of the Statement of Activities. However, temporarily restricted net assets may decrease as the result of net assets released from restrictions and payments to annuity and life income beneficiaries.

Permanently restricted inflows include permanently restricted contributions for endowments and for plant and museum collections that are intended to be maintained permanently. It should be noted that funds held as endowments might be classified in any of the three net asset types. If a donor were to give $1,000,000 to an institution with instructions to invest the money permanently (with income either restricted or unrestricted), then this would be a permanent **endowment** and would be classified as permanently restricted. If a donor were to contribute $1,000,000 with instructions that the funds be invested for 10 years and then released, this would be a **term endowment,** and the assets would be classified as temporarily restricted. If a donor gave $1,000,000 as an unrestricted gift, but the institution's governing board decided to create an endowment, this would be called a **quasi-endowment** and would be unrestricted.

Expenses are to be reported as unrestricted. As was the case in Chapter 10, reclassifications are made from the temporarily restricted class to the unrestricted class as the assets are released from restrictions for time, purpose, or plant acquisition (or depreciation charges) and for the expiration of a term endowment.

Revenue Reduction versus Expenses

An issue particularly relevant to colleges and universities is the distinction between discounts and expenses. In general, revenues and expenses are to be reported separately, rather than netting expenses from revenues. However, if a transaction is deemed to be a discount rather than an expense, the revenue is reported net of the discount.

The most frequent situation where this issue arises is for student financial aid. Scholarship allowances are the difference between the stated charges for tuition and fees and the amount actually billed to the student. Some of these allowances represent discounts and others expenses. NACUBO has issued a position paper titled, "Accounting and Reporting Scholarship Allowances to Tuition and Other Revenues by Higher Education" to address this issue. The paper advises that if the tuition or fee reduction is an employee benefit, the reduction is to be treated as compensation expense, rather than a discount. As a result, tuition waivers associated with graduate assistantships and work-study programs are expenses. However, academic or athletic scholarships that do not require service to the college or university are considered scholarship allowances and treated as reductions in revenue. Interestingly, the NACUBO *Financial Accounting and Reporting Manual* treats estimates of uncollectible accounts as reductions in tuition and fee revenue, rather than bad debt expense.

Academic Terms Encompassing More Than One Fiscal Year

Because colleges and universities commonly use June 30 as fiscal year-end, tuition and other revenues for summer school frequently cover parts of two fiscal years. Under the 1973 *Audits of Colleges and Universities* audit guide, the accepted practice was to recognize revenues and expenses associated with these split sessions in the academic year in which the term was predominantly conducted. Neither *SFAS 116* nor the audit guide, *Not-for-Profit Organizations,* provides any support for this practice. Accordingly, NACUBO requires both revenues and expenses for split sessions to be apportioned to the two fiscal years, following accrual accounting practices similar to those employed by commercial organizations.

Expenses

NACUBO guidelines recommend expenses be classified by function. Functional categories include:

- Educational and General. This includes subcategories for instruction, research, public service, academic support, student services, institutional support, and scholarships and fellowships.
- Auxiliary Enterprises.
- Hospitals.
- Independent Operations.

Academic support includes expenses incurred to provide support for research, instruction, and public service while institutional support includes expenses associated with central executive-level management and long-range planning.

Other Accounting Guidance

Some additional features of accounting for colleges and universities under the jurisdiction of the FASB follow:

- Accrual accounting is used. Revenues and expenses are reported at gross amounts; gains and losses are reported net.
- Depreciation is recorded. When reporting by function, depreciation is allocated to functional categories such as Instruction, Research, and Auxiliary Enterprises.
- If both unrestricted and restricted resources are available for a restricted purpose, the FASB requires that the institution recognize the use of restricted resources first.
- A contribution is recorded as a revenue when the promise to give is unconditional. Multiyear pledges are recorded at the present value of the scheduled receipts.
- As is true for other not-for-profits, plant acquired with either unrestricted or restricted resources may be (1) recorded initially as unrestricted or (2) recorded initially as temporarily restricted and then reclassified in accordance with the depreciation schedule.
- Expenses are reported by function, either in the statements or in the notes. This text illustrates entries and statements leading to functional reporting.
- The FASB requires that investments in stocks with determinable fair values and all debt securities be reported at market value. Unrealized as well as realized gains are reported as a part of the change in net assets.
- Contributed services should be recognized only when the services create or enhance nonfinancial assets or require specialized skills, are provided by individuals possessing those skills, and would typically be purchased if not provided by donation.
- Museum and other inexhaustible collections may or may not be capitalized and recorded in the accounts. If an institution decides not to capitalize these items, extensive note disclosures are required regarding the collections.
- When a private college or university has a foundation, and that foundation receives contributions specifically directed for the benefit of the college or university, the college or university must recognize its interest in the contribution as an asset and as a revenue. The same is true when the college and foundation are financially interrelated.
- As indicated in Chapter 10, if a private college solicits funds, the cost of that solicitation must be considered fund-raising expenses, unless the solicitation meets criteria of purpose, audience, and content. When all of those criteria are met, joint costs can be allocated between fund-raising and other functions.

ILLUSTRATIVE TRANSACTIONS AND FINANCIAL STATEMENTS

A beginning trial balance, entries for typical transactions, and financial statements for a hypothetical private college, the College of St. Michael, are illustrated next (all amounts are in thousands of dollars). Entries for revenues, expenses, gains, losses, and net assets are identified by net asset class, but individual assets and liabilities are not. The fiscal year is the year ending June 30, 2012. Assume the following trial balance for the College of St. Michael as of July 1, 2011:

	Debits	Credits
Cash	$ 1,950	
Accounts Receivable	4,200	
Allowance for Uncollectible Accounts		$ 400
Accrued Interest Receivable	300	
Contributions Receivable	5,400	
Allowance for Uncollectible Contributions		1,000
Loans to Students and Faculty	900	
Long-Term Investments	19,550	
Property, Plant, and Equipment	18,100	
Accumulated Depreciation—Property, Plant, and Equipment		7,500
Accounts Payable		700
Long-Term Debt—Current Installment		100
Long-Term Debt		1,900
Net Assets: Unrestricted—Board Designated		2,000
Net Assets: Unrestricted—Undesignated		15,200
Net Assets: Temporarily Restricted		10,400
Net Assets: Permanently Restricted		11,200
Totals	$50,400	$50,400

Assume it is the policy of St. Michael's to record fixed assets as unrestricted net assets. St. Michael's does not record museum collections, as permitted by the FASB.

Illustrative Transactions

Cash receipts, related to assets at the beginning of the year, include accounts receivable, $3,700; accrued interest receivable, $300; contributions receivable, $4,200; and loans to students and faculty, $500:

	Debits	Credits
1. Cash	8,700	
Accounts Receivable		3,700
Accrued Interest Receivable		300
Contributions Receivable		4,200
Loans to Students and Faculty		500

Cash payments, related to liabilities existing at the beginning of the year, include $700 for accounts payable and $100 for the current installment of long-term debt:

	Debits	Credits
2. Accounts Payable..	700	
Long-Term Debt—Current Installment	100	
Cash		800

Unrestricted revenues include tuition and fees of $15,500. Of this amount, $400 is expected to be uncollectible and $10,500 was collected during registration for classes. Student scholarships for which no service was required amounted to $1,500 and tuition waivers for work-study students (institutional support) amounted to $1,000.

	Debits	Credits
3a. Cash	10,500	
Accounts Receivable	5,000	
Allowance for Uncollectible Accounts		400
Revenues: Unrestricted—Tuition and Fees		15,100
3b. Tuition Discount: Unrestricted—Student Aid.. Scholarship...	1,500	
Institutional Support Expense	1,000	
Accounts Receivable		2,500

Other unrestricted cash receipts included: $1,500 state appropriations, $5,600 contributions (not previously recorded as receivables), $500 investment income on endowment investments, $100 other investment income, and $11,600 sales of services by auxiliary enterprises. An additional $100 of accrued interest is receivable at year-end.

	Debits	Credits
4. Cash	19,300	
Accrued Interest Receivable	100	
Revenues: Unrestricted—State Appropriations		1,500
Revenues: Unrestricted—Contributions...................		5,600
Revenues: Unrestricted—Unrestricted Income on Endowment Investments............................		500
Revenues: Unrestricted—Other Investment Income		200
Revenues: Unrestricted—Sales of Services by Auxiliary Enterprises................................		11,600

Accounts receivable are written off in the amount of $400; uncollectible contributions are written off in the amount of $300.

	Debits	Credits
5. Allowance for Uncollectible Accounts	400	
Allowance for Uncollectible Contributions	300	
Accounts Receivable		400
Contributions Receivable		300

Temporarily restricted pledges for time, purpose, and plant acquisition were received in the amount of $2,250. In addition, $4,000 was received in cash contributions for temporarily restricted purposes; $1,000 of the resources was restricted for plant acquisition.

	Debits	Credits
6. Contributions Receivable	2,250	
Cash	4,000	
Revenues: Temporarily Restricted—Contributions		6,250

Cash in the amount of $1,000 and pledges in the amount of $350 were received, establishing endowments, and are recorded as revenue-increasing permanently restricted net assets:

	Debits	Credits
7. Cash	1,000	
Contributions Receivable	350	
Revenues: Permanently Restricted—Contributions		1,350

Interest income that is temporarily restricted amounts to $760. Of that amount, $570 is received in cash and $190 is accrued at year-end:

	Debits	Credits
8. Cash	570	
Accrued Interest Receivable	190	
Revenues: Temporarily Restricted—Investment Income		760

Expenses, exclusive of depreciation, are as follows: instruction, $17,400; research, $2,300; public service, $1,900; academic support, $600; student services,

$1,000; institutional support, $1,100; and auxiliary enterprises, $8,500. In addition, the college experiences an uninsured fire loss in the amount of $300. Cash is paid in the amount of $32,100, and accounts payable is increased by $1,000:

	Debits	Credits
9. Instruction Expense	17,400	
Research Expense	2,300	
Public Service Expense	1,900	
Academic Support Expense	600	
Student Services Expense	1,000	
Institutional Support Expense	1,100	
Auxiliary Enterprise Expense	8,500	
Fire Loss	300	
Cash		32,100
Accounts Payable		1,000

Depreciation is charged in the amount of $1,500 and is allocated to functions as shown:

10. Instruction Expense	800	
Research Expense	80	
Public Service Expense	60	
Academic Support Expense	30	
Student Services Expense	70	
Institutional Support Expense	90	
Auxiliary Enterprise Expense	370	
Accumulated Depreciation—Property, Plant, and Equipment		1,500

Reclassifications are made in the total amount of $7,000 from temporarily restricted to unrestricted net assets. The $7,000 includes $2,000 reclassified on the basis of expiration of time restrictions, $3,000 reclassified for program restrictions (research), $1,200 for plant (equipment) acquisition, and $800 for the expiration of time endowments:

	Debits	Credits
11. Reclassification from Temporarily Restricted Net Assets— Expiration of Time Restrictions.......................	2,000	
Reclassification from Temporarily Restricted Net Assets— Satisfaction of Program Restrictions	3,000	
Reclassification from Temporarily Restricted Net Assets— Satisfaction of Plant Acquisition Restrictions	1,200	
Reclassification from Temporarily Restricted Net Assets— Expiration of Term Endowments......................	800	
Reclassification to Unrestricted Net Assets— Expiration of Time Restrictions....................		2,000
Reclassification to Unrestricted Net Assets— Satisfaction of Program Restrictions		3,000
Reclassification to Unrestricted Net Assets— Satisfaction of Plant Acquisition Restrictions		1,200
Reclassification to Unrestricted Net Assets— Expiration of Term Endowments...................		800

Research expenses are incurred and equipment is acquired. As indicated earlier, it is the policy of St. Michael's to record plant as increases in unrestricted net assets, one of the options permitted by the FASB. These two entries cause the reclassifications for program and plant purposes above in entry 11:

12. Research Expense......................................	3,000	
Property, Plant, and Equipment	1,200	
Cash		4,200

Long-term investments, with a cost of $3,500, are sold for $3,750. Of the $250 gain, $200 was required by gift agreement to be added to temporarily restricted net assets, and $50 was required by the endowment agreement to be added to endowments.

13. Cash	3,750	
Long-Term Investments...............................		3,500
Gains on Long-Term Investments—Temporarily Restricted...		200
Gains on Long-Term Investments—Permanently Restricted		50

Loans to students and faculty are made in the amount of $750:

14. Loans to Students and Faculty	750	
Cash		750

Long-term investments are purchased in the amount of $5,800:

	Debits	Credits
15. Long-Term Investments................................	5,800	
Cash		5,800

The Board of Trustees of St. Michael's College decides to invest an additional $1,000 of unrestricted resources. These investments are designated by the board for permanent endowment, technically known as a *quasi-endowment*. Two entries are necessary:

16a. Long-Term Investments................................	1,000	
Cash		1,000
16b. Net Assets: Unrestricted—Undesignated...................	1,000	
Net Assets: Unrestricted—Designated...................		1,000

At year-end, it is determined that the fair value of long-term investments has increased by $1,900. Of that amount, $800 is restricted temporarily by donor agreements and $1,100 is restricted for future endowment purposes:

17. Long-Term Investments................................	1,900	
Gains on Long-Term Investments—Temporarily Restricted. . .		800
Gains on Long-Term Investments—Permanently Restricted . .		1,100

The current portion of long-term debt is recognized:

18. Long-Term Debt..	100	
Long-Term Debt: Current Installment....................		100

The closing entry is made for the unrestricted net asset class. Note that revenues and reclassifications have been recorded by net asset class; all expenses are considered unrestricted.

	Debits	Credits
19. Revenues: Unrestricted—Tuition and Fees	15,100	
Revenues: Unrestricted—State Appropriation.	1,500	
Revenues: Unrestricted—Contributions	5,600	
Revenues: Unrestricted—Investment Income on Endowment Investments	500	
Revenues: Unrestricted—Other Investment Income	200	
Revenues: Unrestricted—Sales and Services of Auxiliary Enterprises	11,600	
Reclassification to Unrestricted Net Assets— Expiration of Time Restrictions.	2,000	
Reclassification to Unrestricted Net Assets— Satisfaction of Program Restrictions	3,000	
Reclassification to Unrestricted Net Assets— Satisfaction of Plant Acquisition Restrictions	1,200	
Reclassification to Unrestricted Net Assets— Expiration of Term Endowments.	800	
Tuition Discount—Student Aid		1,500
Instruction Expense.		18,200
Research Expense.		5,380
Public Service Expense		1,960
Academic Support Expense		630
Student Services Expense.		1,070
Institutional Support Expense		2,190
Auxiliary Enterprise Expense.		8,870
Fire Loss.		300
Net Assets: Unrestricted: Undesignated.		1,400

The entry to close accounts for temporarily restricted net assets was made:

	Debits	Credits
20. Revenues: Temporarily Restricted—Contributions.	6,250	
Revenues: Temporarily Restricted—Other Investment Income . .	760	
Gains on Long-Term Investments—Temporarily Restricted.	1,000	
Reclassifications from Temporarily Restricted Net Assets— Expiration of Time Restrictions.		2,000
Reclassifications from Temporarily Restricted Net Assets— Satisfaction of Program Restrictions		3,000
Reclassifications from Temporarily Restricted Net Assets— Satisfaction of Plant Acquisition Restrictions		1,200
Reclassifications from Temporarily Restricted Net Assets— Expiration of Term Endowments.		800
Net Assets: Temporarily Restricted		1,010

Finally, the closing entry is made for the permanently restricted net asset class:

	Debits	Credits
21. Revenues: Permanently Restricted Contributions	1,350	
Gains on Long-Term Investments—Permanently Restricted	1,150	
Net Assets: Permanently Restricted		2,500

Illustrative Financial Statements for Private Colleges and Universities

Financial statements required for private-sector nonprofit colleges and universities include a Statement of Financial Position, Statement of Activities, and Statement of Cash Flows. An acceptable alternative to the Statement of Activities is to present two statements: (1) Statement of Unrestricted Revenues, Expenses, and Other Changes in Unrestricted Net Assets and (2) Statement of Changes in Net Assets. Illustrative financial statements for the College of St. Michael are shown in this section.

Statement of Unrestricted Revenues, Expenses, and Other Changes in Unrestricted Net Assets As mentioned in Chapter 10, several alternatives are acceptable for the Statement of Activities as long as revenues, expenses, and reclassifications are clearly shown and as long as the changes in net assets are shown separately for each of the three net asset classes and in total. Illustration 10–1 presented a four-column Statement of Activities for a performing arts organization with separate columns for each net asset class and a total. Illustration 11–2 presents a Statement of Unrestricted Revenues, Expenses, and Other Changes in Unrestricted Net Assets.

Statement of Changes in Net Assets If an organization prepares a Statement of Unrestricted Revenues, Expenses, and Other Changes in Unrestricted Net Assets in lieu of a complete Statement of Activities, the FASB requires that a Statement of Changes in Net Assets be prepared. One way of preparing it is shown as the Statement of Changes in Net Assets for the College of St. Michael in Illustration 11–3.

Statement of Financial Position The Statement of Financial Position for the College of St. Michael is presented as Illustration 11–4. Note that the statement is not classified, but assets are generally shown in the order of liquidity and liabilities are generally shown in the order of payment dates.

Statement of Cash Flows Illustration 11–5 presents a Statement of Cash Flows for the College of St. Michael. The direct method is used.

SPLIT-INTEREST AGREEMENTS

The *Not-for-Profit Guide* provides guidance to not-for-profit organizations, including those covered in Chapter 10 and this chapter, regarding split-interest agreements. **Split-interest agreements** represent trust or other arrangements with donors

ILLUSTRATION 11–2   Statement of Unrestricted Revenues, Expenses, and Other Changes in Unrestricted Net Assets

COLLEGE OF ST. MICHAEL	
Statement of Unrestricted Revenues, Expenses, and Other Changes in Unrestricted Net Assets	
For the Year Ended June 30, 2012	
(in thousands of dollars)	
Unrestricted Revenues:	
Net Tuition and Fees	$13,600
State Appropriation	1,500
Contributions	5,600
Investment Income on Endowment	500
Other Investment Income	200
Sales and Services of Auxiliary Enterprises	11,600
Total Revenues	33,000
Net Assets Released from Restrictions:	
Expiration of Time Restrictions	2,000
Satisfaction of Program Restrictions	3,000
Satisfaction of Plant Acquisition Restrictions	1,200
Expiration of Term Endowment	800
Total Net Assets Released from Restrictions	7,000
Total Unrestricted Revenues and Other Support	40,000
Expenses and Losses:	
Educational and General:	
Instruction	18,200
Research	5,380
Public Service	1,960
Academic Support	630
Student Services	1,070
Institutional Support	2,190
Total Educational and General Expenses	29,430
Auxiliary Enterprises	8,870
Total Expenses	38,300
Fire Loss	300
Total Expenses and Losses	38,600
Increase in Unrestricted Net Assets	$ 1,400

in which not-for-profit organizations receive benefits that are shared with other beneficiaries. Annuity and life income agreements, discussed earlier in this chapter, are examples. The *Not-for-Profit Guide* categorizes these split-interest agreements into five types: (1) charitable lead trusts, (2) perpetual trusts held by third parties,

ILLUSTRATION 11–3 Statement of Changes in Net Assets

COLLEGE OF ST. MICHAEL Statement of Changes in Net Assets For the Year Ended June 30, 2012 (in thousands of dollars)	
Total Unrestricted Revenues	$33,000
Net Assets Released from Restrictions	7,000
Total Unrestricted Expenses and Losses	(38,600)
Increase in Unrestricted Net Assets	1,400
Temporarily Restricted Net Assets:	
Contributions	6,250
Gains on Long-Term Investments	1,000
Other Investment Income	760
Net Assets Released from Restrictions	(7,000)
Increase in Temporarily Restricted Net Assets	1,010
Permanently Restricted Net Assets:	
Contributions	1,350
Gains on Long-term Investments	1,150
Increase in Permanently Restricted Net Assets	2,500
Increase in Net Assets	4,910
Net Assets, July 1, 2011	38,800
Net Assets, June 30, 2012	$43,710

(3) charitable remainder trusts, (4) charitable gift annuities, and (5) pooled (life) income funds. Each of these is discussed in the following paragraphs.

A **charitable lead trust** is an arrangement whereby a donor establishes a trust in which a portion of the trust is distributed to a not-for-profit organization for a certain term. At the end of the term, the remainder of the trust assets is paid to the donor or other beneficiary. The not-for-profit organization may or may not hold the trust assets. When the trust is created and is irrevocable, the not-for-profit organization recognizes a receivable for the fair value of the assets received and a temporarily restricted revenue at the present value of the anticipated receipts that will be retained by the not-for-profit. If the not-for-profit is the trustee of the trust assets, the difference between the trust assets and the present value of anticipated receipts is recognized as a liability. Year-to-year changes are recognized as Changes in the Value of Split-Interest Agreements, which are recognized as additions to or deductions from the temporarily restricted net asset class in the Statement of Activities.

A **perpetual trust held by a third party** is not exactly a split-interest agreement but is accounted for in a similar fashion. Assume that a person establishes a permanent trust at a bank with the income to go to a not-for-profit organization in

ILLUSTRATION 11–4 Statement of Financial Position

COLLEGE OF ST. MICHAEL
Statements of Financial Position
As of June 30, 2012 and 2011
(in thousands of dollars)

	2012	2011
Assets		
Cash and Cash Equivalents	$ 5,120	$ 1,950
Accounts Receivable (Net of Allowance for Uncollectibles of $400 and $400)	2,200	3,800
Accrued Interest Receivable	290	300
Contributions Receivable (Net of Allowance for Uncollectibles of $700 and $1,000)	2,800	4,400
Loans to Students and Faculty	1,150	900
Long-term Investments	24,750	19,550
Property, Plant, and Equipment (Net of Accumulated Depreciation of $9,000 and $7,500)	10,300	10,600
Total Assets	$46,610	$41,500
Liabilities and Net Assets		
Accounts Payable	$ 1,000	$ 700
Long-term Debt: Current Installment	100	100
Long-term Debt: Noncurrent	1,800	1,900
Total Liabilities	2,900	2,700
Net Assets:		
Board Designated	3,000	2,000
Other Unrestricted	15,600	15,200
Total Unrestricted	18,600	17,200
Temporarily Restricted	11,410	10,400
Permanently Restricted	13,700	11,200
Total Net Assets	$43,710	$38,800
Total Liabilities and Net Assets	$46,610	$41,500

perpetuity. The present value of anticipated receipts (usually the fair value of the assets contributed) is recorded as an asset and as contribution revenue in the permanently restricted net asset class. Income received each year is recorded as either unrestricted or temporarily restricted investment income, depending on the trust agreement. Changes in the value of trust principal are recorded as additions to or deductions from the permanently restricted net asset class.

A **charitable remainder trust** is a trust established by a donor to ensure that a specified dollar amount or a specified percentage of the trust's fair market value is paid to a beneficiary. At the end of the term of the trust, the trust principal is paid to the institution for unrestricted or temporarily restricted purposes or as an

ILLUSTRATION 11–5   Statement of Cash Flows

COLLEGE OF ST. MICHAEL Statement of Cash Flows For the Year Ended December 31, 2012 (in thousands of dollars)	
Cash Flows from Operating Activities:	
Cash Received from Service Recipients	$25,800
Cash Received from State Appropriations	1,500
Cash Received from Contributors	12,800
Interest and Dividends Received	1,470
Cash Paid to Employees and Suppliers	(35,800)
Cash Flows from Operating Activities	5,770
Cash Flows from Investing Activities:	
Acquisition of Property, Plant, and Equipment	(1,200)
Purchase of Investments	(6,800)
Sale of Investments	3,750
Disbursement of Loans to Students and Faculty	(750)
Repayment of Loans to Students and Faculty	500
Cash Flows from Investing Activities	(4,500)
Cash Flows from Financing Activities:	
Proceeds from Contributions Restricted for:	
Investment in Property, Plant, and Equipment	1,000
Investment in Endowments	1,000
Other Financing Activities:	
Payments on Long-term Debt	(100)
Cash Flows from Financing Activities	1,900
Net Increase in Cash and Cash Equivalents	3,170
Cash and Cash Equivalents, July 1, 2011	1,950
Cash and Cash Equivalents, June 30, 2012	$ 5,120
Reconciliation of change in net assets to cash flows from operating activities:	
Change in Net Assets	$ 4,910
Adjustments to Reconcile Change in Net Assets to Net Cash Provided by Operating Activities:	
Depreciation	1,500
Decrease in Accounts Receivable	1,600
Decrease in Accrued Interest Receivable	10
Decrease in Contributions Receivable	1,600
Increase in Accounts Payable	300
Gains on Long-Term Investments	(2,150)
Contribution Restricted to Investment in Property, Plant, and Equipment	(1,000)
Contribution Restricted to Long-term Investment in Endowments	(1,000)
Cash Flows from Operating Activities	5,770

endowment (permanently restricted). The trust assets are recorded at fair market value, the present value of the amounts to be paid to the beneficiary are recorded as a liability, and the difference is recorded as contribution revenue in the appropriate net asset class. Adjustments in the present value of the liability are recorded each year as a change in the value of split-interest agreements in the Statement of Activities.

4) A **charitable gift annuity** is the same as a charitable remainder trust except that no formal trust agreement exists; normally a contract is signed. The accounting is the same as for a charitable remainder trust.

5) A **pooled (life) income fund** represents a situation in which the assets of several life income agreements are pooled together. A life income fund represents a situation in which all of the income is paid to a donor or a beneficiary during his or her lifetime. At the end of the donor's or beneficiary's life, the assets go to the not-for-profit organization for unrestricted or restricted purposes. In a pooled (life) income fund, the assets are recorded and entered into the pool based on the fair value of all assets at the time of entry. A revenue is recognized in the temporarily restricted net asset class, discounted for the time period of the donor's or beneficiary's expected remaining life. The difference between the fair value of the assets received and the revenue is recorded as deferred revenue, representing the amount of the discount for future interest.

Illustrative journal entries are presented in the *Not-for-Profit Guide,* and in the NACUBO *Financial Accounting and Reporting Manual.*

SUMMARY—PRIVATE COLLEGE AND UNIVERSITY REPORTING

Private colleges and universities are required to follow the accounting principles promulgated by the FASB and in the AICPA *Not-for-Profit Guide.* These pronouncements include FASB statements on display, contributions, depreciation, and investments. The *Not-for-Profit Guide,* unlike the *Health Care Guide* (described in Chapter 12), does not prescribe or illustrate reporting format. However, the NACUBO *Financial Accounting and Reporting Manual for Higher Education* provides more detailed guidance and illustrative entries for both private and public institutions.

Governmental colleges and universities are under the jurisdiction of the GASB, for purposes of financial reporting. GASB *Statement 35* requires governmental colleges and universities to follow GASB *Statement 34* guidance for special-purpose entities. Most choose to report as special-purpose entities engaged in business-type activities only. That accounting is described and illustrated in Chapter 9.

Now that you have finished reading Chapter 11, complete the multiple choice questions provided on the text's Web site (www.mhhe.com/copley10e) to test your comprehension of the chapter.

Questions and Exercises

11–1. Obtain a copy of the annual report of a private college or university. Answer the following questions from the report. For examples, try:

Baylor University: http://www.baylor.edu/content/services/document.php/53248.PDF
Harvard University: http://vpf-web.harvard.edu/annualfinancial/
University of Notre Dame: http://cfweb-prod.nd.edu/controller/annual-report/
Stanford University: http://bondholder-information.stanford.edu/home.html
Vanderbilt University: http://financialreport.vanderbilt.edu/

   a. Is the annual report audited? Name the auditing firm.
   b. Does the organization present (1) a single Statement of Activities, or does it present (2) a Statement of Unrestricted Revenues, Expenses, and Other Changes in Unrestricted Net Assets together with a Statement of Changes in Net Assets?
   c. What additional financial statements are presented?
   d. Does the organization have temporarily restricted net assets? What is the amount of the net assets released from restrictions in the current period?
   e. Does the organization have permanently restricted net assets?
   f. Is there a note describing split interest agreements?

11–2. For each of the following, identify (1) which accounting standards–setting body has primary authority, (2) the required financial statements, and (3) the account titles used in the equity section of the balance sheet or equivalent statement.
   a. Public (government-owned) colleges and universities.
   b. Private, not-for-profit colleges and universities.
   c. Investor-owned, proprietary schools.

11–3. With regard to private-sector colleges and universities:
   a. List the three net asset classes required under FASB *Statement 117*.
   b. List the financial reports required under FASB *Statement 117*.
   c. Distinguish between an endowment, a term endowment, and a quasi-endowment. Indicate the accounting required for each.
   d. Outline the accounting required by the FASB for
      (1) An endowment gift received in cash.
      (2) A pledge received in 2011, unrestricted as to purpose but restricted for use in 2012.
      (3) A pledge received in 2011, restricted as to purpose other than plant. The purpose was fulfilled in 2012.
   e. Discuss the requirements necessary before contributed services are recorded as revenues.

11–4. Define and outline the accounting required for each of the following types of agreements:

  a. Charitable lead trusts.

  b. Charitable remainder trusts.

  c. Perpetual trust held by a third party.

11–5. During the year ended June 30, 2012, the following transactions were recorded by St. Ann's College, a private institution:

1. Tuition and fees amounted to $6,800,000, of which $4,500,000 was received in cash. A state appropriation was received in cash in the amount of $600,000. Sales and services of auxiliary enterprises amounted to $3,500,000, all of which was received in cash.

2. Student scholarships were awarded in the amount of $900,000. Recipient students were not required to provide services for this financial aid.

3. The provision for doubtful accounts for the year ended June 30, 2012, amounted to $25,000. During the year, doubtful accounts related to student fees were written off in the amount of $20,000.

4. During the year, contributions received, all in cash, amounted to: unrestricted, $600,000; temporarily restricted for use in the year ended June 30, 2013, $1,100,000 (unrestricted as to purpose); temporarily restricted for certain purposes, $900,000; and restricted for endowments, $1,000,000.

5. During the year, $500,000 was released from restrictions based on time and $700,000 was released from restrictions for program purposes (research). The applicable research expense of $700,000 was paid in cash.

6. Investment income amounted to: unrestricted income from endowments, $150,000; income from endowments for purposes restricted by program, $200,000; and income from endowments required to be added to the endowment, $15,000.

7. During the year, St. Ann's received a gift of $1,500,000, which was to be used for the future construction of an addition to the library.

8. During the year, $1,300,000 was released from restriction for the construction of a new wing to the student services building. The building was constructed using the cash. St. Ann's records all fixed assets in the unrestricted net asset class.

9. Endowment long-term investments, carried at a basis of $2,000,000, were sold for $2,150,000. The total proceeds were reinvested. Income is to remain as permanently restricted.

10. Expenses for the year (in addition to expenses provided for in other parts of the problem) were instruction, $5,050,000; research, $1,300,000; public service, $300,000; academic support, $200,000; student services, $600,000; institutional support, $700,000; and auxiliary enterprises, $3,400,000. Of this, $10,950,000 was paid in cash and $600,000 was credited to Accounts Payable.

11. Depreciation recorded for the year amounted to $540,000. One-third of that amount was charged to instruction, one-third to institutional support, and one-third to auxiliary enterprises.

12. The institution sustained an uninsured fire loss of $230,000. Repairs were paid in cash and charged to the fire loss account.

13. Closing entries were prepared.

    a. Record the transactions on the books of St. Ann's College. Indicate the net asset class for revenues and reclassifications.

    b. Prepare, in good form, a Statement of Unrestricted Revenues, Expenses, and Other Changes in Unrestricted Net Assets for St. Ann's College for the year ended June 30, 2012.

    c. Prepare, in good form, a Statement of Changes in Net Assets for St. Ann's College for the year ended June 30, 2012. The net assets at the beginning of the year amounted to $2,080,000.

11–6. Record the following transactions on the books of Calvin College, which follows FASB standards, for Calvin's fiscal year, which ends on June 30, 2012.

1. During the year ended June 30, 2012, a donor made a cash contribution in the amount of $1,000,000 with the stipulation that the principal be invested permanently and that the income be used for research in biology. The cash was invested.

2. Also during the year ended June 30, 2012, a donor made an unrestricted cash contribution of $500,000. Calvin's governing board decided to establish this gift as a permanent investment and invested the funds.

3. By the end of the year, the investments mentioned in transaction 1 earned $45,000 and the investments mentioned in transaction 2 earned $22,500; both amounts were received in cash.

4. The fair value of investments in transaction 1 increased by $15,000 at year-end.

5. During the year ended June 30, 2013, the biology research was completed, using the income mentioned in transaction 3.

11–7. Record the following transactions on the books of Carnegie College, a private institution that follows FASB standards. The year is 2012.

1. During 2012, Carnegie received a pledge in the amount of $225,000, unrestricted as to purpose, indicating that the amount was to be paid to and used by the college in 2013.

2. Carnegie received $80,000 in cash from a donor who specified that the funds were to be used for research in voting behavior. The university did not conduct the research in 2012.

3. Carnegie conducted certain research on electrical conductivity during 2012, costing $50,000. A grant had been given in 2010 for just that purpose, but Carnegie hoped to use $30,000 of unrestricted resources for

the 2012 research and keep $30,000 of the original grant for future use in research. (*Hint:* Follow the required procedure in this case.)

4. During 2012, Carnegie reclassified $65,000 of funds that had been given in 2011 to support unspecified activities in 2012.

5. During 2011, Carnegie received $750,000 to renovate a dormitory. During 2012, $620,000 of the funds were spent. Carnegie records all plant in the unrestricted net asset class.

11–8. Presented below are the closing entries for Lee College, a private not-for-profit, for the year ended December 31, 2012.

	Debits	Credits
Revenues—Unrestricted—Tuition and Fees	$11,200,000	
Revenues—Unrestricted—Unrestricted Income on Endowment Investments	40,000	
Revenues—Unrestricted—Sales and Services of Auxiliary Enterprises	5,000,000	
Revenues—Unrestricted—Contributions	100,000	
Reclassifications to Unrestricted Net Assets— Satisfaction of Program Restrictions.	640,000	
Reclassifications to Unrestricted Net Assets— Satisfaction of Plant Acquisition Restrictions	1,160,000	
Tuition Discount—Unrestricted—Student Aid.		$ 110,000
Instruction Expense		7,000,000
Research Expense		4,500,000
Public Service Expense		1,200,000
Institutional Support Expense.		700,000
Student Services Expense.		150,000
Auxiliary Enterprise Expense.		3,500,000
Net Assets—Unrestricted—Undesignated		980,000
Revenues—Temporarily Restricted—Contributions	1,500,000	
Revenues—Temporarily Restricted—Grants	950,000	
Reclassifications From Temporarily Restricted Net Assets—Satisfaction of Program Restrictions		640,000
Reclassifications from Temporarily Restricted Net Assets—Satisfaction of Plant Acquisition Restrictions . . .		1,160,000
Net Assets—Temporarily Restricted		650,000
Revenues—Permanently Restricted—Contributions.	2,540,000	
Gains on Long-Term Investments.	750,000	
Net Assets—Permanently Restricted.		3,290,000

Assume the January 1, 2012, net asset balances are as follows: $1,000,000 unrestricted net assets; $300,000 temporarily restricted net assets; and $1,700,000 permanently restricted net assets.

a. Prepare a Statement of Activities using the format presented in Illustration 10–1.

b. Prepare a Statement of Unrestricted Revenues, Expenses, and Other Changes in Unrestricted Net Assets together with a Statement of Changes in Net Assets.

11–9. **Comprehensive Problem.** As of July 1, 2011, the trial balance for Korner College was as follows:

	Debits	Credits
Cash	$ 618,000	
Accounts Receivable	1,350,000	
Allowance for Uncollectible Accounts		$ 60,000
Accrued Interest Receivable	49,000	
Contributions Receivable	5,425,000	
Allowance for Uncollectible Contributions		125,000
Loans to Students and Faculty	350,000	
Long-Term Investments	15,500,000	
Property, Plant, and Equipment	15,450,000	
Accumulated Depreciation— Property, Plant, and Equipment		7,530,000
Accounts Payable		520,000
Long-Term Debt: Current Installment		150,000
Long-Term Debt: Noncurrent		8,500,000
Net Assets—Unrestricted—Board Designated		2,400,000
Net Assets—Unrestricted—Undesignated		3,815,000
Net Assets—Temporarily Restricted		5,555,000
Net Assets—Permanently Restricted		10,087,000
Totals	$38,742,000	$38,742,000

During the year ended June 30, 2012, the following transactions occurred:

1. Cash collections included: accounts receivable, $1,200,000; accrued interest receivable, $49,000; contributions receivable, $5,345,000; and for loans to students and faculty, $155,000. Of the contributions, $1,900,000 was for plant acquisition (use for cash flow statement).

2. Cash payments included accounts payable, $520,000; and the current portion of long-term debt, $150,000.

3. Unrestricted revenues included tuition and fees, $21,800,000; unrestricted income on endowment investments, $400,000; other investment income, $300,000; and sales and services of auxiliary enterprises, $14,740,000. A total of $33,690,000 in cash was received, and the following receivables were increased: accounts receivable, $3,500,000; accrued interest receivable, $50,000.

4. Scholarships, for which no services were required, were applied to student accounts in the amount of $2,200,000.

5. Contributions were received in the following amounts: unrestricted, $4,900,000; temporarily restricted, $5,400,000; permanently restricted, $2,000,000. Of that amount, $7,020,000 was received in cash; contributions receivable increased $5,280,000. None of these contributions were restricted to plant acquisition.

6. Accounts receivable were written off in the amount of $50,000, and contributions receivable were written off in the amount of $20,000. Provisions for bad debts were increased by $125,000 for accounts receivable (tuition and fees) and by $30,000 for unrestricted contributions receivable.

7. Expenses, exclusive of depreciation and uncollectible accounts, were as follows: instruction, $18,460,000; research, $1,980,000; public service, $1,910,000; academic support, $990,000; student services, $1,310,000; institutional support, $1,050,000; and auxiliary enterprises, $13,500,000. The college had an uninsured flood loss in the amount of $600,000. Cash was paid in the amount of $39,200,000, and accounts payable increased by $600,000.

8. Depreciation was charged in the amount of $1,500,000. One-third of that amount was charged each to instruction, institutional support, and auxiliary enterprises.

9. Interest income was earned as follows: addition to temporarily restricted net assets, $30,000; addition to permanently restricted net assets, $35,000. Of those amounts, $55,000 was received in cash and $10,000 was accrued at year-end.

10. Research expense was incurred in the amount of $1,700,000; and property, plant, and equipment were acquired in the amount of $1,400,000. Both were paid in cash.

11. Reclassifications were made from temporarily restricted to unrestricted net assets as follows: on the basis of time restrictions, $1,600,000; for program restrictions (research), $1,700,000; and for fixed asset acquisition restrictions, $1,400,000. Korner records fixed assets as increases in unrestricted net assets.

12. Long-term investments, with a carrying value of $1,700,000, were sold for $1,770,000. Of the $70,000 gain, $40,000 was temporarily restricted by donor agreement and $30,000 is required to be added to permanently restricted net assets.

13. Additional investments were purchased in the amount of $3,970,000. Loans were made to students and faculty in the amount of $200,000.

14. In addition to 13 above, the board of trustees decided to purchase $2,000,000 in long-term investments, from unrestricted net assets, to create a quasi-endowment.

15. At year-end, the fair value of investments increased by $530,000. Of that amount, $300,000 increased unrestricted net assets, $30,000 increased temporarily restricted net assets, and $200,000 increased permanently restricted net assets.

16. $150,000 of the long-term debt was reclassified as a current liability.

17. Closing entries were prepared for (*a*) unrestricted net assets, (*b*) temporarily restricted net assets, and (*c*) permanently restricted net assets.

Required:

a. Prepare journal entries for each of the above transactions.

b. Prepare a Statement of Unrestricted Revenues, Expenses, and Other Changes in Unrestricted Net Assets for Korner College for the fiscal year ended June 30, 2012.

c. Prepare a Statement of Changes in Net Assets for Korner College for the fiscal year ended June 30, 2012.

d. Prepare a Statement of Financial Position for Korner College as of June 30, 2012.

e. Prepare a Statement of Cash Flows for Korner College for the year ended June 30, 2012. Use the indirect method.

Excel-Based Problem

11–10. Presented below are comparative post-closing trial balances for a college. In addition, cash transactions for the year ended December 31, 2012, are summarized in the T-account.

	December 31, 2011	December 31, 2012	Increase (Decrease)
Debits			
Cash	$1,650,000	$1,925,700	$275,700
Student Accounts Receivable	170,000	147,000	(23,000)
Endowment Investments	2,500,000	2,600,000	100,000
Property, Plant, and Equipment	4,875,000	5,167,000	292,000
Credits			
Accumulated Depreciation	2,107,000	2,557,000	450,000
Accounts Payable	37,500	46,200	8,700
Accrued Interest Payable	1,500	1,000	(500)
Long-term Debt	2,282,000	2,189,000	(93,000)
Net Assets	$4,767,000	$5,046,500	$279,500

Cash

Beginning balance 1/1/2012	$1,650,000		
Student Tuition and Fees	1,531,000	$1,200,000	Salaries
State Appropriations	700,000	597,300	Operating Expenses
Contributions to Endowment	105,700	19,700	Interest
Federal Grants	175,000	292,000	Equipment Purchases
Investment Income	66,000	93,000	Payment Principal LT Debt
		$100,000	Purchase Endowment Investments
Ending balance 12/31/2012	$1,925,700		

Comparative activity statements have been prepared for the year ended December 31, 2012, assuming the college is: (*a*) a private not-for-profit (Statement of Activities) and (*b*) a public college (Statement of Revenues, Expenses, and Changes in Fund Net Assets). These are provided in the first tab of the Excel file template.

Using the information above and the Excel template provided, prepare statements of cash flow assuming the college is: (*a*) a private not-for-profit and (*b*) a public college. Assume that all long-term debt is associated with the purchase of property, plant, and equipment.

Accounting for Hospitals and Other Health Care Providers

My doctors told me I would never walk again. My mother told me I would. I believed my mother. (Wilma Rudolph, 1940–1994, three-time Olympic gold medal winner in track)

America's health care system is neither healthy, caring, nor a system. (Walter Cronkite, 1916–2009, anchor of the *CBS Evening News* for 19 years and was known as "the most trusted man in America")

Learning Objectives

- Describe the reporting requirements of varying types of health care organizations.
- Apply the accrual basis of accounting in the recording of typical transactions of a not-for-profit health care organization.
- Prepare the financial statements for a not-for-profit health care organization.

Health care expenditures now exceed $2.5 trillion or 17.6 percent of the gross national product of the United States, and this percentage is expected to grow in the future. A major national debate continues over how health care should be provided and paid for. Health care entities are subject to a complex set of regulatory requirements established by federal and state governments as well as by third-party payors, such as insurance companies. The relationships among physicians, patients, health care entities, insurance companies, and regulators have been changing, and many mergers have taken place, resulting in complex organizations that may include several participants in the health care process. Health care accounting and auditing can provide an exciting and profitable career to individuals who are willing and able to deal with complexity and change.

Health care providers may be private not-for-profits, governmentally owned, or owned by private investors. Like charities and private colleges, private not-for-profit health care organizations follow FASB standards. In particular, several standards are written specifically for not-for-profits, including *Statements 116, 117, 124,* and *136.* If a health care organization is owned or controlled by a government, it is typically considered a special-purpose entity engaged only in business-type activities (GASB *Statement 34*) and would use proprietary fund accounting, similar to government-owned colleges and universities described in Chapter 9. Other health care organizations are privately owned and operated to provide a return to investors. For example, Hospital Corporation of America (HCA) owns or operates hundreds of hospitals in the United States and internationally and its stock is traded on the New York Stock Exchange. HCA and other private for-profit health care organizations follow FASB standards *excluding* those written specifically for not-for-profits.

While the three types of health care organizations follow different sets of generally accepted accounting standards, the differences lie mainly in presentation. All three types of organizations measure assets and liabilities similarly, recognize revenue and expenses under the accrual basis, and present comparable performance (i.e., income) measures. Helping to assure comparability across health care organizations with varying ownership structures, the *AICPA Audit and Accounting Guide: Health Care Organizations* applies equally to private not-for-profit, governmentally owned, and investor-owned health care organizations.[1]

This chapter concentrates on reporting by private not-for-profit health care organizations, the most numerous of the three types. However, unique features of governmental health care reporting are also described in a separate section. For accounting purposes, health care organizations include the following:

- Clinics, medical group practices, individual practice associations, individual practitioners, emergency care facilities, laboratories, surgery centers, and other ambulatory care organizations.
- Continuing care retirement communities.
- Health Maintenance Organizations (HMOs) and similar prepaid health care plans.
- Home health agencies.
- Hospitals.
- Nursing homes that provide skilled, intermediate, and less intensive levels of health care.
- Drug and alcohol rehabilitation centers and other rehabilitation facilities.

Payments for these health care organizations come from many sources, including Medicare, Medicaid, commercial insurance companies, nonprofit insurance companies, state and local assistance programs, and directly from patients.

---

[1] American Institute of Certified Public Accountants, *AICPA Audit and Accounting Guide: Health Care Organizations* (New York: AICPA, 2008).

The *Health Care Guide* makes a distinction between health care organizations and voluntary health and welfare organizations, a distinction that is sometimes difficult in practice. The organizations just listed that are legally nonprofit but raise essentially all revenues from services produced are health care organizations and are subject to the *Health Care Guide.* The *Health Care Guide* calls these organizations Not-for-Profit, Business-Oriented Organizations. If similar organizations raise a significant amount or nearly all their resources from voluntary contributions or grants, then they are subject to the guidance in the *Not-for-Profit Guide* as illustrated in Chapter 10 of this text. The *Health Care Guide* calls these organizations Not-for-Profit Nonbusiness-Oriented Organizations.

ACCOUNTING AND REPORTING REQUIREMENTS OF THE *HEALTH CARE GUIDE*

The AICPA *Health Care Guide* provides certain additional accounting and reporting requirements beyond those required by the FASB (Chapter 10) and the GASB (Chapter 6) standards. As both the FASB and the GASB approved the *Health Care Guide,* its requirements constitute Category B GAAP and must be followed by all health care organizations. Some of the more important requirements follow:

Financial Statements

Illustration 12–1 summarizes the reporting requirements for the three types of health care organizations. While governmental health care organizations follow GASB standards, they typically report as special-purpose entities engaged only in business-type activities. Because they are engaged in business-type activities, governmental health care organizations use the accrual basis and economic resources measurement focus. The result is that public and private-sector health care organizations measure transactions and events similarly. The three types of health care organizations use different equity accounts, reflecting the varying ownership categories. Other differences exist in the format and title of the financial statements. For example, private-sector organizations use the three-category FASB format for the Statement of Cash Flows, while public sector organizations use the four-category GASB format.

The Balance Sheet (or Statement of Net Assets) is required to be presented in a classified format (i.e., assets and liabilities are subdivided into current and non-current categories). The **Statement of Operations** must include a **performance indicator** that reports results from continuing operations; therefore, it is important to distinguish operating revenues and expenses from nonoperating. The Audit and Accounting Guide identifies the following items that should not be included in the determination of the performance indicator:

- Transactions with the owners, other than in exchange for services.
- Transfers among affiliated organizations.
- Receipt of temporarily or permanently restricted contributions.
- Items identified by FASB standards as elements of other comprehensive income (such as foreign currency translation adjustments).

ILLUSTRATION 12–1 Health Care Organization Reporting—Ownership Forms

Type of Entity	Authoritative Standards	Accrual Basis of Accounting	Components of Financial Report	Equity Section of Balance Sheet/Statement of Net Assets
Not-for-Profit, Business—Oriented Organizations	FASB	✓	Balance Sheet/Statement of Financial Position Statement of Operations Statement of Changes in Net Assets Statement of Cash Flows Notes to the Financial Statements	Unrestricted Net Assets Temporarily Restricted Net Assets Permanently Restricted Net Assets
Investor-Owned Health Care Enterprises	FASB	✓	Balance Sheet/Statement of Financial Position Statement of Operations Statement of Changes in Equity Statement of Cash Flows Notes to the Financial Statements	Paid in Capital Retained Earnings
Governmental Health Care Organizations*	GASB	✓	MD&A Statement of Net Assets Statement of Revenues, Expenses, and Changes in Fund Net Assets Statement of Cash Flows Notes to the Financial Statements RSI Other Than MD&A	Net Assets Invested in Capital Assets, Net of Related Debt Restricted Net Assets Unrestricted Net Assets

*Typically these are special-purpose entities engaged in business-type activities.

- Items requiring separate display (such as extraordinary items, discontinued operations, and the effect of changes in accounting principle).
- Unrealized gains and losses on investments other than those classified as trading securities.

Revenues

- Patient service revenues are to be reported net of estimated contractual adjustments (i.e. discounts) with Medicare, Medicaid or insurance companies in the operating statement. Differences between actual contractual adjustments and the amounts estimated are treated as changes in accounting estimates (and do not require re-statement of prior periods). Note disclosure is to indicate the methods of revenue recognition and description of the types and amounts of contractual adjustments.
- Patient service revenue does not include charity care. Management's policy for providing charity care and the level of charity care provided should be disclosed in the notes.
- Operating revenues are often classified as net patient service revenue, premium revenue (from capitation agreements—agreements whereby the entity is to pro-vide service to a group or individual for a fixed fee), and other revenue from ac-tivities such as parking lot, gift shop, cafeteria, and tuition. If significant, tuition revenue may be reported separately. Unrestricted gifts and bequests and invest-ment income for current unrestricted purposes may be reported as either operat-ing or nonoperating revenue, depending on the policy of the entity.

Classifications

- Expenses may be reported by either their natural classifications (salaries, sup-plies, and so on) or their functional classifications (professional care of patients, general services, and so on). Private-sector not-for-profit health care entities must disclose expenses by their functional classifications in the notes, if not provided in the Statement of Operations.
- As is true for other not-for-profits, property, plant, and equipment acquired with either unrestricted or restricted resources may be (1) recorded initially as unre-stricted or (2) recorded initially as temporarily restricted and then reclassified in accordance with the depreciation schedule.
- **Assets whose use is limited** is an unrestricted balance sheet category used in health care reporting to show limitations on the use of assets due to bond covenant restrictions and governing board plans for future use. This category is especially important for private-sector, not-for-profit health care entities as the restricted category is limited to restrictions placed by contributors.
- FASB *Statement 117* reports net assets as permanently restricted, temporarily restricted, or unrestricted. It also requires that the changes in each of the three net asset classifications be shown. As will be described later, GASB standards present net assets of governmental health care organizations using categories different from those of private organizations.

ILLUSTRATIVE TRANSACTIONS AND FINANCIAL STATEMENTS

Entries for typical transactions are listed next as they are assumed to occur in a hypothetical not-for-profit business-oriented hospital. The entries are directly traceable to the financial statements (Illustrations 12–2 through 12–5). All amounts are in thousands of dollars.

Beginning Trial Balance

Assume the beginning trial balance for the Nonprofit Hospital, as of January 1, 2012, is as follows (in thousands):

	Debits	Credits
Cash	$ 2,450	
Patient Accounts Receivable	14,100	
Allowance for Uncollectible Patient Accounts Receivable		$ 1,500
Contributions Receivable	5,250	
Allowance for Uncollectible Contributions		800
Supplies	400	
Investments—Assets Whose Use Is Limited	1,500	
Investments—Other	17,100	
Property, Plant, and Equipment	22,300	
Accumulated Depreciation— Property, Plant, and Equipment		11,300
Accounts Payable		800
Accrued Expenses		900
Long-Term Debt—Current Installment		1,000
Long-Term Debt—Noncurrent		10,800
Net Assets—Unrestricted—Board Designated		1,500
Net Assets—Unrestricted—Undesignated		13,100
Net Assets—Temporarily Restricted		10,100
Net Assets—Permanently Restricted		11,300
Totals	$63,100	$63,100

Assume that the $10,100 of temporarily restricted net assets are restricted as follows: program, $4,000; time, $4,500; plant acquisition, $1,600. Assume that the board designations are all for capital improvements. Note that all property, plant, and equipment are recorded in the unrestricted net asset class—it is the policy of the Nonprofit Hospital to record acquisitions of plant with either unrestricted or restricted resources in the unrestricted net asset class, as permitted by the FASB. Also note that it is the policy to record all gifts, bequests, and investment income as Nonoperating Income.

During the year, gross patient service revenue amounted to $82,656, of which $71,650 was received in cash. Contractual adjustments to third-party payors, such as insurance companies and health maintenance organizations, amounted to $10,000. These amounts do not include charity care, which is not formally recorded in the accounts. In the Statement of Operations, Contractual Adjustments (a contra-revenue account) is offset against Patient Service Revenue, and Net Patient Service Revenue is reported in the amount of $72,656 in accord with the *Audit and Accounting Guide*.

	Debits	Credits
1a. Cash	71,650	
Patient Accounts Receivable	11,006	
Operating Revenues—Unrestricted—Patient Service Revenue...		82,656
1b. Contractual Adjustments—Unrestricted	10,000	
Patient Accounts Receivable		10,000

Patient accounts receivable in the amount of $1,300 were written off. The estimated bad debts for 2012 amounted to $1,500:

2a. Allowance for Uncollectible Patient Accounts Receivable	1,300	
Patient Accounts Receivable		1,300
2b. Bad Debt Expense	1,500	
Allowance for Uncollectible Patient Accounts Receivable		1,500

During the year, premium revenue from capitation agreements amounted to $20,000, all of which was received in cash. Other operating revenues were also received in cash in the amount of $5,460; these included revenues from the gift shop, parking lot, and cafeteria operations and from tuition from nursing students:

3. Cash	25,460	
Operating Revenues—Unrestricted—Premium Revenue		20,000
Operating Revenues—Unrestricted—Other Revenue		5,460

Nonoperating revenues related to undesignated resources amounted to $1,856, all of which was received in cash. This included $822 in unrestricted gifts and bequests, $750 in unrestricted income on investments of endowment funds, and $284 in investment income from other investments:

	Debits	Credits
4. Cash	1,856	
Nonoperating Income—Unrestricted—Gifts and Bequests.....		822
Nonoperating Income—Unrestricted—Income on		
Investments of Endowment Funds......................		750
Nonoperating Income—Unrestricted—Investment Income		284

Investment income related to Assets Whose Use Is Limited amounted to $120, all of which is board designated for future capital improvements:

5. Cash—Assets Whose Use Is Limited.......................	120	
Nonoperating Income—Unrestricted—		
Assets Whose Use Is Limited for Capital Improvements—		
Investment Income.................................		120

Supplies were purchased in the amount of $500; accounts payable and accrued expenses at the beginning of the year were paid:

6. Supplies	500	
Accounts Payable......................................	800	
Accrued Expenses	900	
Cash		2,200

Operating expenses for the year included depreciation of $4,800. Supplies used amounted to $400. Salaries and benefits amounted to $89,006, of which accrued wages totaled $1,000 at year-end. Utilities totaled $10,800, of which $900 remained in accounts payable at year-end. Included in these amounts was $3,500 from resources restricted by the donors for program purposes.

7a. Operating Expenses—Depreciation.......................	4,800	
Accumulated Depreciation—Property, Plant, and Equipment ..		4,800
7b. Operating Expenses—Supplies	400	
Supplies		400
7c. Operating Expenses—Salaries and Benefits	89,006	
Cash		88,006
Accrued Expenses		1,000

	Debits	Credits
7d. Operating Expenses—Utilities	10,800	
Cash		9,900
Accounts Payable		900
7e. Reclassification from Temporarily Restricted Net Assets— Satisfaction of Program Restrictions	3,500	
Reclassification to Unrestricted Net Assets— Satisfaction of Program Restrictions		3,500

Cash was received for pledges made in 2011 in the amount of $4,200. That amount had been reflected as temporarily restricted net assets, based on time restrictions:

	Debits	Credits
8a. Cash	4,200	
Contributions Receivable		4,200
8b. Reclassification from Temporarily Restricted Net Assets— Expiration of Time Restrictions	4,200	
Reclassification to Unrestricted Net Assets— Expiration of Time Restrictions		4,200

Property, plant, and equipment was acquired at a cost of $5,200. Of that amount, $1,200 was from resources temporarily restricted for plant acquisition. Since the policy of the Nonprofit Hospital is to record all plant as unrestricted, the $1,200 is reclassified.

	Debits	Credits
9a. Property, Plant, and Equipment	5,200	
Cash		5,200
9b. Reclassification from Temporarily Restricted Net Assets— Satisfaction of Plant Acquisition Restrictions	1,200	
Reclassification to Unrestricted Net Assets— Satisfaction of Plant Acquisition Restrictions		1,200

Contributions were received as follows: for unrestricted purposes in 2013 and beyond (time restrictions), $4,400; for restricted purposes other than plant, $3,800; $4,300 for the construction of a new maternity wing (scheduled for 2013); $800 for endowment purposes. A total of $5,600 was received in cash, and $7,700 was pledged:

	Debits	Credits
10. Cash	5,600	
Contributions Receivable................................	7,700	
Revenues—Temporarily Restricted—Contributions.........		12,500
Revenues—Permanently Restricted—Contributions.........		800

Endowment pledges receivable at the beginning of the year in the amount of $800 were received. Remaining pledges of $300 were written off:

	Debits	Credits
11. Cash	800	
Allowance for Uncollectible Contributions..................	300	
Contributions Receivable..............................		1,100

Principal on long-term debt was paid in the amount of $1,000; an additional $1,000 was classified as current; and $600 of interest was paid on the last day of the year. Interest is classified as an operating expense in the statement of operations.

	Debits	Credits
12a. Long-Term Debt—Current Installment	1,000	
Cash		1,000
12b. Long-Term Debt—Noncurrent..........................	1,000	
Long-Term Debt—Current Installment		1,000
12c. Operating Expenses—Interest	600	
Cash		600

Investment income, restricted as to purpose, amounted to $200:

	Debits	Credits
13. Cash	200	
Investment Income—Temporarily Restricted		200

Investments, carried at a value of $4,000, were sold for $4,100. The gain was an increase in temporarily restricted net assets:

	Debits	Credits
14. Cash	4,100	
Investments—Other..............................		4,000
Net Realized and Unrealized Gains on Investments—		
Temporarily Restricted............................		100

...6,600 in investments was purchased during the year. This included the ...de for capital improvements in transaction 5:

	Debits	Credits
15. Investments—Assets Whose Use Is Limited................	120	
Investments—Other.....................................	6,480	
Cash—Assets Whose Use Is Limited.....................		120
Cash..		6,480

At year-end, it was determined that the market value of investments (other than board designated) increased in value by $100. However, this is a combination of a gain of $650 in resources held for temporarily restricted purposes and a loss of $550 in resources held for permanently restricted resources.

	Debits	Credits
16. Investments—Other.....................................	100	
Net Realized and Unrealized Losses on Investments— Permanently Restricted	550	
Net Realized and Unrealized Gains on Investments— Temporarily Restricted............................		650

Closing entries are made for the unrestricted net asset class. Two entries are necessary:

	Debits	Credits
17. Operating Revenues—Unrestricted—Patient Service Revenue ..	82,656	
Operating Revenues—Unrestricted—Premium Revenue	20,000	
Operating Revenues—Unrestricted—Other Revenue	5,460	
Nonoperating Income—Unrestricted—Gifts and Bequests......	822	
Nonoperating Income—Unrestricted— Income on Investments of Endowment Funds.............	750	
Nonoperating Income—Unrestricted—Investment Income	284	
Reclassification to Unrestricted Net Assets— Satisfaction of Program Restrictions	3,500	
Reclassification to Unrestricted Net Assets— Expiration of Time Restrictions........................	4,200	
Reclassifications to Unrestricted Net Assets— Satisfaction of Plant Acquisition Restrictions	1,200	
Contractual Adjustments—Unrestricted		10,000
Operating Expenses—Bad Debts.....................		1,500
Operating Expenses—Depreciation....................		4,800
Operating Expenses—Supplies		400
Operating Expenses—Salaries and Benefits		89,006
Operating Expenses—Utilities.......................		10,800
Operating Expenses—Interest		600
Net Assets—Unrestricted—Undesignated..............		1,766

	Debits	Credits
18. Nonoperating Income—Unrestricted—Assets Whose Use Is Limited for Capital Improvements—Investment Income	120	
Net Assets—Unrestricted—Board Designated		120
(see entries 5 and 15)		

The closing entry is made for temporarily restricted net assets:

	Debits	Credits
19. Revenues—Temporarily Restricted—Contributions..........	12,500	
Investment Income—Temporarily Restricted	200	
Net Realized and Unrealized Gains on Investments— Temporarily Restricted.............................	750	
Reclassification from Temporarily Restricted Net Assets— Satisfaction of Program Restrictions		3,500
Reclassification from Temporarily Restricted Net Assets— Expiration of Time Restrictions....................		4,200
Reclassification from Temporarily Restricted Net Assets— Satisfaction of Plant Acquisition Restrictions		1,200
Net Assets—Temporarily Restricted..................		4,550

Finally, the closing entry is made for permanently restricted net assets:

	Debits	Credits
20. Revenues—Permanently Restricted—Contributions..........	800	
Net Realized and Unrealized Losses on Investments— Permanently Restricted		550
Net Assets—Permanently Restricted.....................		250

Illustrative Statements for Private-Sector Not-for-Profit Health Care Entities

Financial statements required for private-sector not-for-profit hospitals include the Statement of Operations, Statement of Changes in Net Assets, Statement of Financial Position, and a Statement of Cash Flows. Illustrative statements for the Nonprofit Hospital are shown as Illustrations 12–2 through 12–5.

Statement of Operations As the FASB permits considerable flexibility for the Statement of Activities, the *Health Care Guide* has prescribed a Statement of Operations and a Statement of Changes in Net Assets, although the two may be combined. Illustration 12–2 reflects a Statement of Operations that meets the requirements of FASB *Statement 117* and the AICPA *Health Care Guide.*

Statement of Changes in Net Assets The Statement of Changes in Net Assets shown in Illustration 12–3 fulfills the FASB requirement to show the changes in net assets by net asset class and in total. As indicated earlier, the information

ILLUSTRATION 12–2 Statement of Operations

NONPROFIT HOSPITAL Statement of Operations For the Year Ended December 31, 2012 (in thousands of dollars)		
Unrestricted Revenues:		
Net Patient Service Revenue		$ 72,656
Premium Revenue		20,000
Other Revenue		5,460
Net Assets Released from Restrictions Used for Operations:		
Expiration of Time Restrictions		4,200
Satisfaction of Program Restrictions		3,500
Total Operating Revenues		$105,816
Operating Expenses:		
Salaries and Benefits	$89,006	
Utilities	10,800	
Supplies	400	
Bad Debts	1,500	
Depreciation	4,800	
Interest	600	
Total Operating Expenses		107,106
Operating Loss		(1,290)
Other Income:		
Unrestricted Gifts and Bequests	$ 822	
Income on Investments of Endowment Funds	750	
Investment Income	284	
Investment Income Limited by Board Action for Capital Improvements	120	1,976
Excess of Revenues over Expenses		686
Net Assets Released from Restrictions Used for Plant Acquisition		1,200
Increase in Unrestricted Net Assets		$ 1,886

presented in Illustration 12–3 might have been combined with the information in Illustration 12–2.

Statement of Financial Position Several format possibilities also exist for the Statement of Financial Position, or Balance Sheet, as long as total assets, liabilities, and net assets as well as the unrestricted, temporarily restricted, and permanently restricted net assets are shown. Illustration 12–4 presents one possibility.

The Statement of Financial Position might be modified in several ways. For example, some of the assets that are set aside for restricted purposes might be reported on separate lines. The restricted net assets might be labeled as to the nature

ILLUSTRATION 12–3 Statement of Changes in Net Assets

NONPROFIT HOSPITAL Statement of Changes in Net Assets For the Year Ended December 31, 2012 (in thousands of dollars)	
Unrestricted Net Assets:	
Excess of Revenues over Expenses	$ 686
Net Assets Released from Restrictions Used for Plant Acquisition	1,200
Increase in Unrestricted Net Assets	1,886
Temporarily Restricted Net Assets:	
Contribution for Future Years	4,400
Contributions for Restricted Purposes Other Than Plant	3,800
Contributions for New Maternity Wing	4,300
Net Realized and Unrealized Gains and Losses on Investments	750
Investment Income	200
Net Assets Released from Restrictions:	
Expiration of Time Restrictions	(4,200)
Satisfaction of Program Restrictions	(3,500)
Satisfaction of Plant Acquisition Restrictions	(1,200)
Increase in Temporarily Restricted Net Assets	4,550
Permanently Restricted Net Assets:	
Endowment Contributions	800
Net Realized and Unrealized Gains and Losses on Investments	(550)
Increase in Permanently Restricted Net Assets	250
Increase in Net Assets	6,686
Net Assets, Beginning of Year	36,000
Net Assets, End of Year	$42,686

of the restrictions. Alternatively, much of that information could be presented in the notes to the financial statements.

Statement of Cash Flows   Illustration 12–5 presents a Statement of Cash Flows for the Nonprofit Hospital using the indirect method. The direct method is also acceptable (see Illustration 11–5) for private not-for-profit organizations and is required for governmental health care organizations (see Illustration 6–5).

FINANCIAL REPORTING FOR GOVERNMENTAL HEALTH CARE ENTITIES

Because health care organizations may be private not-for-profits or governmental, it is important to identify the appropriate set of standards that govern financial reporting. Governmental health care entities that report as special-purpose entities

ILLUSTRATION 12–4 Statements of Financial Position

NONPROFIT HOSPITAL Statements of Financial Position As of December 31, 2012 and 2011 (in thousands of dollars)		
Assets:	2012	2011
Current Assets:		
Cash and Cash Equivalents	$ 2,930	$ 2,450
Patient Accounts Receivable (Net of Allowance for Uncollectibles of $1,700 and $1,500)	12,106	12,600
Contributions Receivable (Net of Allowance for Uncollectibles of $500 and $800)	7,150	4,450
Supplies	500	400
Total Current Assets	22,686	19,900
Noncurrent Assets:		
Investments—Assets Whose Use Is Limited	1,620	1,500
Investments—Other	19,680	17,100
Property, Plant, and Equipment (Net of Accumulated Depreciation of $16,100 and $11,300)	11,400	11,000
Total Assets	$55,386	$49,500
Liabilities and Net Assets:		
Current Liabilities:		
Accounts Payable	$ 900	$ 800
Accrued Expenses	1,000	900
Current Installment of Long-Term Debt	1,000	1,000
Total Current Liabilities	2,900	2,700
Long-term Debt	9,800	10,800
Total Liabilities	12,700	13,500
Net Assets:		
Board Designated	1,620	1,500
Other Unrestricted	14,866	13,100
Total Unrestricted	16,486	14,600
Temporarily Restricted	14,650	10,100
Permanently Restricted	11,550	11,300
Total Net Assets	42,686	36,000
Total Liabilities and Net Assets	$55,386	$49,500

that are engaged only in business-type activities will prepare a Statement of Net Assets; a Statement of Revenues, Expenses, and Changes in Fund Net Assets; and a Statement of Cash Flows. The Statement of Revenues, Expenses, and Changes in Fund Net Assets may be separated into two statements, as shown for private health care entities; however, the reporting framework does not encourage such a presentation.

ILLUSTRATION 12–5   Statement of Cash Flows

NONPROFIT HOSPITAL Statement of Cash Flows For the Year Ended December 31, 2012 (in thousands of dollars)	
Cash Flows from Operating Activities:	
Change in Net Assets	$6,686
Adjustments to Reconcile Change in Net Assets to Net Cash Provided by Operating Activities:	
Depreciation	4,800
Net Unrealized Gains on Investments	(100)
Decrease in Patient Accounts Receivable	494
Increase in Contributions Receivable	(2,700)
Increase in Supplies	(100)
Increase in Accounts Payable	100
Increase in Accrued Expenses	100
Gain on Sale of Investments	(100)
Contribution Restricted to Investment in Property, Plant, and Equipment	(1,300)
Contribution Restricted to Long-Term Investment	(1,300)
Cash Flows from Operating Activities	6,580
Cash Flows from Investing Activities:	
Acquisition of Property, Plant, and Equipment	(5,200)
Purchase of Investments	(6,600)
Sale of Investments	4,100
Cash Flows from Investing Activities	(7,700)
Cash Flows from Financing Activities:	
Proceeds from Contributions Restricted for:	
Investment in Endowment	1,300
Investment in Property, Plant, and Equipment	1,300
Other Financing Activities:	
Payments on Long-term Debt	(1,000)
Cash Flows from Financing Activities	1,600
Net Increase in Cash and Cash Equivalents	480
Cash and Cash Equivalents, January 1	2,450
Cash and Cash Equivalents, December 31	$2,930
Supplemental disclosure of cash flow information:	
Cash paid during the year for interest	600

Governmental health care entities reported as enterprise funds of a state or local government use accrual accounting. The statements are similar to those presented in Chapter 6 (Illustrations 6–3, 6–4, and 6–5) with modifications as required by the AICPA *Health Care Guide.*

The **Statement of Net Assets** (not illustrated) is similar to that presented in Illustration 6–3 or in Illustration 9–4 for public colleges and universities. It is permissible to use a balance sheet format, where assets equal liabilities plus net assets. Net assets are to be categorized as (1) invested in capital assets, net of related debt, (2) restricted, and (3) unrestricted.

The **Statement of Revenues, Expenses, and Changes in Fund Net Assets** (not illustrated) is similar to Illustrations 6–4 and 9–5. Both GASB and the AICPA require presentation of a performance indicator, such as Excess of Revenues over Expenses. In addition, the requirement of the AICPA to place certain items below the performance indicator (such as receipt of restricted contributions) applies.

The **Statement of Cash Flows** (not illustrated) follows GASB standards, as reflected in Illustrations 6–5 and 9–6. The direct method must be used. Four categories of cash flows must be presented. A reconciliation is made between operating income and the cash flows from operating activities.

FINANCIAL REPORTING FOR COMMERCIAL (FOR-PROFIT) HEALTH CARE ENTITIES

Health care entities that are investor-owned and are for-profit enterprises are subject to the FASB (category A GAAP) and the AICPA *Health Care Guide* (category B GAAP). However, none of the FASB pronouncements related to not-for-profit organizations, such as *Statements 116* and *117,* apply. Accrual accounting applies in the same manner as it would for other commercial enterprises. Equity accounts consist of paid in capital and retained earnings. For further information on commercial accounting, consult intermediate and advanced accounting texts.

SUMMARY AND CONCLUSIONS REGARDING HEALTH CARE ACCOUNTING AND REPORTING

Health care entities may be private, not-for-profit, governmental, or commercial (for-profit). Private, not-for-profit, and commercial health care entities have Category A GAAP established by the Financial Accounting Standards Board. State and local governmental health care entities follow the principles of the GASB. All, however, are subject to the AICPA *Health Care Guide,* which is accepted by both FASB and GASB as being Category B GAAP.

This chapter has concentrated on accounting and financial reporting required for private, not-for-profit health care entities, as these are the most numerous. General FASB requirements regarding financial reporting, the use of net asset classes, and so on are supplanted by requirements of the *Health Care Guide.* The financial statements reported as Illustrations 12–2 through 12–5 meet the requirements of both the FASB and the AICPA.

Now that you have finished reading Chapter 12, complete the multiple choice questions provided on the text's Web site (www.mhhe.com/copley10e) to test your comprehension of the chapter.

Questions and Exercises

12–1. Describe the accounting treatment by hospitals and health care organizations for each of the following:

   a. Charity care.

   b. Bad debts.

   c. Contractual adjustments.

12–2. Describe the accounting treatment by hospitals and health care organizations for property, plant, and equipment acquisitions using each of the following:

   a. Unrestricted resources.

   b. Temporarily restricted resources.

12–3. For each of the following transactions and events, indicate the effect it will have on each of the three categories appearing in the Statement of Operations for a not-for-profit health care organization.

   Put an X in the appropriate column. If the net assets are unaffected, leave the column blank.

	Operating Revenues		Operating Expenses		Other Income	
	Increase	Decrease	Increase	Decrease	Increase	Decrease
Ex1			X			
Ex2						

Ex1: Recorded nursing salaries of $16,000.

Ex2: Collected $10,000 on patient accounts receivable.

1. A capital campaign in support of a new building brought in pledges of $50,000.

2. $5,000 was expended from the capital campaign on architects' fees. The organization records all fixed assets in the unrestricted class of net assets.

3. Estimate that the amounts collected from third-party payors will be $22,000 less than the amount billed, due to contractual adjustment.

4. Estimate that the amounts collected from individual patients will be $10,000 less than the amount billed.

5. Performed charity care of $6,000 (at normal billing rates).

6. Unrestricted income on endowments amounted to $5,000.

7. Interest expense totaled $850.

8. Investment income limited by board action for capital improvement amounted to $240.

9. Determined depreciation on plant and equipment to be $12,000.

10. Received $500 in unrestricted contributions.

12–4. Briefly describe the following items related to financial reporting by (a) private not-for-profit health care entities; (b) government-owned health care entities; and (c) commercial health care entites:

(1) Source of Category A and B GAAP.

(2) Equity or net asset account titles.

(3) Required financial statements.

12–5. With regard to accounting for private, not-for-profit health care entities, do the following:

a. Outline the accounting required, under FASB guidance, for a(n):

(1) Endowment gift received in cash.

(2) Pledge received in 2011, unrestricted as to purpose but restricted for use in 2012.

(3) Pledge received in 2011, restricted as to purpose other than acquisition of fixed assets, which is fulfilled in 2012.

b. List those items required to be reported "outside" the performance indicator in the Statement of Operations.

12–6. During 2011, the following transactions were recorded by the Baton Rouge Community Hospital, a private-sector, not-for-profit institution.

1. Gross charges for patient services, all charged to Patient Accounts Receivable, amounted to $1,200,000. Contractual adjustments with third-party payors amounted to $300,000.

2. Charity services, not included in transaction 1, would amount to $100,000, had billings been made at gross amounts.

3. Other revenues, received in cash, were parking lot, $20,000; cafeteria, $15,000; gift shop, $5,000.

4. Cash gifts for cancer research amounted to $20,000 for the year. During the year, $35,000 was expended for cancer research technicians salaries (Debit Operating Expense—Salaries and Benefits).

5. Mortgage bond payments amounted to $50,000 for principal and $40,000 for interest. Assume unrestricted resources are used.

6. During the year, the hospital received, in cash, unrestricted contributions of $40,000 and unrestricted income of $60,000 from endowment investments. (It is the hospital's practice to treat unrestricted gifts as nonoperating income.)

7. New equipment, costing $120,000, was acquired, using donor-restricted cash that was on hand at the beginning of the year. Baton Rouge's policy is to record all equipment in the unrestricted net asset class.

8. An old piece of lab equipment that originally cost $50,000 and that had an undepreciated cost of $10,000 was sold for $8,000 cash.

9. Pledges made in 2011 for use in 2012 that were unrestricted as to purpose were collected in the amount of $80,000. The $80,000 had been

recorded in the Temporarily Restricted Net Asset Class. At the end of 2012, pledges received in the amount of $120,000 are intended to be paid and used for unrestricted purposes in 2013.

10. Cash contributions were received as follows: temporarily restricted for purposes other than plant, $40,000; temporarily restricted for plant acquisition, $30,000.

11. Bills totaling $200,000 were received for the following items:

Utilities	120,000
Insurance	80,000

12. Depreciation of plant and equipment amounted to $70,000.

13. Cash payments on vouchers payable amounted to $180,000. Another $800,000 was expended on wages and benefits. Cash collections of patient accounts receivable amounted to $1,080,000.

14. Closing entries were prepared.

   a. Record the transactions in the general journal of the Baton Rouge Community Hospital.

   b. Prepare, in good form, a Statement of Operations for the Baton Rouge Community Hospital for the year ended December 31, 2012.

12–7. Record the following transactions on the books of Hope Hospital, which follows FASB and AICPA standards. The year is 2012.

1. Hope received $135,000 in cash from pledges made in 2011 that were unrestricted as to purpose but intended to be expended in 2012.

2. Hope received $150,000 in pledges that indicated the money was to be paid in 2013 and used in that year for any purpose desired by the board.

3. Hope expended $37,000 for nursing training, using $30,000 of temporarily restricted resources that had been given in 2011 for that purpose.

4. Hope received $40,000, restricted by the donor for cancer research. The funds were not expended in 2012.

5. Hope received $50,000 in cash. The board decided to invest the funds for future plant expansion.

12–8. St. Joseph's Hospital follows FASB standards of accounting and reporting. On January 1, 2011, St. Joseph's received $1,400,000, restricted to the purchase of cancer diagnostic equipment. On January 1, 2012, the equipment was purchased with the cash. The equipment is expected to last six years and have a salvage value of $200,000 at the end of its useful life. Straight-line depreciation is used by St. Joseph's.

1. Record the journal entries on January 1, 2011, January 1, 2012, and December 31, 2012 (to record depreciation), assuming St. Joseph's follows the policy of recording all fixed assets as unrestricted.

2. Record the journal entries on January 1, 2011, January 1, 2012, and December 31, 2012 (to record depreciation), assuming St. Joseph's follows the policy of recording all fixed assets as temporarily restricted.

3. Compute the amount that would be included in net assets (after closing the books on December 31, 2012) for (a) unrestricted net assets and (b) temporarily restricted net assets under requirements (1) and (2). What incentives might exist for St. Joseph's to choose either (1) or (2)?

12–9. As of January 1, 2012, the trial balance for Haven Hospital was as follows:

	Debits	Credits
Cash	$ 430,000	
Patient Accounts Receivable	3,200,000	
Allowance for Uncollectible Patient Accounts Receivable		$ 650,000
Contributions Receivable	2,930,000	
Allowance for Uncollectible Contributions Receivable		353,000
Supplies	130,000	
Investments—Board Designated	1,300,000	
Investments—Other	11,500,000	
Property, Plant, and Equipment	6,500,000	
Accumulated Depreciation— Property, Plant, and Equipment		3,100,000
Accounts Payable		600,000
Long-term Debt—Current Installment		200,000
Long-term Debt—Noncurrent		4,600,000
Net Assets—Unrestricted—Board Designated		1,300,000
Net Assets—Unrestricted—Undesignated		2,036,000
Net Assets—Temporarily Restricted		6,144,000
Net Assets—Permanently Restricted		7,007,000
Totals	$25,990,000	$25,990,000

During the fiscal year ended December 31, 2012, the following transactions occurred:

1. Patient service revenue amounted to $21,200,000, all recorded on account. Contractual adjustments were recorded in the amount of $4,200,000. Bad debts are estimated to be $460,000. Cash was received on account in the amount of $17,600,000.

2. Other revenue (cafeteria, parking lot, etc.) amounted to $2,530,000, all received in cash.

3. Patient accounts in the amount of $430,000 were written off.

4. Unrestricted gifts and bequests were received in cash in the amount of $600,000. Unrestricted income on investments of endowment funds amounted to $400,000. (It is the hospital's practice to treat unrestricted gifts as nonoperating revenue.)

5. Investment income on board designated funds, which is limited by board policy to provide renewals and replacements, amounted to $120,000 and was received in cash. Do not increase board designated net assets at this stage but close out the revenue account to board designated net assets in entry 19.

6. Investment income, restricted for current restricted purposes was received in cash in the amount of $300,000. Investment income, required by donor agreement to be added to endowment balances, was received in cash in the amount of $200,000.

7. Cash contributions were received in the following amounts: $2,200,000 for current restricted purposes; $2,500,000 for future plant expansion; and $1,000,000 required by the donor to be invested permanently in an endowment.

8. Pledges receivable in the amount of $2,100,000 were received in cash. These pledges were on hand at the beginning of the year (reflected in temporarily restricted net assets, for purposes of time) and were unrestricted as to purpose. In addition, pledges for endowment purposes were collected in the amount of $450,000.

9. $1,600,000 in temporarily restricted net assets was expended, as the donors stipulated, for cancer research. Debit Operating Expense—Salaries and Benefits, $1,400,000; and Operating Expense—Supplies, $200,000. (Assume the supplies were purchased with cash and used in the same year.)

10. $2,400,000 in temporarily restricted net assets was expended for equipment, as provided for by the donor. The policy of Haven Hospital is to record all property, plant, and equipment as unrestricted.

11. A pledge drive during 2012 resulted in $2,700,000 in pledges that are intended by the donors to be used in 2013 for any purposes desired by the donor. In addition, $600,000 was received in pledges for endowment purposes. It was decided that the allowance for contributions was sufficient.

12. Supplies were purchased in the amount of $750,000, on account.

13. Operating expenses (in addition to those already recorded in entries 1 and 9) for the year included: depreciation of $600,000; supplies used of $690,000; and salaries and benefits of $21,325,000 (paid in cash). In addition the following expenses were recorded through Accounts Payable: utilities of $515,000 and insurance of $320,000.

14. Accounts payable were paid in the amount of $1,775,000.

15. Current installments of long-term debt were paid in the amount of $200,000. The portion to be paid next year is $300,000. Interest was paid in the amount of $280,000 and is reported as an operating expense.

16. Investments, carried at a basis of $4,000,000, were sold for $4,050,000. The $50,000 gain is considered to be temporarily restricted.

17. Cash in the amount of $6,530,000 was invested. Of that amount, $120,000 was from Cash—Assets Whose Use Is Limited and is designated by the board for renewals and replacements (see entry 5).

18. A reading of the financial press indicated that investments increased in market value by $800,000. Of that amount, $250,000 was in investments designated by the board for renewals and replacements, $350,000 is required by donors to be added to endowment balances, and the remainder is unrestricted.

19. Closing entries were prepared.

Required:

a. Prepare journal entries for each of the previous transactions.

b. Prepare a Statement of Operations for Haven Hospital for the year ended December 31, 2012.

c. Prepare a Statement of Changes in Net Assets for Haven Hospital for the year ended December 31, 2012.

d. Prepare a Statement of Financial Position for Haven Hospital as of December 31, 2012.

e. Prepare a Statement of Cash Flows for Haven Hospital for the year ended December 31, 2012, using the indirect method.

f. Using the direct method, prepare the Cash Flows from Operating Activities section of the Cash Flow Statement for Haven Hospital for the year ended December 31, 2012.

Excel-Based Problem

12–10. Presented below are account balances for Monterey Hospital. In addition, cash transactions for the year ended December 31, 2012, are summarized in the T-account.

	December 31, 2011	December 31, 2012
BALANCE SHEET ACCOUNTS		
Debits		
Cash	$1,650,000	$3,620,700
Patient Accounts Receivable (net)	1,700,000	1,970,000
Contributions Receivable	10,000	12,500
Investments—Endowment	1,500,000	1,600,000
Property, Plant, and Equipment	4,875,000	5,167,000
Credits		
Accumulated Depreciation	2,107,000	2,557,000
Accounts Payable	37,500	46,200
Long-term Debt	2,282,000	2,682,000
Net Assets—December 31, 2011	5,308,500	
Net Assets—December 31, 2012		7,085,000

	December 31, 2012
ACTIVITY ACCOUNTS	
Debits	
Contractual Adjustments	$1,040,000
Operating Expenses—Bad Debts	33,500
Operating Expenses—Depreciation	450,000
Operating Expenses—Salaries	5,200,000
Operating Expenses—Supplies	2,200,000
Reclassification from Temporarily Restricted Net Assets (Time Restrictions)	19,600
Net Losses on Investments—Permanently Restricted	50,000
Credits	
Patient Service Revenue—Unrestricted	10,520,000
Income on Endowments—Unrestricted	25,000
Reclassification to Unrestricted Net Assets	19,600
Contribution Revenue—Unrestricted	30,000
Contribution Revenue—Endowment	150,000
Contribution Revenue—Temporarily Restricted for Future Years	25,000

CASH

Beginning balance January 1, 2012	$1,650,000		
Collections from patients	2,966,500	$5,200,000	Salaries
Collections from third parties	6,210,000	2,191,300	Operating expenses
Contributions to Endowment	150,000		
Other Contributions	52,500	292,000	Equipment purchases
Investment Income	25,000	100,000	Payment principal LT Debt
Proceeds - LT debt	500,000	150,000	Purchase Endowment Investments
	- -		
Ending Balance December 31, 2012	$3,620,700		

Required:

Using the information above and the Excel template provided, prepare:

a. A Statement of Operations and a Statement of Changes in Net Assets for the year ended December 31, 2012.

b. Statements of Cash Flow assuming:

1. Monterey Hospital is a private not-for-profit.

2. Monterey Hospital is a government-owned hospital.

Auditing, Tax-Exempt Organizations, and Evaluating Performance

If the confidence of the public in the integrity of accountants' reports is shaken, their value is gone. (Arthur Andersen 1885–1947, founder of what was once the world's largest professional services firm. In 2002, the firm lost its auditing license in the United States as a result of involvement in the Enron collapse.)

The hardest thing in the world to understand is the income tax. (Albert Einstein, 1879–1955)

Learning Objectives

- Describe the unique characteristics of audits of governmental and not-for-profit entities.
- Describe the major requirements of the Single Audit Act.
- Describe the process of applying for tax-exempt status and the reporting requirements of the Form 990.
- Identify when a not-for-profit organization is subject to the unrelated business income tax and describe how the tax is determined.
- Identify financial ratios commonly used to evaluate governmental and not-for-profit entities and describe how they are calculated and interpreted.
- Identify the elements of service efforts and accomplishments reporting and explain why governments and not-for-profits report nonfinancial performance measures.

Chapters 2 through 12 present accounting and financial reporting requirements of state and local governments and not-for-profit organizations. This chapter describes (1) the unique aspects of auditing governments and not-for-profit organizations, (2) the taxation and tax filing requirements of not-for-profit organizations, and (3) the use of financial and nonfinancial measures to evaluate the performance and financial position of government and not-for-profit organizations.

GOVERNMENTAL AUDITING

Auditing of governmental and not-for-profit entities has much in common with auditing of business enterprises, including making judgments about internal controls, selectively testing transactions, assessing the fairness of financial statements, and issuing audit reports. However, governmental auditing, like governmental accounting, follows a unique set of professional guidelines established by a separate governing organization.

Governmental units and many not-for-profit organizations are subject to *Government Auditing Standards* in addition to the *Statements on Auditing Standards,* issued by the American Institute of Certified Public Accountants (AICPA). *Government Auditing Standards* are issued by the U.S. Government Accountability Office (GAO), and apply to audits conducted to satisfy the requirements of the Single Audit Act as well as other governmental audits. In common terminology, the standards issued by the AICPA are known as **GAAS (Generally Accepted Auditing Standards),** and the standards issued by the GAO are known as GAGAS (Generally Accepted Government Auditing Standards).

Government Auditing Standards, published in a document commonly known as the Yellow Book, incorporate the AICPA standards and provide extensions that are necessary due to the unique nature of public entities. These extensions, for example, require auditor knowledge of government accounting and auditing, public availability of audit reports, written evaluations of internal controls, and distribution of the reports and availability of working papers to federal and state funding authorities. The standards also emphasize the heightened importance of government audits in a democratic society: "In an audit of a government entity or entity that receives government assistance, auditors may need to set lower materiality levels than in audits in the private sector because of the public accountability of the audited entity, the various legal and regulatory requirements, and the visibility and sensitivity of government programs, activities and functions" (paragraph 4.27). Additional guidance for audits of state and local governments is found in the *AICPA Audit and Accounting Guide: State and Local Governments* (2009) and the *AICPA Audit Guide: Government Auditing Standards and Circular A-133 Audits* (2008).

Types of Governmental Audits *Government Auditing Standards* identify four categories of professional engagements: financial audits, attestation engagements, performance audits, and nonaudit services. These are described in Illustration 13–1. Nonaudit services are not covered by *Government Auditing Standards* and differ from the other types of engagements in that the auditors are providing information to a requesting party without providing verification or evaluation of the information. These engagements may result in a report but not an opinion on the information.

Financial audits must comply with the AICPA's generally accepted auditing standards for fieldwork and reporting as well as *Government Auditing Standards.*

ILLUSTRATION 13–1   Types of Governmental Audits and Attestation Engagements

1. *Financial audits* primarily concern providing reasonable assurance about whether financial statements are presented fairly in all material respects in conformity with generally accepted accounting principles or with a comprehensive basis of accounting other than GAAP.
2. *Attestation engagements* concern examining, reviewing, or performing agreed upon procedures on a subject matter or an assertion about a subject matter and reporting on the results. . . . Attestation engagements can cover a broad range of financial or nonfinancial objectives and can be part of a financial audit or other type of engagement.
3. *Performance audits* are an objective and systematic examination of evidence to provide an independent assessment of the performance and management of a program against objective criteria or an assessment of best practices and other information. Performance audits provide information to improve program operations and facilitate decision making by parties with responsibility to oversee or initiate corrective action, and improve public accountability.
4. *Nonaudit services* consist of gathering, providing, or explaining information requested by decision makers or providing advice or assistance to management officials.

Source: Comptroller General of the United States, *Government Auditing Standards* (Washington, DC: U.S. Government Accountability Office, 2007).

Governmental standards prescribe additional fieldwork and reporting requirements beyond those provided by the AICPA. For example, auditors are specifically required to test compliance with laws and regulations and internal control over financial reporting. With regard to communications, governmental auditors should communicate not only with officials of the audited organization, but also with parties that have oversight responsibility for the audited organization such as legislative members or staff.

Attestation engagements encompass a wide range of activities. These include reporting on an entity's: (1) system of internal control, (2) compliance with laws and regulations, (3) prospective financial information, and (4) costs under contracts. Similar to financial audits, attestation engagements must comply with both the AICPA's attestation standards and *Government Auditing Standards.*

Performance audits encompass a variety of objectives and may be more analogous to the functions normally performed by internal auditors in the private sector, except that the results are made public. Generally they are undertaken to assess: program effectiveness and results; economy and efficiency; internal controls as they relate to program management and reporting; and compliance with legal requirements and other program matters. Effectiveness audits measure the extent to which a program is achieving its goals while economy and efficiency audits are concerned with whether an organization is acquiring, protecting, and using its resources in the most productive manner to achieve program objectives. For example, an auditor performing an economy and efficiency audit of a Head Start program might observe purchasing procedures and evaluate transportation routes, classroom sizes, and general office procedures. An auditor performing an effectiveness audit would look to the original legislation to determine explicit or implicit objectives, develop criteria to determine whether the objectives were being met, and evaluate the relative benefit of alternative approaches. The audit team will often include specialists outside of accounting who are better prepared to assess program effectiveness. Performance audits are not intended to be done on an annual basis but are expected to be performed periodically as a means of holding government accountable for carrying out its legislative mandates.

The Yellow Book was revised in 2007. Many of the changes are intended to provide standardized language between governmental and other auditing standards. Perhaps the most notable change in the 2007 revision is a heightened emphasis on ethical principles guiding governmental audits. The standards describe five ethical concepts:

1. *Public interest* focuses auditors' attention on serving the citizenry and honoring the public trust.
2. *Integrity* requires auditors to conduct their work with an attitude that is objective, fact-based, and nonpartisan.
3. *Objectivity* includes independence in fact and appearance and being free of conflict of interests.
4. *Proper use of government information, resources, and position* precludes auditors from using sensitive or classified information or resources for personal gain.
5. *Professional behavior* includes auditors conducting their services in accordance with technical and professional standards.

The GAO Web site (http://www.gao.gov/govaud/ybk01.htm) provides a summary of major changes in the 2007 Yellow Book as well as PowerPoint slides.

Opinion Units In response to changes brought about by GASB *Statement 34,* the *AICPA Audit and Accounting Guide: State and Local Governments* developed the concept of opinion units. In any audit engagement, the auditor must determine a level of materiality. This determination is then used to plan, perform, and evaluate the results of audit procedures. Because of the various levels of reporting by governments (government-wide, fund-type, and individual fund), it was not clear which level was most appropriate for determining materiality.

The guide requires a separate (quantitative) materiality evaluation at each opinion unit. Each of the following is considered an opinion unit:

- Governmental activities.
- Business-type activities.
- Each major fund (both governmental and enterprise).
- The aggregate of all discretely presented component units.
- The aggregate of all remaining fund information.

The first two categories relate to information contained in the government-wide financial statements and the remaining three relate to information contained in the fund-basis financial statements. The final category includes nonmajor governmental and enterprise funds, internal service funds, and fiduciary funds.

One effect of reporting on opinion units is that some opinion units may receive unqualified or clean opinions while others receive modified opinions. For example, failure to report infrastructure assets could result in an adverse opinion regarding the governmental activities and an unqualified opinion for the business-type, major fund, aggregate component unit, and aggregate of all remaining fund information. Audit reports are discussed in the next section.

Audit Reports Reporting requirements are a combination of requirements of the *Government Auditing Standards* and the single audit requirements (described in the next section). A reporting package is due to a designated federal repository nine months after the end of the fiscal year. Part of the reporting is done by the auditor and part by the audited organization. The auditor is required to prepare up to five reports:

1. A report containing an opinion on the financial statements.
2. A report discussing the evaluation and testing of internal control and compliance with laws and regulations.
3. A report discussing significant deficiencies in internal controls.
4. A report describing instances of fraud, illegal acts, or other material noncompliance.
5. A report containing the views of responsible officials of the audited organization regarding any reported significant deficiencies.

Unlike private-sector audits, the auditor is required to report directly to appropriate officials, such as funding agencies or legislative bodies, as well as to the organization's board or audit committee. Additionally, the auditor must report the existence of any privileged or confidential information not contained in the audit reports.

Guidelines for conducting and reporting on financial audits of state and local governments are contained in the 2009 AICPA *Audit and Accounting Guide: State and Local Governments.* The AICPA has developed standard wording for auditor's reports to make clear the responsibility the auditor is accepting. If the financial statements are prepared in conformity with generally accepted accounting principles, the auditor expresses an "unqualified" or clean opinion. An example of an independent auditor's report expressing an **unqualified opinion** for a government subject to *Government Auditing Standards* is shown in Illustration 13–2. Note that the title of the report stresses that the auditor is independent. The report contains five paragraphs. The first paragraph, the introductory paragraph, states that the financial statements were audited, that the financial statements are the responsibility of the city's management, and that the auditor's responsibility is to express an opinion on the financial statements based on the audit. The basic financial statements are the minimum that should be prepared under GAAP and contain the government-wide financial statements, fund financial statements, and notes to the financial statements.

The first paragraph also indicates (for each opinion unit) which financial statements were audited. Normally these include the financial statements of:

- The governmental activities.
- The business-type activities.
- Each major governmental and enterprise fund.
- The aggregate discretely presented component units.
- The aggregate remaining fund information (i.e., the nonmajor governmental and enterprise funds, the internal service funds, and the fiduciary funds).

ILLUSTRATION 13–2 **Unqualified Opinions on Basic Financial Statements Accompanied by Required Supplementary Information and Supplementary Information**

Independent Auditor's Report

We have audited the accompanying financial statements of the governmental activities, the business-type activities, the aggregate discretely presented component units, each major fund, and the aggregate remaining fund information of the Village of Elizabeth, as of and for the year ended December 31, 2012, which collectively comprise the basic financial statements as listed in the table of contents. These financial statements are the responsibility of the Village of Elizabeth's management. Our responsibility is to express opinions on these financial statements based on our audit.

We conducted our audit in accordance with auditing standards generally accepted in the United States of America. Those standards require that we plan and perform the audit to obtain reasonable assurance about whether the financial statements are free of material misstatement. An audit includes examining, on a test basis, evidence supporting the amounts and disclosures in the financial statements. An audit also includes assessing the accounting principles used and significant estimates made by management, as well as evaluating the overall financial statement presentation. We believe that our audit provides a reasonable basis for our opinions.

In our opinion, the financial statements referred to above present fairly, in all material respects, the respective financial position of the governmental activities, the business-type activities, the aggregate discretely presented component units, each major fund, and the aggregate remaining fund information of the Village of Elizabeth, as of December 31, 2012, and the respective changes in financial position and cash flows, where applicable, thereof for the year then ended in conformity with accounting principles generally accepted in the United States of America.

The [*identify accompanying required supplementary information, such as management's discussion and analysis and budgetary comparison information*] are not a required part of the basic financial statements but are supplementary information required by the Governmental Accounting Standards Board. We have applied certain limited procedures, which consisted principally of inquiries of management regarding the methods of measurement and presentation of the required supplementary information. However, we did not audit the information and express no opinion on it.

Our audit was conducted for the purpose of forming opinions on the financial statements that collectively comprise the Village's basic financial statements. The [*identify accompanying supplementary information, such as the introductory section, combining and individual nonmajor fund financial statements, and statistical tables*] are presented for purposes of additional analysis and are not a required part of the basic financial statements. The [*identify relevant supplementary information, such as the combining and individual nonmajor fund financial statements*] have been subjected to the auditing procedures applied in the audit of the basic financial statements and, in our opinion, are fairly stated in all material respects in relation to the basic financial statements taken as a whole. The [*identify relevant supplementary information, such as the introductory section and statistical tables*] have not been subjected to the auditing procedures applied in the audit of the basic financial statements and, accordingly, we express no opinion on them.

[Signature] [Date]

Source: American Institute of Certified Public Accountants, *Audits of State and Local Governments* (New York: AICPA, 2009), Example A-1. 14.79.

The basic financial statements should be accompanied by required supplementary information (RSI), such as management's discussion and analysis and budgetary comparison schedules. Unless the auditor is engaged to render an opinion on the RSI, auditors are required to perform only limited procedures to make sure the information is not misleading. Information other than required supplemental information may be presented in a CAFR, such as the letter of transmittal, statistical section, and combining statements for nonmajor funds. Unless auditors are engaged to render an opinion on this supplemental information, professional standards require the auditor only to read this *nonrequired* supplemental information and consider whether the information or the manner of its presentation is materially inconsistent with the financial statements. If the auditor believes this information or the RSI is misleading, the auditor should include an explanatory paragraph in the auditor's report to explain the situation. The reporting requirements for supplemental information are complex and are presented in flowchart form in Exhibit 14.1 of the AICPA *Audit and Accounting Guide: State and Local Governments.*

The second paragraph includes these elements:

- A statement that the audit was conducted in accordance with generally accepted auditing standards (which include both GAAS and GAGAS).
- A statement that generally accepted auditing standards require that the auditor plan and perform the audit to obtain reasonable assurance about whether the financial statements are free of material misstatement.
- A statement that an audit includes:
  a. Examining, on a test basis, evidence supporting the amounts and disclosures in the financial statements.
  b. Assessing the accounting principles used and significant estimates made by management.
  c. Evaluating the overall financial statement presentation.
- A statement that the auditor believes that the audit provides a reasonable basis for the opinion.

The third paragraph, the opinion paragraph, presents the auditor's opinion as to whether the financial statements present fairly, in all material respects, the financial position of the government as of the balance sheet date and the changes in financial position and cash flows, in conformity with generally accepted accounting principles.

The fourth paragraph indicates the extent of the auditor's evaluation of required supplementary information. This evaluation consists primarily of inquiries of management. A fifth paragraph indicates the extent to which supplemental disclosures are subject to the audit opinion. If they are not, the paragraph indicates that no opinion is being expressed with regard to this information. Note that the paragraph is very specific as to which supplemental disclosures are subject to audit and which are not.

In addition to issuing the unqualified opinion shown in Illustration 13–2, independent auditors also issue qualified opinions and adverse opinions. In some circumstances the auditor may disclaim an opinion. The AICPA *Statement on Auditing Standards* and *Audit and Accounting Guide: State and Local Governments* provide guidance for when each opinion type is appropriate. Three conditions require a departure from an unqualified report: (1) the scope of the audit has been restricted, (2) the financial statements have not been prepared in accordance with generally accepted accounting principles, and (3) the auditor is not independent. The appropriate opinion depends on the type and severity of the condition:

- *Qualified opinion* A qualified opinion may result from either a limitation on the scope of the audit or failure to follow generally accepted accounting principles (conditions 1 or 2). The opinion states that, except for the effects of the matter(s) to which the qualification relates, the financial statements are fairly presented.

- *Adverse opinion* An adverse opinion is used when the auditor believes that the financial statements are so materially misstated or misleading that they do not present fairly the financial position and results of operations (and cash flows, if applicable) in accordance with generally accepted accounting principles (condition 2).

- *Disclaimer of opinion* A disclaimer of opinion is appropriate if the auditor is not satisfied that the financial statements are fairly presented because of a severe scope limitation (condition 1). A disclaimer is also appropriate if the auditor is not independent, as defined by the *Code of Professional Conduct* (condition 3). In a disclaimer, the auditor states that no opinion is being expressed.

The Single Audit Act and Amendments

History Federal financial assistance has been an important source of financing operating and capital expenditures of state and local governments and not-for-profit organizations for many years. Federal grants-in-aid and federal contracts, in the past, were subject to accounting, reporting, and auditing requirements that varied depending on which agency of the federal government administered the grant program or contract. Efforts were made during the 1960s and 1970s to standardize requirements but met with only moderate success.

The Single Audit Act of 1984 was enacted to provide statutory authority for uniform requirements for audits of state and local organizations receiving federal financial assistance. Following the legislation, the Office of Management and Budget (OMB) issued Circular A–128 to provide guidance for federal agencies in administering the Single Audit Act. A few years later, OMB issued Circular A–133 providing requirements for federal agencies in administering grants for nongovernmental, not-for-profit organizations, even though those organizations were not covered under the 1984 act. In addition, the American Institute of Certified Public Accountants issued Statements of Position (SOPs) to provide guidance for CPAs when conducting audits of federal assistance, and those SOPs are included in the appropriate audit and accounting guides.

Congress enacted the Single Audit Act Amendments of 1996 that extended the 1984 law to include federal assistance to nongovernmental, not-for-profit organizations. These groups are covered in Chapters 10, 11, and 12 of this text (state and local governments and public colleges and universities were covered under the

1984 act and continue to be covered). Whereas the 1984 act required a single audit for organizations receiving $100,000 or more in federal assistance (those receiving $25,000 to $100,000 could have a program-by-program audit or a single audit), the amount was later raised to $500,000.

In 1997 the Office of Management and Budget issued revised Circular A–133, *Audits of States, Local Governments, and Non-Profit Organizations.* This circular replaced the two previous circulars for state and local governments and for not-for-profit organizations. The American Institute of Certified Public Accountants issued Statement of Position 98–3, *Auditing of States, Local Governments, and Not-for-Profit Organizations Receiving Federal Awards,* providing additional guidance for CPAs auditing recipients of federal funds.

Purpose   The main objective of the single audit process is to create a mechanism whereby those auditors conducting the regular financial audits of state and local governments and not-for-profit organizations can provide assurance to the federal government that federal and state funds are expended in accordance with grant agreements and with financial management and other standards promulgated by the federal government. This is more efficient than having grant-by-grant audits supervised by each agency that provides funds. Governments and not-for-profit organizations that expend $50 million in federal awards are assigned **cognizant agencies** (normally the federal agencies that provide the most funding). Organizations receiving smaller amounts are expected to use **oversight agencies** (again, the agencies providing the most funding). Cognizant agencies are required to monitor the audit process and resolve findings and questioned costs. Oversight agencies may do the same, at their option. Audits are conducted according to the requirements of the Single Audit Act, as amended, OMB Circular A–133, and a *Compliance Supplement* issued by OMB that includes OMB-approved special requirements for many of the grants.

In the 1980s the General Accounting Office conducted several studies to determine the effectiveness of audits performed under the Single Audit Act.[1] A substantial proportion of these audits were found to not be in compliance with professional standards. Since then, the GAO has modified the standards to require firms conducting governmental audits to implement specialized continuing education programs (24 hours of government-specific training and 80 hours in total every two years), internal quality control programs, and external peer reviews. In addition, the GAO provides guidance to audited organizations concerning auditor solicitation and evaluation and limits the nature of consulting services that may be provided by an organization's auditing firm. This latter requirement is intended to assure the independence of external auditors.

AICPA Statement of Position 98–3 and OMB Circular A–133 provide guidance for the auditor in implementing the single audit requirement. First, a determination must be made as to whether a client is subject to the single audit act. Entities that

---

[1] General Accounting Office, *CPA Audit Quality: Many Governmental Audits Do Not Comply with Professional Standards.* Report to the House Committee on Government Operations. (Washington, DC: GAO, August 1986).

expend $500,000 or more in federal awards in a fiscal year have either a single audit (when several grantors are involved) or a program-specific audit (usually when only one grantor is involved). This includes, in some cases, certain governments or not-for-profit organizations that act as **pass-through entities,** organizations that receive federal awards to be sent to **subrecipients.** The pass-through entities have responsibilities for reporting funding to the subrecipients, and the auditor must be aware of these arrangements.

The auditor is required to test controls to gain an understanding of internal controls for use in selecting programs for audit, in determining whether the auditee is low risk, and in reporting.

Major Programs   A major program is a program selected for audit under the single audit approach. The auditor is required to express an opinion on compliance on major programs, which generally must add up to 50 percent of the federal funds expended by the auditee. This is reduced to 25 percent if the auditee is determined by the auditor to be a **low-risk auditee.** A low-risk auditee is one that for the past two years has met certain criteria such as unqualified opinions, no material weakness in internal controls, and no material noncompliance on major programs.

Major programs are determined on a **risk-based approach.** First, the programs are classified into Type A and Type B programs. Type A programs are the larger programs and Type B programs are the smaller programs. Type A programs are considered major programs unless they are determined to be low risk. In order for this to happen, a Type A program must have been audited during the past two years as a major program and have had no major audit findings. Type B programs are included as major programs only if the auditor determines that they are high risk. Risk assessments are generally required for Type B programs that exceed $100,000 for most auditees and $300,000 for larger auditees.

For example, assume that an auditee that is not determined to be low risk has five programs, two Type A and three Type B, as follows:

Type A

Housing and Urban Development, $350,000, audited last year with no major control problems or compliance findings
Environmental Protection Agency, $400,000, not audited during the past two years

Type B

Department of Education, $200,000
Department of Energy, $150,000
Department of Agriculture, $50,000

The total amount of grant expenditures is $1,150,000, so at least $575,000 must be audited as major programs. The Environmental Protection Agency grant must be audited, as it does not meet the criteria of low risk, not having been audited in the past two years. Then the auditor must choose grants adding up to $175,000.

The other Type A program could be audited, or the auditor could select Type B programs, based on a risk assessment. The auditor would choose either the Department of Education ($200,000) or the programs from the Departments of Energy and Agriculture, which also add up to $200,000. If the auditee were considered low risk, then only 25 percent of the grant expenditures would be required as major programs; if risk assessments showed that the Departments of Education and Energy were low risk, then the EPA grant could be the only grant audited as a major program.

The Sarbanes-Oxley Act

The Sarbanes-Oxley Act was signed into law in 2002 in response to accounting scandals in the business sector. The Act is intended to improve corporate governance and limit the services accounting firms may provide to their audit clients. While the Act applies only to corporations filing with the Securities and Exchange Commission, it has changed the way public accounting firms relate to all their clients, including governmental and not-for-profit organizations. The Act has also influenced governing boards and many not-for-profit boards have begun to model themselves on corporate governance "best practices" initiated by the Sarbanes-Oxley Act. Several of the provisions of the Act already existed in governmental auditing standards. In particular, auditors are to report deficiencies in the design or operation of internal controls. Additionally, GAO standards for independence prohibit auditors from performing many nonaudit services.

As a result of heightened public awareness for the importance of accountability and independence, other provisions of the Sarbanes-Oxley Act are being voluntarily adopted by not-for-profit organizations. These include:

- Establishing audit committees composed of non-management board members and assigning the committee responsibility for the appointment, compensation, and oversight of the auditor.
- Requiring the chief executive and chief financial officers to publicly attest to the accuracy and completeness of the financial report and the adequacy of the system of internal controls.
- Requiring audit partner rotation and a concurring partner review of the reports.
- Having all nonaudit services performed by the auditors to be approved by the audit committee.
- Establishing a code of conduct for the organization and a mechanism for whistle-blowing by employees.

Additional pressure to adopt these practices has come from funding foundations that have announced that Sarbanes-Oxley compliance will be a factor in the awarding of grants.

Summary   Like governmental accounting, governmental auditing follows a unique set of professional guidelines. *Government Auditing Standards* are established by the U.S. Government Accountability Office. These standards differ from those governing audits of private businesses. In particular, governmental standards require auditors to evaluate and report on the system of internal controls and compliance with laws and regulations. Governmental auditors are required to report to funding agencies or oversight bodies in addition to the management of the organization under audit.

Frequently state and local governments and not-for-profit organizations receive funding under a variety of federal programs. Many of these organizations are subject to the requirements of the Single Audit Act and its amendments. Auditors of these organizations must be familiar with governmental auditing standards as well as specific requirements under the act for determining major programs subject to audit.

TAX-EXEMPT ORGANIZATIONS

Accountants working for, auditing, or providing consulting services to not-for-profit organizations must be aware of certain tax issues related to those organizations. Generally, not-for-profit organizations are exempt from federal income taxes. However, it is possible for them to engage in activities that result in **unrelated business income** that is taxable. This section of the chapter discusses the provisions in the tax code that provide exemption for certain types of not-for-profit organizations, discusses and illustrates the tax form that is used for many of these organizations **(Form 990),** and concludes by examining the unrelated business income sections of the tax code that may cause an exempt organization to pay taxes or even lose its exempt status.

Tax Code Section 501 provides that nonprofit organizations organized for charitable purposes may be exempt from federal income taxes. These include corporations organized under an Act of Congress as a U.S. instrumentality, **501(c)(3) entities,** civic leagues, trade and professional associations, social clubs and country clubs, fraternal societies, and veterans organizations. In order to qualify as tax exempt, the entity must have a limited purpose, must not have the authority to engage in activities other than exempt purposes, and must not be engaged in political activities.

The most common form of tax-exempt organization is the 501(c)(3) organization, which will be the focus of the remainder of this section. A 501(c)(3) organization is a "corporation and any community chest, fund, or foundation organized and operated exclusively for religious, charitable, scientific, testing for public safety, literary or educational purposes, or to foster national or international amateur sports competition (so long as none of its activities involve the providing of athletic facilities or equipment) or for the prevention of cruelty to children or animals, no part of the net earnings of which inures to the benefit of any private shareholder or individual, no substantial part of the activities of which is carrying on propaganda, participate or intervene in any political campaign."[2] To apply for tax-exempt status, an organization should file IRS Form 1023, *Application for Recognition of Exemption Under Section 501(c)(3) of the Internal Revenue Code.* Certain special rules apply to churches and to private foundations, as distinguished from **public charities.**

[2] U.S. Internal Revenue Code Section 501(c)(3).

A public charity is defined as (1) a church, school, hospital, governmental unit, or publicly supported charity; (2) an organization that receives more than one-third of its support from a combination of contributions, membership fees, and gross receipts from exempt activities and no more than one-third of its support from a combination of investment income and net unrelated business income after taxes; (3) an organization operated exclusively for the benefit of organizations already described; or (4) an organization founded and operated exclusively for public safety. The remainder of this section will concentrate on public charities.

Applying for Tax-Exempt Status

Organizations that receive substantial support from outside contributors find it particularly important to have Section 501(c)(3) status. Contributions made to such organizations are deductible when computing income taxes as well as estate taxes. For this reason, many donors require proof of Section 501(c)3 status before making contributions. Because state laws govern sales taxes, 501(c)(3) status does not exempt the organization from sales taxes. The ability to deduct donations reduces the net cost of contributions to the donor but places some restrictions on the activities of the tax-exempt organization and imposes reporting requirements. For example, exempt organizations are prohibited from supporting political candidates or campaigning to influence legislation. Reporting requirements are described in the next section of this chapter.

To qualify for tax-exempt status, the organization must:

1. Have an Employer's Identification Number (IRS form SS–4).
2. Be organized as a corporation, trust, or association.
3. Complete IRS form 1023, *Application for Recognition of Exemption.*
4. Receive notice from the IRS that the organization has been determined to be tax exempt.

Form 1023 requires the organization to provide information regarding its purpose and activities and provide up to four years of financial information or budgets. Copies of the organizing documents (articles of incorporation or association, bylaws, or trust agreement) must accompany the application. Again state law determines what an organization must do to incorporate. Many times it is easier for the organization to prepare Articles of Association, but these articles must include specific language regarding the purpose of the organization, the distribution of any earnings, and disposition of assets in the event the organization is dissolved. Example articles of association for a Boy Scout troop appear in Illustration 13–3.

Federal Filing Requirements

Many tax-exempt organizations are required to file an annual information return (Form 990) with the IRS. The first page of this form is reproduced in Illustration 13–4. The purpose of Form 990 is to promote tax compliance by assuring that tax-exempt entities remain within their exempt purpose and to provide the IRS and the public with a transparent and comprehensive view of the organization. Revised in 2008, Form 990

ILLUSTRATION 13–3 Example Articles of Association

Boy Scout Troop 388
Watkinsville, Georgia
Articles of Association

First: The name of the organization shall be Boy Scout Troop 388, herein referred to as Troop 388.

Second: The place in this state where Boy Scout Troop 388 is to be based is the Town of Watkinsville, Oconee County, Georgia.

Third: Said Troop 388 is organized exclusively for educational and charitable purposes. The purpose of Troop 388 is to provide an educational program for boys and young adults to build character, to train in the responsibilities of participating citizenship, and to develop personal fitness and to contribute to the community through charitable and service projects.

Fourth: The names and addresses of the persons who are the initial trustees of the organization are as follows:

_____   _____

_____   _____

Fifth: No part of the net earnings of Troop 388 shall inure to the benefit of, or be distributable to its members, officers or other private persons, except that Troop 388 shall be authorized and empowered to pay reasonable compensation for services rendered and to make payments and distributions in furtherance of the purposes set forth in Article Third hereof. No substantial part of the activities of Troop 388 shall be the carrying on of propaganda, or otherwise attempting to influence legislation, and Troop 388 shall not participate in, or intervene in (including the publishing or distribution of statements) any political campaign on behalf of or in opposition to any candidate for public office. Notwithstanding any other provision of these articles, Troop 388 shall not carry on or engage in any activities or exercise any powers that are not in furtherance of the purposes of Troop 388.

Sixth: Upon the dissolution of the organization, assets shall be distributed for one or more exempt purposes within the meaning of section 501(c)(3) of the Internal Revenue Code, or corresponding section of any future federal tax code, or shall be distributed to the federal government, or to a state or local government, for a public purpose. Any such assets not disposed of shall be disposed of by the Court of Common Pleas of the county in which the principal office of the organization is then located, exclusively for such purposes or to such organization or organizations, as said Court shall determine, which are organized and operated exclusively for such purposes.

Dated this 15th day of November 2009.

(Include signatures of three principal officers)

---

now provides descriptions of the organization's service accomplishments, governance, and finances. Major sections of Form 990 include:

- **Statement of Program Accomplishments** This section requires the organization to report its mission and services. The organization is required to provide specific measures of its service accomplishments.

ILLUSTRATION 13–4   Page 1 of Form 990

Form **990**	**Return of Organization Exempt From Income Tax**	OMB No. 1545-0047
	Under section 501(c), 527, or 4947(a)(1) of the Internal Revenue Code (except black lung benefit trust or private foundation)	2008
Department of the Treasury Internal Revenue Service	▶ The organization may have to use a copy of this return to satisfy state reporting requirements.	**Open to Public Inspection**

A For the 2008 calendar year, or tax year beginning _____ , 2008, and ending _____ , 20 __

B Check if applicable:	Please use IRS label or print or type. See Specific Instructions.	**C** Name of organization				**D** Employer identification number
☐ Address change		Doing Business As				
☐ Name change		Number and street (or P.O. box if mail is not delivered to street address)		Room/suite		**E** Telephone number
☐ Initial return						( )
☐ Termination		City or town, state or country, and ZIP + 4				
☐ Amended return						**G** Gross receipts $
☐ Application pending	**F** Name and address of principal officer:					**H(a)** Is this a group return for affiliates? ☐ Yes ☐ No
						H(b) Are all affiliates included? ☐ Yes ☐ No If "No," attach a list. (see instructions)

I Tax-exempt status: ☐ 501(c) ( ) ◀ (insert no.) ☐ 4947(a)(1) or ☐ 527

J Website: ▶ _____   **H(c)** Group exemption number ▶ _____

K Type of organization: ☐ Corporation ☐ Trust ☐ Association ☐ Other ▶ ___   **L** Year of formation: ___   **M** State of legal domicile: ___

Part I   Summary

Activities & Governance

1 Briefly describe the organization's mission or most significant activities: _____

2 Check this box ▶ ☐ if the organization discontinued its operations or disposed of more than 25% of its assets.

3 Number of voting members of the governing body (Part VI, line 1a)	**3**	
4 Number of independent voting members of the governing body (Part VI, line 1b)	**4**	
5 Total number of employees (Part V, line 2a)	**5**	
6 Total number of volunteers (estimate if necessary)	**6**	
7a Total gross unrelated business revenue from Part VIII, line 12, column (C)	**7a**	
b Net unrelated business taxable income from Form 990-T, line 34	**7b**	

Revenue

		Prior Year	Current Year
8 Contributions and grants (Part VIII, line 1h)			
9 Program service revenue (Part VIII, line 2g)			
10 Investment income (Part VIII, column (A), lines 3, 4, and 7d)			
11 Other revenue (Part VIII, column (A), lines 5, 6d, 8c, 9c, 10c, and 11e) . .			
12 Total revenue—add lines 8 through 11 (must equal Part VIII, column (A), line 12)			

Expenses

13 Grants and similar amounts paid (Part IX, column (A), lines 1–3)		
14 Benefits paid to or for members (Part IX, column (A), line 4)		
15 Salaries, other compensation, employee benefits (Part IX, column (A), lines 5–10)		
16a Professional fundraising fees (Part IX, column (A), line 11e)		
b Total fundraising expenses (Part IX, column (D), line 25) ▶ _____		
17 Other expenses (Part IX, column (A), lines 11a–11d, 11f–24f)		
18 Total expenses. Add lines 13–17 (must equal Part IX, column (A), line 25). .		
19 Revenue less expenses. Subtract line 18 from line 12		

Net Assets or Fund Balances

		Beginning of Year	End of Year
20 Total assets (Part X, line 16)			
21 Total liabilities (Part X, line 26)			
22 Net assets or fund balances. Subtract line 21 from line 20			

Part II   Signature Block

Under penalties of perjury, I declare that I have examined this return, including accompanying schedules and statements, and to the best of my knowledge and belief, it is true, correct, and complete. Declaration of preparer (other than officer) is based on all information of which preparer has any knowledge.

Sign Here	▶ _____ Signature of officer	_____ Date
	▶ _____ Type or print name and title	

Paid Preparer's Use Only	Preparer's signature ▶ _____	Date _____	Check if self-employed ▶ ☐	Preparer's identifying number (see instructions)
	Firm's name (or yours if self-employed), address, and ZIP + 4 ▶ _____		EIN ▶	
			Phone no. ▶ ( )	

May the IRS discuss this return with the preparer shown above? (see instructions) . . . . ☐ Yes ☐ No

For Privacy Act and Paperwork Reduction Act Notice, see the separate instructions.   Cat. No. 11282Y   Form **990** (2008)

• **Governance, Management, and Disclosures**   In this section the organization describes its governing body, business relationships, management structure, and key policies including: fundraising, compensation, code of ethics, whistleblowing, document retention, and whether the organization receives a financial audit.

- **Compensation Schedules** Schedules are provided for the compensation of officers, directors, trustees, and highest-paid employees and independent contractors.
- **Financial Information** These include a Statement of Revenues, Statement of Functional Expense, and Balance Sheet.

The financial information required by Form 990 is similar to that required under FASB standards for private not-for-profits except that a cash flow statement and notes are not required. Illustration 13–5 reproduces the balance sheet required in Form 990. Note that pledge receivables are recognized and that the Net Asset classifications are consistent with FASB standards.

Churches, governmental organizations, political parties, and organizations whose gross receipts are less than $25,000 are exempt from Form 990 filing requirements. The Taxpayer Bill of Rights (1996) called for an increase in public disclosures of tax-exempt organizations. Exempt organizations are required to provide copies, upon request, of the three most recent annual Form 990s. Many organizations choose to satisfy the requirement to provide copies by placing their documents on their Web page or on that of another entity as part of a database of similar documents.

State Filing Requirements

In addition to having federal filing requirements, an organization has a number of state filing requirements. Many require a copy of Form 990, and others supplement this form with additional requirements. It should be noted that not-for-profit organizations are normally corporations created under the laws of individual states; as such, they are subject to state laws and regulations as well as those of the federal government.

Unrelated Business Income Tax (UBIT)

A tax-exempt organization is required to pay tax at the corporate or trust rate on income generated from any trade or business activities unrelated to the entity's tax-exempt purposes. The purpose of this requirement is to eliminate advantages that tax-exempt organizations have over profit-making organizations. For example, a college bookstore, when selling certain items to nonstudents, would be competing with private business engaged in the same activities.

This provision has created some controversy. Many activities could be judged by some to be related to the tax-exempt purposes of a not-for-profit and by others as unrelated. As a result, a body of case law has evolved, and certain specific situations have been addressed by legislation.

The existence of one or more of the following conditions will exempt income-producing activities from UBIT: (1) the business is not regularly carried on; (2) volunteers perform most of the labor; (3) the not-for-profit sells donated merchandise; and (4) it is operated for the convenience of employees, patients, students, and so on. Additional exceptions have been provided in legislation. These include, among others, (1) royalties, dividends, interest, and annuities (except from controlled corporations); (2) income of a college or university or hospital from research performed for a person or governmental unit; (3) income from qualified public

ILLUSTRATION 13–5 Part 10 of Form 990 (Balance Sheet)

Form 990 (2008) Page 11

Part X Balance Sheet

			(A) Beginning of year		(B) End of year
Assets	1	Cash—non-interest-bearing		1	
	2	Savings and temporary cash investments		2	
	3	Pledges and grants receivable, net		3	
	4	Accounts receivable, net		4	
	5	Receivables from current and former officers, directors, trustees, key employees, or other related parties. Complete Part II of Schedule L		5	
	6	Receivables from other disqualified persons (as defined under section 4958(f)(1)) and persons described in section 4958(c)(3)(B). Complete Part II of Schedule L		6	
	7	Notes and loans receivable, net		7	
	8	Inventories for sale or use		8	
	9	Prepaid expenses and deferred charges		9	
	10a	Land, buildings, and equipment: cost basis 10a			
	b	Less: accumulated depreciation. Complete Part VI of Schedule D 10b		10c	
	11	Investments—publicly traded securities		11	
	12	Investments—other securities. See Part IV, line 11		12	
	13	Investments—program-related. See Part IV, line 11		13	
	14	Intangible assets		14	
	15	Other assets. See Part IV, line 11		15	
	16	**Total assets.** Add lines 1 through 15 (must equal line 34)		16	
Liabilities	17	Accounts payable and accrued expenses		17	
	18	Grants payable		18	
	19	Deferred revenue		19	
	20	Tax-exempt bond liabilities		20	
	21	Escrow account liability. Complete Part IV of Schedule D		21	
	22	Payables to current and former officers, directors, trustees, key employees, highest compensated employees, and disqualified persons. Complete Part II of Schedule L		22	
	23	Secured mortgages and notes payable to unrelated third parties		23	
	24	Unsecured notes and loans payable		24	
	25	Other liabilities. Complete Part X of Schedule D		25	
	26	**Total liabilities.** Add lines 17 through 25		26	
Net Assets or Fund Balances		**Organizations that follow SFAS 117, check here ▶ ☐ and complete lines 27 through 29, and lines 33 and 34.**			
	27	Unrestricted net assets		27	
	28	Temporarily restricted net assets		28	
	29	Permanently restricted net assets		29	
		Organizations that do not follow SFAS 117, check here ▶ ☐ and complete lines 30 through 34.			
	30	Capital stock or trust principal, or current funds		30	
	31	Paid-in or capital surplus, or land, building, or equipment fund		31	
	32	Retained earnings, endowment, accumulated income, or other funds		32	
	33	Total net assets or fund balances		33	
	34	Total liabilities and net assets/fund balances		34	

Part XI Financial Statements and Reporting

			Yes	No
1	Accounting method used to prepare the Form 990: ☐ Cash ☐ Accrual ☐ Other			
2a	Were the organization's financial statements compiled or reviewed by an independent accountant?	2a		
b	Were the organization's financial statements audited by an independent accountant?	2b		
c	If "Yes" to lines 2a or 2b, does the organization have a committee that assumes responsibility for oversight of the audit, review, or compilation of its financial statements and selection of an independent accountant?	2c		
3a	As a result of a federal award, was the organization required to undergo an audit or audits as set forth in the Single Audit Act and OMB Circular A-133?	3a		
b	If "Yes," did the organization undergo the required audit or audits?	3b		

Form **990** (2008)

entertainment activities in connection with a fair or exposition; (4) income from labor, agricultural, and horticultural organizations and business trade associations from qualified convention or trade show activities; and (5) income from the rental or exchange of membership lists.

Assume a sheltered workshop sold goods assembled by the clients of the workshop. It is likely that the revenue produced by those sales would be related to the tax-exempt purpose, as the clients would be engaged in a meaningful activity. On the other hand, instead assume the sheltered workshop operated a business across town, selling manufactured goods that were produced by regular employees, with the sole intent of raising money for the organization. It is likely that this would be perceived as unrelated to the tax-exempt purpose and, therefore, subject to the UBIT.

When computing the unrelated business income tax, not-for-profit organizations are allowed to deduct ordinary and necessary business expenses directly connected with their trade or business (as would any other business), a $1,000 special deduction, charitable contributions, and many of the other deductions available to business organizations. The applicable tax return is Form 990T. Estimated tax payments are required, when applicable.

IRS Oversight

The Internal Revenue Service (IRS) recently announced that it considers tax-exempt organizations to be one of its four highest enforcement priorities. Several of the areas of concern are cost allocations, excess executive compensation, and organizations operating outside their tax-exempt purpose. The program expense ratio, described in Chapter 10, is commonly used to evaluate not-for-profit organizations and is favorably affected when costs are allocated from fund-raising to program expenses. The IRS is concerned that financial information reported in Form 990 is accurate and may be relied upon by donors. The issue of cost allocations arose when the IRS observed that many tax-exempt organizations that reported contribution revenue also reported zero fund-raising expenses.

Another area of concern is executive compensation. If the IRS deems wages and benefits to be in excess of reasonable amounts, the IRS may impose intermediate sanctions on the individual receiving the benefits and the organization managers who approved it. Benefits are defined broadly and include salaries, deferred compensation, insurance, loans, and medical benefits. The term "intermediate sanctions" refers to penalties imposed by the IRS when individuals associated with a tax-exempt organization receive excess benefits. Prior to the existence of intermediate sanctions, the only sanction available to the IRS was revoking the organization's tax-exempt status, an effective death sentence for many tax-exempt organizations.

In the event compensation is found to be unreasonable, the executive is required to pay back the excess benefit to the tax-exempt organization. In addition, there is a tax penalty of 25 percent of the excess benefit on the individual receiving the compensation and a penalty of 10 percent on the individuals responsible for approving it. If the executive receiving the excess benefits fails to repay the amount in a timely manner, an additional tax equal to 200 percent may be imposed.

Summary and Some Conclusions Related to Exempt Entities

A major portion of the practice of CPAs and a major concern of not-for-profit organizations is the obtaining and preservation of tax-exempt status and the avoidance or minimization of unrelated business income tax. During the initial organizing of a nonprofit, care must be taken to define and limit its purpose to tax-exempt activities. Decisions ınd-raising activities must constantly be monitored to determine the impact Some not-for-profit organizations create separate, related organizations that e tax exempt to ensure that the primary organization does not lose its tax-

⌣.. atus. While the taxation of tax-exempt entities may seem to be a contradiction in terms, not-for-profit organizations must be continually vigilant and prepared to file the necessary forms and meet the regulations of the federal and state governments.

EVALUATING PERFORMANCE

Our attention to this point in the text has been on the preparation of financial statements by state and local governments and a variety of not-for-profit organizations. Now we will focus on the use of financial and nonfinancial information in evaluating the performance and financial position of not-for-profit organizations and governments. When organizations vary greatly in size, it is difficult to evaluate their relative performance based on gross amounts reported in the financial statements. To facilitate comparisons, many users of financial statement calculate ratios. We describe commonly used ratios in the following sections.

Analysis of Not-for-Profit Organization Financial Statements

As indicated in Chapter 10, the most frequently used measure of not-for-profit efficiency is the **program expense ratio.** This is calculated as program service expenses divided by total expenses and provides an indication of the extent to which a not-for-profit is dedicating its resources to programs as opposed to administration, fund-raising, and membership development. The program expense ratio may be calculated from the Statement of Activities or from information reported in the Form 990. For example, the program expense ratio for the Performing Arts Organization in Illustration 10–1 is 67 percent, calculated as ($6,906 + $7,020 + $1,760 + $960)/$24,774. Alternative measures of efficiency decompose the expenses into program, administration, and fund-raising, each expressed as a percentage of total expenses. The Better Business Bureau recommends a program expense ratio of not less than 65 percent and maintains a Web site with financial information for a variety of charities (www.give.org).[3] The Web site presents pie charts of not-for-profits' expenses (program, administration, and fund-raising).

Fund-raising efficiency is another measure of performance that expresses how much an organization spends in raising a dollar of donations. The fund-raising efficiency ratio is calculated as fund-raising expense divided by contribution revenues. Generally membership development is combined with fund-raising expenses. The fund-raising efficiency ratio for the Performing Arts Organization in Illustration 10–1 is < $.05, calculated as ($1,292 + $1,152)/$50,303. The interpretation is that the organization spends less than five cents to raise a dollar of contributions.

Working capital ratio is the ratio of working capital (current assets − current liabilities) divided by total expenses. The ratio provides a measure of how long a

[3] Better Business Bureau, *Wise Giving Alliance Standards for Charity Accountability,* http://www.bbb .org/us/Charity-Standards/.

not-for-profit could sustain its operations without generating new revenue. Entities with high working capital ratios would be less likely to eliminate programs or staff during periods of economic downturn. The working capital ratio for the Performing Arts Organization in Illustration 10–1 is .390, calculated as ($10,218 + $4,344 + $360 + $240 + $180 − $28 − $120 − $5,520)/$24,774. This ratio is commonly expressed in terms of months. In this example the organization has approximately 4 1/2 months (.39 × 12 months) of operating expenses available in working capital. Note, this is different from a similarly titled ratio commonly used to evaluate businesses (current assets/current liabilities).

Analysis of State and Local Government Financial Statements

In a study for the Governmental Accounting Standards Board, Jones and others listed three primary groups of users of governmental financial reports: (1) citizen groups, (2) legislative and oversight officials, and (3) investors and creditors.[4] They suggest that citizen groups use financial reports to:

1. Evaluate efficiency and effectiveness.
2. Compare results of the current year with previous years.
3. Assess financial operations and financial condition.
4. Determine compliance with the budget.
5. Advocate certain programs or actions.

The study indicated that legislative and oversight officials use governmental financial reports to:

1. Evaluate executive branch funding and spending proposals.
2. Determine compliance with the budget and other finance-related requirements.
3. Monitor fund activity and financial position and analyze fund balances.

Finally, investors and creditors use reports to ascertain the ability of government to repay its debt. The study considered investors and creditors to be investors, bond raters, bond insurers, and underwriters.

This section of the chapter provides suggestions as to how readers might use governmental financial statements to gather information that would meet the needs just described.

Public Finance Market   The public finance market includes many types of bonds, short-term notes, and other financing arrangements. Often described as the municipal bond market, participants include issuers, investors, underwriters, and financial advisors, rating agencies, bond attorneys, and debt insurers. This text previously differentiated **general obligation bonds,** which carry the full faith and credit of the governmental unit and its taxing power, from **limited obligation** and **revenue bonds,** which are serviced from the revenues of particular facilities.

---

[4] See Jones et al., *The Needs of Users of Governmental Financial Reports* (Norwalk, CT: Governmental Accounting Standards Board, 1985), pp. 26–31.

Debt-rating services, such as Moody's, Standard & Poor's, and Fitch's Investors Service, assist investors by rating bonds and other forms of debt. Ranging from highest to lowest, Moody's rates bonds as Aaa, Aa, A, Baa, Ba, B, Caa, Ca, and C.[5] Bonds insured with certain insurance companies are automatically Aaa, as payments of interest and principal are guaranteed.

While rating agencies, underwriters, and large institutional investors in the public finance market can obtain information directly from issuers, other investors depend upon publicly available information. When bonds are initially issued an "official statement" is prepared. The Government Finance Officers Association and the National Federation of Municipal Analysts have prepared disclosure guidelines for these official statements. After initial issuance, many in the investment community depend on the Comprehensive Annual Financial Report for information related to municipal governments, especially in the secondary market (the market for bonds after initial issuance).

Analysis of the Comprehensive Annual Financial Report As you have seen, governmental financial statements differ in many ways from those of commercial enterprises. As a result, many citizens and some elected officials do not understand the financial statements issued by local governments. If citizens fail to understand these statements, the GASB has failed to meet one of its primary objectives. To address this problem, the GASB published two user's guides: *What You Should Know about Your Local Government's Finances* (GASB, September 2000) and *What You Should Know about Your School District's Finances* (GASB, November 2000). The guides have no standing in the formal hierarchy of generally accepted accounting principles, but are written from the user's perspective and provide plain-language interpretations of the financial statements.

Financial ratios are another means to help users understand and interpret financial information. This section presents financial statement analysis using the Village of Elizabeth financial statements contained in this book. Of course, a final decision regarding the financial viability of a government involves many factors, only some of which are available from the financial statements. An analyst has many sources available which list ratios that might be useful. This text uses information from GASB,[6] Standard & Poor's,[7] Moody's Investors Service,[8] and Chaney, Mead, and Schermann.[9] In this example, the population of the Village of Elizabeth is assumed to be 10,000, and the market value of property in the government is assumed to be $100 million.

[5] Moody's Public Finance Department, *1997 Medians: Selected Indicators of Municipal Performance* (New York).

[6] Dean Michael Mead, *An Analyst's Guide to Government Financial Statements* (Norwalk, CT: GASB, 2001).

[7] Standard & Poor's, *Public Finance Criteria* (New York: Standard & Poor's, 2000).

[8] See footnote 5.

[9] Barbara A. Chaney, Dean Michael Mead, and Kenneth R. Schermann, "The New Governmental Financial Reporting Model: What It Means for Analyzing Government Financial Condition," *Journal of Government Financial Management* (Spring 2002), pp. 26–31.

ILLUSTRATION 13–6 Summary: Financial Ratios for State and Local Governments

Net debt per capita	$$\dfrac{\text{General obligation debt* – debt service fund balance**}}{\text{Population}}$$
Net debt to fair value of property	$$\dfrac{\text{General obligation debt* – debt service fund balance**}}{\text{Market value of property}}$$
Net debt to assets	$$\dfrac{\text{General obligation debt* – debt service fund balance**}}{\text{Total assets governmental activities*}}$$ $$\dfrac{\text{Debt from business-type activities* (e.g. revenue bonds)}}{\text{Total assets business-type activities*}}$$ $$\dfrac{\text{Total debt primary government* – debt service fund balance**}}{\text{Total assets primary government*}}$$
Debt service to total expenditures	$$\dfrac{\text{Principal and Interest Expenditures**}}{\text{Total expenditures: General and debt service funds**}}$$
Net assets/expenses	$$\dfrac{\text{Total net assets governmental activities*}}{\text{Total expenses from governmental activities*}}$$ $$\dfrac{\text{Total net assets business-type activities*}}{\text{Total expenses from business-type activities*}}$$ $$\dfrac{\text{Total net assets primary government*}}{\text{Total expenses from primary government*}}$$
Unrestricted net assets/expenses	$$\dfrac{\text{Unrestricted net assets governmental activities*}}{\text{Total expenses from governmental activities*}}$$ $$\dfrac{\text{Unrestricted net assets business-type activities*}}{\text{Total expenses from business-type activities*}}$$ $$\dfrac{\text{Unrestricted net assets primary government*}}{\text{Total expenses from primary government*}}$$
Unreserved fund balance/revenues	$$\dfrac{\text{General Fund unreserved fund balance**}}{\text{General Fund total revenues**}}$$
Governmental revenues per capita	$$\dfrac{\text{Total revenues: governmental funds**}}{\text{Population}}$$
Interest coverage– revenue bonds	$$\dfrac{\text{Operating income: enterprise funds***}}{\text{Interest expense***}}$$
Operating ratio– enterprise funds	$$\dfrac{\text{Operating expenses – depreciation expense***}}{\text{Operating revenues***}}$$

Sources: *Government-wide financial statements.
**Governmental funds financial statements.
***Enterprise funds financial statements.

Ten common ratios are summarized in Illustration 13–6 and are demonstrated in the following pages. Remember that sophisticated analysis would include many more factors and a trend analysis of governments over time.

Net debt per capita is a measure of the ability of the citizens to pay general government debt; a high figure indicates that citizens of a government bear an above-average burden. The government-wide Statement of Net Assets (Illustration 8–6) indicates that the Village of Elizabeth has $1,090,800 in general obligation bonds outstanding. The Village of Elizabeth governmental funds Balance Sheet

(Illustration 5–3) indicates that $36,500 is on hand for payment of debt; thus the net debt is $1,054,300. The net debt per capita, then, is

$$\$1{,}054{,}300/10{,}000 = \$105.43$$

Standard & Poor's indicates that anything below $1,000 would indicate low fiscal stress. As a result, it is clear that the Village of Elizabeth has low fiscal stress from this factor. When analyzing debt, analysts also consider other long-term liabilities, such as capital leases, compensated absences, and unfunded pension obligations. They also consider overlapping debt (see Chapter 8) to determine the overall impact of debt on the citizens of a municipality.

Net debt to fair value of property measures the ability of the government to pay its long-term debt based on the fair value of its property subject to tax. As is the case for net debt per capita, a high ratio indicates the possibility of stress. Using the same net debt factor as for net debt per capita, the net debt to fair value of property would be:

$$\$1{,}054{,}300/\$100{,}000{,}000 = 1.054\%$$

Standard & Poor's indicated that anything below 3 percent indicates low fiscal stress, 3 to 6 percent indicates medium stress, and more than 6 percent indicates high stress.

Net debt to assets is a measure of solvency that is included in both the GASB and the Chaney, Mead, and Schermann materials. This can be obtained from the government-wide Statement of Net Assets and can be computed separately for governmental activites, business-type activities, and the total primary government. Following the sources, the amount available (used in previous computations) is ignored. The computations for the Village of Elizabeth, taken from Illustration 8–6, are

Governmental Activities: $1,090,800/$39,282,290 = 2.78%

Business-type Activities: $2,700,000/$4,399,120 = 61.4%

Primary Government: $3,790,800/$43,681,410 = 8.68%

Debt service to total expenditures—General and debt service funds measures the degree to which expenditures are tied up in debt service charges. Governments that have low ratios have more flexibility for operations and ability to incur more debt. Standard & Poor's indicates that 5 percent or below represents a low carrying charge, 10 percent represents a moderate carrying charge, and 15 percent or greater represents a high carrying charge. This information is obtained from the Statement of Revenues, Expenditures, and Changes in Fund Balances for the governmental funds for the Village of Elizabeth (Illustration 5–4):

$$(\$120{,}000 + \$96{,}000)/(\$5{,}030{,}300 + \$216{,}000) = 4.12\%$$

The Village of Elizabeth, then, is carrying a relatively low debt burden, in terms of governmental operating expenditures.

Net assets/expenses is a measure of overall financial position, according to GASB and Chaney, Mead, and Schermann. This can be computed for governmental activities, business-type activities, and the total primary government. For the Village of

Elizabeth, this information would be found in the government-wide Statement of Net Assets (Illustration 8–6) and Statement of Activities (Illustration 8–5):

Governmental Activities: $37,400,190/$8,421,600 = 4.44

Business-type Activities: $1,600,520/$828,100 = 1.93

Primary Government: $39,000,710/9,249,700 = 4.22

Unrestricted net assets/expenses provides a more conservative measure of the availability of resources to meet expenses. This information comes from the same financial statements as the previous measure. For the Village of Elizabeth, the factors are

Governmental Activities: = $886,990/$8,421,600 = 0.11

Business-type Activities: = $402,255/$828,100 = 0.49

Primary Government: = $1,289,245/$9,249,700 = 0.14

Unreserved fund balance/revenues—General Fund is a liquidity measure long used in financial statement analysis. For the Village of Elizabeth, the information would be found in the General Fund column of the governmental funds Balance Sheet (Illustration 5–3) and the governmental funds Statement of Revenues, Expenditures, and Changes in Fund Balances (Illustration 5–4):

$790,990/$6,081,290 = 13.01%

Standard & Poor's indicate that a figure above 8 percent is strong. Many governments establish a policy regarding this figure.

Governmental revenues per capita measures the demand for services for a particular jurisdiction. The total governmental revenues for the Village of Elizabeth can be obtained from Illustration 5–4:

$8,001,290/10,000 = $800.13

Interest coverage—revenue bonds is a measure of an enterprise's ability to pay the interest on its enterprise debt. In many cases, a government may have several enterprises; in some cases, revenue bonds are payable specifically out of the revenues of each individual enterprise. In that case, this and the following ratio should be computed separately for each enterprise. The Village of Elizabeth has a single enterprise, reported as a Water Utility Fund. This ratio divides the net revenues (total revenues minus operating expenses) by the interest charges. For the Village of Elizabeth, both of these figures can be found in the proprietary funds Statement of Revenues, Expenses, and Changes in Fund Net Assets (Illustration 6–4). Total operating revenues (the Village of Elizabeth reports no nonoperating revenues) amount to $1,053,100, operating expenses amount to $659,900, and interest charges are $171,200:

($1,053,100 − $656,900)/$171,200 = 2.31 times

Some enterprises do not have debt, and analysts will not be able to calculate this ratio. Note that some governments may issue general obligation bonds to be paid by enterprise revenues; in this case, the bonds (and the interest) would be reported in the enterprise funds.

Operating ratio—enterprise funds provides a measure of the expense coverage of an enterprise, based on operations. This ratio can be calculated, whether or not an enterprise has debt. A high ratio indicates stress. This ratio divides the operating expenses, excluding depreciation, by the operating revenues. Both figures can be obtained from Illustration 6–4.

$$(\$656,900 - \$122,800)/\$1,053,100 = 50.72\%$$

The apparent inconsistency between the results of this ratio and the interest coverage ratio is caused by the fact that the Village of Elizabeth Water Utility Fund has a relatively high interest payment. Note in the government-wide Statement of Net Assets (Illustration 8–6) or the proprietary funds Statement of Net Assets (Illustration 6–3) that $2,700,000 in revenue bonds are outstanding.

Additional Analysis   Citizen groups, legislative and oversight officials, and investors and creditors would want to examine financial statements in much greater depth than is suggested by listing only 10 ratios. Population trends, trends in assessed and market value of property, economic indicators, budget to actual figures, analysis of individual enterprise funds related to separate revenue bond issues, tax rate limitations and margins, debt limitations and margins, growth or contraction of employee numbers, management of pension liabilities, analysis of infrastructure and other capital facility maintenance, and examination of the notes to uncover any contingent liabilities are examples of additional analysis. The analyst must be aware of how financial statements are prepared and of the limitations in the numbers when making judgments. Nevertheless, the Comprehensive Annual Financial Report contains much that is useful to those who make political and financial decisions affecting governmental units.

Service Efforts and Accomplishments Reporting

Governmental financial statements, notes, and required supplementary information meet many of the needs of citizens, creditors, and oversight authorities. Similarly, the financial statements of private not-for-profits are useful to donors, government regulators, and creditors. However, neither governmental nor not-for-profit financial statements are particularly effective in measuring organizational effectiveness. The fundamental problem is that government and not-for-profit effectiveness cannot be expressed solely in financial terms. Effectiveness in nonbusiness organizations must be measured in terms of the quality of the service provided or the extent to which an organization fulfills its mission. For this reason, many governments and not-for-profits report nonfinancial information in addition to their financial statements. The framework for combining financial and nonfinancial information to more effectively communicate organizational effectiveness is termed **Service Efforts and Accomplishments (SEA)** reporting.

The Governmental Accounting Standards Board has been engaged in a major effort related to service efforts and accomplishments. GASB Concepts Statement 2, *Service Efforts and Accomplishments Reporting,* was issued in 1994. In addition, a series of research reports related to colleges and universities, economic development programs, elementary and secondary education, fire department programs, hospitals, mass transit, police department programs, public assistance programs, public health, road maintenance, sanitation collection and disposal, water and wastewater treatment, and other activities has been issued. A summary research report includes chapters for each of these areas.

According to the GASB, reporting on SEA is necessary to make governmental financial reporting complete. No decisions have been made as to how the information should be reported—as a part of the Comprehensive Annual Financial Report, as a special report, or in some other form. However, according to the GASB, "The Objective of SEA reporting is to provide more complete information about a governmental entity's performance than can be provided by the operating statement, balance sheet, and budgetary comparison statements and schedules."

Having completed its original agenda, the GASB expressed an interest in providing standards addressing the reporting of nonfinancial performance measures (i.e., service efforts and accomplishments). In November 2006, the Financial Accounting Foundation (the organization that funds the FASB and GASB) affirmed that the GASB has the jurisdictional authority to include service efforts and accomplishments in its financial accounting and reporting standard-setting activities for state and local governments. This has proven to be a controversial stance.

Following that action, eight professional groups publicly objected to the GASB, adding a project on performance measurement reporting. Most notable among these groups is the Government Finance Officers Association, whose executive board concluded "that the GASB's time has now come and gone, and that some other vehicle would better meet the authentic need of state and local governments for *accounting* standards."[10] In a 2007 position document, the GFOA's leadership proposed dissolving the GASB and moving jurisdictional authority for state and local government reporting to the FASB. Although it is unlikely the GASB will be dissolved, the position paper demonstrates the strength of opinion over the GASB's involvement in the reporting of nonfinancial measures.

SEA Measures Service efforts are defined as "measures of costs or inputs; the financial and nonfinancial resources applied to provide services." For example, direct costs include salaries and benefits for police officers who are directly engaged in crime prevention, detection, and apprehension of offenders. To the extent that the costs are separately identifiable, occupancy, vehicle, and equipment costs are directly allocated. Indirect costs of the police department and general government may also be allocated. Inputs may also include nonfinancial measures such as number of personnel and hours expended.

Service accomplishments include outputs and outcomes. According to the GASB, output measures are the quantity of a service provided or the quantity of a service that meets a certain quality requirement. Examples of output measures for a police department include number of responses, number of arrests, and the hours of patrol.

---

[10] Government Finance Officers Association, 2007, http://www.gfoa.org/gasb.shtml.

Output measures should be distinguished from measures of outcome. Outcomes measure the extent to which results are achieved or needs are met at least partially due to the services provided. Examples of outcome measures are the number of violent crimes committed, the value of property lost due to crime, and response time.

Efficiency measures relate costs and other inputs to output measures, such as the number of responses per dollar spent or per police officer. Cost-outcome measures relate inputs to outcomes, such as the value of property lost to crime per dollar spent.

A variety of measures should be presented. Those measures should be reported consistently, in a timely manner, and in a way that is easily understood. Comparisons with prior periods and with other governments are also useful. Explanatory variables, such as socioeconomic data, should be included to help readers understand that not all the results are controllable.

Some cautions are in order regarding SEA reporting. Until standards are developed and commonly reported and used, there is a risk that governments will present only that information that is favorable. Audit opinions are not associated with this information, and it is unlikely they will be for some time. Problems exist in the measurement and allocations of costs, not to mention the measurement of outputs and outcomes. Even with the problems, however, SEA reporting is viewed by many as essential for measuring the performance of a government or an activity of a government. SEA measures are now a part of the budget process of many governments. Standardization and public reporting would make the SEA measures more useful.

Example of SEA Reporting: School Report Cards   Many states require school systems or individual schools to publish annual "school report cards." Illustration 13–7 provides Web sites for school report cards by state. These reports are an example of service efforts and accomplishments reporting for an important and highly visible government service, public schools. The content of these report cards is frequently dictated by the state government and varies by state. However most of these reports contain the following types of information:

Service Inputs:	Tax revenues, state appropriations, and federal grants. Number of teachers, administrators, and support personnel. Education level (certificate levels) of teachers and administrators. Demographics of student population (income, race, language).
Service Outputs:	Enrollment. Gifted or alternative programs. Degrees conferred.
Service Outcomes:	Standardized test scores. Dropout rates. Competency tests and high school graduation tests. Accreditation results.

Now that you have finished reading Chapter 13, complete the multiple choice questions provided on the text's Web site (www.mhhe.com/copley10e) to test your comprehension of the chapter.

ILLUSTRATION 13-7   State Web sites for School Performance Reports

Alabama	http://www.alsde.edu/html/ed_dir_menu.asp
Alaska	http://www.eed.state.ak.us/stats/
Arizona	http://www.ade.az.gov/srcs/find_school.asp?rdoYear=2009
Arkansas	http://normessasweb.uark.edu/schoolperformance/District/District.php
California	http://api.cde.ca.gov/reports.asp
Colorado	http://reportcard.cde.state.co.us/reportcard/CommandHandler.jsp
Connecticut	http://www.csde.state.ct.us/public/cedar/districts/index.htm
Delaware	http://www.doe.k12.de.us/reports_data/sd.shtml
Florida	http://schoolgrades.fldoe.org/
Georgia	http://reportcard2005.gaosa.org/k12/Systems.asp
Hawaii	http://doe.k12.hi.us/myschool/
Idaho	http://www.sde.idaho.gov/ipd/reportcard/SchoolReportCard.asp
Illinois	http://webprod.isbe.net/ereportcard/publicsite/getSearchCriteria.aspx
Indiana	http://www.doe.in.gov/data/
Iowa	http://www.iowaschoolprofiles.com/profilesdist.asp?new=1
Kansas	http://online.ksde.org/rcard/searchpage.aspx
Kentucky	http://applications.education.ky.gov/schoolReportCardArchive/
Louisiana	http://www.doe.state.la.us/lde/saa/2394.asp
Maine	http://portalx.bisoex.state.me.us/pls/doe/eddev.profiles.find_school
Maryland	http://www.msp.msde.state.md.us/
Massachusetts	http://profiles.doe.mass.edu/
Michigan	https://oeaa.state.mi.us/ayp/index.asp
Minnesota	http://education.state.mn.us/ReportCard2005/index.do
Mississippi	http://orsap.mde.k12.ms.us:8080/MAARS/index.jsp
Missouri	http://dese.mo.gov/schooldata/school_data.html
Montana	http://www.opi.state.mt.us/ReportCard/
Nebraska	http://reportcard.nde.state.ne.us/Main/Home.aspx
Nevada	http://www.nevadareportcard.com/
New Hampshire	http://reporting.measuredprogress.org/nhprofile/
New Jersey	http://education.state.nj.us/rc/nclb08/index.html
New Mexico	http://www.ped.state.nm.us/AssessmentAccountability/AcademicGrowth/
	DistrictReportCards.html
New York	https://www.nystart.gov/publicweb/AllDistrict.do?year=2008
North Carolina	http://www.ncreportcards.org/src/
North Dakota	http://www.dpi.state.nd.us/dpi/reports/profile/index.shtm
Ohio	http://ilrc.ode.state.oh.us/Default.asp
Oklahoma	http://www.schoolreportcard.org/approach.asp
Oregon	http://www.ode.state.or.us/data/reportcard/reports.aspx
Pennsylvania	http://paayp.emetric.net/
Rhode Island	http://www.infoworks.ride.uri.edu/2009/reports/district.asp
South Carolina	http://ed.sc.gov/topics/researchandstats/schoolreportcard/2008/District/
South Dakota	http://doe.sd.gov/ofm/applications/statdigest/default.asp
Tennessee	http://edu.reportcard.state.tn.us/pls/apex/f?p=200:1:4325015781100374::NO:::
Texas	http://ritter.tea.state.tx.us/perfreport/src/2008/campus.srch.html
Utah	http://u-pass.schools.utah.gov/u-passweb/DistrictData.jsp?report=10
Vermont	http://crs.uvm.edu/schlrpt/
Virginia	https://p1pe.doe.virginia.gov/reportcard/
Washington	http://reportcard.ospi.k12.wa.us/summary.aspx?year=2008-09
West Virginia	http://wveis.k12.wv.us/nclb/pub/
Wisconsin	http://www2.dpi.state.wi.us/spr/
Wyoming	http://www.k12.wy.us/statistics/index.html

Questions and Exercises

13–1. Using the annual financial report obtained for Exercise 1–1, answer the following questions:

 a. Examine the auditor's report. Is the auditor identified as an independent CPA firm? A state audit agency? Other? Is the wording of the auditor's report the same as illustrated in this chapter? Does the scope paragraph indicate exactly what is covered by the auditor's opinion? If the auditor is expressing an opinion only on the basic financial statements, what responsibility is taken for the combining and individual fund statements? Is the opinion unqualified? If not, what are the qualifications?

 b. Does the annual financial report contain a single audit section? If not, does the report refer to the existence of a single audit report? If so, does the report include a Schedule of Federal (and State) Financial Assistance? Are all of the reports illustrated in this chapter included? Can you identify the major programs, if any?

13–2. Go to the Better Business Bureau's Wise Giving Alliance Web site (http://www.bbb.org/us/charity/). Click on Charity Reports and select a charity. Be sure it is one that presents financial information.

 a. State the name of the organization and its mission.

 b. What are the two largest programs in terms of expenses?

 c. What are the two largest sources of funds?

 d. Calculate the program expense ratio.

 e. Calculate the fund-raising efficiency ratio.

13–3. Using the annual financial report obtained for Exercise 1–1, answer the following questions:

 a. Report the following ratios, using the text material for the Village of Elizabeth as a guide:

  (1) Net debt per capita.

  (2) Net debt to fair value of property.

  (3) Net debt to assets.

  (4) Debt service to total expenditures—General and debt service funds.

  (5) Net assets/expenses.

  (6) Unrestricted net assets/expenses.

  (7) Unreserved fund balance/revenues—General Fund.

  (8) Governmental revenues per capita.

  (9) Interest coverage—revenue bonds.

  (10) Operating ratio—enterprise funds.

 b. Write a memorandum, based on the ratios you calculated in part (*a*) of this problem, giving a recommendation as to whether to purchase (1) general obligation or (2) revenue bonds of your governmental unit.

13–4. Use the Web sites provided in Illustration 13–7 to access your high school or school system school report card (or any other school report card of your choice). Answer the following questions:

  a. What measures of service inputs are presented on the report card?

  b. What measures of service outputs are presented on the report card?

  c. What measures of service outcomes are presented on the report card?

  d. What information is presented to provide comparisons between the school selected and other schools in the state?

13–5. Presented below are the computed amounts of ratios for the Village of Elizabeth example appearing in the chapter.

	Village of Elizabeth	**City of Salem**
Net debt per capita	$ 105.43	
Net debt to fair value of property	1.054%	
Net debt to assets		
Governmental activities	2.78%	
Business-type activities	61.4%	
Primary government	8.68%	
Debt service to total expenditures	4.12%	
Net assets/expenses		
Governmental activities	4.44	
Business-type activities	1.93	
Primary government	4.22	
Unrestricted net assets/expenses		
Governmental activities	0.1053	
Business-type activities	0.4858	
Primary government	0.1394	
Unreserved fund balance/revenues	13.01%	
Governmental revenues per capita	$800.13%	
Interest coverage — revenue bonds	2.31 times	
Operating ratio — enterprise funds	50.72%	

  a. Using the financial statements provided in Illustrations 2–5 through 2–11, compute ratios for the City of Salem. Assume the population of Salem is 41,000 and the fair value of property totals $850 million.

  b. For each ratio, indicate which of the two governments has a stronger financial position.

13–6. Presented below are financial statements (except cash flows) for two not-for-profit organizations. Neither organization has any permanently restricted net assets.

Statement of Activities	ABC Not-for-Profit		XYZ Not-for-Profit	
	Unrestricted	Temporarily Restricted	Unrestricted	Temporarily Restricted
Revenues				
Program service revenue	$6,595,000		$2,250,000	
Contribution revenues	2,327,500	$750,000	3,200,000	
Grant revenue		96,000		$1,025,000
Net gains on endowment investments	17,500			
Net assets released from restriction				
Satisfaction of time restrictions	325,000	(325,000)		
Satisfaction of program restrictions	125,000	(125,000)	377,000	(377,000)
Total revenues	9,390,000	396,000	5,827,000	648,000
Expenses				
Public service expenses	116,000			
Education program expenses	5,505,000		1,659,000	
Research program expense	1,256,000		3,256,000	
Total program service expenses	6,877,000		4,915,000	
Fund-raising	456,000		256,000	
Administration	650,000		229,000	
Total supporting service expenses	1,106,000		485,000	
Total expenses	7,983,000		5,400,000	
Increase in net assets	1,407,000	396,000	427,000	648,000
Net assets January 1	4,208,000	759,000	1,037,500	320,000
Net assets December 31	$ 5,615,000	$1,155,000	$1,464,500	$968,000

STATEMENT OF NET ASSETS	ABC Not-for-profit	XYZ Not-for-profit
Current assets		
Cash	$ 105,000	$ 256,000
Short-term investments	365,000	99,000
Supplies inventories	32,000	150,000
Receivables		
Accounts (net)	79,000	82,000
Pledges (net)	45,000	
Accrued interest	15,500	6,500
Total current assets	641,500	593,500
Noncurrent assets		
Pledges receivable	365,000	
Long-term investments	2,690,000	
Land, buildings, and equipment (net)	3,275,000	1,968,000
Total noncurrent assets	6,330,000	1,968,000
Total assets	$ 6,971,500	$ 2,561,500

	ABC Not-for-profit	XYZ Not-for-profit
Current liabilities		
Accounts payable	$ 78,000	129,000
Total current liabilities	78,000	129,000
Noncurrent liabilities		
Notes payable	123,500	
Total noncurrent liabilities	123,500	
Total liabilities	201,500	129,000
Net Assets		
Unrestricted	5,615,000	1,464,500
Temporarily restricted	1,155,000	968,000
Permanently restricted	0	0
Total net assets	6,770,000	2,432,500
Total liabilities and net assets	$ 6,971,500	$ 2,561,500

    a. Calculate the following ratios:
- Program expense.
- Fund-raising efficiency.
- Working capital.

    b. For each ratio, explain which of the two organizations has the stronger ratio.

13–7. With regard to the Government Auditing Standards:

    a. Differentiate among the different types of professional engagements.

    b. Assume you are auditing a city that has a summer youth employment program. List some factors you might investigate in terms of (1) financial statement audits and (2) performance audits.

13–8. You have been assigned the task of writing the audit report for the City of X. The scope includes the basic financial statements, although the report is attached to a complete Comprehensive Annual Financial Report.

    a. Write the opinion paragraph.

    b. Differentiate among opinions that are unqualified, qualified, adverse, and disclaimed. Give examples of situations that might cause you to (1) qualify an opinion, (2) issue an adverse opinion, and (3) disclaim an opinion.

13–9. With respect to the Single Audit Act of 1984 and amendment of 1996 relating to state and local governments and not-for-profit organizations:

    a. Distinguish between major and nonmajor programs.

    b. List the criteria used to determine whether an entity is subject to the Single Audit Act.

    c. List the audit reports that should be included in a single audit report.

    d. List some of the sources of information that an auditor would need to conduct an audit of a government subject to the Single Audit Act. List both GAAP and audit sources.

13–10. A local government has five federal grants. Expenditures amounted to $2,000,000 during the year, as follows:

Type A	
HUD grant, new and never audited	$600,000
HHS grant, audited last year, no major findings	500,000
Type B	
EPA grant	400,000
Summer Youth Employment grant	450,000
Dept. of Agriculture grant	50,000

Describe how you, as an auditor, would determine major programs for audit, assuming (*a*) the local government is not a low-risk auditee, and (*b*) the local government is a low-risk auditee.

13–11. With regard to tax-exempt organizations:

a. Define a 501(c)(3) organization.

b. Define a public charity.

13–12. With regard to filing requirements for 501(c)(3) organizations:

a. List those entities that are not required to file.

b. What are the three financial statements required in Form 990?

13–13. With regard to Unrelated Business Income Tax (UBIT), answer the following questions:

a. Which four conditions will automatically exempt entities from UBIT?

b. What are some exceptions to UBIT provided by legislation?

c. How is UBIT computed? What deductions are allowed?

13–14. You and a few friends have decided to establish a not-for-profit organization in your community to help provide shelter and food to the homeless and transients. Outline the steps you would take to obtain tax-exempt status, avoid paying unrelated business income tax, and so on. Consider the creation of a related entity, a foundation, as a part of your planning.

13–15. With regard to service efforts and accomplishments reporting, define the following terms:

a. Service efforts.

b. Service accomplishments.

c. Inputs.

d. Outputs.

e. Outcomes.

f. Efficiency measures.

g. Cost-outcome measures.

13–16. Assume you are an analyst charged with the responsibility of advising investors regarding the general obligation and revenue bonds of 10 cities. You have Comprehensive Annual Financial Reports for the 10 cities, and each report has received a Certificate of Achievement for Excellence in Financial

Reporting from the Government Finance Officers Association. You have decided to investigate the following ratios:

(1) Net debt per capita.

(2) Net debt to fair value of property.

(3) Net debt to assets.

(4) Debt service to total expenditures—General and debt service funds.

(5) Net assets/expenses.

(6) Unrestricted net assets/expenses.

(7) Unreserved fund balance/revenues—General Fund.

(8) Governmental revenues per capita.

(9) Interest coverage—revenue bonds.

(10) Operating ratio—enterprise funds.

Required:

a. Indicate precisely where in the CAFR you would find data needed to compute each of the ratios. Be specific.

b. Indicate briefly the purpose of each of the ratios. What would you learn from the numbers calculated?

13–17. Indicate the information you would extract and some ratios you might calculate from the Comprehensive Annual Financial Report for each of the following major areas. Do not limit your answer to the 10 ratios listed in the text.

a. Analysis of the ability to repay revenue bonds for the Water and Sewer Fund.

b. Analysis of the ability to repay general obligation debt of a government.

c. Analysis of the ability to repay a short-term loan to a local bank.

d. Analysis of the ability to increase services next year without raising taxes.

e. Analysis of the ability to provide raises to employees next year without raising taxes.

f. Analysis of the ability to raise taxes next year.

g. Analysis to see if the budget is under control.

Continuous Problem

Available on the text's Web site (www.mhhe.com/copley10e).

Financial Reporting by the Federal Government

It's time to fundamentally change the way that we do business in Washington. To help build a new foundation for the 21st century, we need to reform our government so that it is more efficient, more transparent, and more creative.

What Washington needs is adult supervision. (Barack Obama, 44th president of the United States)

Learning Objectives

- Describe the reporting requirements of federal agencies[1] and the U.S. government.
- Understand the purpose and composition of the required financial statements of federal government units.
- Prepare journal entries for typical transactions of a federal government unit, applying budgetary and proprietary accounting practices.

*W*e the People of the United States, in Order to form a more perfect Union, establish Justice, ensure domestic Tranquility, provide for the common defense, promote the general Welfare, and secure the Blessings of Liberty to ourselves and our Posterity, do ordain and establish this Constitution for the United States of America. [Preamble to the United State Constitution.]

The federal government of the United States, as it is known today, did not come into existence on July 4th, 1776, but was created by the Constitutional Convention of 1787. The Convention's initial goal was to modify the existing *Articles of Confederation* to curtail growing divisiveness among the state governments. With George Washington presiding, the convention delegates (notably James Madison and Alexander Hamilton) took on a more ambitious agenda and created the Constitution. The Constitutional Convention concluded with a speech by Benjamin Franklin and the Constitution was sent to the state legislatures for ratification.

---

[1] The term *agency* is used throughout this chapter to represent subunits of the federal government and includes departments, commissions, services, and other distinct organizational units.

It was not clear that the Constitution would be accepted by the states. Patrick Henry, Samuel Adams, and other important patriots in the American Revolution fought against ratification. In reply, Madison, Hamilton and John Jay wrote the *Federalist Papers*, which argued for a strong central government and are used to this day to interpret the Constitution. By June 1788, nine states (the number necessary for ratification) had accepted the Constitution. The key components of the Constitution are a two-house legislature, executive branch, and judiciary with a system of interrelated checks and balances across the three branches. The Constitution also establishes the role of financial reporting by the federal government:

> *No money shall be drawn from the Treasury, but in consequence of appropriations made by law; and **a regular statement and account of the receipts and expenditures of all public money shall be published from time to time*** (Section 9).

FEDERAL GOVERNMENT ACCOUNTING STANDARDS

It took more than 200 years for the federal government to truly begin to fulfill this constitutional requirement to publish meaningful and comprehensive financial reports. The Chief Financial Officers' Act of 1990 was passed with the purpose of improving the federal government's financial management. The Act created the Office of Federal Financial Management within the **Office of Management and Budget (OMB)** to carry out financial management directives. The Act also created the position of chief financial officer within federal departments and agencies and charged those officials with issuing audited financial statements.

The Office of Management and Budget, together with the **Government Accountability Office (GAO)** and the **Department of the Treasury** are the primary organizations charged with financial management of the federal government. OMB and Treasury are within the executive branch of government whereas GAO is an agency in the legislative branch. Treasury maintains a government-wide system of accounts and prepares the federal government's consolidated financial statements. GAO assists Congress in oversight of the executive branch, establishes governmental auditing standards, and audits the financial statements of some federal agencies and the consolidated statements of the federal government.

To implement the reporting requirements of the 1990 Chief Financial Officers' Act, the Secretary of the Treasury, Director of the OMB, and Comptroller General (GAO) established the **Federal Accounting Standards Advisory Board (FASAB).** The purpose of the FASAB is to develop and issue federal accounting standards. The Board comprises ten members: two from the executive branch, two from the legislative, and six who are not employees of the federal government. The Board is considered "advisory" in that the standards must be approved by the three founding organizations (Treasury, OMB, and GAO). The standards (called *Statements of Federal Financial Accounting Standards*) are recognized as the highest level of authoritative standard in the AICPA's Code of Professional Conduct for federal government entities.

Like the FASB and GASB, the FASAB has developed a conceptual framework to guide the Board in the development of new standards. The Concept Statements are

ILLUSTRATION 14–1   Comparison FASAB and GASB Financial Statement Elements

Federal Government	State and Local Governments[2]
An *asset* is a resource that embodies economic benefits or services that the federal government controls.	*Assets* are resources with present service capacity that the government presently controls.
A *liability* is a present obligation of the federal government to provide assets or services to another entity at a determinable date, when a specified event occurs, or on demand.	*Liabilities* are present obligations to sacrifice resources that the government has little or no discretion to avoid.
Net position or its equivalent, net assets, is the arithmetic difference between the total assets and total liabilities.	*Net position* is the residual of all other elements presented in a statement of financial position.
A *revenue* is an inflow of or other increase in assets, a decrease in liabilities, or a combination of both that results in an increase in the government's net position.	An *inflow of resources* is an acquisition of net assets by the government that is applicable to the reporting period.
An *expense* is an outflow of or other decrease in assets, an increase in liabilities, or a combination of both that results in a decrease in the government's net position.	An *outflow of resources* is a consumption of net assets by the government that is applicable to the reporting period.

not authoritative but they identify user needs, the objectives of the financial reports, and definitions of the reporting entity and the elements of the financial statements. The FASAB's elements of the financial statements (presented in Illustration 14–1) are similar to those of the GASB.

FINANCIAL REPORTING BY FEDERAL AGENCIES

The annual financial report of an agency or other organization following federal government reporting standards includes the following:

- Management's discussion and analysis: This includes a discussion of the organization's mission and performance goals as well as the most recent year's financial information.
- Audit report: This will include an opinion on the financial statements, as well as reports on internal controls and compliance with laws and regulations.
- Basic financial statements and notes, including:
  - Balance Sheet
  - Statement of Net Cost
  - Statement of Changes in Net Position

[2] Statement of Federal Financial Accounting Concepts 5: *Definitions of Elements and Basic Recognition Criteria for Accrual-Basis Financial Statements,* Federal Accounting Standards Advisory Board, 2007 and Concepts Statement No. 2: *Elements of Financial Statements.* Governmental Accounting Standards Board, 2007.

- Statement of Budgetary Resources
- Statement of Custodial Activity (if applicable)
- Statement of Social Insurance (if applicable)
- Required supplemental information: this may include a statement of stewardship assets

The first five financial statements listed above are examined in the following sections. A statement of social insurance is required for federal agencies administering social insurance programs such as Social Security and Medicare. The statement projects income and benefit payments so that users of the statements can evaluate the long-term viability of the programs.

Balance Sheet

The Balance Sheet of the U.S. Securities and Exchange Commission is presented in Illustration 14–2.[3] Assets and liabilities are measured on the accrual basis and separated into intragovernmental (between federal government entities) and other. The difference between assets and liabilities is *net position* and is composed of *unexpended appropriations* and the *cumulative result of operations*. Unexpended appropriations are amounts provided by Congress that are not yet expended or committed (obligated). The cumulative result of operations is the difference between appropriations and revenues over expenses over the life of the organization.

Statement of Net Cost

The Statement of Net Cost of the U.S. Securities and Exchange Commission (SEC) is presented in Illustration 14–3. This statement displays the cost (measured on the accrual basis) of the federal agency by strategic goal. The SEC has four strategic goals. Similar to the government-wide Statement of Activities for state and local governments, program revenues are subtracted to determine the net cost of government services. Many federal agencies will have no earned revenues. In the case of the SEC, the Commission charges corporations and investment companies when they register securities for sale. Since this is a Statement of Net *Cost* and the SEC has revenues in excess of cost, the bottom line appears as a negative. Typically the bottom line will be a net cost (positive), rather than income.

Statement of Changes in Net Position

The Statement of Changes in Net Position of the U.S. Securities and Exchange Commission is presented in Illustration 14–4. This statement begins with the beginning balance in the equity account, *net position*, and identifies all financing sources used to support its operations. The statement articulates with *net position* appearing on the balance sheet. For most government agencies, the primary source of resources is appropriations resulting from congressional legislation and signed by the president. Other sources can include dedicated taxes, donations, and transfers.

---

[3] For presentation purposes, only one year of information is presented. However, two years of information are required on all statements. Additionally, some information has been condensed for presentation purposes.

ILLUSTRATION 14–2 Balance Sheet

U.S. SECURITIES AND EXCHANGE COMMISSION
Balance Sheet
As of September 30, 2008
Dollars in thousands

Assets

Intragovernmental:

Fund Balance with Treasury	$6,011,310	Most agencies do not have cash balances but deposit/ draw cash with the U.S. Treasury
Investments, Net	2,982,542	
Accounts Receivable	45	
Advances and Prepayments	3,936	
Total Intragovernmental	8,997,833	

Governmental:

Accounts Receivable, Net	135,470	
Advances and Prepayments	1,032	Assets (including noncurrent) are measured on the accrual basis.
Property and Equipment, Net	84,007	
Total Assets	$9,218,342	

Liabilities

Intragovernmental:

Accounts Payable	15,588	Intragovernmental balances are receivables or payables between federal government entities.
Employee Benefits	4,433	
Unfunded FECA and Unemployment Liability	1,340	
Custodial Liability, Net	2	
Total Intragovernmental	21,363	

Governmental:

Accounts Payable	39,122	
Accrued Payroll and Benefits	22,970	
Accrued Leave	38,829	Amounts (penalties) collected from securities law violators are deposited with Treasury and paid as restitution to the harmed investors. This represents the amount due to those investors.
Registrant Deposits	51,793	
Actuarial FECA Liability	5,604	
Liability for Disgorgement and Penalties	3,108,367	
Other Accrued Liabilities	27,005	
Total Liabilities	3,315,053	

Net Position

Unexpended Appropriations	0
Cumulative Results of Operations	5,903,289
Total Net Position	5,903,289
Total Liabilities and Net Position	$9,218,342

Statement of Budgetary Resources

The Statement of Budgetary Resources is presented in Illustration 14–5. Unlike the previous statements it follows the budgetary (not accrual) basis of accounting. Budgetary accounting practices are described later in this chapter. The statement

ILLUSTRATION 14–3 Statement of Net Cost

U.S. SECURITIES AND EXCHANGE COMMISSION Statement of Net Cost For the year ended September 30, 2008 Dollars in thousands		
COSTS BY STRATEGIC GOAL **Enforce compliance with federal** **securities laws**		Costs are measured on the accrual basis.
Total Gross Cost	$595,327	
Promote healthy capital markets through **an effective and flexible regulatory** **environment**		
Total Gross Cost	102,822	
Foster informed investment decision making		
Total Gross Cost	133,487	
Maximize the use of SEC resources		
Total Gross Cost	99,267	
Total Entity		
Total Gross Program Cost	930,903	
Less: Earned Revenue Not Attributed to Programs	956,317 ◄	These are the fees the SEC charges to register and
Net Cost (Income) from Operations	$(25,414)	sell securities.

provides information on how budgetary resources were obtained and the status (e.g., expended, obligated, etc.) of those resources at year-end. The budgetary basis of accounting is prescribed by OMB, not FASAB.

Statement of Custodial Activity

The Statement of Custodial Activity for the U.S. Securities and Exchange Commission is presented in Illustration 14–6. This statement is required only if the government agency collects nonexchange funds to be turned over to the Treasury. Because the collecting entity cannot use the funds, the activities are analogous to an agency fund of a state or local government. In addition to the SEC, the U.S. Customs and Border Protection and the Internal Revenue Service perform custodial functions and include this statement within their annual reports.

CONSOLIDATED FINANCIAL REPORT OF THE U.S. GOVERNMENT

The annual financial report of the U.S. government is prepared by the Department of the Treasury and audited by the Government Accountability Office. Similar to state and local governments, the annual financial report contains: Managements' Discussion and Analysis, Financial Statements, unaudited Supplemental and Stewardship Information, and the auditor's (i.e., GAO's) report. The GAO report contains an

ILLUSTRATION 14–4 Statement of Changes in Net Position

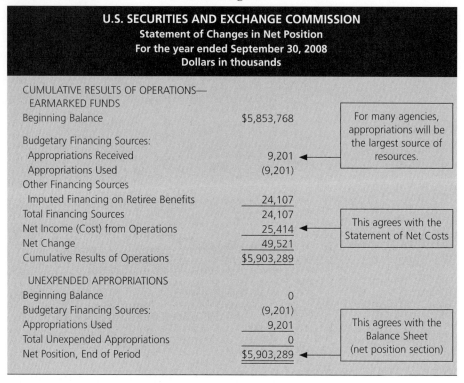

U.S. SECURITIES AND EXCHANGE COMMISSION
Statement of Changes in Net Position
For the year ended September 30, 2008
Dollars in thousands

CUMULATIVE RESULTS OF OPERATIONS—EARMARKED FUNDS		
Beginning Balance	$5,853,768	For many agencies, appropriations will be the largest source of resources.
Budgetary Financing Sources:		
Appropriations Received	9,201	
Appropriations Used	(9,201)	
Other Financing Sources		
Imputed Financing on Retiree Benefits	24,107	
Total Financing Sources	24,107	
Net Income (Cost) from Operations	25,414	This agrees with the Statement of Net Costs
Net Change	49,521	
Cumulative Results of Operations	$5,903,289	
UNEXPENDED APPROPRIATIONS		
Beginning Balance	0	
Budgetary Financing Sources:	(9,201)	
Appropriations Used	9,201	This agrees with the Balance Sheet (net position section)
Total Unexpended Appropriations	0	
Net Position, End of Period	$5,903,289	

audit opinion as well as reports on internal controls and compliance with laws and regulations. The financial statements include:

- Statement of Net Cost
- Statement of Operations and Changes in Net Position
- Reconciliation of Net Operating Cost and Unified Budget Deficit
- Statement of Changes in Cash Balance from Unified Budget and Other Activities
- Balance Sheet
- Statement of Social Insurance
- Notes to the financial statements

The report is nearly 200 pages long and is available for review on the GAO's Web site: http://www.gao.gov/financial/fy2008/08frusg.pdf.

The Statement of Net Cost, Balance Sheet, and Statement of Social Insurance have been previously described. The *Statement of Operations and Changes in Net Position* presents the results of the federal government's operations, measured on the accrual basis. The format of the statement is similar to the fund-basis statement of state and local governments. It begins with revenues, deducts costs, and adds (subtracts) intragovernmental transfers. It is then reconciled to net position on the

ILLUSTRATION 14–5   Statement of Budgetary Resources

U.S. SECURITIES AND EXCHANGE COMMISSION
Statement of Budgetary Resources
For the year ended September 30, 2008
Dollars in thousands

BUDGETARY RESOURCES

Unobligated Balance, Brought Forward, October 1	$ 90,012
Recoveries of Prior-Year Unpaid Obligations	38,384
Budget Authority:	
Spending Authority from Offsetting Collections	
Earned	
Collected	985,997
Change in Receivables from Federal Sources	167
Subtotal	986,164
Temporarily Not Available Pursuant to Public Law	(141,039)
Total Budgetary Resources	$ 973,521

> This statement is prepared using the budgetary basis of accounting.

> This section provides information on how budgetary resources became available.

STATUS OF BUDGETARY RESOURCES

Obligations Incurred:	
Direct	$ 916,512
Unobligated Balance Not Available	57,009
Total Status of Budgetary Resources	$ 973,521
Obligated Balance, Net	
Unpaid Obligations, Brought Forward, October 1	$ 254,660
Obligations Incurred Net	915,825
Gross Outlays	(881,127)
Recoveries of Prior-Year Unpaid Obligations, Actual	(38,384)
Total, Unpaid Obligated Balance, Net, End of Period	$ 250,807

> This section reflects whether the resources were obligated during the year.

NET OUTLAYS

Gross Outlays	$ 881,127
Offsetting Collections	(985,997)
Distributed Offsetting Receipts	(3,779)
Net Outlays/(Collections)	$(108,649)

Balance Sheet. The *Reconciliation of Net Operating Cost and Unified Budget Deficit* reconciles the net operating result (revenue or cost) from the Statement of Operations and Changes in Net Position with the cash-based federal budget. As such, it is similar to the reconciliation of the Statement of Activities to the governmental funds Statement of Revenues, Expenditures, and Changes in Fund Balance required by state and local governments. Finally, the *Statement of Changes in Cash Balance from Unified Budget and Other Activities* shows the relationship between the cash-based budget deficit and the change in the federal government's operating cash balance.

The federal government also publishes an annual *Citizen's Guide to the Financial Report of the U.S. Government* (http://www.gao.gov/financial/citizensguide2008.pdf).

ILLUSTRATION 14–6   Statement of Custodial Activity

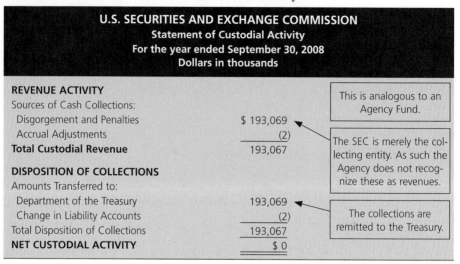

U.S. SECURITIES AND EXCHANGE COMMISSION Statement of Custodial Activity For the year ended September 30, 2008 Dollars in thousands		
REVENUE ACTIVITY		This is analogous to an Agency Fund.
Sources of Cash Collections:		
Disgorgement and Penalties	$ 193,069	
Accrual Adjustments	(2)	The SEC is merely the collecting entity. As such the Agency does not recognize these as revenues.
Total Custodial Revenue	193,067	
DISPOSITION OF COLLECTIONS		
Amounts Transferred to:		
Department of the Treasury	193,069	
Change in Liability Accounts	(2)	The collections are remitted to the Treasury.
Total Disposition of Collections	193,067	
NET CUSTODIAL ACTIVITY	$ 0	

The guide presents plain language explanations of key terms, such as annual versus accumulated deficit. It provides graphic displays of revenues by source and the cost of operating the government by function. A condensed financial report is also presented and appears in Illustration 14–7. The condensed financial statements contain a brief activity statement beginning with costs and deducting program revenues and

ILLUSTRATION 14–7   Citizen's Guide to the 2008 Financial Report of the United States Government

A SNAPSHOT OF THE GOVERNMENT'S FINANCIAL POSITION & CONDITION Billions of dollars			
	2008	**2007**	**2006**
Gross Costs	$ (3,891.6)	(3,157.3)	(3,127.7)
Earned Revenues	250.9	247.8	226.4
Net Cost	(3,640.7)	(2,909.5)	(2,901.3)
Total Taxes and Other Revenues	2,661.4	2,627.3	2,440.8
Other	(29.8)	6.7	11.0
Net Operating Cost	$ (1,009.1)	(275.5)	(449.5)
Assets	$ 1,974.7	1,581.1	1,496.5
Less: Liabilities, comprised of:			
Debt Held By the Public	(5,836.2)	(5,077.7)	(4,867.5)
Federal Employee & Veteran Benefits	(5,318.9)	(4,769.1)	(4,679.0)
Other Liabilities	(1,023.1)	(940.1)	(866.4)
Total Liabilities	(12,178.2)	(10,786.9)	(10,412.9)
Net Position (Assets Minus Liabilities)	$ (10,203.5)	(9,205.8)	(8,916.4)

then tax revenues to arrive at the current period deficit (termed *net operating cost*). Following that is a highly condensed balance sheet showing total assets, total liabilities, and the accumulated deficit (termed *net position*). In 2008, the net position is an accumulated deficit in excess of $10 trillion. The Citizen's Guide also provides a measure of the present value of projected obligations for Social Security, Medicare, and other social insurance programs. These obligations, which are not currently recognized as liabilities in the consolidated balance sheet, are estimated to be in excess of $40 trillion.

BUDGETARY AND PROPRIETARY ACCOUNTING

The accounting systems of federal agencies must serve both the external financial reporting needs mandated by the Chief Financial Officers' Act and the necessity of having internal budgetary controls over the spending of public resources. This is accomplished through the maintenance of two self-balancing sets of accounts, termed *budgetary and proprietary accounts.*

Budgetary Accounts

The purpose of **budgetary accounts** is to provide a record by which federal expenditures can be traced back to the budgetary authority granted by Congress through appropriations. The budgetary authority process is depicted in Illustration 14–8 and representative journal entries are presented in Illustration 14–9. Journal entries are recorded at each step in the budgetary authority process so that the budgetary accounts always reflect the status of those resources in the spending cycle.

The process begins with Congress passing an *appropriation*, a spending bill that is signed by the President. The Department of Treasury then issues a warrant verifying the appropriation and establishment of a line of credit for the agency that will be disbursing the funds. The federal agency records its entire appropriation when it receives the warrant from Treasury. The OMB issues an *apportionment,* which is an allocation of the total appropriation to specific time periods (frequently three month periods). The purpose of apportionment is to prevent the federal agency from spending the appropriation too rapidly and having to request a supplemental appropriation later in the year.

The federal agency then has authority to divide the funds among its offices or programs in accordance with the spending bill. These are called *allotments.* At this point, the subunits of the agency can begin to place orders for goods or services. Similar to encumbrance accounting by state and local governments, federal entities record these commitments in an account termed *obligations—undelivered orders.* When the goods or services are received, the status is changed to *expended appropriations.*

Under federal budgetary accounting, budgetary resources (appropriations) are represented by debits. Credits reflect the status of the resources within the spending process. For the example appearing in Illustration 14–9, Congress appropriated

ILLUSTRATION 14–8   Federal Government Budgetary Authority Process

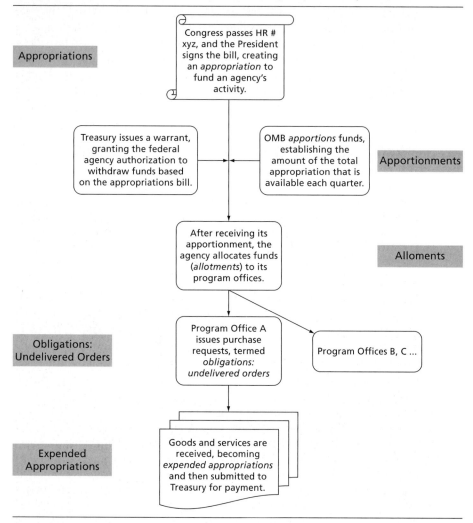

$12,000,000 for the year. The status of that appropriation at the end of the first quarter is as follows:

Amount	Status
$ 9,000,000	**Unapportioned authority:** this amount will be apportioned to the agency by OMB over the remaining 3 quarters of the year.
500,000	**Apportionments:** current quarter resources that have not yet been allotted by the head of the agency to specific subunits of the agency.
600,000	**Allotments:** resources currently available to agency offices, but have not yet been committed by placing orders for goods or services.

(Continued)

ILLUSTRATION 14–9   Comparative Journal Entries

TYPICAL JOURNAL ENTRIES: FEDERAL AGENCY
COMPARISON OF BUDGETARY AND PROPRIETARY ACCOUNTING

Event Description	Budgetary Accounting		Proprietary Accounting	
	Debits	Credits	Debits	Credits
Appropriations: Treasury notifies the agency that Congress passed legislation (signed by the President) granting budgetary authority to fund its activities.	Appropriations realized 12,000,000 Unapportioned authority	12,000,000	Fund balance with Treasury 12,000,000 Unexpended appropriations	12,000,000
Apportionment: OMB apportions ¼ of the appropriated amount which may now be expended for first quarter activities.	Unapportioned Authority 3,000,000 Apportionments	3,000,000	No journal entry required	
Allotment: The head of the agency allots a portion of the apportionment to the heads of subunits within the agency. The subunits may now expend resources.	Apportionments 2,500,000 Allotments	2,500,000	No journal entry required	
Obligations (commitments): A unit of the agency places orders for goods and services related to its activities.	Allotments 1,900,000 Obligations— undelivered orders	1,900,000	No journal entry required	
Expenditure: Some of the items ordered above (equipment of $100,000 and services of $800,000) are received and approved for payment.	Obligations —undelivered orders 900,000 Expended Appropriations	900,000	Equipment 100,000 Operating (program) expense 800,000 Accounts payable Accounts payable 900,000 Fund balance with Treasury	900,000 900,000

431

Amount	Status
1,000,000	**Obligations for undelivered orders:** commitments for outstanding purchase orders for goods and services that have not yet been received.
900,000	**Expended appropriations:** amounts that have been expended on goods and services received.
$12,000,000	Total appropriation

Proprietary Accounts

Proprietary accounts are those accounts that comprise the accrual basis financial statements prepared by the federal governments and its agencies. Proprietary accounts measure assets, liabilities, revenues, and expenses (including depreciation) in much the same manner as accrual basis accounts of state and local governments. The entry to record appropriations is notable because it involves the use of account titles that are unique to the federal government. The account, *Unexpended appropriations,* is credited at the time of an appropriation. This represents a source of funds to the federal agency and is similar to a *transfer in* account in a state or local government fund. Federal agencies do not typically maintain cash balances. Instead, the ability to draw cash from the Treasury is recognized as an asset at the time of an appropriation with the account *Fund Balance with Treasury.* Payments made by Treasury on behalf of the agency are reflected with a credit to this account. Illustrative transactions, journal entries, and financial statements are presented in the appendix to this chapter.

SUMMARY OF FEDERAL GOVERNMENT REPORTING

Section 9 of the U.S. Constitution requires that the federal government publish financial reports. The Federal Accounting Standards Advisory Board (FASAB) establishes the accounting and reporting standards for the U.S government overall and for federal agencies and departments. The AICPA's Code of Professional Conduct recognizes FASAB standards as the highest level of authoritative standard for federal government agencies. Like the FASB and GASB, the FASAB issues concepts statements to guide the Board in the development of new standards.

Federal agency financial reports contain a management's discussion and analysis, an audit report, financial statements and notes, and required supplemental and stewardship information. The primary accrual basis financial statements include a Balance Sheet, Statement of Net Cost, and Statement of Changes in Net Position. The Statement of Budgetary Resources is prepared using the budgetary basis and provides information on the status of budgetary resources. In some cases, a Statement of Custodial Activity and Statement of Social Insurance can also be required. Because federal entities have both budgetary and financial reporting requirements, a dual-track accounting system is employed using budgetary and proprietary accounts.

Now that you have finished reading Chapter 14, complete the multiple choice questions provided on the text's Web site (www.mhhe.com/copley10e) to test your comprehension of the chapter.

APPENDIX: ILLUSTRATIVE EXAMPLE

Assume the National Subarctic Ornithology Agency is a federal agency dedicated to the study and protection of penguins. The agency began the fiscal year with the following balances:

NATIONAL SUBARCTIC ORNITHOLOGY AGENCY
TRIAL BALANCE
October 1, 2011

	Debits	Credits
Fund Balance with Treasury	$ 150,000	
Supplies	35,000	
Equipment	1,200,000	
Accumulated Depreciation		$ 380,000
Accounts Payable		26,000
Cumulative Results of Operations		979,000
	$1,385,000	$1,385,000

Congress passed a spending bill providing $8,000,000 to fund the agency's operations for the year. Entries are required in both the budgetary and proprietary accounts.

	Debits	Credits
1a. *Budgetary Accounts*		
Appropriations Realized...........................	8,000,000	
Unapportioned Authority.........................		8,000,000
1b. *Proprietary Accounts*		
Fund Balance with Treasury.......................	8,000,000	
Unexpended Appropriations......................		8,000,000

The Office of Management and Budget approves quarterly apportionments. Entries are made each quarter.

	Debits	Credits
2. *Budgetary Accounts*		
1st quarter:		
Unapportioned Authority...........................	2,000,000	
Apportionments		2,000,000
Total for other quarters:		
Unapportioned Authority...........................	6,000,000	
Apportionments		6,000,000

During the year the agency allotted the entire apportionment to its two departments.

	Debits	Credits
3. *Budgetary Accounts*		
Apportionments	8,000,000	
Allotments—(Department A).........................		3,000,000
Allotments—(Department B).........................		5,000,000

During the year the agency approved purchase orders and contracts in the following amounts:

Purpose	Total	Dept. A	Dept. B
Salaries and benefits	$1,200,000	$ 500,000	$ 700,000
Supplies	800,000	500,000	300,000
Contracted services	1,500,000	1,500,000	——
Grants	3,000,000	——	3,000,000
Equipment	1,500,000	500,000	1,000,000
Total	$8,000,000	$3,000,000	$5,000,000

4. *Budgetary Accounts*		
Allotments—(Department A).........................	3,000,000	
Allotments—(Department B).........................	5,000,000	
Obligations—Undelivered Orders—(Department A).......		3,000,000
Obligations—Undelivered Orders—(Department B).......		5,000,000

Assume all items were received. The beginning accounts payable of $26,000 and $7,890,000 of the current year obligations were processed and paid before year-end.

5. *Budgetary Accounts*		
Obligations—Undelivered Orders—(Department A).........	3,000,000	
Obligations—Undelivered Orders—(Department B).........	5,000,000	
Expended Appropriations—(Department A)		3,000,000
Expended Appropriations—(Department B)		5,000,000
Proprietary Accounts		
Supplies	800,000	
Equipment	1,500,000	
Operating Expenses—(Department A)...................	2,000,000	
Operating Expenses—(Department B)...................	3,700,000	
Accounts Payable................................		8,000,000
Accounts Payable................................	7,916,000	
Fund Balance with Treasury........................		7,916,000

Ending supplies totaled $25,000 (a decrease of $10,000 from the balance at the beginning of the year). Assume the beginning and ending supplies inventories all relate to Department A. The entry to record supplies expense is:

	Debits	Credits
6. *Proprietary Accounts*		
Operating Expenses—(Department A)...................	510,000	
Operating Expenses—(Department B)...................	300,000	
Supplies		810,000

The entry to record depreciation on the agency's fixed assets is:

	Debits	Credits
7. *Proprietary Accounts*		
Operating Expenses—(Department A)...................	70,000	
Operating Expenses—(Department B)...................	200,000	
Accumulated Depreciation...........................		270,000

In this example, the agency expended its full appropriation. Typically budgetary authority that is not obligated by year-end would be returned to Treasury. The entry to record this would credit the budgetary account *Appropriations Withdrawn*. The corresponding proprietary entry would reverse entry (1b) to the extent of the unused appropriation.

The Statement of Net Costs is presented in Illustration 14–10. Assume the agency has two strategic goals, corresponding to the two departments. This statement is prepared on the accrual basis using expense information appearing in the proprietary journal entries 5, 6, and 7.

The Statement of Changes in Net Position is also prepared on the accrual basis and reconciles the beginning balance of net position to the end of year balance. This statement appears in Illustration 14–11. Note that *Net Cost from Operations* agrees

ILLUSTRATION 14–10 Statement of Net Costs

NATIONAL SUBARCTIC ORNITHOLOGY AGENCY Statement of Net Cost For the Year Ended September 30, 2012	
Costs by Strategic Goal	
Penguin Habitat and Protection	$ 2,580,000
Penguin Research	4,200,000
Total Gross Costs	6,780,000
Less Earned Revenues	—
Net Cost from Operations	$ 6,780,000

ILLUSTRATION 14–11 Statement of Changes in Net Position

NATIONAL SUBARCTIC ORNITHOLOGY AGENCY Statement of Changes in Net Position For the Year Ended September 30, 2012		
	Cumulative Results of Operations	Unexpended Appropriations
Beginning Balance	$ 979,000	——
Appropriations Received		$ 8,000,000
Appropriations Used	8,000,000	(8,000,000)
Other Financing Sources	——	——
Total Financing Sources	8,979,000	——
Net Cost of Operations	6,780,000	——
Ending Balance	$2,199,000	——

ILLUSTRATION 14–12 Balance Sheet

NATIONAL SUBARCTIC ORNITHOLOGY AGENCY Balance Sheet As of September 30, 2012	
Assets	
Intragovernmental:	
Fund Balance with Treasury	$ 234,000
Governmental:	
Supplies	25,000
Equipment (Net of Accumulated Depreciation)	2,050,000
Total Assets	$ 2,309,000
Liabilities	
Governmental:	
Accounts Payable	110,000
Net Position	
Unexpended Appropriations	0
Cumulative Results of Operations	2,199,000
Total Liabilities and Net Position	$ 2,309,000

with the bottom line of the Statement of Net Costs. Illustration 14–11 uses a columnar format, in contrast to that used by the SEC in Illustration 14–4.

The agency's Balance Sheet appears in Illustration 14–12. Note that the balances appearing under *Net Position* agree with the bottom line of the Statement of Changes in Net Position. Assets and liabilities are displayed within the categories of *Intragovernmental* (between government agencies) or *Governmental*.

Now that you have finished reading Chapter 14, complete the multiple choice questions provided on the text's Web site (www.mhhe.com/copley10e) to test your comprehension of the chapter.

Questions and Exercises

14–1. What are the required financial statements of a federal agency?

14–2. What are the required financial statements of the U.S. government?

14–3. What bodies are responsible for establishing accounting standards for the federal government and its agencies?

14–4. The 2008 financial statements of the U.S. Government are available at: http://www.gao.gov/financial/fy2008/08frusg.pdf. Use these to answer the following questions:

　a. Statement of Net Costs

　　1. What are the three largest government units based on net cost?

　　2. Which government department operates at the largest net profit?

　b. Statement of Operations and Changes in Net Position

　　3. What are the two largest sources of revenue to the federal government?

　　4. Which item on this statement articulates (agrees) with the Statement of Net Costs?

　c. Balance Sheet

　　5. What are the two largest liabilities reported on a balance sheet?

　　6. Which item on this statement articulates with the Statement of Operations and Changes in Net Position?

14–5. The 2008 financial statements of the Internal Revenue Service are available at: http://www.gao.gov/new.items/d09119.pdf. Use these to answer the following questions:

　a. Statement of Net Costs

　　1. What are the IRS's two largest programs based on net cost?

　b. Statement of Changes in Net Position

　　2. What is the largest source of financing for the activities of the IRS?

　c. Statement of Custodial Activity

　　3. What activity is reported in this statement? (i.e., what is the IRS doing?)

14–6. Assume a federal agency has the following events:

　1. Receives a warrant from the Treasury notifying the agency of appropriations of $2,400,000.

　2. OMB apportions one-fourth of the appropriation for the first quarter of the year.

　3. The director of the agency allots $590,000 to program units.

　4. Program units place orders of $550,000.

　5. Supplies ($100,000) and services ($320,000) are received during the first quarter. Supplies of $80,000 were used in the quarter.

Required:

Prepare any necessary journal entries to reflect the events described above. Identify whether the entry is a budgetary or proprietary type.

14–7. Using the information from exercise 14–6, prepare a schedule showing the status of the appropriation at the end of the first quarter.

14–8. The Mosquito Abatement Commission is a newly organized federal agency with three primary programs: Coordination of state government abatement functions, conduct research on mosquito abatement, and promote abatement through public education. The following information is available at the end of the first quarter (December 31, 2012):

	Government Coordination	Research	Public Education	Total
Apportionments from OMB				$5,000,000
Allotments—first quarter	$2,500,000	$1,500,000	$1,000,000	5,000,000
Salaries paid	1,400,000	600,000	720,000	2,720,000
Accrued salaries payable	25,000	15,000	18,000	58,000
Supplies ordered and received	156,000	357,000	136,000	649,000
Supplies used	107,000	355,000	120,000	582,000
Depreciation	35,000	27,000	8,000	70,000
Equipment purchases	850,000	500,000	37,000	1,387,000
Program Revenue: Charges for services			100,000	100,000

Required:

Prepare a Statement of Net Costs for the quarter ended December 31.

14–9. Assume the Federal Interstate Commission began the fiscal year with the following account balances:

FEDERAL INTERSTATE COMMISSION
TRIAL BALANCE
October 1, 2012

	Debits	Credits
Fund Balance with Treasury	$ 750,000	
Supplies	135,000	
Equipment	1,300,000	
Accumulated Depreciation		$ 480,000
Accounts Payable		126,000
Wages Payable		79,000
Cumulative Results of Operations		1,500,000
	$2,185,000	$2,185,000

1. Congress passed a spending bill providing $12,000,000 to fund the agency's operations for the year.

2. During the first quarter the commission processed the following items for payment (all items were paid by Treasury in the first quarter).

Beginning balances

Accounts payable	$ 126,000
Wages payable	79,000
Salaries and benefits	500,000
Supplies	500,000
Contracted services	1,000,000
Grants	1,000,000
Equipment	500,000
Total	$3,705,000

3. Unpaid wages at the end of the quarter totaled $25,000.
4. In addition to the items paid in item 2, the commission received supplies of $12,000 and contracted services of $70,000 that are to be processed for payment in January.
5. Unused supplies on hand totaled $209,000 at December 31.
6. Depreciation for the quarter is $60,000.

Required:

a. Prepare journal entries in the proprietary accounts for the events described above.
b. Prepare a Statement of Changes in Net Position for the quarter ended December 31. (Assume the amount of appropriations used is $3,607,000 and use the format appearing in Illustration 14–11.)
c. Prepare a Balance Sheet as of December 31.

Governmental and Not-for-Profit Accounting Terminology

A

accounting entity Where an entity is established for the purpose of accounting for a certain activity or activities. See *fiscal entity.*

accrual basis Basis of accounting under which revenues are recorded when earned and expenditures (or expenses) are recorded as soon as they result in liabilities for benefits received, notwithstanding that the receipt of cash or the payment of cash may take place, in whole or in part, in another accounting period.

acquisition method A method of accounting for mergers among not-for-profit organizations in which the acquiring entity records the acquired assets and liabilities at their fair values, not at the acquired entity's book values.

activity Specific and distinguishable line of work performed by one or more organizational components of a governmental unit for the purpose of accomplishing a function for which the governmental unit is responsible. For example, "Food Inspection" is an activity performed in the discharge of the "Health" function. See also *Function.*

actuarial basis Basis used in computing the amount of contributions to be made periodically to a fund so that the total contributions plus the compounded earnings thereon will equal the required payments to be made out of the fund. The factors taken into account in arriving at the amount of these contributions include the length of time over which each contribution is to be held and the rate of return compounded on such a contribution over its life. Commonly used to compute annual required contributions (q.v.) to pension and other postemployment benefit plans.[1]

additions GASB term for fiduciary fund financial reporting, replacing the term *revenues.* Additions are reported on the accrual basis.

ad valorem In proportion to value. Basis for levy of taxes on property.

advance refunding A bond refunding (q.v.) in which the proceeds are placed in an escrow account pending the call date or the maturity date of the existing debt. In this case, the debt is said to be *defeased* (q.v.) for accounting purposes.

advances, interfund Long-term loans between funds. A long-term loan to another fund would be represented in the account Advances to Other Funds. A long-term loan from another fund would be represented in the account Advances from Other Funds. Should be contrasted with Due to and Due from accounts, which represent short-term interfund loans.

adverse opinion Audit report in which the auditor states that the financial report "does not present fairly" due to major departures from generally accepted accounting principles (q.v.).

agency fund Fiduciary fund consisting of resources received and held by the governmental agent for others; for example, taxes collected and held by a municipality for a school district.

---

[1] The letters *q.v.* signify *which see.*

agent multiple-employer defined benefit pension plan   Statewide pension plan in which separate account balances are maintained for each participating employer; expected to fund any deficits. Contrast with cost-sharing multiple-employer defined benefit pension plan.

allotment   Portion of an apportionment directed to subunits of a federal agency that provides authority to expend funds.

American Institute of Certified Public Accountants (AICPA)   Organization of Certified Public Accountants that provides auditing guidance, including the GAAP Hierarchy (q.v.) and accounting and auditing guidance, in the case of *Audit and Accounting Guides,* when approved by the FASB (q.v.) and/or the GASB (q.v.).

annual required contributions (ARC)   Term used by GASB to determine the amount required by a retirement fund (including other postemployment benefit plans) to be contributed, including normal cost and funding of past service cost. Used in the Schedule of Employer Contributions (q.v.).

annuity   Series of equal money payments made at equal intervals during a designated period of time. In governmental accounting, the most frequent annuities are accumulations of debt service funds for term bonds and payments to retired employees or their beneficiaries under public employee retirement systems.

apportionment   Portion of a federal appropriation allotted to a federal agency. Typically this is done quarterly.

appropriation   Authorization granted by a legislative body to incur liabilities for purposes specified in the appropriation act (q.v.).

appropriations, expenditures, and encumbrances ledger   Subsidiary ledger used by governmental funds in which a budget is recorded to track the appropriations, expenditures, and encumbrances that apply to the subsidiary account. Using this ledger, a department head, for example, could determine the unencumbered balance in the department.

ARC   The actuarially computed *annual required contribution* by an entity to pension or other postemployment benefit plans.

assessed valuation   Valuation set on real estate or other property by a government as a basis of levying taxes. A state government may provide that the local governments within its jurisdiction assess property at 100 percent, 33$\frac{1}{3}$ percent, or other percentages of market value.

assessment   (1) Process of making the official valuation of property for purposes of taxation. (2) Valuation placed on property as a result of this process.

asset impairment   An unexpected decline in the usable capacity of a capital asset. An asset is deemed to be impaired if the decline is not part of the normal life cycle of an asset and the amount of the decline in service utility is large.

assets whose use is limited   Account title used by health care organizations to indicate those assets that are unrestricted but limited by board action, bond resolutions, or the like.

assigned fund balance   A classification of fund balance reported in governmental-type funds to indicate net resources of the fund that the government intends for a specific purpose. Assigned resources differ from committed in that constraints imposed on assigned resources are more easily modified or removed. For governmental funds other than the General Fund, this is the category for all (positive) residual fund balances.

attestation agreements   Under Government Auditing Standards (q.v.), concerns examining, reviewing, or performing agreed upon procedures on a subject matter or an assertation about a subject matter and reporting on the results.

audit   Examination of documents, records, reports, systems of internal control, accounting and financial procedures, and other evidence and the issuance of a report relating to the examination.

auditor's report   Report included with financial statements that expresses an opinion of the fairness of the material presented.

authority   Governmental unit or public agency created to perform a single function or a restricted group of related activities. Usually such units are financed from service charges, fees, and tolls, but in some instances they also have taxing powers.

auxiliary enterprises   Activities of a college or university that furnishes services to students, faculty, or staff on a user-charge basis. Charge is directly related to, but not necessarily equal to, the cost of the service. Examples are college unions, residence halls, stores, faculty clubs, and intercollegiate athletics.

available   One condition that must be met before a revenue can be recognized under modified accrual accounting. The amount must be available in time to pay expenditures related to the current period.

B

balance sheet Format where assets equal liabilities plus net assets (fund balance). Required governmental funds basic statement; may be used as government-wide and proprietary fund statements in lieu of Statement of Net Assets.

basic financial statements The primary financial statements required by the GASB in order for state and local governments to meet GAAP. The nature of the government (general-purpose, special-purpose) and of the governmental activities (governmental-type, business-type, and fiduciary-type) determine which statements are basic.

basis of accounting Rule (or rules) used to determine the point in time when assets, liabilities, revenues, and expenses (expenditures) should be measured and recorded as such in the accounts of an entity. An organization might use the cash, modified accrual, or accrual basis of accounting.

blending, blended presentation One method of reporting the financial data of a component unit in a manner similar to that in which the financial data of the primary government are presented. Under this method, the component unit data are combined with the appropriate fund types of the primary government and reported in the same columns as the data from the primary government. See *discrete presentation.*

bonded debt That portion of indebtedness represented by outstanding bonds.

bonds, authorized and unissued Bonds that have been legally authorized but not issued and that can be issued and sold without further authorization. *Note:* This term must not be confused with the term *legal debt margin,* which represents the difference between the legal debt limit (q.v.) of a governmental unit and the debt outstanding against it.

budget Plan of financial operation embodying an estimate of proposed expenditures for a given period and the proposed means of financing them. Used without any modifier, usually indicates a financial plan for a single fiscal year.

budgetary accounts (federal) Accounts that provide a record by which federal expenditures can be traced back to the budgetary authority granted by Congress through appropriations. They include appropriations, apportionments, allotments, and obligations.

budgetary accounts (state and local) Accounts that reflect budgetary operations and conditions, such as Estimated Revenues, Appropriations, and Encumbrances, as distinguished from proprietary accounts (q.v.). Other examples include Estimated Other Financing Sources, Estimated Other Financing Uses, Budgetary Fund Balance, and Budgetary Fund Balance Reserved for Encumbrances. As distinguished from actual revenues, expenditures, etc.

budgetary comparison schedule Schedule, part of RSI (q.v.) where actual revenues and expenditures are compared with the original and revised budget. Required for General Fund and major special revenue funds for which an annual budget is legally adopted. A basic statement may be prepared in lieu of this schedule.

budgetary fund balance Budgetary account for state and local governmental funds that reflects the difference between estimated revenues and estimated other financing sources compared with appropriations and estimated other financing uses. Closed at the end of the year.

budgetary fund balance reserved for encumbrances Budgetary account for state and local governmental funds that reflects the amount offsetting Encumbrances (q.v.), or purchase orders or contracts issued during the current year.

business-type activities Business-type activities are reported separately in the government-wide statements and include activities normally accounted for in enterprise funds.

C

CAFR See *Comprehensive Annual Financial Report.*

capital and related financing activities Cash flow statement category required by GASB. Includes proceeds from bond issues, payment of debt, acquisition of fixed assets, and payment of interest on capital-related debt.

capital assets Term used by GASB to include land, improvements to land, easements, buildings, building improvements, vehicles, machinery, equipment, works of art and historical treasures, infrastructure, and all other tangible or intangible assets that are used in operations and that have initial useful lives extending beyond a single reporting period.

capital lease Lease that substantively transfers the benefits and risks of ownership of property to the lessee. Any lease that meets certain criteria specified in applicable accounting and reporting standards. See also *operating lease.*

capital outlays   Expenditures that result in the acquisition of or addition to fixed assets. One of the Character classifications, the others being Current and Debt Service.

capital projects fund   Fund created to account for financial resources restricted, committed, or assigned for the construction or acquisition of designated fixed assets by a governmental unit except those financed by proprietary or fiduciary funds.

carryover method   A method of accounting for mergers among not-for-profit organizations in which the two merging organizations' asset and liability book balances are "carried over" to the new reporting entity.

cash basis   Basis of accounting under which revenues are recorded when received in cash and expenditures are recorded when cash is disbursed.

cash equivalent   Short-term, highly liquid investments that are both readily convertible into known amounts of cash and so near their maturity (with original maturities of three months or less) that they present insignificant risk of changes in value due to changes in interest rates.

character classification   Grouping of expenditures on the basis of the fiscal periods they are presumed to benefit. The three groupings are (1) current expenditures, presumed to benefit the current fiscal period; (2) debt service, presumed to benefit prior fiscal periods primarily but also present and future periods; and (3) capital outlay, presumed to benefit the current and future fiscal periods.

charitable gift annuity   Split interest agreement that exists when no formal trust agreement is signed but that otherwise is similar to a charitable remainder trust (q.v.) in which a specified amount or percentage of the fair value of assets is paid to a beneficiary during the term of the agreement; at the end of the agreement, the trust assets go to the not-for-profit organization.

charitable lead trust   Split interest (q.v.) agreement in which an organization receives a fixed amount (charitable lead annuity trust) or a percentage of the fair value of the trust (charitable lead unitrust) for a certain term. At the end of the term, the remainder of trust assets is paid to the donor or other beneficiary.

charitable remainder trust   Split interest (q.v.) agreement in which a fixed dollar amount (charitable remainder annuity trust) or a specified percentage of the trust's fair market value (charitable remainder unitrust) is paid to a beneficiary. At the end of the term of the trust, the trust principal is paid to a not-for-profit organization.

codification   A listing of GASB or FASB pronouncements by topic. In contrast to a chronological listing in the *GASB (FASB) Original Pronouncements.*

cognizant agency   Under Single Audit Act and amendments, an agency that deals with the auditee, as representative of all federal agencies. Is assigned by the U.S. Office of Management and Budget (q.v.) for auditees with more than $50 million in federal awards.

collection   Under both FASB and GASB standards, collections are works of art, historical treasures, etc., that are (1) held for public exhibition, education, or research in furtherance of public service, other than financial gain; (2) protected, kept unencumbered, cared for and preserved; and (3) subject to an organizational policy that requires the proceeds from sales of collection items to be used to acquire other items for collections. Collections may or may not be capitalized and depreciated.

combining financial statements   CAFR section where nonmajor funds are presented. The total column of the nonmajor funds in the combining statements is equal to the nonmajor funds column in the basic financial statements.

committed fund balance   A classification of fund balance reported in governmental-type funds to indicate net resources of the fund that the governing body has specified for particular use. To be classified as committed, the resources should have been designated through ordinance or resolution by the government's highest level of authority.

compliance audit   Audit designed to provide reasonable assurance that a governmental entity has complied with applicable laws and regulations. Required for every audit performed in conformity with *Government Auditing Standards.*

compliance supplement   Supplement to OMB Circular A–133 (q.v.) that provides specific guidance to use when conducting audits of certain programs.

component unit   Separate governmental unit, agency, or nonprofit corporation that, pursuant to the criteria in the GASB *Codification*, Section 2100, is combined with other component units and the primary government to constitute the reporting entity (q.v.).

Comprehensive Annual Financial Report (CAFR)   A governmental unit's official annual report prepared and published as a matter of public record. In addition to the basic financial statements (q.v.) and required supplementary information, the CAFR should contain introductory material, schedules to demonstrate compliance, and statistical tables specified in the GASB *Codification*.

Comptroller General of the United States Head of the U.S. Government Accountability Office. One of the Principals that reviews the recommendations of the Federal Accounting Standards Advisory Board (FASAB) (q.v.).

concepts statements Documents issued by the GASB (q.v.), FASB (q.v.), and FASAB (q.v.) to provide guidance to those boards and a conceptual framework that can be used to establish future standards.

condition Under both FASB and GASB, a condition is an event that must take place in order for a donation or grant to be recognized, such as a requirement for a matching pledge. Neither FASB nor GASB permits a pledge containing a condition to be recorded as a revenue.

construction work in progress Cost of construction work that has been started but not yet completed. Fixed asset account.

consumption method Refers to method used to recognize expenditures for govern-mental funds (q.v.) in which an expenditure (q.v.) is recognized when inventory is consu-med. Similar to the method of expense recog-nition used by commercial organizations.

contingencies Term used by both GASB and FASB. Something must happen (for example a matching requirement) before a revenue (expense) can be recognized. For GASB, an eligibility requirement.

contributions Amounts given to an individual or to an organization for which the donor receives no direct private benefits. Contributions may be in the form of pledges, cash, securities, materials, services, or fixed assets.

control account Account in the general ledger in which are recorded the aggregate of debit and credit postings to a number of identical or related accounts called *subsidiary accounts* (q.v.). For example, Expenditures is a control account supported by the aggregate of individual balances in individual departmental expenditure accounts.

cost-sharing multiple-employer defined benefit pension plan Statewide pension plan in which separate account balances are not maintained for each participating employer. Contrast with *agent multiple-employer defined benefit pension plan*.

current Term that, applied to budgeting and accounting, designates the operations of the present fiscal period as opposed to past or future periods. One of the Character classifications of expenditures.

current financial resources measurement focus Measurement focus used for governmental funds by GASB that measures current financial resources, not fixed assets and long-term debt. Contrast with *economic resources measurement focus* (q.v.).

current refunding A bond refunding (q.v.) in which new debt is issued, and the proceeds are used to call in the existing debt. Contrast with *advance refunding* (q.v.).

D

debt limit Maximum amount of gross or net debt that is legally permitted.

debt margin Difference between the amount of the debt limit (q.v.) and the net amount of outstanding indebtedness subject to the limitation.

debt service fund Fund established to report financial resources that are restricted, committed, or assigned for the payment of interest and principal on tax-supported long-term debt, including that payable from special assessments in which the government assumes some level of liability.

deductions GASB term for fiduciary fund financial reporting, replacing the term *expenses*. Deductions are reported on the accrual basis.

defeased In an advanced refunding (q.v.) where proceeds are placed in an escrow account pending the call date or maturity date of the existing debt, the old debt is considered not to exist and to be replaced by the existing debt.

deferred revenues or deferred credits In governmental or nonprofit accounting, items that may not be recognized as revenues of the period in which received and the related asset (cash or receivable) is first recognized.

deferred serial bonds Serial bonds (q.v.) in which the first installment does not fall due for two or more years from the date of issue.

deficit (1) Excess of liabilities and reserved equity of a fund over its assets. (2) Excess of expenditures and encumbrances over revenues during an accounting period; or, in the case of Enterprise and Internal Service Funds, excess of expense over revenue during an accounting period.

defined benefit retirement plans   Retirement plans in which the benefit is defined, normally as a percentage multiplied by average or highest salaries multiplied by the number of years worked.

defined contribution retirement plans   Retirement plans in which the amount to be paid at retirement is based on employee and employer contributions and interest income.

delinquent taxes   Taxes remaining unpaid on and after the date on which a penalty for nonpayment is attached. Even though the penalty may be subsequently waived and a portion of the taxes may be abated or canceled, the unpaid balances continue to the delinquent taxes until abated, canceled, paid, or converted into tax liens.

derived tax revenues   One of the four classes of nonexchange transactions established by GASB. Examples are sales taxes and income taxes.

designated   (1) In nonprofit accounting, assets, or equity set aside by action of the governing board, as distinguished from assets or equity set aside in conformity with requirements of donors, grantors, or creditors, which are properly referred to as *restricted.* (2) In governmental accounting, equity that is unreserved but set aside by the governing board, as opposed to equity that is committed or otherwise tied up beyond the control of the governing board, which is *reserved.*

direct debt   Debt that a governmental unit has incurred in its own name or assumed through the annexation of territory or consolidation with another governmental unit. See also *overlapping debt.*

direct method   Method for cash flow statements in which operating cash flows are presented "directly" such as receipts from customers, payments to suppliers and employees, etc. Contrast with *indirect method* (q.v.). GASB requires the direct method, whereas FASB permits either the direct or indirect method.

disclaimer of opinion   Audit report in which the auditor does not provide an opinion due to a severe scope limitation or for other reasons.

discrete presentation   Method of reporting financial data of component units (q.v.) in a column or columns separate from the financial data of the primary government (q.v.).

donated services   Services of volunteer workers who are unpaid or who are paid less than the market value of their services. In certain circumstances, donated services are recognized as revenues of nonprofit organizations.

E

economic resources measurement focus   Term used by GASB to indicate measurement focus for government-wide, proprietary fund, and fiduciary fund statements. The economic resources measurement focus measures all economic resources, including fixed assets and long-term debt. Contrast with *current financial resources measurement focus* (q.v.).

eligibility requirements   Term used by GASB, in *Statement 33,* that describes certain conditions or events that must be met before a nonexchange revenue can be recognized. The four eligibility requirements are (1) required characteristics of recipients, (2) time requirements, (3) reimbursements, and (4) contingencies.

encumbrances   The estimated amount of purchase orders, contracts, or salary commitments chargeable to an appropriation.

endowments   Exist when a donor contributes an amount, never to be expended by donor restriction. The income from endowments may or may not be *restricted* (q.v.). See also *term endowment.*

enterprise fund   Fund used in state and local government accounting. Established to finance and account for the acquisition, operation, and maintenance of governmental facilities and services that are entirely or predominantly self-supporting by user charges; or for which the governing body of the governmental unit has decided periodic determination of revenues earned, expenses incurred, and/or net income is appropriate. Government-owned utilities and hospitals are ordinarily accounted for by enterprise funds.

escheat property   Private property that reverts to government ownership upon the death of the owner if there are no legal claimants or heirs.

estimated other financing sources   Amounts of financial resources estimated to be received or accrued during a period by a governmental or similar type fund from interfund transfers or from the proceeds of noncurrent debt issuances. Budgetary account.

estimated other financing uses   Amounts of financial resources estimated to be disbursed or accrued during a period by a governmental or similar type fund for transfer to other funds. Budgetary account.

estimated revenues   Budgetary account providing an estimate of the revenues that will be recognized during an accounting period by a governmental fund, such as the General Fund.

estimated uncollectible taxes (credit) Provision out of tax revenues for that portion of taxes receivable that it is estimated will never be collected. Amount is shown on the balance sheet as a deduction from the Taxes Receivable account in order to arrive at the net taxes receivable.

exemption Statutory reduction in the assessed valuation of taxable property accorded to certain taxpayers. Typical examples are senior citizens and war veterans.

exchange transactions A transaction in which each party receives and gives up essentially equal values. FASB and GASB require that exchange transactions be recognized when the exchange takes place. See *nonexchange transactions.*

exchange-like transactions Where the parties to an exchange may not be independent of each other (such as between funds). Recognized in same manner as *exchange transactions* (q.v.).

expendable Resources, where focus is on the receipt and expenditure of resources; for example, modified accrual accounting. See *nonexpendable.*

expended Term describing outflow of resources or reduction of liabilities associated with receipt of goods or services. Especially used in budgetary accounting, e.g., when an appropriation (q.v.) is expended.

expenditures Recorded when liabilities are incurred pursuant to authority given in an appropriation (q.v.). Designates the cost of goods delivered or services rendered, whether paid or unpaid, including current items, provision for interest and debt retirement, and capital outlays. Used for governmental funds of governmental units.

F

face value As applied to securities, the amount of liability stated in the security document. Sometimes called *par value.*

fair value Amount at which an investment could be exchanged in a current transaction, other than a forced or liquidation sale, between willing parties. Certain investments are required by the FASB and GASB to be reported at fair value.

Federal Accounting Standards Advisory Board (FASAB) Standards-setting body that promulgates federal government accoun-ting and financial reporting standards.

fiduciary activities Fiduciary activities are not included in the government-wide statements but are included, as fiduciary funds, in the fund financial statements.

fiduciary funds Any fund held by a governmental unit in a fiduciary capacity, ordinarily as agent or trustee. Also called *trust and agency funds.* Four categories exist: agency funds, pension trust funds, investment trust funds, and private-purpose trust funds.

Financial Accounting and Reporting Manual (FARM) Issued by the National Association of College and University Business Officers (NACUBO) (q.v.) as additional illustrative guidance for accounting and financial reporting for both public and private institutions of higher education.

Financial Accounting Foundation (FAF) Parent organization of the Financial Accounting Standards Board (FASB) and the Governmental Accounting Standards Board (GASB). Responsible for overall policy direction, raising funds, and selecting board members, but not for setting standards.

Financial Accounting Standards Board (FASB) Independent seven-member body designated to set accounting and financial reporting standards for commercial entities and nongovernmental not-for-profit entities.

financial audits Under Government Auditing Standards (q.v.), type of governmental audit that provides assurance about the fairness of financial statements.

financial reporting entity See *reporting entity.*

financial section One of the three major parts of the Comprehensive Annual Financial Report (q.v.). Contains the auditor's opinion, the MD&A, the basic financial statements, required supplementary information, and any combining and individual fund financial statements and schedules.

financing activities Cash flow statement category required by FASB. Includes all borrowing and repayment of debt.

fiscal agent Bank or other corporate fiduciary that performs the function of paying interest and/or principal on debt when due on behalf of the governmental unit, nonprofit organization, or other organization.

fiscal entity Where assets are set aside, for example in a fund, for specific purposes. See *accounting entity.*

501(c)(3) entities Not-for-profit organizations that receive tax-exempt status through Section 501(c)(3) of the Internal Revenue Code.

forfeiture   Automatic loss of cash or other property as a punishment for not complying with legal provisions and as compensation for the resulting damages or losses.

Form 990   Tax form information return filed by certain tax exempt organizations under Section 501(c)(3)(q.v.) of the Internal Revenue Code.

full faith and credit   Pledge of the general taxing power for the payment of debt obligations. General obligation bonds are backed by the full faith and credit of a given governmental unit.

function   Group of related activities aimed at accomplishing a major service or regulatory responsibility for which a governmental unit is responsible. For example, public health is a function. The GASB provides for functional reporting of expenditures for governmental funds, and the FASB provides for functional reporting of expenses for private-sector not-for-profit organizations.

functional classification   Grouping of expenditures on the basis of the principal purposes for which they are made. Examples in government are public safety, public health, and public welfare. Examples in not-for-profit organizations are the various programs, fund-raising, management and general, and membership development.

functional expenses, statement of   Statement that displays, in a matrix format, expenses reported by function (q.v.) and expenses reported by object (q.v.). Required by the FASB for voluntary health and welfare organizations and recommended for other not-for-profit organizations, either as a statement or in the notes.

fund   Fiscal and accounting entity with a self-balancing set of accounts recording cash and other resources together with all related liabilities, net assets or fund balances, and changes therein that are segregated for the purpose of carrying on specific activities or attaining certain objectives in accordance with special regulations, restrictions, or limitations.

fund accounting   Accounting system organized on the basis of funds, each of which is considered a separate accounting entity. The operations of each fund are accounted for with a separate set of self-balancing accounts that comprise its assets, liabilities, fund equity, revenues, and expenditures, or expenses, as appropriate.

fund balance   Term used for governmental funds (q.v.) representing the difference between assets and liabilities. Fund balance may be restricted, committed, assigned for various purposes or unassigned. (q.v.).

fund balance—reserved for encumbrances   see budgetary fund balance—reserved for encumbrances.

fund balance with treasury   Account used by federal agencies, it represents the ability of the agency to draw cash from the Treasure Department and is recognized as an asset at the time of appropriation.

fund equity   Excess of fund assets and resources over fund liabilities. A portion of the equity of a governmental fund may be reserved (q.v.) or designated (q.v.).

fund financial statements   Fund financial statements are required by GASB *Statement 34* as well as government-wide statements. Statements include those for governmental funds (q.v.), proprietary funds (q.v.), and fiduciary funds (q.v.).

G

GAAP hierarchy   Priority listing of Generally Accepted Accounting Principles (GAAP) (q.v.) established by the GASB, FASB and FASAB for governmental and nongovernmental units.

general capital (or fixed) assets   Capital assets of a governmental unit that are not accounted for by a proprietary or fiduciary fund.

general fund   Fund used to account for all transactions of a governmental unit that are not accounted for in another fund.

general long-term debt   Long-term debt legally payable from general revenues and backed by the full faith and credit of a governmental unit.

general obligation bonds   Bonds for whose payment the full faith and credit of the issuing body is pledged. More commonly, but not necessarily, considered to be those payable from taxes and other general revenues (q.v.). In some states, called *tax-supported* bonds.

general-purpose government   Includes states, counties, municipalities, and other governments that have a range of purposes. General-purpose governments are by definition primary governments. In addition, general-purpose governments are required to prepare the full range of basic financial statements, including government-wide and fund.

general revenues (governmental)   All tax revenues and those other revenues that are not associated directly with a particular function or program. Deducted from net program costs in Statement of Activities (q.v.).

Generally Accepted Accounting Principles (GAAP) Body of accounting and financial reporting standards as defined by Rule 203 of the American Institute of Certified Public Accountants (AICPA). "Level A" GAAP is set by the FASB, the GASB, and the FASAB.

Generally Accepted Auditing Standards (GAAS) Standards prescribed by the American Institute of Certified Public Accountants to provide guidance for planning, conducting, and reporting audits by Certified Public Accountants.

Government Accountability Office, U.S. Legislative Branch Agency of the federal government that prepares *Government Auditing Standards* (q.v.); responsible for audit of U.S. government executive branch.

Government Auditing Standards (GAS) Auditing standards set forth by the Comptroller General of the United States to provide guidance for federal auditors and state and local governmental auditors and public accountants who audit federal organizations, programs, activities, and functions. Also referred to as *Generally Accepted Government Auditing Standards (GAGAS)*.

Government Finance Officers Association (GFOA) Association of government finance officials, primarily state and local. Sponsored by the National Council on Governmental Accounting (NCGA), the predecessor standards-setting body to the GASB. Administers the Certificate of Achievement programs to encourage excellence in financial reporting and budgeting by state and local governments.

Governmental Accounting Standards Board (GASB) Independent agency established under the Financial Accounting Foundation in 1984 to set accounting and financial reporting standards for state and local governments and for governmentally related not-for-profit organizations.

governmental activities Governmental activities are reported separately in the government-wide statements and include activities normally accounted for in the governmental funds and internal service funds.

governmental funds Generic classification used by the GASB to refer to all funds other than proprietary and fiduciary. Includes the General Fund, special revenue funds, capital projects funds, debt service funds, and permanent funds.

government-mandated nonexchange transactions One of the four classes of nonexchange transactions established by GASB. Example would be a grant to a school district to carry out a mandated state program.

government-wide financial statements Government-wide statements included in the financial reporting requirements of GASB *Statement 34* include the Statement of Net Assets and Statement of Activities.

grant Contribution by one governmental unit to another unit. The contribution is usually made to aid in the support of a specified function (for example, education), but it is sometimes also for general purposes or for the acquisition or construction of fixed assets.

H-I

Health Care Guide The AICPA (q.v.) *Auditing and Accounting Guide: Health Care Organizations,* which provides guidance for all health care entities, governmental, not-for-profit, and for-profit.

imposed tax revenues One of the four classes of nonexchange transactions established by GASB. Examples are property taxes and fines and forfeits.

indirect method Method for cash flow statement in which operating cash flows begin by reconciling from change in net assets to cash flows from operations. Contrast with *direct method* (q.v.). GASB prohibits the indirect method, whereas FASB permits either the direct or the indirect method.

infrastructure assets Long-term assets including roads, bridges, storm sewers, etc. Under *Statement 34,* governments are required to capitalize and depreciate infrastructure, or to use the modified approach (q.v.).

in-substance defeasance Transaction in which low-risk U.S. government securities are placed into an irrevocable trust for the benefit of debt holders and the liability for the debt is removed from the accounts of the entity even though the debt has not been repaid.

interfund loans and advances Interfund transaction where one fund provides a short-term loan or a long-term advance to another. Type of reciprocal interfund transaction (q.v.). One fund recognizes a receivable and the other a liability.

interfund reimbursements Type of interfund transaction in which one fund reimburses another for expenditures already incurred. One fund recognizes an expenditure or expense; the other reduces an expenditure or expense.

interfund services provided and used   Interfund transaction in which one fund provides service to another. Type of reciprocal interfund transaction (q.v.). One fund recognizes a revenue and the other fund recognizes an expenditure or expense. Replaces the term *quasi-external transaction.*

interfund transactions   GASB term to describe transactions between funds. Four types of interfund transactions exist. Reciprocal interfund transactions (q.v.) include interfund loans and advances (q.v.) and interfund services provided and used (q.v.). Nonreciprocal interfund transactions include interfund transfers (q.v.) and reimbursements (q.v.).

interfund transfers   Type of interfund transaction in which one fund transfers resources to another, without an exchange transaction. One fund recognizes an Other Financing Source (q.v.) (or Transfer In) and the other fund recognizes an Other Financing Use (q.v.) (or Transfer Out).

intergovernmental revenue   Revenue from other governments, a source classification of revenues in governmental accounting. Includes grants, shared revenues, and entitlements.

internal service fund   Fund established to finance and account for services and commodities furnished by a designated department or agency to other departments and agencies within a single governmental unit or to other governmental units. Type of proprietary fund. Resources used by the fund are restored either from operating earnings or by transfers from other funds so that the original fund capital is kept intact.

interpretations   Documents issued by the GASB (q.v.), FASB (q.v.), and FASAB (q.v.), that provide guidance regarding previously issued statements (q.v.).

introductory section   One of the three major parts of the Comprehensive Annual Financial Report (CAFR)(q.v.), including the letter of transmittal, organization chart, and list of principal officials.

invested in capital assets, net of related debt   Equity account, used for government-wide and fiduciary fund statement of net assets (q.v.) that represents the amount reported for capital assets (q.v.), net of accumulated depreciation, less debt issued to obtain those capital assets.

investing activities   Cash flow statement category required by both FASB and GASB. FASB and GASB have differing content requirements for this category.

investment trust fund   Fiduciary fund that accounts for the external portion of investment pools reported by the sponsoring government.

IRS 457 Deferred Compensation Plans   Tax deferred plans allowed by law to be offered by state and local governmental units. In some cases, reported as Pension Trust Funds.

J-L

lapse   As applied to appropriations, denotes the automatic termination of an appropriation. As applied to encumbrances, denotes the termination of an encumbrance (q.v.) at the end of a fiscal year.

levy   To impose taxes, special assessments, or service charges for the support of govern-mental activities. Total amount of taxes, special assessments, or service charges imposed by a governmental unit.

limited obligation debt   Debt secured by a pledge of the collections of a certain specified tax (rather than by all general revenues).

low-risk auditee   Auditee determined by an auditor who is auditing under the Single Audit Act (q.v.) to have met certain criteria.

M

major funds   Major funds must be displayed in the basic statements for governmental and proprietary funds. Funds are considered major when both of the following conditions exist: (1) total assets, liabilities, revenues, or expenditures/expenses of that individual governmental or enterprise fund constitute 10 percent of the governmental or enterprise activity; and (2) total assets, liabilities, revenues, or expenditures/expenses are 5 percent of the governmental and enterprise category.

major programs   Programs that must be audited under the provisions of the Single Audit Act (q.v.). Determined by a risk-based approach. Auditors must audit larger (Type A) programs unless they judge them to be low risk; auditors must audit smaller (Type B) programs if they judge them to be high risk.

Management's Discussion and Analysis (MD&A)   Required part of the financial section of a CAFR that provides an opportunity for management to explain, in plain-English terms, an overview of the government's financial activities. Considered Required Supplementary Information (q.v.) by the GASB.

matured bonds payable Bonds that have reached their maturity but remain unpaid.

matured interest payable Bond interest that is due but remains unpaid.

measurable One condition that must be met before a revenue can be recognized under the modified accrual basis of accounting. The amount must be measurable.

measurement focus Nature of the resources, claims against resources, and flows of resources that are measured and reported by a fund or other entity. For example, governmental funds measure and report current financial resources, whereas proprietary and fiduciary funds measure and report economic resources.

mill Tax rate (q.v.) expressed in thousands per net assessed valuation. For example, a tax rate of $2.50 per $100 net assessed valuation would be $25.00 per $1,000 net assessed valuation, or 25 mills.

modified accrual basis of accounting Basis of accounting required for use by governmental funds (q.v.) in which revenues are recognized in the period in which they become available and measurable, and expenditures are recognized at the time a liability is incurred except for principal and interest on long-term debt, which are recorded when due.

modified approach (infrastructure) When a government chooses not to depreciate infrastructure assets (q.v.). Under this approach, improvements and additions would be capitalized; expenditures that extend the life would be expenses. When using the modified approach, a government must provide certain RSI (q.v.) schedules that demonstrate that infrastructure is maintained at a certain level.

N

National Association of College and University Business Officers (NACUBO) Association of college and university financial vice presidents, controllers, budget officials, and other finance officers that produces and distributes *Financial Accounting and Reporting Manual for Higher Education* (q.v.).

National Council on Governmental Accounting (NCGA) Body that established accounting and financial reporting standards for state and local governments prior to the formation of the Governmental Accounting Standards Board.

net assets Difference between total assets and total liabilities. Used by the FASB and GASB to describe equity accounts.

net assets—invested in capital assets, net of related debt (governmental) The portion of net assets of a governmental unit representing capital assets less accumulated depreciation less debt associated with the capital assets.

net assets—permanently restricted (not-for-profit) Used in accounting for not-for-profit organizations indicating the amount of net assets whose use is permanently restricted by an external donor.

net assets—restricted (governmental) That portion of net assets of a governmental unit or proprietary fund that is restricted. See *restricted (governmental)*.

net assets—temporarily restricted (not-for-profit) Used in accounting for not-for-profit organizations indicating the amount of net assets whose use is temporarily restricted by donors or grantors. Released by program, time, plant acquisition, and term endowments.

net assets—unrestricted (governmental and not-for-profit) Used in accounting for governmental and not-for-profit organizations indicating that portion of net assets that is unrestricted.

net increase/decrease in fair value of investments Account title used by governments to report realized and unrealized gains or losses on investments.

net pension obligation (NPO) In a pension plan, the accumulated difference between the employer's required (see actuarial basis) and actual contributions.

nominal interest rate Contractual interest rate shown on the face and in the body of a bond and representing the amount of interest to be paid, in contrast to the effective interest rate (q.v.).

nonaudit services Under Government Au-diting Standards (q.v.), gathering, providing, or explaining information requested by deci-sion makers or providing advice or assistance to management officials.

noncapital financing activities Cash flow statement category required by GASB. Includes cash flows from financing not related to capital acquisition, including borrowing and transfers to and from other funds.

nonexchange transactions Transactions that are not the result of arms-length exchange between two parties that are bargaining for the best position. Contrasted with exchange transactions, such as sales and services for user charges. Examples are taxes and contributions. GASB has established accounting rules for nonexchange transactions in *Statement 33.*

nonexpendable Resources, which are maintained, and focus is on the recognition of revenues and expenses; for example, in accrual accounting. See *expendable.*

nonmajor funds All funds other than major. Nonmajor funds are not required to be presented separately in the basic fund financial statements of governmental and enterprise funds. See *major funds.*

nonreciprocal interfund transactions
Type of interfund transaction where the direction is "one-way." Includes interfund transfers and interfund reimbursements. The interfund equivalent of nonexchange transactions (q.v.).

nonspendable fund balance A classification of fund balance reported in governmental-type funds to indicate net resources of the fund that cannot be spent. Nonspendable resources include inventories, prepaid items, and the corpus of permanent funds.

normal cost Amount that would be required to be contributed to a retirement plan (or other postemployment benefit plan) and charged as expenditure/expense, assuming the plan was currently funded; present value of future payments based on current earnings.

Not-for-Profit Guide AICPA (q.v.) *Audits of Not-for-Profit Organizations,* which provides guidance for private-sector colleges and universities, voluntary health and welfare organizations, and other not-for-profit organizations, excluding health care.

not-for-profit organization An entity that possesses the following characteristics: (1) receives significant resources from donors who do not expect equivalent value in return; (2) operates for purposes other than to provide goods or services at a profit; and (3) lacks an identifiable individual or group of individuals who hold a legally enforceable residual claim. Entities that fall outside this definition include all investor-owned enterprises and other organizations that provide economic benefits to the owners, members, or participants.

notes to the financial statements
Required part of the basic financial statements for state and local governments. Includes a summary of significant accounting policies, other required, and optional disclosures.

O

object As used in expenditure classification, applies to the article purchased or the service obtained (as distinguished from the results obtained from expenditures). Examples are personal services, contractual services, materials, and supplies.

object classification Grouping of expenditures on the basis of goods or services purchased. See also *Functional Classification, Activity Classification,* and *Character Classification.*

objectives statements Issued by the FASB, FASAB, and GASB for guidance and reference when preparing standards of accounting and financial reporting.

Obligations A term used in federal government accounting when an agency places an order for goods or services. A budgetary account, it is similar to encumbrances in state and local government reporting.

Office of Management and Budget, U.S. (OMB) Executive agency of the federal government responsible for the preparation of the executive budget proposal and for the form and content of agency financial statements. The director is one of the Principals (q.v.) that approves the recommendations of the Financial Accounting Standards Advisory Board (FASAB) (q.v.).

OMB Circular A–133, *Audits of States, Local Governments, and Not-for-Profit Organizations Receiving Federal Awards*
Replaces former OMB Circular A–128 for state and local governments and A–133 for not-for-profit organizations. Provides guidance for auditors when engaged in audits required by the Single Audit Act. See *compliance supplement.*

OPEB obligation The cumulative difference between the amounts provided by a government to fund other postemployment benefits and the actuarially determined annual required contributions (ARC).

operating activities Cash flow statement category required by both FASB and GASB. Includes receipts from customers, payments to suppliers and employees, etc.

operating lease Rental-type lease in which the risks and benefits of ownership are substantively retained by the lessor and that does not meet the criteria in applicable accounting and reporting standards of a capital lease (q.v.).

opinion units Under the AICPA *State and Local Government Guide* (q.v.), opinion units are reporting levels where materiality is set and audit reporting is done. Opinion units are (1) governmental activities (q.v.), (2) business-type activities (q.v.), (3) each major governmental and enterprise fund (q.v.), (4) the aggregate of all discretely presented component units (q.v.), and (5) the aggregate of all remaining fund information.

other financing sources   Operating statement classification in which financial inflows other than revenues are reported; for example, proceeds of general obligation bonds and transfers in.

other financing uses   Operating statement classification in which financial outflows other than expenditures are reported; for example, operating transfers out.

other not-for-profit organizations
Term describing category of not-for-profit organizations. Includes all but *voluntary health and welfare organizations* (q.v.), colleges and universities, and health care organizations.

other postemployment benefits   Health plan payments for retirees and other payments made pursuant to agreements between employers and employees. Resources available to pay these benefits are reported in pension (and other employee benefit) trust funds.

overlapping debt   Proportionate share of the debts of local governmental units located wholly or in part within the geographic borders of the government reporting entity that must be borne by property owners within each governmental unit.

oversight agency   Under Single Audit Act and amendments, agency that deals with auditee, as representative of all federal agencies. Agency with the most dollars expended by the auditee assumes the role.

P

pass-through entity   Entity that receives federal funds and transfers some or all of the funds to other entities, called *subrecipients* (q.v.).

pension (or other employee benefit) trust fund   One of the fiduciary fund types. Accounts for pension and other employee benefit plans when the governmental unit is trustee.

performance audits   Under Government Auditing Standards (q.v.), an independent assessment of the performance and management of a program against objective criteria.

performance indicator   Used in *Health Care Guide* (q.v.) to describe a measure of operations.

Required in the Statement of Operations (q.v.) by the *Health Care Guide.*

permanent fund   Governmental fund that is restricted so that only earnings, not principal, may be expended, and for purposes to benefit the government and its citizenry.

permanently restricted net assets   Category used by FASB in not-for-profit accounting to describe *net assets* (q.v.) as being permanently restricted by donors. Permanent *Endowments* (q.v.) represent an example.

perpetual trust held by a third party   Split interest (q.v.) agreement in which trust assets are held by a third party but the income is to go to a not-for-profit organization.

pooled life income fund   Split-interest agreement described in AICPA *Not-for-Profit Guide* (q.v.) in which several life income agreements are pooled together. A life income fund represents a situation where all of the income is paid to a donor or beneficiary during his or her lifetime.

primary government   State government or general-purpose local government. Also, special-purpose government that has a separately elected governing body, is legally separate, and is fiscally independent of other state or local governments.

principals   The Director of the Office of Management and Budget (q.v.), the Secretary of the Treasury (q.v.), and the Comptroller General of the United States (q.v.). These three individuals review standards passed by the FASAB (q.v.) and, unless they object, those standards become GAAP (q.v.).

private organizations   Organizations and entities that are not owned or controlled by any governments. They include for-profit and not-for-profit organizations. In contrast to public organizations.

private-purpose trust fund   All trust arrangements other than pension and investment trust funds under which principal and income benefit individuals, private organizations, or other governments.

proceeds of bonds (or long-term notes)   Account used in governmental accounting for governmental funds to indicate the issuance of long-term debt. Considered an "other financing source." (q.v.)

program expense ratio   The most common financial ratio used to evaluate not-for-profit organizations. It is computed as program services expenses divided by total expenses.

program revenues (governmental)
Charges for services, operating grants, and

contributions, and capital grants and contributions that are related to specific programs and subtracted from those programs in the Statement of Activities (q.v.) to obtain net program costs.

program services Category of functional expenses used by many not-for-profit organizations to describe expenses related to fulfilling the mission of the organization. Contrasted with *supporting services.* Program expenses are listed individually with all direct and allocated costs assigned.

property taxes Taxes levied by a legislative body against agricultural, commercial, residential, or personal property pursuant to law and in proportion to the assessed valuation of said property, or other appropriate basis. See *ad valorem.*

proprietary accounts Accounts used by federal agencies in the accrual basis financial statements.

proprietary funds One of the major fund classifications of governmental accounting, the others being governmental (q.v.) and fiduciary (q.v.). Sometimes referred to as *income determination or commercial-type funds.* Includes enterprise funds and internal service funds.

public charity Churches, schools, hospitals, governmental units, and publicly supported charities and certain other entities. Distinguished from private foundations, which are subject to different tax rules.

Public Employee Retirement Systems (PERS) Organizations that collect retirement and other employee benefit contributions from government employers and employees, manage assets, and make payments to qualified retirants, beneficiaries, and disabled employees.

public organizations Organizations owned or controlled by a government, including government authorities, instrumentalities, and enterprises. In contrast to private organizations.

purchases method Refers to method used to recognize expenditures for governmental funds (q.v.) in which an expenditure (q.v.) is recognized when inventory is acquired.

Q-R

qualified opinion Audit report in which the auditor provides an "except for" opinion, due to failure to follow generally accepted accounting principles (q.v.) or due to a scope limitation.

quasi-endowment Term to describe a situation where a governing board of a not-for-profit organization takes resources that are unrestricted and sets

them aside "as if" those resources were an endowment; the intent is to never expend those funds. Such funds continue to be unrestricted for financial reporting purposes.

quasi-external transaction Outdated term. See *interfund services provided and used.*

reciprocal interfund transactions Type of interfund transaction where all funds receive benefit. Includes interfund loans and advances (q.v.) and interfund services provided and used (q.v.). The interfund equivalent of exchange transactions (q.v.).

reclassification Term created by the FASB to describe the transfer of net assets from temporarily restricted to unrestricted. Done when restrictions have expired, for expiration of time restriction, for expiration of term endowments, for satisfaction of program restrictions, or for satisfaction of plant acquisition restrictions.

reconciliation As used in state and local government accounting, reconciliations are required between fund statements and government-wide statements. Specifically, a reconciliation is required between the governmental fund Balance Sheet and the government-wide Statement of Net Assets. Also, a reconciliation is required between the governmental fund Statement of Revenues, Expenditures, and Changes in Fund Balances and the government-wide Statement of Activities.

refunding bonds Bonds issued to retire bonds already outstanding. May be sold for cash and outstanding bonds redeemed in cash or may be exchanged with holders of outstanding bonds.

reimbursements An eligibility requirement imposed by GASB. A nonexchange revenue (or expense) cannot be recognized until the resources are expended, when a grant or contribution makes this requirement. Also, see *interfund reimbursements.*

reporting entity Primary government and all related component units, if any, combined in accordance with the GASB *Codification* Sec. 2100 constituting the governmental reporting entity.

repurchase agreement Agreement wherein a governmental unit transfers cash to a financial institution in exchange for U.S. government securities and the financial institution agrees to repurchase the same securities at an agreed-upon price.

required characteristics of recipients An eligibility requirement imposed by GASB.

A nonexchange revenue (or expense) cannot be recognized unless the recipient government meets the characteristics specified by the provider.

Required Supplementary Information (RSI) Information required by GASB to be reported along with basic financial statements. Includes MD&A (q.v.) and, when applicable, the Schedule of Funding Progress, the Schedule of Employer Contributions, Budgetary Comparison Schedules, and information about infrastructure assets required using the modified format.

restricted (governmental) According to GASB, a restriction on resources of a state or local government is (*a*) externally imposed by creditors (such as through debt covenants), grantors, contributors, or laws or regulations of other governments, and (*b*) imposed by law through constitutional provisions or enabling legislation. See *net assets—restricted.*

restricted (not-for-profit) According to FASB, in order to report resources as restricted, those resources must be restricted by a contributor or grantor. See *permanently restricted assets* and *temporarily restricted net assets.*

restricted assets Assets (usually of an enterprise fund) that may not be used for normal operating purposes because of the requirements of regulatory authorities, provisions in bond indentures, or other legal agreements but that need not be accounted for in a separate fund.

restricted fund balance A classification of fund balance reported in governmental-type funds to indicate net resources of the fund that are subject to constraints imposed by external parties or law.

revenue bonds Bonds whose principal and interest are payable exclusively from earnings of a public enterprise.

revenues Additions to fund financial resources other than from interfund transfers (q.v.) and debt issue proceeds.

revenues ledger Subsidiary ledger used in accounting for governmental funds that records budgets to support the Revenues control account. Normally established by revenue source.

reverse repurchase agreement Agreement in which a broker-dealer or financial institution (buyer-lender) transfers cash to a governmental entity (seller-borrower); the entity transfers securities to the broker-dealer or financial institution and promises to repay the cash plus interest in exchange for the same securities or for different securities.

risk-based approach Approach to be used by auditors when conducting audits with the newly revised A–133 to determine major programs, based on perceived risk as well as size of programs.

risk management Policies adopted by a governmental or not-for-profit organization to manage risk that might result in liabilities for health care, accidents, and so on, including the purchase of insurance, self-insurance, and participation in public entity or other risk pools.

RSI See *Required Supplementary Information.*

S

Sarbanes-Oxley Act A federal act intended to improve corporate governance and limit the services accounting firms may provide to their audit clients. While the Act applies only to corporations filing with the Securities and Exchange Commission, many of the Act's best practices have been adopted by governments and not-for-profit organizations.

Schedule of Employer Contributions Schedule required by the GASB to be presented as Required Supplementary Information (RSI) (q.v.) for public employee retirement systems, other postemployment benefit plans, and pension trust funds. Compares the annual required contributions with the contributions actually made.

Schedule of Funding Progress Schedule required by the GASB to be presented as Required Supplementary Information (RSI) (q.v.) for public employee retirement systems, other postemployment benefit plans, and pension trust funds. Compares the actuarial accrued liability with the actuarial value of plan assets.

schedules Explanatory or supplementary statements that accompany the balance sheet or other principal statements periodically prepared from the accounts.

segment information Note disclosures required in general-purpose financial statements to report the financial condition and operating results of individual enterprise activities.

self-insurance Decision of an entity not to purchase insurance but instead to accept the risk of claims as a part of its risk-management policy. When a government uses one fund to report that risk, it is required to use either the General Fund or an internal service fund.

serial bonds   Bonds the principal of which is repaid in periodic installments over the life of the issue.

Service Efforts and Accomplishments Conceptualization of the resources consumed (inputs), tasks performed (outputs), and goals attained (outcomes), and the relationships among these items in providing services in selected areas (e.g., police protection, solid waste garbage collection, and elementary and secondary education).

shared revenue   Revenue levied by one governmental unit but shared, usually on a predetermined basis, with another unit of government or class of governments.

single audit   Audit prescribed by federal law for state and local governmental units, colleges and universities, and not-for-profit organizations that receive federal financial assistance above $500,000.

Single Audit Act Amendments of 1996   Legislation that extended the single audit to not-for-profit organizations and provided for a risk-based approach to determine major programs.

solid waste landfill   Landfill accepting waste from citizens and also waste manage-ment firms. Charges are normally levied against those depositing waste. Managed by government. Due to certain federal environmental requirements to maintain those landfills many years, the GASB (q.v.) has adopted accounting requirements that bring forward future charges to offset current revenues.

special assessment   Compulsory levy made against certain properties to defray part or all of the cost of a specific improvement or service that is presumed to be a general benefit to the public and of special benefit to such properties.

special assessment bonds   Bonds payable from the proceeds of special assessments (q.v.).

special district   Independent unit of local government organized to perform a single governmental function or a restricted number of related functions. Examples of special districts are water districts, drainage districts, flood control districts, hospital districts, fire protection districts, transit authorities, port authorities, and electric power authorities.

special item   Classification by GASB in financial statements to indicate that a revenue, expense, gain, or loss is either unusual or infrequent and within the control of management.

special-purpose government   Governments that are not general-purpose (q.v.) governments and have a more limited range of purposes. Often includes townships, park districts, sanitation districts, and authorities.

special revenue fund   Fund used to report resources from specific taxes or other earmarked revenue sources that are restricted or committed to finance particular functions or activities of government.

split-interest agreement   Agreement between a donor and a not-for-profit organization in which the donor (or beneficiary) and the organization "split" the income and/or principal of the gift. Examples are charitable lead trusts (q.v.) and charitable remainder trusts (q.v.).

State and Local Government Guide AICPA (q.v.) *Audits of State and Local Governmental Units,* which provides guidance for state and local governmental units.

statement of activities (not-for-profit accounting)   One of the three statements required for not-for-profit organizations by FASB *Statement 117.* Requirements are to show revenues, expenses, gains, losses, and reclassifications (q.v.) and to show the change in net assets by net asset class (unrestricted, temporarily restricted, permanently restricted).

statement of activities (governmental accounting)   Required basic government-wide financial statement in which program revenues are subtracted from expenses to get net program costs. General revenues are then deducted, to get the change in net assets.

statement of budgetary resources   A financial statement required of federal agencies that describes how budgetary resources were obtained and the status of those resources at year-end. It is prepared using the budgetary basis of accounting.

statement of cash flows   Required basic statement for proprietary funds for governmental units and for public colleges and universities. Also required statement for non-governmental not-for-profit organizations.

statement of changes in net position   A financial statement required of federal agencies which reconciles the beginning and ending net position of the agency using the accrual basis.

statement of custodial activity A financial statement required of federal agencies that collect non-exchange funds to be turned over to Treasury. It is analogous to an agency fund of a state or local government.

Statement of Federal Financial Accounting Concepts (SFFACs) Concepts statements passed by the FASAB that provide objectives of accounting and financial reporting for the federal government. Do not have the authoritative status of statements.

Statement of Fiduciary Changes in Net Assets Required basic statement for fiduciary funds. Reported by fund type.

Statement of Fiduciary Net Assets Required basic statement for fiduciary funds where assets less liabilities equals net assets. Reported by fund type.

statement of financial accounting concepts Concepts statements passed by the FASB that provide objectives of accounting and financial reporting for nongovernmental entities. Do not have the authoritative status of statements.

statement of financial position Required basic statement that reports assets, liabilities, and net assets.

statement of functional expenses Statement required by FASB *Statement 117* for voluntary health and welfare organizations (q.v.). Shows a matrix of expenses by function (q.v.) and by object classification (q.v.).

statement of net assets Balance sheet format where assets less liabilities equal net assets. Encouraged for government-wide statements and may be used for proprietary and fiduciary fund statements.

statement of net cost A financial statement required of federal agencies that displays costs by strategic goal.

statement of operations Required by the *Health Care Guide* (q.v.) to be prepared by all health care organizations. Includes a performance indicator (q.v.).

statement of revenues, expenditures, and changes in fund balances Basic operating statement for governmental funds, included in the CAFR.

statement of revenues, expenses, and changes in fund net assets Basic statement used for proprietary funds to reflect operations and changes in net assets.

statements Issues by the GASB (q.v.), FASB (q.v.), and FASAB (q.v.) outlining accounting principles for those entities under each board's

jurisdiction. Constitutes GAAP (q.v.). Also principal financial presentations of governments and not-for-profit organizations.

statistical section One of the three major parts of the Comprehensive Annual Financial Report (CAFR) (q.v.), listing schedules that assist users in evaluating the financial condition of a government and its community.

subrecipient Entity that receives federal funds through another government or not-for-profit entity. For example, a state may pass through funding to certain local governments. See *pass-through entities*.

subsidiary account One of a group of related accounts that support in detail the debit and credit summaries recorded in a control account. An example is the individual property taxpayers' accounts for taxes receivable in the general ledger.

subsidiary ledger Group of subsidiary accounts (q.v.) the sum of the balances of which is equal to the balance of the related control accounts. This text illustrates the Revenues Ledger (q.v.) and the Appropriations, Expenditures, and Encumbrances Ledger (q.v.).

supporting services Functional expense category recommended, but not required, by the FASB for not-for-profit organizations. Includes fund-raising, management and general, and membership development expenses.

T

tax agency fund Agency fund, usually maintained by a county official, to handle the collection of all property taxes within the county or other jurisdiction and the distribution of proceeds to all governments within the borders of that county or other jurisdiction.

tax increment debt Debt issued by a governmental unit to finance improvements in a Tax Increment Financing (TIF) District; the incremental taxes from those improvements are dedicated to the repayment of the debt.

tax rate Amount of tax stated in terms of a unit of the tax base; for example, $2.50 per $100 of net assessed valuation, or 25 mills (q.v.).

tax supported bonds Bonds supported by the full faith and credit of the governmental unit, by specific taxes.

technical bulletins Issues by the staffs of the standards-setting bodies and approved by the boards, providing additional information regarding questions and answers that might be addressed by those bodies.

temporarily restricted net assets Category used by FASB to describe *net assets* (q.v.) as being restricted by donors, but are not *permanently restricted net assets* (q.v.). Temporarily restricted net assets may be restricted for purpose, time, plant acquisition, or *term endowments* (q.v.).

term bonds Bonds for which the principal is paid at the end of the term. Contrast with serial bonds (q.v.).

term endowments Exist when a donor contributes an amount, which is not to be expended for a certain period of time. Term endowments are classified as *temporarily restricted net assets* (q.v.) by FASB.

time requirements An eligibility requirement imposed by GASB. A non-exchange revenue (or expense) cannot be recognized until the time specified by the donor or grantor or contributor for expenditure.

transfers As used in state and local government accounting, the shifting of resources from one category to another. In fund reporting, the transfer of resources from one fund to another. In government-wide reporting, the transfer of resources from one type of activity to another, such as from governmental activities to business-type activities. Transfers may be regularly recurring and routine (formerly called "operating transfers") or nonroutine (formerly called "equity transfers").

Treasury, U.S. Department of Federal executive branch agency; prepares Consolidated Financial Statements of the Federal Government. One of the "principals" that approves FASAB standards of financial reporting for the Federal Government.

trust fund Fund consisting of resources received and held by the governmental unit as trustee, to be expended or invested in accordance with the conditions of the trust. In governmental accounting, includes investment (q.v.), private-purpose (q.v.), and pension trust (q.v.).

U-Z

unassigned fund balance A classification of fund balance reported in governmental-type funds. This is the residual fund balance category for the General Fund and is used to report negative fund balances in other governmental funds.

unexpended appropriation Proprietary account used by federal agencies. It represents a source of funds to the federal agency and is similar to a transfer in account in a state or local government. This account is credited at the time spending approval is passed by Congress and signed by the President.

unfunded actuarial liability In a pension plan, difference between the actuarially computed accrued liability and the net assets available for benefits. Included in the RSI.

unqualified opinion Audit report in which the auditor states that the financial statements are "fairly presented."

Unrelated Business Income Tax (UBIT) Tax that applies to business income of otherwise tax-exempt not-for-profit entities. Determined by relationship to exempt purpose and other criteria.

unrestricted net assets Portion of the excess of total assets over total liabilities that may be utilized at the discretion of the governing board of a not-for-profit entity. Separate classification provided in FASB *Statement 117* and in GASB *Statement 34.*

voluntary health and welfare organizations Not-for-profit organizations formed for the purpose of performing voluntary services for various segments of society. They are tax exempt, supported by the public, and operate on a not-for-profit basis.

voluntary nonexchange transactions One of the four classes of nonexchange transactions established by GASB. Examples are contributions and grants for restricted purposes but which purposes are not mandated independent of the grant.

Index

4820 180 Place S
Lynwood 98037